Everyman, I will go with thee,
and be thy guide

THE EVERYMAN
LIBRARY

*The Everyman Library was founded by J. M. Dent
in 1906. He chose the name Everyman because he wanted
to make available the best books ever written in every
field to the greatest number of people at the cheapest possible
price. He began with Boswell's 'Life of Johnson';
his one-thousandth title was Aristotle's 'Metaphysics',
by which time sales exceeded forty million.*

*Today Everyman paperbacks remain true to
J. M. Dent's aims and high standards, with a wide range
of titles at affordable prices in editions which address
the needs of today's readers. Each new text is reset to give
a clear, elegant page and to incorporate the latest thinking
and scholarship. Each book carries the pilgrim logo,
the character in 'Everyman', a medieval morality play,
a proud link between Everyman
past and present.*

WOMEN
PHILOSOPHERS

Edited by
MARY WARNOCK
University of Cambridge

EVERYMAN
J. M. DENT . LONDON
CHARLES E. TUTTLE
VERMONT

Consultant Editor for this Volume
DAVID BERMAN
Trinity College, Dublin

Introduction, notes and other critical apparatus
© J. M. Dent 1996

This edition first published in Everyman in 1996
Reprinted 1997
For the copyright of the texts
see the Acknowledgements

J.M Dent
Orion Publishing Group
Orion House, 5 Upper St Martin's Lane,
London WC2H 9EA
and
Charles E. Tuttle Co., Inc.
28 South Main Street,
Rutland, Vermont 05701, USA

Typeset in Sabon by Deltatype Ltd, Ellesmere Port, Cheshire
Printed in Great Britain by
The Guernsey Press Co. Ltd, Guernsey, C.I.

British Library Cataloguing-in-Publication Data
is available upon request

ISBN 0 460 87721 6

CONTENTS

NOTE ON THE EDITOR

MARY WARNOCK is a Life Fellow of Girton College, Cambridge, of which she was Mistress from 1985–91. She is a Life Peer. She was educated in Winchester and at Lady Margaret Hall, Oxford. She has been a Fellow and Tutor in Philosophy at St Hugh's College, Oxford, and has lectured in Australia, New Zealand and the USA. Her main philosophical interests are in ethics, education and the philosophy of mind. Among her publications are *Imagination* (Faber, 1976), *Ethics Since 1900* (Oxford University Press, third edition 1978), *A Common Policy for Education* (Oxford University Press, 1989) and *Imagination and Time* (Blackwell, 1994).

CHRONOLOGY OF THE PHILOSOPHERS' LIVES

Year	Lives
1631	Birth of Anne Conway (née Finch)
1651	Anne Conway marries the third Viscount Conway
1670	Anne Conway writes *The Principles of the Most Ancient and Modern Philosophy*
1679	Death of Anne Conway Birth of Catharine Cockburn (née Trotter)
1690	Publication of Anne Conway's *Principles*, in Latin translation
1692	Publication of English version of Anne Conway's *Principles*
1701	Catharine Cockburn, *Defence of Locke*

CHRONOLOGY OF THEIR TIMES

Year	Cultural and historical events
1588	Birth of Thomas Hobbes
1596	Birth of René Descartes
1632	Birth of John Locke and Benedict de Spinoza
1636	Hobbes meets Galileo in Florence
1637	Descartes, *Discourse on Method*
1644	Descartes, *Principles of Philosophy* (dedicated to Princess Elizabeth of Bohemia)
1646	Birth of Gottfried Wilhelm Leibniz
1649	Execution of Charles I; England a republic
1651	Hobbes, *Leviathan*
1660	Restoration of Charles II
1677	Death of Spinoza; *Ethics* published posthumously
1679	Death of Hobbes
1685	Birth of George Berkeley
	Death of Charles II; accession of James II
	Birth of J. S. Bach and G. F. Handel
1687	Isaac Newton, *Principia*
1688	Overthrow of James II
1689	Accession of William and Mary
1690	Locke, *Essay concerning Human Understanding* and *Two Treatises of Civil Government*
1692	Birth of Joseph Butler
1701	Act of Settlement ensures Hanoverian succession
1702	Death of William III; accession of Queen Anne
1704	Death of Locke
	Duke of Marlborough's victory at Blenheim

Year	Lives
1708	Catharine Cockburn marries
1709	Catharine Cockburn converts to Catholicism
1724	Catharine Cockburn defends Locke on the subject of the Resurrection
1737	Catharine Cockburn's work published in *The Gentleman's Magazine*
1750	Death of Catharine Cockburn
1751	Collected works of Catharine Cockburn published by Thomas Birch

Year	Cultural and historical events
1707	Act of Union of Scotland and England
1709	Berkeley, *Essay towards a New Theory of Vision*
	First Copyright Act
1710	Berkeley, *A Treatise concerning the Principles of Human Understanding*
1711	Birth of David Hume
	Accession of Charles VI of the Holy Roman Empire
1712	Birth of Jean-Jacques Rousseau
	Last execution for witchcraft in England
1714	Leibniz writes *Monadology*
	Death of Queen Anne; accession of George I
1716	Death of Leibniz
1723	Birth of Adam Smith
	Death of Christopher Wren
1724	Birth of Immanuel Kant
1725	Accession of Catherine I of Russia
1726	Butler, *Fifteen Sermons* (preached at Rolls Chapel)
1728	F. Hutcheson, *Essay on the Nature and Conduct of the Passions with Illustrations on Moral Sense*
1730	Accession of Anne of Russia
1731	*Gentleman's Magazine* first published
1732	Alexander Pope, *Essay on Man*
1736	Butler, *Analogy of Religion*
	Repeal of English statutes against witchcraft
1739	Hume, *Treatise of Human Nature*
1740	Accession of Frederick II of Prussia and Marie-Theresa of Austria; Frederick II introduces liberty of press and worship
1741	First performance of Handel's *Messiah*, in Dublin
1746	Death of Hutcheson
1748	Birth of Jeremy Bentham
	Hume, *Enquiry concerning Human Understanding*
1750	Death of J. S. Bach

Year	Cultural and historical events
1752	Hume, *Political Discourses*
	Death of Butler
1753	Death of Berkeley
	British Museum founded
1755	Hume, *Natural History of Religion*
	Samuel Johnson, *Dictionary of the English Language*
1756	Birth of W. A. Mozart
	Beginning of the Seven Years' War
1757	Birth of William Blake
1759	Smith, *The Theory of Moral Sentiments*
	Death of Handel
	Birth of Friedrich von Schiller
1762	Rousseau, *The Social Contract*
1770	Birth of G. F. Hegel and Ludwig van Beethoven
1773	Boston Tea Party
1776	Death of Hume
	American Declaration of Independence
1777	First Constitution of United States of America
1778	Death of Rousseau
	Relief Act for Roman Catholics in England
1781	Kant, *Critique of Pure Reason*
	Rousseau, *Confessions*
1783	England officially recognizes United States of America
1786	Frederick II dies and is succeeded by Frederick William II
1788	Birth of Arthur Schopenhauer
	Kant, *Critique of Practical Reason*
1789	Declaration of Rights of Man
	Fall of the Bastille
	Blake, *Songs of Innocence*
1790	Kant, *Critique of Judgement*
	Burke, *Reflections on the French Revolution*
1791	James Boswell, *Life of Johnson*
	Thomas Paine, *The Rights of Man*

Year	Cultural and historical events
1795	Schiller, *Letters concerning the Aesthetic Education of Mankind*
1797	Kant, *Metaphysic of Morals* Frederick William II dies and is succeeded by Frederick William III
1800	Beethoven, First Symphony
1804	Death of Kant
1805	Death of Schiller
1806	Birth of John Stuart Mill
1812	Birth of Charles Dickens
1807	Hegel, *Phenomenology of Spirit*
1813	Schopenhauer, *On the Fourfold Root of the Principle of Sufficient Reason*
1818	Schopenhauer, *The World as Will and Idea* Birth of Karl Marx
1820	Death of George III and accession of George IV Birth of Florence Nightingale
1827	Death of Beethoven Death of Blake
1829	Catholic Emancipation Act in Britain
1830	Bentham, *Constitutional Code* Death of George IV and accession of William IV Birth of Emily Dickinson
1832	Death of Bentham
1833	Slavery abolished throughout British Empire
1837	Death of William IV and accession of Victoria
1838	National Gallery opened Dickens, *Oliver Twist*
1839	Birth of C. S. Peirce
1842	Birth of William James
1845	Potato Famine in Ireland
1847	British Museum opened
1848	Marx and Engels, *The Communist Manifesto* Mill, *Principles of Political Economy*
1856	Birth of Sigmund Freud and George Bernard Shaw

Year	Lives
1863	The Hon. Victoria marries Sir William Welby-Gregory. Birth of Mary Whiton Calkins
1876	Death of Harriet Martineau
1885	Birth of L. Susan Stebbing
1889	Mary Whiton Calkins appointed as instructor in Greek at Wellesley College, Massachusetts
1891	Mary Whiton Calkins appointed as instructor in Psychology at Wellesley and establishes the first psychology laboratory at a women's college
1895	Birth of Susanne K. Langer

Year	Cultural and historical events
1859	Darwin, *Origin of Species*
	Mill, *On Liberty*
	Birth of John Dewey
1860	Death of Schopenhauer
1865	Lincoln assassinated
	Slavery abolished in United States of America
1867	Marx, *Das Kapital*
	Birth of Marie Curie
1869	Mill, *The Subjection of Women*
	Suez Canal opened
1870	Death of Dickens
	Papal infallibility announced by Pius IX
1872	Birth of Bertrand Russell
	Secret Ballot Act introduced in Britain
1873	Birth of G. E. Moore
	Death of Mill
1875	London Medical School for Women founded
1877	Queen Victoria proclaimed Empress of India
1882	Birth of James Joyce
	Married Woman's Property Act
1883	Birth of Karl Jaspers
1885	Death of Marx
1886	Death of Emily Dickinson
	Irish Home Rule Bill defeated
1887	Sir Arthur Conan Doyle, *A Study in Scarlet* (first Sherlock Holmes novel)
	Celluloid film invented
	Queen Victoria's Golden Jubilee
1889	Birth of Ludwig Wittgenstein
	Birth of Martin Heidegger
1891	Birth of R. Carnap
1895	Freud publishes first work on psychoanalysis (*Studies in Hysteria*) with Breuer
1897	James, *The Will to Believe*
	Queen Victoria's Diamond Jubilee

Year	Cultural and historical events
1898	Marconi's first radio transmission
1900	Birth of Gilbert Ryle
	Freud, *The Interpretation of Dreams*
1901	Death of Queen Victoria; accession of Edward VII
1902	James, *The Varieties of Religious Experience*
	End of the Boer War
1903	Moore, *Principia Ethica*
	Lenin becomes Bolshevik leader
1905	Birth of Jean-Paul Sartre
1906	Movement for women's suffrage becomes active in Britain
1907	James, *Pragmatism*
	Labour Bill to give vote to women defeated
	Fifty-seven suffragettes arrested in London
1908	Birth of W. V. O. Quine
	Mrs Pankhurst imprisoned
1910	Death of James
	Birth of A. J. Ayer
	Death of Edward VII; accession of George V
	Death of Florence Nightingale
1911	Birth of J. L. Austin
	Marie Curie awarded Nobel Prize for Chemistry
1912	Russell, *The Problems of Philosophy*
	Titanic disaster
1914	Assassination of Archduke Franz Ferdinand of Austria at Sarajevo
	Outbreak of First World War
	Death of Peirce
	Russell, *Our Knowledge of the External World*
1916	Easter Rising in Ireland
	Battle of Verdun
1917	Revolution in Russia
	America enters the war
1918	Collapse of Central Powers ends First World War
	Vote given to women over 30 and men over 21
	Countess Markiewicz is first woman elected to Parliament

Year	Lives
1919	Birth of Iris Murdoch, Mary Midgley (née Scrutton) and G. E. M. Anscombe
1920	Birth of Philippa Foot (née Bosanquet)
1923	L. Susan Stebbing returns to teach at Girton College
1927	L. Susan Stebbing, *A Modern Introduction to Logic*
1929	Birth of Judith Jarvis Thomson
1930	Death of Mary Whiton Calkins
1933	L. Susan Stebbing made Professor of Philosophy at Bedford College, University of London, and becomes first woman Professor of Philosophy in Britain
1937	L. Susan Stebbing, *Philosophy and the Physicists*
1939	L. Susan Stebbing, *Thinking to Some Purpose*
1941	Birth of Onora O'Neill L. Susan Stebbing, *Ideals and Illusions* G. E. M. Anscombe obtains a Research Fellowship at Newnham College, Cambridge Hannah Arendt escapes Europe to America
1942	Susanne K. Langer, *Philosophy in a New Key*
1943	Death of L. Susan Stebbing

Year	Cultural and historical events
1919	Birth of R. M. Hare
	Prohibition in America
	First flight across the Atlantic, by Alcock and Brown
1920	Degrees first open to women at Oxford University
1921	Russell, *The Analysis of Mind*
	Irish Free State established
1922	Joyce, *Ulysses*
	Wittgenstein, *Tractatus Logico-Philosophicus* (English translation)
1924	Death of Lenin
1927	Russell, *The Analysis of Matter*
	Heidegger, *Being and Time*
1928	Women given equal suffrage to men
1929	Wall Street Crash
1930	Birth of Donald Davidson
1933	Adolf Hitler appointed Chancellor of Germany
	Thirteen women elected to British Parliament
1934	Death of Marie Curie
	Hitler assumes title of *Führer*
1936	Ayer, *Language, Truth and Logic*
	Death of George V and accession of Edward VIII
	Abdication of Edward VIII after 325 days
1937	Accession of George VI
1939	Death of Freud
	Second World War begins
1940	Ayer, *The Foundations of Empirical Knowledge*
	Russell, *An Enquiry into Meaning and Truth*
	Quine, *Mathematical Logic*
	Battle of Britain
1941	Death of Joyce
	Hitler invades Russia
	America enters war
1942	Carnap, *Introduction to Semantics*
	Start of Hitler's 'Final Solution'
1944	D-Day invasion of Europe

Year	Cultural and historical events
1945	End of Second World War
	Mussolini executed
	Hitler's suicide
	Atomic bomb dropped on Hiroshima and Nagasaki
1946	Austin, *Other Minds*
	First meeting of UN General Assembly
1947	Carnap, *Meaning and Necessity*
1948	State of Israel proclaimed 14 May
	Russell, *Human Knowledge, its Scope and Limits*
1949	Ryle, *The Concept of Mind*
	Mao Tse-Tung proclaims People's Republic of China
1950	Carnap, *Logical Foundations of Probability*
	Death of Shaw
1951	Death of Wittgenstein
1952	Death of Dewey
	Hare, *The Language of Morals*
	Death of George VI and accession of Elizabeth II
1953	Wittgenstein, *Philosophical Investigations*
1955	Quine, 'From a logical point of view'
	Moore, *Some Main Problems of Philosophy*
1956	Russell, *Logic and Knowledge*
	Ayer, *The Problem of Knowledge*
1957	Austin, 'A Plea for Excuses'
1958	Death of Moore
	Wittgenstein, *The Blue and Brown Books*
	First women peers introduced to House of Lords (21 October)
1960	Death of Austin
	Quine, *Word and Object*
	John F. Kennedy elected President of United States of America
1961	Trial of Eichmann in Jerusalem
1962	Eichmann executed in Israel
	Austin, *How to Do Things with Words*

Year	Cultural and historical events
1963	First woman astronaut (Bykovsky/Tereshkova space flight)
	Assassination of President Kennedy
	Black civil rights 'freedom march' on Washington
1964	Enactment of US Civil Rights Bill
	Nobel Peace Prize awarded to Dr Martin Luther King
1965	US troops sent to Vietnam
	Appointment of first woman high court judge in Britain
1967	Outbreak of Six-Day War in Middle East
	Abortion Act passed in Britain
1968	Assassination of Martin Luther King
1969	Death of Jaspers
	Wittgenstein, *On Certainty*
	Mrs Martin Luther King becomes first woman to preach at St Paul's
	US astronauts land on moon
	Death penalty abolished in United Kingdom
1970	Death of Russell
	Quine, *Set Theory and its Logic*
	Death of Carnap
1971	Decimal currency introduced in Britain
1973	Paris Peace Settlement ends Vietnam War
	Ireland, Britain and Denmark join European Community
1974	Watergate scandal
1978	UN peace force sent to Lebanon
1979	First direct elections for European Parliament take place in all nine member states
1980	Death of Sartre
	Richard Rorty, *Philosophy and the Mirror of Nature*
	Solidarity Trade Union confronts Communist government in Poland

Year	Lives
1983	Philippa Foot, 'Moral realism and moral dilemmas', *Journal of Philosophy*
1985	Death of Susanne K. Langer
1986	Death of Simone de Beauvoir
	Judith Jarvis Thomson, *Rights, Restitution, and Risk*
	Onora O'Neill, *Faces of Hunger*
	G. E. M. Anscombe retires from Cambridge Chair
1987	Iris Murdoch receives honorary degree from Oxford and becomes DBE
1989	Onora O'Neill, *Constructions of Reason*
1992	Iris Murdoch, *Metaphysics as a Guide to Morals*
	Onora O'Neill elected Principal of Newnham College, Cambridge
1993	Susan Haack, *Evidence and Inquiry*

Year	Cultural and historical events
1982	Rorty, *Consequences of Pragmatism*
	Falklands War between Britain and Argentina
1986	US space shuttle (Challenger) explodes on take-off
	Chernobyl nuclear disaster in Soviet Union
1989	Fall of the Berlin Wall
1991	Break-up of Soviet Union
	Gulf War; Iraq driven out of Kuwait
1992	Break-up of Yugoslavia
1993	Ratification of Maastricht Treaty on European unity

INTRODUCTION

When I was choosing the work of women philosophers for inclusion in this collection, the first question to arise was 'Who counts as a philosopher?' If one were thinking only of the twentieth century, the answer would be comparatively easy. A philosopher is someone who holds a teaching or research position in a university philosophy department. Yet even this is not quite right. There are people, especially in Europe, who are generally regarded as philosophers but who either have never held such a post or have held it for only a short time (such as Jean-Paul Sartre, for example). If one goes back to the nineteenth century, and further back still, it is quite obvious that this simple criterion will not do. Some of the most acclaimed philosophers of the more distant past have not held university posts. J. S. Mill is one example. No one would deny his philosophical credentials, but he never held a university post, having spent most of his working life in the East India Company and, briefly, as an MP. Again, John Locke, though a Student of Christ Church, Oxford, was then a medical scientist. Most of his philosophical works were written when he was physician and private secretary to the first Earl of Shaftesbury. Apart from Plato and Aristotle, who certainly flourished in an academic environment, it seems that it was not until that highly professional philosopher Kant, and his German successors, that it was generally a help to hold an academic post in order to count philosophically. And of course before the end of the nineteenth century there were no women academic philosophers at all, because there were no women academics. And so we have to look for other tests. I have included in this collection women from the seventeenth century onwards who seemed to satisfy different criteria.

The question is 'What makes someone a philosopher, apart from being deemed such by a university?' First, I think, a writer must be concerned with matters of a high degree of generality, and must be at home among abstract ideas. It is not enough to seek the truth, for truth can be established with regard to particular facts; it can be the aim of historians, or of novelists who seek imaginatively to tell things, in some sense, as they are A philosopher would doubtless also claim to be seeking the truth, but would be interested in whatever lies behind the particular facts of experience, the details of history; a philosopher is concerned with the underlying meaning of the language that we habitually and unthinkingly use, the categories into which we sort our experience. Thus he or she would claim not only to seek the truth, but to seek a truth, or theory, that will explain the particular and the detailed and the everyday.

One very great philosopher who exemplified these characteristics was the eighteenth-century Scotsman David Hume. He never held any academic post (though he once unsuccessfully tried for one); most of his writings were of that particularly Scottish kind, the essay; and his essays were on a variety of social, political and economic subjects. But his great philosophical work, the *Treatise of Human Nature*, which he completed when he was only twenty-six years old, was designed to establish the foundations of a genuinely empirical science of human nature. From these foundations, he hoped, could be built up an account of all human knowledge, including scientific knowledge, and all morality, including political morality. Here was generality, and indeed vast explanatory ambition. Hume also satisfied another criterion by which to judge a true philosopher: he was concerned not merely with stating his views, but with arguing for them. This concern has almost always led, among philosophers, to a passionate interest in one another's work; to dissenting from, and if possible refuting, the arguments of other philosophers; to expounding theories by means of dialogue, spoken or written. Sometimes, as in the case of Plato, Berkeley or Hume, these dialogues were fictional; sometimes they were real, and took the form, as in Descartes's case, of replies to objections, or the exchange of letters. Philosophers are by nature talkers or correspondents; only rarely do they prefer to sit and think, isolated from their kind.

The women whose work appears in this collection, then, are (or were) mostly philosophers in the same sort of sense as, all would agree, Hume was a philosopher. And it is these generalizing, explanatory and argumentative aspects of their works that I have tried to present here. When we reach the twentieth century, most, though not quite all, of them also held university posts in philosophy. Thus, in putting together the collection I have hardly widened the scope of what is generally thought to be covered by the concept of philosophy. That scope has, however, changed somewhat in recent years, and I shall say something about the role that women have had in this change below.

First, however, I must try to explain some omissions that will be noticed in the women's writing that follows. The first explanation is concerned with religion, the second with feminism. The gradual secularization of the West, the age of Enlightenment, spanning the seventeenth and eighteenth centuries, brought about the beginning of what we now call specialization. Science began to be distinct from philosophy; philosophy itself could be distinguished from theology. But it must not be thought that these three increasingly distinct subjects were necessarily, and from the beginning, at war with each other. It is true that the Catholic Church of the Counter-Reformation anathematized not only other forms of Christianity, but also such scientists as Giordano Bruno, who was burned to death in Rome in 1600, and Galileo, who was condemned in 1633 for his publication of the revolutionary heliocentric theory of the universe. And it is true that Descartes, alarmed by the fate of Galileo, hesitated to finish or publish his theory of scientific method, the *Rules for the Direction of the Understanding*, at least until he had placed God firmly in the centre of both his science and his philosophy, in the *Discourse on Method* and in the *Meditations*. But gradually, especially in England and the Netherlands, Christianity itself was increasingly influenced by the secularization of society, by the spread of literacy, by the refusal to believe in hell-fire and by the ideal of 'reasonable Christianity'. This ideal was widespread, especially among philosophers such as John Locke, but among theologians as well. We still find an overlap between science and philosophy, as in Descartes, and between philosophy and theology, as in Bishop Butler. It is certainly the case that a writer concerned with the proper subjects of philosophy, those general and explanatory arguments that are the philosophical hallmark, might start from certain Christian assumptions which he or she chose not to question, or indeed positively defended. Nevertheless, from the seventeenth century onwards it becomes increasingly possible to exclude some writings from the category of philosophy and deem them instead to be either works of theology or works of a personal religious kind, works of piety. This has entailed that a number of women writers have been excluded from this collection who might have been thought to have some claim to philosophical status. And even of those included, some may seem to be almost too unquestioningly Christian in their outlook and approach, and the overlap between philosophy and religion too complete, for them to qualify. For as we move from the eighteenth into the nineteenth century, women, especially among Protestants, took on increasingly the role of preserving and upholding religion in the home. Religion became not only a personal, but also a family concern. Women were brought up and educated in an atmosphere of piety and charitable works. Those women brave and intelligent enough to be interested in strictly philosophical questions, and often to correspond with other philosophers, may nevertheless have had their interest aroused within the context of religion, and may have found it most natural to go on, for example, to argue against the materialism of Hobbes (like Anne Conway), using arguments which could be taken to be more or less in favour of religion (though Anne Conway's version of Christianity was anything but orthodox).

Even when the education of women spread, and the new girls' schools were opened in the second half of the nineteenth century, followed soon after by the women's colleges in Cambridge, Oxford and London, the heads of these establishments, though they wrote much about morality and education, and even sometimes about the truly philosophical questions of what was the foundation of the first or the purpose of the second, nearly always did so from a religious or pietistic point of view. Whether this was a matter of conviction or of prudence it is difficult to establish. For one of the often-expressed terrors concerning the new education of girls was that it would turn them from their piety as well as from their duty; they might cease to be the angels in the house. Thus the discourses of Emily Davies, the founder of Girton College, and of others no less sensible but much more academic than she, can have no place in a book of philosophy. They are too much akin to sermons, and sermons bereft of argument. I have accordingly omitted the writings of women who, to put it crudely, seem to rely more on dogma, revelation or mystical experience than on argument, and this means that I have had to exclude some astonishingly powerful writings by the fourteenth-century Julian of Norwich; likewise I have excluded the strange effusions on theosophy and spiritualism of Helena Blavatsky and Annie Besant (her follower), in the nineteenth century; and, in the twentieth century, I have excluded, for the same reasons, the works of Simone Weil. Such judgements might well be challenged, but I think that no one would dispute that the task of separating philosophy from religion is far more difficult in the case of women than of men.

There is another kind of writing about which I have had considerable difficulties, and that is writing about what used to be called 'the Women Question'. There is, understandably, an enormous quantity of broadly 'feminist' literature written by women. How much of this should count as philosophy? A great deal of what has been written plainly satisfies my criteria of generality and of the hoped-for explanation of phenomena; a great deal is concerned to go behind the superficial and to expose the presuppositions of society as a whole. Increasingly in the 1980s and 1990s, there has been a flood of books and articles concerned with the theory of knowledge from a feminist standpoint. Thus, for example, in 1983 Sandra Harding and Merrill B. Hintikka edited a collection of articles entitled *Discovering Reality: Feminist Perspectives on Epistemology, Methodology and the Philosophy of Science* (Dordrecht [etc.]: Reidel, 1983). In 1989, Ann Garry and Marilyn Pearsall edited a volume entitled *Women, Knowledge and Reality: Explorations in Feminist Philosophy* (London: Unwin Hyman, 1989). In the same year there appeared another collection, edited by Alison M. Jagger and Susan R. Bordo, called *Gender/Body/Knowledge: Feminist Reconstructions of Being and Knowledge* (New Brunswick, NJ: Rutgers University Press, 1989). And in these collections all the writers, as well as the editors, were women. In 1987 Lorraine Code published a book entitled *Epistemic Responsibility: Feminist Theory and the Construction of Knowledge* (Ithaca, NY: Cornell University Press, 1987). In 1990 Susan J. Hekman published a book called *Gender and Knowledge: Elements of Post-Modern Feminism* (Cambridge: Polity Press, 1990). And so on. There are literally dozens of such books, all plausibly purporting to be philosophical. What indeed could be more philosophical than investigations of the nature of knowledge or studies of the representation of the world? Yet, just as in the case of religion, there tends to be too much unexamined dogma in these writings, too much ill-concealed proselytizing, too little objective analysis, to allow them to qualify for inclusion among philosophical writing proper. Moreover, as we look at these titles and others like them it becomes clear that they fail, after all, the test of generality. For the great subjects of philosophy, the nature of human knowledge, the limits of science, the foundations of morality or of aesthetics, the relation between our language and the world, must be concerned with 'us' in the sense in which 'we' are all humans. The truths which philosophers seek must aim to be not merely generally, but objectively, even universally, true. Essentially they must be gender-indifferent. Those who deny that any such truth is possible – who argue, as postmodernists, that there is an infinite variety of points of view, no one to be preferred to any other; that there is no common shared world, but that we each construct our own world and use what metaphors we choose to explain that construction – are engaged, it seems to me, not in philosophy but in a species of anthropology. And there are many feminists, and many postmodernist critics, who would not deny this. And so, with some misgivings, I decided to represent the most famous and one of the earliest of feminists, Mary Wollstonecraft, and no one else who published under that banner. Her rambling book *A Vindication of the Rights of Woman* was published in 1792 and, though mainly an outburst against the inequalities and injustice suffered by women, was nevertheless wider in its implications than that would suggest. It is a work of political philosophy, concerned with justice and equality for everyone, not only for women. It is a work of genuine socialism. Equality must mean equality among all mankind; and this means not only between men and women, but between the rich and the poor, the privileged and the oppressed, whichever their gender. In this spirit, she was concerned above all with the fundamental political importance of education. And it is this topic that is represented below.

My other reason for omitting most writing that would be called specifically feminist is that I wanted to show the variety of philosophical topics on which women have written, and written well. It may still be asked whether or not women have a particular 'voice' as philosophers, but it would prejudge the answer to that question if too great a proportion of the extracts I selected were concerned with 'women's' subjects. The only thing that tempted me to break my own rule was that I was prevented by it from extracting any part of Janet Radcliffe Richards's book *The Sceptical Feminist*, first published in 1980. I can only say of it that it is by far the best and the most philosophical study of the subject that I know.

Before we turn to those who have been included, there are two more omissions to be explained. First, one of the earliest of the women philosophers who began gradually to emerge in the first half of the seventeenth century was Princess Elizabeth of Bohemia, the shrewd and energetic correspondent of Descartes. I have found it impossible to include any extracts from her letters, because it is impossible to make them free-standing. They are unintelligible without Descartes's replies. She may sometimes have been right where Descartes was wrong or confused, but the difficulty of showing her as the thinker she undoubtedly was is a presentational one, as far as this book is concerned, and cannot be overcome. (An annotated edition of both sides of the correspondence would be worth undertaking.)

The other woman philosopher who is, sadly, not represented is absent for the excellent reason that she never wrote anything. I refer to J. S. Mill's friend and eventual wife, Harriet Taylor. We know how deeply his writing was influenced by her; during the period of their marriage he wrote the essay *Enfranchisement of Women*, and wrote and revised perhaps his most famous work, *On Liberty*. Immediately after her death, he embarked on *The Subjection of Women*. The passionate plea for individuality, and the denunciation of the 'tyranny of the majority', which make *On Liberty* such an instantly appealing book, especially to the young, make far better sense if they are seen in the context of women's war against oppression. There is some sense in which we should be able to ascribe all these works to Harriet Taylor/Mill herself. But, however great her influence over Mill may have been, we cannot. (For a persuasive account of this matter, see Gertrude Himmelfarb, *On Liberty and Liberalism: The Case of John Stuart Mill* (New York, 1974).)

So at last for the inclusions: I start with Anne Conway, to whom I have already referred. Like many, if not all, philosophers of her time, including Descartes, Hobbes, Spinoza and Leibniz, she was above all interested in the question of what things there are in the universe and how they are divided up one from another. What are the things, or substances, to which attributes are ascribed? This led to the further fundamental question of how substances change. To what extent can an individual thing change and still be the same individual thing? The notion of a substance, that which 'has' attributes, had been at the centre of philosophical thought since Aristotle, and in the Middle Ages had been central both to logic and to theology. Anne Conway, too, raised the question of substance in a theological context. God, she held, is essentially incorporeal and essentially the creator. God is the unique member of one distinct class of substances. The second distinct kind of substance also has one member, namely Christ, who was essentially both man and God, corporeal and incorporeal. The third and last class of substances contains everything else that exists. To hold this view entails asserting that there is no essential difference between, say, tables and chairs on the one hand, and humans or other animals on the other. There is a huge number of essentially separate individual items in the world, which have been created separate but to which attributes or properties come and go as the separate items react to or reflect other items. There is a continuum of such reflection: at one end what we should call 'thought', at the other what would be referred to, I suppose, as reactive change. In principle an individual man, created to be a separate substance, could so change as to become a chair or a table, but he would still be the same individual as he was, even though no one might recognize this. In propounding this highly original theory Anne Conway rejected the materialism of Hobbes, who had held that there is only one kind of stuff, or matter, and that it is broken up into individual bits arbitrarily, according to the words we choose to use of it. She also, though with more difficulty, rejected Descartes's theory that there were just two distinct kinds of substance, *res cogitans* and *res extensa* ('thinking thing' and 'extended thing').

Anne Conway's work was known to Leibniz and admired by him. There is an obvious similarity between her created individuals and his monads, each of which reacts to or 'mirrors' the activity of all the rest, and which form a series, parts of which are more active than others, but of which none is totally active (for only God is totally active) and none totally inactive. Indeed the word 'monad' seems first to have been used by the Cambridge theologian Henry More, who taught both Anne Conway's brother and her husband, and who spent many years living in the Conways' house as librarian and resident Thinker. Prototypes of the monads, and the consequential relativity of space and time, are to be found in Anne Conway's book. She has, indeed, been described as a 'proto-Leibniz'. And the question of influence, as opposed to similarity, is one that it would be worth trying to disentangle. Eccentric and sometimes wild though her writing is,

Anne Conway seems to me to be one of the few women philosophers who may be said to have been unjustly neglected.

The next philosopher represented is Catharine Cockburn, a very different figure indeed, and in some ways a characteristically eighteenth-century writer, though one of her main philosophical concerns was with the work of John Locke. She wrote various defences of Locke, on the subject of the Resurrection, in this contributing to a long-standing argument which had started in the correspondence between Locke and Edward Stillingfleet, Bishop of Worcester, and had been carried on by them until 1699, when it was taken over by others. That apart, it seems that she was mostly interested in social and political questions, in sovereigns' rights over their people, and in the origins of morality. She was certainly interested in argument, as the extracts I have chosen demonstrate.

We come now to the fiery and enthusiastic figure of Mary Wollstonecraft, whose *Vindication of the Rights of Woman* I have referred to above. She is followed by Harriet Martineau, perhaps the woman with the least right to be deemed a philosopher of those whom I have included. But she was a determined and independent thinker, publishing in 1851 a strongly anti-theological book, the *Laws of Man's Nature and Development*. In the extracts I have chosen from her correspondence with Atkinson (which belongs to the same year) she shows herself determined to bridge what was generally assumed to be a total gap between the mind and the body; while this preoccupation may in some ways be reminiscent of Anne Conway, much more seriously it looks forward to arguments on the 'mind/body problem' that became familiar in the twentieth century.

The next philosopher, Victoria Lady Welby, brings us almost, but not quite, into the era of professional women philosophers. She was born just too early (in 1837) for the great revolution in the education of girls brought about by the founding of the girls' day-schools of the 1870s and onwards. In any case these schools were mainly designed for the middle classes, that is, for girls who would ultimately earn their livings. She was not of this class. She was a god-daughter of Queen Victoria and became one of her maids of honour. Her philosophical studies were entirely those of an amateur, and the long list of her publications, as well as the genuine originality of her interest in meaning, is all the more to her credit. Yet, though she published in learned journals (and the extract I have chosen is from *Mind* 1898), there is still something markedly non-professional in her style. She rambles a bit; she protests too often against what she calls 'linguistic anarchy'. Having had a good idea, she is in danger of running it to death. But that it was a good idea is indisputable. In her first book, *Links and Clues* (1881), she was primarily concerned with the nature of religious belief, and from this she derived her interest in the meanings of the words making up the religious vocabulary. She argued that language always follows experience, and that meanings therefore change over time. She wrote to Bishop Talbot, that formidable theological figure: 'When the Fathers of the Church, the great divines of three centuries ago, are quoted to me, I have always the same answer: are you able to tell me positively, of your own knowledge, that what they said then they would say now, here in this room, knowing all we know and belonging to these times?' Rather than attempting to reconcile science with religion, she regarded it as her task to restructure religious belief through science.

Victoria Welby was constantly in touch, through her correspondence, not only with theologians but with fellow-philosophers. She wrote a long article on her new invention, 'significs', for the eleventh edition of the *Encyclopaedia Britannica*, and there survives an important correspondence that she had with the American philosopher Charles Peirce.

So far the women whose work is included here have all, necessarily, been amateurs. Therefore there is little or no point in considering whether they have had a common influence or followed a common road; they have followed their own inclinations and have not, on the whole, contributed much to the history of philosophy as pursued in the universities. Moreover, being, all of them, determinedly individualistic (otherwise they would not have become engaged in philosophy, which was, after all, not a particularly 'feminine' occupation), they would be the last to wish to see anything common to all women philosophers. They pursued what subjects they personally thought important or interesting, in whatever way, and in whatever time, was available to them.

We move on now to the professionals, and of them there may be more point in asking whether or not they speak with a recognizable common voice. The first of them is Mary Whiton Calkins. Mary Calkins, an American, and a pupil of Josiah Royce and William James, taught for many years at Wellesley College, Massachusetts. I have selected from her writings part of her introduction to philosophy, derived from her lectures to first-year undergraduates. I chose this extract (instead of, for example, something from her discussion of the difference between the concept of the soul and that of the self, or from her work on moral philosophy) because it seemed to me of interest to consider what she thought philosophy was, and her views as to the direction in which philosophical studies must lead. She was, above all else, like her master, Royce, an idealist. Idealism flourished in many different forms in America long after it had died in Europe. Mary Calkins has been described as 'an indomitable absolutist'. She doubtless had an influence on numbers of her students at Wellesley; but beyond that, in spite of her professionalism, it is doubtful if much wider influence could be ascribed to her.

Next comes Susan Stebbing, a most remarkable person, the first woman professor of philosophy in Britain, holding the chair of moral philosophy at Bedford College in the University of London, after a fellowship at Girton College, Cambridge. She had been much influenced by G. E. Moore at Cambridge. She was primarily a logician and had been in Cambridge during the most exciting developments of the 'new' formal logic. But it was largely the Moore of *The Defence of Common Sense* that appealed to her. Her style of argument is so well exemplified in the extract here reproduced that hardly any more need be said, except that the general purpose to debunk, to prick pretentious balloons, became the hallmark of philosophy after the Second World War (perhaps especially in Oxford, but generally as well) and that Susan Stebbing was a brilliant teacher within this overall purpose.

Another woman who fell under the spell of the 'new' symbolic logic was the American Susanne K. Langer, from whose *Philosophy in a New Key* I have included an extract. She was a pupil of Alfred North Whitehead, and wrote on symbolic logic in 1937, and then, imaginatively though not wholly originally, extended the idea of the symbol to include a far wider field, including aesthetics and religion. She attempted here to give art the claim to meaning that science could be given, through the analysis of symbolic modes. She distinguished non-discursive symbols in art, especially music, from the discursive symbols of scientific language and argued that art is a highly articulated form of expression symbolizing direct or intuitive knowledge of emotion. She was much influenced in this work by the exile from Europe Ernst Cassirer, who became professor of philosophy at Yale in

1932 (Yale was then and for long the centre both of idealism and of continental philosophy, of all the kinds most despised both in many other universities in the USA and by many British universities, again especially Oxford). Susanne Langer's work was widely read; *Philosophy in a New Key* went into many editions, and she was an early exemplar of the important link between philosophy as practised in Europe and in the English-speaking world.

In this connection, it is necessary to say something of a general kind about philosophy in England in the period following the Second World War. Before the war, a bombshell had exploded in the philosophical world, the effects of which were felt, indeed, beyond the confines of academic philosophy. It took the form of A. J. Ayer's slim book *Language, Truth and Logic*, which introduced to England the teachings of the Vienna Circle and seemed to have the power to show that not only metaphysics but theology, moral philosophy and aesthetics were all strictly nonsensical, being couched in language that was unverifiable and therefore without meaning. It was not only moral philosophy but morality itself, not only theology but religion, that appeared to be undermined, and therefore the reaction to the new logical positivism was almost hysterical. But this excitement had not had time to die down before war broke out, and for six years philosophy hardly existed in the universities. After the war, when professional philosophers came back and, more important, new young men and women were recruited to the ranks to teach all the numerous ex-servicemen and women returning to the universities, a spirit of revolution prevailed. But the mood, not just in philosophy but in all academic subjects, was cool. The new broom offered by Ayer before the war was not taken up; instead, philosophers began to work on a limited scale, trying to get things right one by one. The essentially Kantian challenge of trying to work out the relation between the words and concepts we employ and the world we live in began to be explored piecemeal, in all sorts of different philosophical areas. At the same time the new works of Wittgenstein (not the wideranging, bold, almost Leibnizian and dotty *Tractatus Logico-Philosophicus*, which had been published in 1922, but those concerned with the living use of language, and the nature of traditional philosophical problems) began to become known. At first, this new work was handed about in typewritten sheets, reported on little by little from hearsay, or as a result of lectures by those who, like Elizabeth Anscombe, were disciples of Wittgenstein. But at last, in 1953, *The Philosophical Investigations* appeared, in a translation by Elizabeth Anscombe, and it became apparent just how pervasive the influence of Wittgenstein had already become during the previous five years. There is no doubt that, if for nothing other than the transmission of the work of Wittgenstein, Elizabeth Anscombe would have to be counted as one of the most important philosophers in the post-war academic world. I shall return to her original contribution, in my view no less remarkable, in a moment.

Meanwhile, the casualties in this flowering of philosophy were moral and political philosophy. These subjects were still taught in the universities, because they were still part of the undergraduate syllabus, but the current interest in language had placed a dead hand on them; for it was supposed that moral philosophers (and those interested in political philosophy were in no better case) could do no more than examine the nature of what was supposed to be a special kind of language, namely the evaluative. There were, it was admitted, real-life moral or political problems, but it was not for philosophers to talk about these: their concern must be with the language in which such problems were posed and answered ('What ought I to do?' 'You should do x or y') and with whatever it was that one had to understand by such questions and answers, that is, with the meaning of the phrases involved. There was thought to be one way in which 'factual' expressions had meaning, and a quite different way in which 'evaluative' expressions had meaning. There might be some disagreement about what constituted evaluative meaning (for example, some argued that evaluative expressions were all of them 'emotive', either expressing or evoking emotions, while others supposed that they were imperative, concerned cryptically or overtly with commands to action), but it was common ground that the two kinds of meaning, evaluative and factual, were totally distinct. The consequence drawn from this dichotomy was that, while disputes about matters of fact could be settled, at least in principle, by observation, disputes about matters of morality could not. Therefore there was ultimately no arguing about morals or politics. Either one had to say, 'I feel horror at such and such a course of action, even though you do not', and leave it at that; or one had to turn 'You ought to do this or that' into 'Do this or that', a command for which no reason need be given and to which, of course, no obedience could be exacted otherwise than by force. Not unnaturally, moral philosophy came to seem both rather empty and rather easy. It was, on the whole, seen as a subject fitted more for women than for men. It is against this background that Philippa Foot's article, reproduced below (p. 224) must be read. It seemed revolutionary in 1958 to suggest that a judgement might be designated a *moral* judgement, or refused that title, on grounds not of the language in which it was couched but of its content. A certain realism began to creep in. In the same year as Philippa Foot's article appeared, John Rawls published an article entitled 'Justice as Fairness' (which later became part of his book *A Theory of Justice*), in which he argued that the idea of justice was the central concept of morality and began to explore its nature. Another highly influential outbreak of realism had occurred.

In Europe, a different brand of philosophy altogether was flourishing at this time. Jean-Paul Sartre's *Being and Nothingness* was written in 1943; its English translation was published in 1957. However, many of Sartre's novels and plays were already known in this country and in the USA. In 1953 Iris Murdoch published a book called *Sartre: Romantic Rationalist*, which discussed primarily the novels and plays but also the philosophy, and which, for many people, was their first introduction to existentialism as a philosophical mode. There was not such a complete divorce between existentialism and English-speaking philosophy as has sometimes been supposed (and as was certainly supposed in Britain in the mid-1950s). There was a great deal of common ancestry, not least in Husserl, who was a revelation both to Sartre, and to Gilbert Ryle in Oxford, whose *Concept of Mind* owes much to him. Nevertheless, the manner and the purpose of existentialism were markedly alien to the kind of cool style and disinterested analysis that characterized most British philosophy at that time. Iris Murdoch wrote this of Sartre:

> A driving force in all his writing is his serious desire to change the life of his reader. It is perhaps this which makes his philosophical conscious-ness stop short of a critical awareness of language. When one is concerned to persuade and communicate one is, as Sartre himself put it, too much inside language to see it as a structure of the external world. It is certainly his rhetorical anxiety to persuade, as well as his psychological picture-making technique, which is responsible for what is open to criticism in Sartre's theories.[1]

I have included in this collection three women who may roughly be called existentialist philosophers. First, Hannah Arendt. She was, in the first place, always concerned not with analysis only, but also with persuasion. She never failed to be engaged with actual political issues. Though at her best, in my view, when concerned with the examination of particular political concepts (as she is in the piece I have included), she is not afraid (far from it) to tackle vast subjects (as in her book *The Human Condition*, 1958). On the other hand, she could also exemplify the 'picture-painting' side of existentialism, in that she could use real-life situations from which to draw wide philosophical conclusions, as she did from her reporting of the Eichmann trials.[2]

The second existentialist philosopher is Iris Murdoch herself. In *The Sovereignty of Good*, from which I have extracted a chapter, she is highly critical of existentialist moral theory. Yet her immersion in the real world makes it not inappropriate so to describe her. The third writer is Simone de Beauvoir. I had considerable difficulty in deciding whether or not to include her in this collection, but I have done so, briefly, though with some remaining doubts. It is not that she does not write in some way philosophically; it is more that one cannot easily disentangle her philosophical thoughts from those of her close companion Sartre. It is rather like trying to decide between the thoughts of Wordsworth and those of Coleridge at the height of their friendship. In one way, such a distinction makes no sense: they thought the same thoughts. So with Sartre and Simone de Beauvoir. It may be, for all we know, that she originated some of the philosophical ideas that lie behind her novels, her autobiography *The Second Sex*, *Old Age* (from which my extract comes) and all her other many publications; it may be that they all come from Sartre, and that she merely used them. But her manner of weaving these ideas into her descriptions, the way in which they structure her understanding of the world, is so totally characteristic of the existentialist mode that she had to be included. Not all philosophers, after all, not even all of those here represented, are original thinkers or innovators. From the standpoint of an anthologist, the real drawback to Simone de Beauvoir's inclusion is the extreme difficulty of picking out parts from the endless, unstructured end-on quotations that constitute her preferred style.

I have no doubt that existentialism changed moral philosophy in this country and made it less arid and depressing than it had been in the period immediately after the Second World War; and there is no doubt either that women philosophers were influential in this change. I have already argued that Philippa Foot, though in no way to be described as an existentialist, in her 1958 and subsequent articles was breaking away from the rigidity of the distinction between 'factual' and 'evaluative' language as constituting the sole subject-matter of moral philosophy, and was introducing a new spirit of realism.

From the late 1960s onwards there were extraneous factors as well which changed the nature of moral and political philosophy. Students had long been liable to disappointment at what they were offered under the title of Morals and Politics. They had long hoped for something 'relevant', for an academic discipline which would help them address actual moral or political issues. It was clear that there existed immediate problems, at least in the USA, which their teachers could not refuse to discuss. Philosophy was obliged to turn its techniques and its arguments on to such issues as the ethics of draft-dodging or the possibility of a just war. The whole student body, in America, in France and finally in Britain, was politicized as never before. It seemed (truly or falsely) that quite new and urgent moral issues were arising every day and could not be avoided. Something akin to the existentialist mode, at any rate the application of philosophy to live issues, began to appear in almost all philosophy departments, even if sometimes the professionals might seem to drag their feet. But on the whole they willingly, indeed enthusiastically, adopted the developing style. 'Applied philosophy' was a new concept, and books and articles began to appear in great numbers on environmental, medical and jurisprudential issues. The habit of taking real examples or defending actual positions steadily grew. As a result (or partly so), in public life moral philosophers became increasingly accustomed to being recruited as members of the large number of official committees or Royal Commissions set up to examine the kinds of problems thought to be too complicated or controversial to be left to ministers and their civil servants.

Both men and women entered this arena, of course. Professor Bernard Williams, who chaired the Commission on Obscenity and Film Censorship (1977-9), was one of the first. But there is no doubt that the realistic manner (and I prefer this term to 'applied philosophy') suited women well. Certainly as moral philosophers they had long been good at examining real complexities and at using philosophy to unravel what lay behind real differences of view. I have included two extracts from the work of women who exemplify these virtues. The first is an article by Judith Jarvis Thomson on abortion, which has become a standard text; the second a chapter from Mary Midgley's influential and justly popular book *Beast and Man*, which among all the large numbers of books on animal rights or human duties towards animals stands out as the best, the most fundamental and the most firmly grounded in philosophy. The final extract on moral philosophy is from Onora O'Neill. Although she is engaged in numerous public inquiries and is the very type of the woman philosopher the government most needs and uses, and although she has written extensively on real and live issues, I have chosen to represent her by a theoretical and general discussion of the nature of morality, because it shows that adopting the realistic mode of philosophy does not entail losing sight of those probing, analytic and universal aspects of the subject, attention to which (as I said at the beginning) entitles a writer to be deemed a philosopher. Indeed, the realistic mode would soon become futile, as well as unconvincing, if it lost itself in the particular and the non-explanatory and forgot its philosophical pretensions.

It will be immediately apparent that, among living women philosophers, the majority of those I have selected have been concerned, more or less, with moral or political philosophy. This, I suppose, lends some colour to the view prevalent in the 1950s and 1960s, to which I have already referred, that moral philosophy was a woman's subject, a kind of soft option. It is certainly true that there are many women who are good at moral philosophy. But this is not to say that women have not worked successfully in other fields as well. Julia Annas, for example, has written outstandingly well on Plato. But I believe it to be true that one of the most original contributions of women in recent years has been in the reviving, one might almost say resurrecting, of moral philosophy from the moribundity of the immediate post-war period. Therefore what might seem like a misleading bias in the collection is not, I think, without some justification.

In any case, I have told only half the story. Just as after the Second World War there was a decline in moral philosophy, so more recently there has been a decline in, or undermining of, the theory of knowledge. In 1980 Richard Rorty published a book entitled *Philosophy and the Mirror of Nature*.[3] Rorty, citing as his 'heroes' Dewey, Wittgenstein, Sellars and Kuhn, sought to demonstrate that the concept of knowledge as 'truthfulness to reality' was basically mistaken, and that therefore all epistemology from Plato to Kant and beyond was barking up some doubtless honourable but essentially wrong tree. His book was not alone, nor especially original. He was in fact caught up in the enormous wave of relativism associated with Foucault and Derrida and such of their English and American followers as Don Cupitt and many of the feminist writers I have already mentioned. This relativism, generally known as postmodernism, has had an obfuscating effect not only on epistemology but, more notoriously, on history, theology and, above all, literary criticism. But there are signs that, at least among philosophers, there is a growing tendency to fight back, and women have played an important part in this renaissance, as well as the other.

Elizabeth Anscombe would probably deny the suggestion that Wittgenstein belongs with Dewey and Rorty's other heroes as a founder of the relativist tradition; but, whether that is so or not, she herself has been apparently unaffected by the relativizing trend and has continued steadily to write on topics in metaphysics and the theory of knowledge as well as on moral philosophy. She is probably best known for her book on intention, and for her other writings in the philosophy of mind and in metaphysics. I have therefore chosen her inaugural lecture, delivered in Cambridge after her election to the chair of philosophy there, on the central philosophical topic of causation, both to represent the authoritative and commanding nature of her philosophical style and to demonstrate the continued possibility of treating this kind of traditional subject in an original and properly philosophical manner.

My last extract is from Susan Haack, who confronts head-on the recent relativistic undermining of epistemology. The extract I have chosen, the first chapter of her book *Evidence and Inquiry: Towards Reconstruction in Epistemology*, is a serious attempt to get away from the destructive dichotomy between a kind of realism on the one hand and an ultimate relativism on the other, and to re-establish the possibility of epistemology. Her book is, in my view, highly important and will be influential in any serious critique of postmodernism, or indeed of certain aspects of feminism as a whole.

Any such collection as this must obviously be in part a matter of personal preference. Other people would undoubtedly have chosen some different philosophers, and, if they had chosen the same, would have chosen different extracts from their work. It has to be admitted that there are philosophers, including those who write roughly in the existentialist mode, from whose work it is extremely difficult to extract, their style being cumulative, full of quotations and, above all, very long. I have tried to include nothing that is not more or less coherent, but even in this modest aim I may not always have succeeded. For this, and for inevitable omissions, I can only apologize. In the end, I have not found any clear 'voice' shared by women philosophers. I have enjoyed reading their works, some more than others, and I have been filled with admiration for the leisured women who, before they had access to any university, took up philosophy as a hobby and became so relatively expert. But it would have been very unrealistic to expect to find, among such determined and individualistic women, anything shared except these qualities of character. As for the professionals, they turn out, unsurprisingly, to be as various as their male colleagues. I believe this is a matter not for disappointment but for pride.

References

1. Iris Murdoch, *Sartre* (Cambridge: Bowes & Bowes, 1953), p. 8.

2. Hannah Arendt, *Eichmann in Jerusalem: A Report on the Banality of Evil* (London: Faber & Faber, 1963–4).

3. Richard Rorty, *Philosophy and the Mirror of Nature* (Princeton, NJ: Princeton University Press, 1979; Oxford: Basil Blackwell, 1980).

WOMEN
PHILOSOPHERS

ANNE CONWAY (1631–79)

Anne Conway, née Finch, was born in 1631 and died in 1679. In 1651 she married the third Viscount Conway, and they lived at Ragley in Warwickshire. Her book *The Principles of the Most Ancient and Modern Philosophy* was probably written in 1670. It was written in English but later translated into Latin, in which language it was published in 1690. This Latin version was certainly read, and referred to, by Leibniz. In 1692 an English version of the Latin text was produced, without reference to the original English text, which may already have been lost. It is from this version that most of chapters 6 and 7 are reproduced below. Both Latin and subsequent English texts are in the British Library, but I have used a publication of English and Latin texts together, edited by Peter Lopston and published by Martinus Nijhoff, The Hague, in 1982.

In these chapters, which are central to the book, Anne Conway argues that there exist exactly three kinds of substance, which are *essentially* different one from another. The first is that which is wholly immutable, i.e. God; the second is that which in its essence is both mutable and immutable, i.e. the Logos or Christ; the third is the mutable, i.e. everything else that exists. Mutability entails motion, and motion is the origin of time, which is relative to motion and change. It is impossible for one of these kinds of substance to change into any other kind; but the third kind of substance, all creation, shares the same nature, and therefore it is theoretically possible for any one item of the created world to change into any other. This theoretical possibility is distinct from the fact that in the world we inhabit, according to the laws we understand, a man will not change into another, still less into a horse. The impossibility of Peter's changing into Paul in the world we have is, however, different from the essential impossibility (impossibility *de re*) of a man or any other created thing changing into God. Things stand like this because of the goodness of God, who has chosen to make a perfectible universe.

There are three systems to which Anne Conway's theories are opposed: first, she is opposed to the materialism of Thomas Hobbes, who held matter or substance to be divided up only according to the arbitrary categories which language imposes on it; secondly, she is opposed to the dualism of Descartes, who held that there were two, and only two kinds of substance – thinking substance, and material or extended substance – and that humans were essentially thinking beings; thirdly, she is opposed to the theory of Spinoza, according to whom the whole of nature is identical with God but seen under a different aspect.

The obvious objection to Anne Conway's system is that in real life all created things do not appear to be of the same substance: the distinction, central to Descartes, between mind and matter seems too important to be simply overlooked. Her response would be that everything thinks or reacts to other things, but some things (especially humans) think more coherently and more clearly than others. The apparent differences between, for example, stones and men are real differences and can be confirmed by all kinds of observed regularities in the world, but they are not *essential* differences. Where Anne Conway posits 'thinking' as the characteristic of all created things, Leibniz was later to posit 'activity' as the characteristic of all monads. Things in the universe appear different from one another, and one can describe these differences systematically, to account for apparent motion and change in the world; but in essence, according to Leibniz, monads are distinguished from one another only by the degree of their activity. There is no doubt that there are striking similarities between Leibniz's monadology and Anne Conway's theory of substance. Indeed, it is easier to make sense of her somewhat bizarre-seeming theory by comparing it with that of Leibniz, who reached his position by logical as well as metaphysical and theological arguments. I have therefore added some works by and about Leibniz in the reading-suggestions below.

Further Reading

Anne Conway, *The Principles of the Most Ancient and Modern Philosophy*, ed. Peter Loptson, International Archives of the History of Ideas (The Hague: Martinus Nijhoff, 1982)

Leibniz, *Monadology*, 1714 (*The Philosophical Writings of Leibniz*, ed. Parkinson)

The Concise Encyclopaedia of Western Philosophy and Philosophers, ed. J. O. Urmson (London: Hutchinson, 1960), s.n. Leibniz.

William and Martha Kneale, *The Development of Logic* (Oxford: Clarendon Press, 1962), pp. 320–36.

From The Principles of the Most Ancient and Modern Philosophy, *ed. Peter Loptson (The Hague: Martinus Nijhoff, 1982), chapters vi–vii*

1. That all Creatures in their own Nature are changeable, the distinction between God and Creatures, duly considered, evidently evinces, and the same is by daily experience confirmed. Now if any Creature be in its own Nature changeable, it hath this Mutability, as it is a Creature, and consequently all Creatures will have the same, according to that Rule: Whatsoever agrees to any thing as placed under this or that *Species*, agrees to all comprehended under the same *Species*; but Mutability agrees to a Creature (which is the most general name of that *Species*, under which all Creatures are comprehended,) and from thence it is manifest; for otherwise there would be no distinction between God and Creatures: For if any Creature were of it self, and in its own Nature unchangeable, that Creature would be God, because Immutability is one of his incommunicable Attributes.

2. Now let us consider how far this Mutability may reach, or be extended; and, First, whether one Individual can be changed into another of the same or a different *Species*: This, I say, is impossible; for then the very Essences of Things would be changed, which would make a great confusion, not only in the Creatures, but in the Wisdom of God, which made all Things: As for Example: If this Man could be changed into that, *viz. Paul* into *Judas*, or *Judas* into *Paul*, then he that sinned would not be punished for his sin, but another in his stead, who was both Vertuous and Innocent; so then a Good Man would not receive the reward of his Vertue, but a Vicious Man in his stead: But if we suppose one good Man to be changed into another, as *Paul* into *Peter*, and *Peter* into *Paul*, *Paul* would not receive his own proper

Reward, but *Peter's* nor *Peter* his, but *Paul's*, which would be a confusion, and unbecoming the Wisdom of God. Moreover, if the very individual Essences of Things could be changed one into another, it would follow, Creatures were not true in themselves; and so we could not be assured, nor have any certain knowledge of any thing; and then all the inbred Notions and Dictates of Truth, which Men generally find in themselves, would be false, and by consequence the Conclusions drawn from thence; for every true Science, or certainty of Knowledge, depends upon the Truth of the Objects, which are commonly called *Veritates Objectivae*, or *Objective Truths*: If therefore these Objective Truths should be changed the one into the other, certainly the Truth of the Propositions depending thereon would be changed also; and so no Proposition could be unchangeably true, no not the most clear and obvious as these are; the whole is greater than its part, and two halves make a whole.

3. The Second Thing to be considered is, Whether one *Species* of Things can be changed into another? Where we must diligently observe after what manner the *Species* of Things are distinguished one from another; for there be many *Species* of Things, which are commonly so called, and yet in Substance of Essence differ not one from another, but in certain Manners or Properties, and when those Modes or Properties are changed, that thing is said to have changed its *Species*: Now whether or no this be not a certain manner of Existence, and not the Essence or Being of the Thing it self that is so changed? As when Water indeed is not changed, but remains the same, and cold coagulates it, which before was fluid: When Water is changed into a Stone, certainly there is no reason, why we should here suppose a greater change of its Substance, than in the former Example of Water turned into Ice. And again when a Stone is changed into soft and tender Earth, here is made no change of its Substance; and so in all other Mutations which we observe in Things, the Substance or Essence always remains the same, and there is only a change of *Modus* or Manner; so that when a Thing ceases to be after this manner, it then begins to be after another manner. And indeed the same Reasons do prove, that one *Species* essentially or substantially distinct from another, cannot be changed into another, even as one Individual cannot be changed into another: For the *Species* of Things are nothing else but Individuals digested, or comprehended, under one general

Idea of the Mind, or Common Term of speaking: As a Man, inasmuch as he is a *Species*, comprehends under him all the Individuals of Men; and a Horse is a *Species*, comprehending every individual Horse. Now if one Man cannot be changed into another, much less can this Man be changed into another Individual of a differing *Species*. For Example: If *Alexander* cannot be changed into *Darius*, he cannot be changed into his own Horse *Bucephalus*.

4. In order to know how far the Mutations of Things can reach, we must examine how many *Species* of Things there be, which as to Substance or Essence are distinct one from another; and if we diligently inquire thereinto, we shall find only Three, as before was said, *viz*. God, Christ, and the Creatures, and that these Three in respect of Essence, are really distinct one from another, is already proved; but there can be no Reason alledged to prove, that there is any Fourth kind of Being distinct from the other Three; yea, a Fourth kind of Being seems wholly superfluous: And because all the *Phaenomena* in the whole Universe may be sufficiently resolved into these Three before-mentioned, as into their proper and original Causes, there is no necessity to acknowledge any other, according to this Rule: (Which if rightly understood, it is most true and certain) Beings are not to be multiplied without necessity; for seeing the Three before-mentioned remove all the Specifical Differences in Substances, which possibly can be conceived in our Minds; and so by these alone is that vast and infinite possibility of Things filled up: How then can there be room or place found for a Fourth, Fifth, Sixth, or Seventh Being? And that it is performed by these Three is already before demonstrated; to wit, that whatsoever can be in any wise called a Being, the same is either wholly unchangeable, and such is God the Supreme Being, or is wholly changeable, *viz*. to good, or evil, and such is the creature or lowest being, or that which is partly unchangeable, *viz*. in respect of Evil, or partly changeable, to wit, in respect of Good; by which is understood Christ, the Son of God; that Middle Being between God and the Creatures; into what *Classis* or Rank therefore shall we bring a certain Fourth, Fifth, Sixth, or Seventh Being, &c. which is neither wholly changeable, nor wholly unchangeable; nor partly changeable, nor partly unchangeable: Besides, he that supposeth a certain Fourth Being, essentially or

substantially distinct from the three before-mentioned, over-throws that most excellent Order we find in the universality of Things, to wit, that there is not only one *Medium* between God and the Creatures, but two, three, four, five, six, or as many as can be supposed between first and latter. Moreover, it is very consentaneous to sound Reason, and so also to the Order of Things, that as God is but One, neither hath he two, three, or more distinct Substances in him; and Christ but one Christ, neither hath in him more distinct Substances, inasmuch as he is the heavenly Man, and very First *Adam*; so likewise the Creature, or whole Creation, is but one only Substance or Essence in *Specie*, although it comprehends many Individuals placed in their subordinate *Species*, and indeed in Manner, but not in Substance or Essence distinct one from another. And so that which *Paul* speaketh concerning Man, may in like manner be understood of all Creatures, (who in their Original State were a certain *Species* of Man so called for their Excellencies, as hereafter shall be shown;) to wit, that God made all Nations, or Armies of Creatures, out of one Blood: And certainly here the reason of both is the same; for as God made all Nations out of one Blood, to the end they might love each other, and stand in a mutual Sympathy, and help each other; so hath he implanted a certain Universal Sympathy and mutual Love in Creatures, as being all Members of one Body, and (as I may so say) Brethren, having one common Father, to wit, God in Christ, or the Word made Flesh; and so also one Mother, *viz.* that Substance or Essence alone, out of which they proceeded, and whereof they are real Parts and Members; and albeit Sin hath in a wonderful Manner impaired this Love and Sympathy, yet it hath not destroyed it.

5. Those Three distinct Beings, before-mentioned, being granted, and no more, which are wholly inconvertible the one into the other, we shall tread in a secure path, in the mid-way of Truth, leaving these grand Errors and Confusions about Entity, both on the Right Hand and the left: For, First, there are some, who teach, that there is but one Being of all Things, whereof the Creatures are real and Proper Parts, and these confound God and the Creatures together, as though both were but one single Essence; so that Sin and Devils would be nothing else but Parts, or at least Modifications of that Divine Being, from whence do arise very dangerous consequences. Although I would not have it misinterpreted to

those who are unwarily faln into this Opinion; yet I would warn the Reader, that he may the better consider whereunto such Principles tend, and avoid their absurdity. There are others again who allow only two *Species* of Things, *viz.* God the Supreme Being, wholly unchangeable; and the Creature the lowest Being, wholly changeable; but these do not duly consider that excellent Order by us above described, which is apparent in all Things; because else peradventure they would have taken notice, that besides these Two Extreams, there is a certain *Medium*, which is partaker of both, and this is Jesus that Christ, whom not only the wiser sort of the *Jews*, but also some among the *Gentiles* so called, have acknowledged, *viz.* maintaining that there is such a *Medium*, which they called by divers Names, as *Logos*, the Son of God, the First Begotten of God, Mind, Wisdom, heavenly *Adam* &c. So that some also do call him the Eternal *Medium*: Which Things, if duly considered, may not a little conduce to the propagation and furthering of the true Faith, and Christian Religion, among the *Jews*, as well as *Turks*, and other Infidel Nations; that is to say, if it appears we are able to prove that there is a mediator between God and Man; yea, between God and all Creatures, by as solid Reasons as those are, which prove God to be a Creator: And so they that believe on that, may be said truly to believe on Christ Jesus, though they should not as yet have known, or been convicted, that he came in the Flesh: For if they yield to the former, they will undoubtedly be forced (if ingenious) whether they will or no, to grant the latter. Others there are, who do as it were infinitely multiply the Specifical Beings of Things, in their distinct Essences and Essential Attributes; which wholly subverts that excellent Order of Things, and greatly obscures and darkens the Glory of the Divine Attributes, so that it cannot shine forth in its due Splendor and Brightness in the Creatures: For so every Creature is so exceeding straitly bounded, and strictly included and imprisoned within the narrow limits of its own *Species*, that the Mutability of Creatures is wholly taken away: Neither can any Creature variously exercise any greater participation of Divine Goodness, or be advanced or promoted to any farther perfection.

6. All which we shall demonstrate by one or two Examples: And First, let us take an Horse, which is a Creature indued with divers degrees of perfection by his Creator, as not only strength of Body,

but (as I may so say) a certain kind of knowledge, how he ought to serve his Master, and moreover also Love, Fear, Courage, Memory, and divers other Qualities which are in Man: which also we may observe in a Dog, and many other Animals: Seeing therefore the Divine Power, Goodness, and Wisdom, hath created every Creature good; and indeed so, that it might by continual augmentations (in its Mutability) be advanced to a greater degree of Goodness, *ad infinitum*, whereby the Glory of those Attributes do more and more shine forth: And seeing such is the Nature of every Creature, that it is always in Motion or Operation, which doth most certainly tend unto an higher degree of Goodness, as the Reward and Fruit of its Labour; unless the Creatures hinder that good by a voluntary Transgression, and abuse of that indifferency of Will which God placed in them in their Creation. Now I demand, unto what higher perfection and degree of Goodness, the Being or Essence of an Horse doth or may attain after he hath done good service for his Master, and so performed his Duty, and what is proper for such a Creature? Is a Horse then a mere Fabrick or dead Matter? or hath he a Spirit in him, having Knowlege, Sence, and Love, and divers other Faculties and Properties of a Spirit? if he hath, which cannot be denied, what becomes of this spirit when the Horse dies? if it be said it passeth into Life, and takes upon it another Body of an Horse, so that it becomes a Horse as before, which Horse may be stronger and fairer, and of a more excellent Spirit than before. Very well! But if he shall die, two, three, or four times, &c. shall he always remain a Horse, though he be still better, and more excellent, by how much the oftner his Spirit revolves. Now I demand, whether the Spirit of an Horse hath in it such infinite perfection, that a Horse may always become better and better *ad infinitum*, and yet so as to remain a Horse? For as the common received Opinion is, this visible Earth shall not always remain in the same State, which may be confirmed by undeniable Reasons: Now it necessarily follows, that the continual Generation of Animals in these gross Bodies shall cease also; for if the Earth shall take on it another Form, neither any longer bring forth Grass, Horses and other Animals shall cease to be such as they were before: And seeing they want their proper Aliment, they cannot remain in the same *Species*; yet nevertheless they are not annihilated, as may be easily conceived; for how can any thing be annihilated, seeing the Goodness of God towards his Creatures always remains the same; and the conservation or continuation of Creatures is a continued Creation, as is generally granted, and already before demonstrated, that God is a perpetual Creator; and as he is the most free, so also the most necessary Agent: But if it be denied, that the Earth is unchangeable, as before was said, then it will come to pass that Horses and other Animals, according to their proportion, will be in like manner changed with the Earth, and the Earth according to the same proportion, will again produce or yield them Aliment or Food agreeable to their changed condition; then I demand, Whether they shall always remain in the same *Species* under such a change? Or, whether there will not be some difference between that State and this? As for Example: There is between a Cow and a Horse, which is commonly granted to be Specifical. Again, I ask whether the *Species* of Creatures do so infinitely one excel another, that an Individual of one particular *Species* may still go forward in perfection, and approach nearer unto another *Species*, but yet never reach so far as to be changed into that *Species*? As for instance: An Horse in divers Qualities and Perfections draws near unto the Nature and *Species* of a Man, and that more than many other Creatures; Is therefore the nature of a Man distant from the Nature of an Horse, by Infinite Degrees, or by Finite only? If by Finite, then certainly a Horse may in length of Time be in some measure changed into a Man, (I mean his Spirit; as for his Body that is a thing evident:) If infinitely distant; then unto any Man, even one of the vilest and basest Nature and Disposition, may be attributed a certain Infinite Excellence in Act, such as only agrees to God and Christ, but to no Creature; for the highest Excellence of a Creature is to be Infinite only, in *potentia*, not in *actu*; that is, to be still in a possibility of attaining a greater Perfection and Excellence, *ad infinitum*, though it can never reach this Infinite; for how far soever an Finite Being may proceed, yet that is still Finite, although there be no limits to its progression . . . As if there should be supposed a certain Ladder, which should be infinitely long, containing Infinite Steps, yet those Steps are not infinitely distant one from another, otherwise there could be no ascension nor descension made thereon; for Steps (in this Example) signifie the various *Species* of Things, which cannot be infinitely distant one from another, or from those which are next unto them; yea daily experience teaches us, that the *Species* of divers Things are changed, one into another, as Earth into Water, and Water into Air, and Air into Fire or Aether; and the contrary, as Fire into Air, and Air into Water, &c. which yet are distinct *Species* of Things; and so also Stones are changed into Metals, and one Metal into another; but least some should say these are only naked Bodies and have no Spirit, we shall observe the same not only in Vegetables, but also in Animals, like as Barley and Wheat are convertible the one into the other, and are in very deed often so changed, which is well enough known to House-keepers in many Provinces, and especially in *Hungary*, where if Barley be sown Wheat springs up instead thereof; but in other places more barren, and especially in Rocky Places, such as are found in *Germany*, if Wheat be sown, Barley cometh up, and Barley in other places becomes mere Grass: And in Animals, Worms are changed into Flies, and Beasts, and Fishes that feed on Beasts, and Fishes of a different kind, do change them into their own Nature, and *Species*: And doth not also a corrupted Nature, or the Body of Earth and Water, produce Animals without any previous Seed of those Animals? And in the Creation of this World, did not the Waters at the Command of God, produce Birds and Fishes? And did not the Earth also at the same Command bring forth Beasts and Creeping Things; which for that Cause were real and proper Parts of the Earth and Waters? And as they had their Bodies from the Earth, so likewise they had their Spirits or Souls from the same; for the Earth brought forth Living Souls, as the *Hebrew* Text speaketh, but not mere Corporeal Figures, wanting Life and Soul; wherefore there is a very remarkable difference between Humane Creatures and Brutes: Of Man it is said, God made him after his own Image, and breathed into him the Breath of Life, and he became a Living Soul; so that from hence Man received his Life, that principle part of him, (by which he is become a Man,) which is really distinct from that Divine Soul or Spirit which God breathed into him.

And seeing the Body of Man was made out of the Earth, which (as is proved) had therein divers Spirits, and gave Spirits to all Brute Beasts; then unto Man, no doubt, She committed the best and most excellent Spirits whom he was to contain; but all these Spirits were of a far inferiour *Species*, in regard of the Spirit of Man, which he received from above, and not from the Earth: And the Spirit of Man ought to have Dominion over these Spirits, (which were all but Earthly,) so as to subdue them to himself, and exalt them to an higher degree, (*viz.*) into his own proper Nature, and that would have been his true Increase and Multiplication; for all this he suffered the Earthly Spirits existing within him, to get Dominion over him, and so became like them; wherefore it is said, Earth thou art, and unto Earth thou shalt return, which hath no less a Spiritual than a Literal Signification.

7. Now we see how gloriously the Justice of God appears in this Transmutation of Things out of one *Species* into another; and that there is a certain Justice which operates not only in Men and Angels, but in all Creatures, is most certain; and he that doth not observe the same may be said to be utterly Blind: For this Justice appears as well in the Ascension of Creatures, as in their Descension; that is, when they are changed into the better, and when into the worse; when into the better, this Justice distributes to them the Reward and Fruit of their Good Deeds; when into the worse, the same punishes them with due Punishments, according to the Nature and Degree of the Transgression. And the same Justice hath given a Law to all Creatures, and written the same on their natures; and every Creature whatsoever, that transgresseth this Law, is punished for it: But that Creature that observes and keeps it, hath this Reward *viz.*, to become better . . .

God hath also put the same instinct of Justice in Man, towards Beasts and Trees of the Field; for whosoever he be that is a good and just Man, the same loves his Beasts that serve him, and taketh care of them that they have their Food and Rest, and what else is wanting to them; and this he doth not do only for his own profit, but out of a Principle of true Justice; for should he be so cruel to them as to require their labour, and yet deny them their necessary Food, then certainly he transgresseth that Law which God hath written on his Heart; and if he kills any of them, only to fulfil his own pleasure, he acts unjustly, and the same measure will again be measured unto him; so likewise a Man that hath a certain Fruitful Tree in his Orchard, that prospereth well, he dungs and cleanses the same, that it may wax better and better; but if it be barren, and incumbers the ground, then he heweth it down with an Ax, and burns it with Fire. And so here is a certain Justice in all these, as in all the Transmutation of Things from one *Species* into another, whether it be by ascending from the Ignobler or Baser unto the Nobler, or by descending into the contrary, there may be found the same Justice . . .

Chapter VII

Now that I may more clearly demonstrate, that every Body is a certain Spirit or Life in its own Nature, and that the same is a certain intelligent Principle, having Knowledge, Sense, Love, Desire, Joy, and Grief; as it is this or that way affected; and by consequence hath Activity and Motion, *per se*; so that it can remove it self whithersoever it desires to be: I say, in its own Nature, wherein it was originally created, and as it shall be again, when it shall be reduced to its primitive State, and delivered from that Confusion and Vanity, to which it is subject by reason of Sin. I shall produce these following Reasons . . .

1. The first hereof shall be from the Order of Things, before-mentioned, which I have already proved to be but Three; to wit, God the Supreme or Chiefest, Christ the *Medium* or Middle, and the Creature the lowest in Order; which Creature is but one Essence or substance, as to Nature or Essence, as is above demonstrated, so that it only differs *secundum modos existendi*; or, *according to the manners of existence*; among which one is Corporiety; whereof also there are many degrees; so that a Thing may more or less approach to, or recede from the State and Condition of a body or a Spirit; but because a Spirit (between these two) is more excellent in the Natural Order of Things, and by how much the more a Creature is a Spirit, (if at least wise it doth not any otherwise degenerate) so much the nearer it approaches to God, who is the chiefest Spirit. Hence a Body may always be more and more Spiritual, *ad infinitum*; because God who is the First and Supreme Spirit is Infinite, and doth not nor cannot partake of the least Corporiety; whence such is the Nature of a Creature, unless it degenerates, that it always draws nearer and nearer unto God in likeness: But because there is no Being, which is every way contrary to God, (*viz.* there is no Being, which is infinitely and unchangeably Evil, as God is infinitely and unchangeably Good; nothing infinitely Dark, as God is infinitely Light; nor any thing infinitely a Body, having nothing of Spirit, as God is infinitely a Spirit, having nothing of Body;) hence it is manifest that no Creature can become more and more a Body, *ad infinitum*, although the same may become more and more a Spirit, *ad infinitum*, and nothing can become infinitely more dark, though it may become infinitely more light: By the same reason nothing can

be Evil *ad infinitum*, although it may become more and more Good *ad infinitum*: And so indeed, in the very Nature of Things, there are limits or bounds to Evil; but none unto Good . . .

And hence may be inferred, that all the Creatures of God, which heretofore degenerated and fell from their primitive Goodness, must after certain periods be converted and restored, not only to as good, but unto a better State than that was in which they were created: For Divine Operation cannot cease: And hence it is the Nature of every Creature to be still in Motion, and always to change either from Good to Good, or from Good into Evil, or from Evil again into Good; and because it cannot proceed infinitely to Evil, for that there is no Infinite Example thereof, hence it must necessarily return or slide into Eternal Silence, which is contrary to the Nature of it . . .

And so we see how a Thing (the same Substance still remaining) may be marvellously changed in respect of the manners of its Existence; so that a certain Holy and Blessed Spirit, or Angel of Light, could by his voluntary Action, become a Wicked and Cursed Spirit of Darkness; which Change, or Metamorphosis, certainly is as great as if a Spirit were changed into a Body. And if it be here demanded, Whether those Spirits became more Corporeal by their Transgression, than they were in their Primitive State before they fell? I answer, Yes; but because, as I have already shown, that a Spirit is capable of Corporiety, *Secundum majus & minus*, or more and less; although not infinitely, yet in many degrees. Hence it is, they could remain for many Ages, and have nothing of such a Corporeal Crassitude, as Things in this visible World have, such as are hard Stones, or Metals, or the Bodies of Men and Women: For certainly the Bodies of the worst Spirits have not such a Crassitude as any visible body, and yet all that grossness of visible Bodies came from the Fall of Spirits from their First State: And so the Spirits after long and various periods, could contract this grossness to themselves, although they could not together, and at one and the same time fall into a universal grossness, so that the whole Body of any fallen Spirit should be in all its parts equally gross; but some parts become grosser and grosser, and the other Corporeal parts of this Spirit (which are its immediate Vehicle, and wherewith it is most intimately united) retain a certain Tenuity or Subtility, without which the Spirit could not be so moveable and active as otherwise it would; and with these subtiler and more tenuious Parts of the Body, the principal Spirit (together with its ministring Spirits, so many of them as it can possibly gather together) departs out of those thicker Parts of the Body, which it leaves as so many cadaverous Bodies, which are no longer fit to serve the said Spirits in those Operations which they exercise in their present State.

And we may observe this departure of the subtiler and stronger Spirits, out of the harder and grosser parts of the Body, into the more soft and tenuious, in a certain Spirituous Liquor, which is congealed with great cold, where the stronger Spirits (forsaking the harder Parts which are outward, and chiefly exposed to the cold) do gather themselves into the middle Part of the Body, which is always subtile and thin, so that one only drop of that Liquor (which is not congealed, but remaineth still liquid in the innermost Part of the congealed Body) hath in it the augmented force of all those Parts which are congealed; so that here is a two fold grossness and hardness of Bodies, the one palpable and visible to our External Senses; the other invisible and impalpable, which nevertheless is as gross as the other, yea, often grosser and harder, which may be truly perceived by the Internal Senses, although the External Senses may be insensible thereof; for the invisible and impalpable grossness or hardness is that which is proper to those Bodies, which are so small, that our External Senses cannot perceive them, when nevertheless they are really exceeding hard, yea, harder than any Flint or Metal, which we can handle with our Hands. And out of these hard and small Bodies, visible Waters are for the most part composed, although they appear to us very soft, fluid, and tenuious, by reason of the great Plenty of certain other subtile Bodies which continually agitate, and move the said hard Particles; so that Water seems to our gross Senses to be one thing Homogeneal, Simple, and Uniform, although it consisteth of many Heterogeneous and Dissimilar or differing Parts, more than many other Bodies; and many of these Parts are exceeding hard and stony, whence proceeds Gravel, bubbling forth, and all other little Sands and Stones, which have their Original and Birth from the Waters springing from the bottom of the Earth; and when those little Stones, or stony Particles of Water, grow into visible Sand and Stones, the same after some time do again lose this hardness, and become more soft and tenuious, than when they belonged to the Waters; for Stones do rot, and are converted into soft Earth, and out of this proceed Animals; so also Stones putrifying, do often become Water again; but this Water is of another *Species* than the former, for one is petrefying, the other mollifying; as it is observed that from one Mountain in *Helvetia* two Kinds of Water flow, one whereof being drunken breeds the Stone, and the other is a proper remedy against it; so that one Water is changed into a Stone, and the other Water proceeds from that Stone, whilst it is in Corruption, and so it alters and loseth its former hardness: And so from what hath been said may the better be understood, how the Heart and Spirit of a Wicked Man may be said to be hard and stony; because indeed his Spirit hath in it a real hardness, such as is found in those little stony Particles of certain Waters; when on the contrary the Spirits of good Men are soft and Tender; which internal softness and hardness of Spirits, we may also really feel, and every Good Man doth as sensibly perceive the same, as the external hardness of gross Bodies is discerned by the outward touch; but such who are dead in their Sins, have not this sense of the hardness or softness of Good or Evil Spirits; and therefore they call these only metaphorical Speeches, when indeed the Things are really so in a proper sence, and that without any Figure.

2. The Second Reason, that created Spirits are convertible into Bodies, and Bodies into Spirits, I shall deduce from a serious and due consideration of the Divine Attributes; from which, as from a Treasury of Instructions, may be manifested the Truth of all Things: For seeing God is infinitely Good, and communicates his Goodness infinite ways to his Creatures; so that there is no Creature which doth not receive something of his Goodness, and that very largely: And seeing the Goodness of God is a living Goodness, which hath Life, Power, Love, and Knowledge in it, which he communicates to his Creatures, How can it be, that any dead Thing should proceed from him, or be created by Him, such as is mere Body or Matter, according to their Hypothesis, who affirm, that the same is wholly inconvertible, to any degree of Life or Knowledge? It is truly said of one that God made not Death, and it is as true, that he made no dead Thing: For how can a dead Thing depend of him, who is infinitely Life and Charity? Or how can any creature receive so vile and diminutive an Essence from him, (who is so infinitely Liberal and Good,) that should partake nothing of Life or Knowledge, nor ever be able to aspire to it, no not in the least degree? Hath not God created all his Creatures for

this end, that in him they might be Blessed, and enjoy his Divine Goodness, in their several States and Conditions? But how can this be without Life or Sense? Or how can any Thing, that wanteth Life, enjoy Divine Goodness? But we shall urge this Argument a little farther, The Divine Attributes are commonly and rightly distinguished, into communicable, and incommunicable; the incommunicable are, that God is a Being, subsisting by himself, Independent, Unchangeable, absolutely Infinite, and most Perfect: The communicable are, that he is a Spirit, Life, and Light, that he is Good, Holy, Just, Wise, &c. But now there are none of these communicable Attributes, which are not living, yea Life it self: And because every Creature hath a Communication with God in some of his Attributes, now I demand, In what Attribute dead Matter hath it, or a Body that is uncapable of Life and Sense for ever? If it be said, It agrees with God in Entity, or that it is an Essence, I Answer, In God there is no dead Being, whereof he is or can be Partaker: Whence, therefore, shall this have its dead Essence? Moreover the Entity or Being of a Thing is not properly an Attribute thereof; but an Attribute is properly, *tale quid*, or something that is predicated or affirmed of that Being: Now what Attributes or Perfections can be attributed to dead Matter, which do analogically Answer to those which are in God? If we diligently enquire thereinto, we shall find none at all; for all his Attributes are living; yea, Life it self. Moreover, seeing the Creatures of God, so far as they are Creatures, ought necessarily in some things to resemble their Creator; now I demand, in what dead matter is like unto God? If they say again in naked Entity, I Answer, There is none such in God or his Creatures: And so it is a mere *non ens*, or nothing.

But as touching the other Attributes of Matter, *viz*, Impenetrability, Figurability, and Mobility; certainly none of these have any place in God, and so are not of his communicable Attributes; but rather Essential Differences or Attributes of Diversity, whereby the Creature, as such, is distinguished from God; as also Mutability is of the Number of those differential Attributes, whence it cannot be said that Mutability is of the communicable Attributes of God: And in like manner, Impenetrability, Figurability, and Mobility, do not pertain unto the communicable Attributes of God; but to those only in which the Creatures differ from him. And seeing dead Matter doth not partake of any of the communicable Attributes of God, we must certainly conclude, that the same is a mere *non ens*, or nothing, a false Fiction or Chimaera, and so a thing impossible. If they say, it hath a metaphysical Goodness and Truth, even as every Being is Good and True: Again; I demand What is that Goodness and Truth? For if it hath no participation with any of the communicable Attributes of God, it will be neither Good nor True, and so a mere Fiction, as before was said. Moreover, seeing it cannot be said, wherein dead Matter doth any way partake of Divine Goodness, much less can it be shown, how it may be capable always to acquire a greater Perfection, *ad infinitum*, which is the nature of all Creatures, *viz.* to increase, and infinitely advance towards a farther Perfection as is before demonstrated. But what farther progress in Goodness or perfection hath a dead Matter? Because after it hath suffered Infinite Changes of Motion and Figure it is constrained always to remain dead, as before; and if Motion and Figure contribute nothing to the receiving of Life, then certainly this is made never the better; nay, is not in the least degree promoted in Goodness: For suppose this dead Matter had undergone all Forms, and been transmuted into all Kinds of Figures, even the most regular and exact: What doth this profit this Matter or Body, because it wants all Life and Sense? So let us suppose the same to have undergone Infinite Kinds of Motion, from slowness to swiftness; Wherein, therefore, is it better, by the way of its Intrinsecal Melioration? For the Argument speaketh of Intrinsecal Melioration, which is such a Melioration as the Nature of the Thing it self requireth, and which is performed thereby; but a mere dead Body, or Matter, requires no kind of Motion or Figure; nor, in it self, is perfected more by one Motion, or Figure, than by another: for it is alike indifferent to all Motions and Figures whatsoever, and by consequence is not perfected or bettered by any of them. And then what advantage will it have from all these helps, if it always remain a dead and impassible Thing?

3. My Third Reason is drawn from the great Love and Desire that the Spirits or Souls have towards Bodies, and especially towards those with which they are united, and in which they have their Habitation: But now the Foundation of all Love or Desire, whereby one Thing is carried unto another, stands in this, That either they are of the same Nature and substance with them, or like unto them, or both; or that one hath its Being from the other, whereof we have an Example in all living Creatures which bring

forth their young; and in like manner also in men, how they love that which is born of them: For so also even Wicked Men and Women (if they are not extremely perverse, and void of Parental Love) do Love their Children, and cherish them with a Natural Affection, the cause whereof certainly is this, That their Children are of the same Nature and Substance, *viz.* as though they were Parts of them; and if they are like them, either in Body, Spirit, or Manners, hereby their Love is the more increased: So also we observe that Animals of one *Species* love one another more than those that are of a different *Species*; whence also Cattle of one Kind feed together; Birds of a Kind flock together; and Fishes of a Kind swim together; and so Men rather converse with Men, than with any other Creatures: But besides this particular Love, there remains yet something of Universal Love in all Creatures, one towards another, setting aside that great confusion which hath fallen out since, by reason of Transgression; which certainly must proceed from the same Foundation, *viz.* in regard of their First Substance and Essence, they were all one and the same Thing, and as it were Parts and Members of one Body. Moreover, in every *Species* of Animals, we see how the Male and Female Love one another, and in all their Propagations (which are not Monstrous, and contrary to Nature) they respect each other; and that proceeds not only from the unity of Nature, but also by reason of a certain eminent similitude or likeness between them. And both these Foundations of Love between a Man and a Woman, are expresly mentioned in *Genesis*; but that which *Adam* spoke concerning his Wife, *This is Bone of my Bone, and Flesh of my Flesh, &c.* pertains unto the Unity of Nature; for she was taken out of him, and was a part of him, and therefore he loved her. Moreover also, concerning Similitude, it is said, there was no Help found for him, or before his Face, as it is in the *Hebrew* (i.e.) among all Creatures he saw not his like, with whom he would converse, until *Eve* was made for him. But there is yet another cause of Love, when Beings, that love each other, are not one Substance, but one gave Being to the other, and is the proper and real cause thereof. And so it is in the case between God and Creatures; for he gave to all, Being, Life, and motion; and therefore he loves all Creatures; neither can he not love them; yea, at the same time when he seems to hate and be angry with them, this his Anger, and what proceeds therefrom, *viz.* Punishments and Judgments, turns to their Good, because he perceiveth they have need of them. So, on the contrary, the Creatures which have not wholly degenerated, and lost all sense of God, do love him; and this is a certain Divine Law, and Instinct, which he put in all rational Creatures, that they might love him, which is the fulfilling of the whole Law: But those Creatures which draw most near unto God in similitude or likeness, do love him the more, and are the more loved of him. But if it be thought there is another principal cause of Love, to wit, Goodness, which is the most vehement or powerful *Magnet* thereof, whence also God is above all the most to be loved; because he is the best; which Goodness is in some measure in Creatures, either really or apparently; wherefore such are loved of their Fellow-Creatures: I Answer: It must be granted indeed, that Goodness is a great, yea the greatest Cause of Love, and the proper Object of it; but this Goodness is not a distinct Cause from those before laid down, but is comprehended in them. Wherefore do we call a Thing Good? But because it either really or apparently pleases us, for the unity it hath with us, or which we have with it: Hence it comes to pass, that Good Men love Good Men, and not otherwise; for Good Men cannot love Evil, nor Evil Men Good Men as such; for there is no greater similitude than between Good and Good: For the reason why we call or esteem a Thing Good, is this, that it benefits us, and that we are made Partakers of its Goodness, and so here the First Cause of Similitude is still Militant: So likewise, when one Thing gives being to another, as when God and Christ give Being to Creatures (as from whom have every true Essence proceeded,) here is in like manner a certain Similitude; for it is impossible that the Creatures should not in some Things be like their Creator, and agree with him in some Attributes or Perfections.

This being supposed a Touch-stone, we shall now return to our subject matter, (i.e.) to examine, whether Spirits and Bodies are of one Nature and Substance, and so convertible one into another? Therefore, I demand, What is the reason, That the Spirit or Soul so loveth the Body wherewith it is united, and so unwillingly departs out of it, that it has been manifestly notorious, the Souls of some have attended on, and been subject to their Bodies, after the Body was dead, until it was corrupted, and dissolved into dust. That the Spirit or Soul gave a distinct Being to the Body, or the Body to the Spirit, cannot be the reason of this Love; for that were Creation in a strict sence; but this (*viz.*) to give Being unto Things agrees only to God and Christ; therefore that necessarily comes to pass by reason of that similitude they have one with another, or some

Affinity in their Natures: Or, if it be said, there is a certain Goodness in the Body, which moves the Spirit to love it, certainly this Goodness must necessarily answer to something in the Soul which is like it, otherwise it could not be carried unto it; yea, let them inform us what that Goodness in the Body is, for which the Soul doth so fervently love it? or in what Attributes or Perfections a Body is like a Spirit; if a Body is nothing but a dead Trunk, and a certain Mass which is altogether uncapable of any degree of Life, and Perfection? if they say a Body agrees with a Spirit *Ratione entis*, or in respect of Being; that is to say; as this hath Being so that hath the same; this is already refuted in the former Argument; for if this Being hath no Attributes or Perfections wherein it may agree with the Being of a Spirit, then it is only a mere Fiction; for God created no Naked *Ens*, or Being, which should be a mere Being, and have no Attributes that may be predicated of it; besides also, *Ens*, is only a Logical Notion or Term, which Logicians do call *Genus generalissimum*, or the most General Kind, which in the naked and abstracted Notion of it, is not in the Things themselves, but only in the Conception of Humane Intellect. And therefore every true Being is a certain single Nature, whereof may be affirmed such and such Attributes: Now what are those Attributes of Body, wherein it resembles a Spirit? Let us examine the principal Attributes of Body, as distinct from a Spirit, according to their Opinion, who so much dispute, that Body and Spirit are so infinitely distant in Nature, that one can never become the other: The Attributes are these, That a Body is impenetrable of all other Bodies, so that the parts thereof cannot penetrate each other; but there is another Attribute of Body, *viz.* to be discerpible or divisible into parts: But the Attributes of Spirit (as they define it) are penetrability and indiscerpibility, so that one Spirit can penetrate another; also, that a thousand Spirits can stand together one within another, and yet possess no more Space than one Spirit. Moreover, that a Spirit is so simple, and one in it self, that it cannot be rent asunder, or actually divided into separate parts. If now the Attributes of Body and Spirit are compared together, they are so far from being like one another, or having any Analogy of Nature (in which nevertheless the true Foundation of Love and Unity doth consist, as before was said,) that they are plainly contrary; yea, nothing in the whole World can be conceived so contrary to any Thing, as Body and Spirit, in the opinion of these Men. For here is a pure and absolute contrariety in all their Attributes; because

Penetrability and Impenetrability are more contrary one to another than black and white, or hot and cold: For that which is black may become white, and that which is hot may become cold: But (as they say) that which is impenetrable cannot be made penetrable; yea, God and Creatures do not so infinitely differ in Essence one from another; as these Doctors make Body to differ from Spirit: For there are many Attributes, in which God and the Creatures agree together; but we can find none, wherein a Body can any way agree with a Spirit, and by consequence, nor with God, who is the chiefest and purest of Spirits; wherefore it can be no Creature, but a mere Non-entity or Fiction: But as Body and Spirit are contrary in the Attributes of Penetrability and Impenetrability; so are they no less contrary in Discerpibility and Indiscerpibility: But if they alledge, that Body and Spirit do agree in some Attributes, as Extension, Mobility, and Figurability; so that Spirit hath Extension, and can reach from one place to another, and also can move it self from place to place, and form it self into whatsoever Figure it pleaseth, in which cases it agrees with a Body, and a Body with it: To this I Answer: Supposing the first, that a Spirit can be extended (which yet many of them deny, yea most, who teach that Body and Spirit are essentially distinct) yet the Extension of Body and Spirit, as they understand it, do wonderfully differ; for the Extension of Body is always impenetrable; yea, to be extended, and impenetrable, as pertaining to Body, is only one real Attribute proposed in two Mental and Logical Notions, or ways of speaking; for what is Extension, unless the Body (wheresoever it is) be impenetrable of its own proper parts? But remove this Attribute of Impenetrability from a Body, and it cannot be conceived any longer, as extended. Moreover also, the Extension of Body and Spirit, according to their Notion, infinitely differ; for whatsoever Extension a Body hath, the same is so necessary and essential to it, that it is impossible for it to be more or less extended; when nevertheless a Spirit may be more or less extended; as they affirm; and seeing to be moveable and figurable, are only consequential Attributes of Extension, (for that a Spirit is far otherwise moveable and figurable than a Body, because a Spirit can move and form it self as a Body cannot:) The same Reason which is good against the one is good against the other also.

4. But, Secondly, How can they prove Impenetrability is an Essential Attribute of Body; or that Penetrability is an Essential

Attribute of Spirit? Why may not Body be more or less impenetrable, and Spirit more or less penetrable, as it may, and indeed doth happen in all other attributes? For *ex. gr.* some Body may be more or less heavy or light, condensed or rarefied, solid or liquid, hot or cold; then why may it not also be more or less penetrable or impenetrable? If it be said, that in all those other Mutations we always observe, that a Body remains impenetrable, as Iron when it is heat red-hot, yet remains still impenetrable: I Answer, I grant it may remain impenetrable of any other Body of equal thickness; yet may, and is entirely penetrated of a more subtile Body, *sc.* of the Fire which hath entred into it, and penetrated all its parts, whereby 'tis made so soft; and if the Fire be stronger, begins wholly to melt. But if, against this, they Object, that the ingress of Fire into the Iron, is not penetration in a Philosophical Sence, nor as they understand it, *viz.* as though the Fire and Iron did possess but one place, and so the one could be intrinsecally present in the other; because it is manifest to the contrary, that Iron (if it be made candent or glowing hot) it swelleth and acquireth a greater Bulk, than when it is cold; and as it waxeth cold again, it returneth to its former dimension. To this I Answer: If they mean such a Penetration, which we call Intrinseck Presence, *viz.* that one Homogeneal Substance should enter into another, both being of equal Dimensions, and yet the bulk or quantity not increased, that seems wholly irrational: and it would be a mere impossibility and contradiction to grant such an intimate Presence in Creatures, which only agrees unto God and Christ as Creators, whose Prerogative it is to be intrinsecally present in Creatures; whereas no Creature can have that Intrinseck Presence in its Fellow Creature, because then it would cease to be a Creature and obtain one of the incommunicable Attributes of God and Christ, which is Intrinseck Presence. This (I say) is primarily to be attributed to God, and secondarily to Christ, in as much as he is *Medium quid*, or a certain *Medium* between God and Creatures, and who as he is Partaker of Mutability and Immutability, of Eternity and Time; so he may be said to be Partaker of Body and Spirit, and consequently of Place and Extension: For, in as much as his Body is of another Substance than the Bodies of all other Creatures, (as of whom he is the nearest Beginning to God,) it may be truly said, he is intrinsecally present in them, and yet not so as to be confounded with them. For to suppose one Creature intrinsecally present in another, so as to be mingled and most perfectly united with it, and yet its Quantity or Extension not increased, that confounds the Creatures, and maketh two or more to be but one: Yea, according to this Hypothesis, it may be said the whole Creation is reducible into the quantity of the least Grain or Dust, because every part would be supposed to penetrate another, and no greater extension follow than of one Part. But if it be said, that only proves that Spirits may be reduced into so small a space but not Bodies: Because Bodies are Impenetrable. I Answer, This is but a begging of the question, because they have not yet proved that Body and Spirit are distinct Substances; which, unless they are, it follows that one Nature is not more penetrable than the other, according to their sense. And indeed it seems very consentaneous to Reason, that as Times are each of them so extended into their due Measures and Extensions, that they cannot exceed those Bounds, and so cannot be intrinsecally present one with another; as (*ex. gr.*) the First Day of the Week cannot be present with the Second Day of the same Week; nor the First Hour of the Day with the Second; neither is the First Minute of an Hour present with the Second Minute thereof; because such is the Nature and Essence of Time, that it is successive, and hath *partes extra partes*, or parts, one without another. When nevertheless God is really and intrinsecally present in all Times, and is not changed, which cannot be said of the Creature, *sc.* that that is present in all or more Times, and not changed; for the Creature is perpetually changed with Times, seeing Times are nothing else but the Motion or Change of the Creature from one State or Condition into another. And as it is in the case of Time, and Creatures which are in Time, so also in the case of Place, Bulk, or Quantity; for as in God there is no Time, so also in him there is no Bulk or Corporeal Quantity; but in Creatures there is both Time and Corporeal Quantity; because otherwise they would be either God, or Nothing, which is impossible. For whatsoever Quantity, Bulk, or Extension any Creature hath, it retains the same, as something which is of its own Essence; as it is the Essence of Time to consist of more parts, and those again of more, and so *ad infinitum*: For it may be easily conceived how a less Time is in a greater, *ex. gr.* how so many Minutes are in an Hour, and so many Hours in a Day; and one Hour doth immediately touch the next, but cannot be present in it, the same is to be understood of the Creatures, in regard of their Quantity or Bulk; for indeed one Creature may immediately touch another, but cannot be present in all its parts, but only a less may

be in a greater, and a subtiler in a grosser; and this is more properly
Penetration which agrees to Bodies as well as Spirits; as some
Body, that is less gross may penetrate another that is more gross;
but two Bodies of an equal thickness cannot penetrate each other:
The same may be said of Spirits which have their degrees of more
or less grossness, as Bodies have: Neither is there any other
difference between Body and Spirit, (if Body be not taken in their
sence, who teach that it is a Thing merely Dead, and void of Life or
a Capacity thereof; but in a proper sence: *sc.* that it is an excellent
Creature having Life and Sense, which either actually or potentially agrees to it) but this that a Body is the grosser part of a thing,
and Spirit the subtiler, whence also Spirit hath its name from the
Air, which is the most subtile nature in this visible World.

Neither doth this hinder, that we observe, how some very small
Body may be extended into a Space a Thousand times greater than
it had; even as Gun-Powder, if it be set on Fire doth marvellously
extend itself; for all this Extension is made by Division of Parts
into Parts, still less and less, which indeed do not fill all that Space
so great as it seems, when in the mean while each part hath neither
greater nor lesser Extension than it had before. Supposing this, it
must be concluded that all Creatural Spirits, which are present in
Bodies, are either in the Pores of the said Bodies, or in certain
Concavities made there, as Moles make in the Earth; or else they
cause the said Bodies to be puffed up, and acquire a greater
Extension; as when Fire copiously enters Iron, it notably puffs up
and extends the same: And although this Turgescency, or puffing
up of Bodies, cannot be always observed by our External Senses;
yet it cannot therefore be denied: For 'tis possible, that a certain
Body may considerably grow or increase in its dimensions, and
become intirely greater, and yet this increase of Magnitude may
shun all outward Observation; yea, it may be so subtile that it
cannot be expressed by Numbers; *ex. gr.* let us suppose some
Body, whose Solidity or Cube may contain 64 Parts, and another
whose Solidity contains 100, where the root of the former Body
whose Cube is 64 is 4; so that the side of the Body contains four
Longitudes of the Parts so divided; but the side or root of the other
Body, whose Cube is 100, can be expressed by no Number; for it is
greater than 4, and less than 5, and no Fraction can determine the
same: Therefore Bodies (as was said) may be considerably swoln
or puffed up, (if more Spirits or subtiler Bodies enter into them,)

and yet so as that our gross Senses may judge them not at all greater. Now that we may come to the other Attribute, which is said to be of Body but not of Spirit, *viz.* Discerpibility; if they understand it so; that one only Body, even the least that can be conceived (if any such Body can be conceived) may be divided; that is certainly impossible; for it is a contradiction in terms, and supposes every the least Body to be discerpible into lesser Parts. But if Body be taken individually only for one single Body, that is indiscerpible; and that which we call the Discerpibility of Body means only this, *sc.* That we may divide one Body from another, by placing some Third Body between them; and according to this sence Spirits are no less discerpible than Bodies; for although one single Spirit cannot become two or more Spirits, yet more Spirits co-existing in one Body, are no less separable one from another than Bodies; for however Bodies or Spirits may be divided or separated from one another in the whole Universe, yet they still remain united in this separation; seeing the whole Creation is still but one Substance or Entity, neither is there a *Vacuum* in it; How then can any thing be separated from it self? I mean, from that which is its proper Nature, as considered Originally, or in its Beginning, or First Being? But as there is a General Unity of All Creatures one with another, so that none can be separated from his Fellow-Creatures; so there is a more special and particular Unity between the Parts of one particular *Species*: As when the Body is divided, or torn asunder, and the Members removed one from another unto a certain distance, so long as these Members are not corrupted, and changed into another *Species*, they still send certain subtile Particles one to another, and to the Body from whence they came, and the Body sends the like unto them, (which we call Spirits, and Bodies, or Spirits, for they are either,) by means whereof the Parts and Members so apparently separated, still retain a certain real Unity and Sympathy, as is manifest from sundry Examples; and especially the two following: The First of which is this: A certain Man wanting a Nose, ordered one to be made for him out of the Flesh of another Man, which being vitally agglutinated, (as a Scion or Graft is united with the Trunk of the Tree into which it is put;) when the other Man died, and his Body corrupted, this Nose was likewise corrupted, and fell from the Body of this living Man. The Second Example is of a Man whose Leg was cut off; which Leg being removed some considerable distance from the rest of the Body, when a certain Chirurgeon cut it, this Man complained of Pains, and showed in what part the said Leg was wounded, which manifestly proves that there is a certain Union of Parts, though separated at a great distance one from another: And so also Individuals of one *Species* or such who have a singular Affinity in *Specie*, have a Union one with another, although locally distant, which is yet more manifest in Humane Kind: For if two Men intirely love one another, they are by this love so united, that no distance of place can divide or separate them; for they are present (one with another) in Spirit; so that there passeth a continual Efflux, or Emanation of Spirits, from the one to the other, whereby they are found together, and united as with Chains: And so whatsoever a Man loves, whether it be Man or Beast, whether a Tree, or whether Silver or Gold, he is united with the same, and his Spirit passeth into that very Thing; and here is to be observed, that though the Spirit of Man is commonly spoken in the Singular, as though it were but one Thing; yet the said Spirit is a certain composition of more, yea innumberable Spirits; as the Body is a composition of more Bodies, and hath a certain Order and Government in all its Parts, much more the Spirit which is a great Army of Spirits, wherein there are distinct Offices under one governing Spirit. And so from hence it appears that Impenetrability and Indiscerpibility, are not more Essential Attributes of Body, than of Spirit; because in one sence they agree unto either, in another sence unto neither.

CATHARINE COCKBURN (1679–?1750)

Catharine Cockburn was the daughter of a naval captain, David Trotter, RN. Her mother was a member of the Scottish aristocracy, related to the Duke of Lauderdale and the Earl of Perth. Catharine Cockburn's collected works, in two volumes, were edited and published by her friend Thomas Birch in 1751, and it is from the second volume that the following extracts are taken. The book never went into another edition.

Catharine Cockburn was educated from an early age in Latin grammar, and logic. Her *Defence of Locke* was published in 1701. She married in 1708 and, according to Thomas Birch, was 'intirely diverted from her studies for many years, by attending upon the duties of a wife and mother'. But in 1724 she was again defending Locke, on the subject of the Resurrection. (She had become a Catholic in 1709.)

The first of the extracts is taken from *The Gentleman's Magazine* of 1737. *The Gentleman's Magazine* had been started in 1731, and was founded and edited by Edward Cave (a friend of Samuel Johnson), who used the pseudonym Sylvanus Urban. The magazine soon became a forum for serious literary and political articles and, as the extract shows, for philosophical puzzles.

The second extract is concerned with a more general topic, the foundations of morality. Though the work that Catharine Cockburn is here attacking is rather obscure (we do not know who the author was, or where it was published) the arguments deployed against it are relatively clear, and I have chosen it because it well illustrates Catharine Cockburn's combative style. The first question addressed is whether God ordains what is good and evil, right and wrong, arbitrarily, according to his will, or because (as the author holds) of an antecedent fitness or unfitness for the purposes of creation. The second question is whether gratitude could ever be a proper response towards favours received if there were no hope of further favours in the future. The final question follows from this: namely, whether there can ever be a motive to duty or virtue other than the expectation of pleasure – whether, that is to say, duty and interest must not necessarily coincide. This was a question much debated in the eighteenth century (as, for example, in the sermons and discourses of Bishop Joseph Butler (1692–1752). Butler was specifically recommended by Catharine Cockburn in 1738 to her niece, with whom she was at that time engaged in a long philosophical correspondence.) Catharine Cockburn here robustly concludes that the motive to virtue is, or can be, to do 'what is fit and right'.

She expanded on this conclusion in one of the letters to her niece:

> The power we have to act or not act, as conscience directs, is, I think, what constitutes us free agents. And . . . whilst our modern moralists have contended to establish moral virtue, some on the moral sense alone, some on the essential difference and relation of things, some on the sole will of God, they have all been deficient; for neither of those principles is sufficient exclusive of the others, but all three together make an immoveable foundation for and obligation to moral practice; the moral sense or conscience and the essential difference of things discovering to us what the will of our maker is.

Towards the end of her life, Catharine Cockburn was engaged in a long correspondence with the Reverend Thomas Sharp on the same topic, the foundation of morality. Much of this is concerned with possible different meanings of the word 'foundation', a subject of considerable philosophical interest. Catharine Cockburn comes out of the argument better, on the whole, than her opponent.

Further Reading

Butler's Fifteen Sermons preached at the Rolls Chapel, and A Dissertation of the Nature of Virtue, ed. T. A. Roberts (London: SPCK, 1970)

From The Works of Mrs Catharine Cockburn, Volume II *(London: Thomas Birch, 1751)*

Answer to a question in The Gentleman's Magazine
In the Magazine for May 1737, is proposed the following

question: If self-preservation be the prime law of nature, and the sole end for which men enter into society; and if the magistrate has no power but what is derived from the people; and if the people have no power over their own lives; whether the jurisdiction of the magistrate can lawfully, and consistently with these principles, extend to the life of the subject? And if it does, will not the same reasons justify suicide?

Yours etc.

Clemens.   East Lothian, May 23rd.

The Question Answered

Mr Urban,

Your Magazine for May last did not reach us at this distance till the middle of July; otherwise I should sooner have sent an answer to the question, proposed in it on p. 260, dated from East Lothian, and signed Clemens. Perhaps others have been beforehand with me: however as different solutions of important difficulties are of use, you may please to insert the following answer in your next.

If self-preservation be the prime law of nature (as is supposed in the question), it is plain that no man can have a right to take away his own life, because this would be a right inconsistent with that prime law, and imply a contradiction, viz. a right to do a thing, which by the prime law of nature he is obliged not to do. But on the other hand, if self-preservation be the prime law of nature, it must follow that every man has a right to defend his own life against any other who attacks it, even at the expense of the life of the other, if he can no way else secure himself. This then is that right (the right of self-defence) which every man in society has given up to the magistrate, excepting cases of extreme exigence, where recourse cannot be had to public authority.

If the people had a right (for I choose to use that word rather than power) over their own lives, and upon entering into society had resigned that right, it would follow that the supreme magistrate might take away every man's life at pleasure. But as the people never could have such a right, all the right they can give, and all the magistrate can derive from them, is a right of defending the innocent against the injurious; which can only extend to the life of the subject, so far as is necessary for the security of the society, a reason which will in no case justify suicide.

I shall be glad to hear that this gives satisfaction to your correspondent, and am,

Sir, your humble servant,

  C. C.   Aberdeen, July 22nd, 1737.

Mr Urban,

I find there are several answers to Clemens, in your magazine for July, before I had so much as heard of his question; and I think your ingenious correspondents have said enough to shew the Gentleman who in *June* p. 344 remarks upon it that those who derive the authority of the supreme magistrate from the people need not be puzzled by Clemens's query, viz. 'Whether the people have not as good a right to take away their own lives as to give the magistrate authority to do it.' Yet I do not see that any of their answers have superseded mine: the solution I have given may serve to enforce the truths they have asserted, and to obviate some objections, to which they may be liable for want of having explicitly shown, as I have plainly done, how the whole body of the people can give the civil magistrate a right to take away life, though not one of them has a right to take away his own; since it is certain, as the Gentleman in p. 344 justly remarks, that no man can give more authority to another than he has himself, which objection my answer has entirely removed; and two of your correspondents . . . do indeed imply that, which I have more directly laid down to be the only solid foundation for the authority of the magistrate over the life of the subject, as derived from the people, viz. their having given up to him that right, which every man must have by the law of nature, to defend his life or property against anyone who attacks it. But as this is not expressed in either of their answers, I am persuaded mine will not be thought unuseful to set that important matter in the clearest light. This is a foundation which leaves not the least ground upon which to justify the unnatural crime of suicide, and takes off all necessity of having recourse to the immediate appointment of God for the authority of the civil magistrate to punish with death. And I believe the gentleman who asserts this to be the case would be more puzzled to show at what time, or in what manner, God has given any authority to supreme magistrates, distinct from that which himself owns they receive from the people, who, he says, 'have a power of choosing and assigning over this sovereign authority to one or many, according to the constitutions of the several states and kingdoms in the world'. But how could they do this, if that authority was not first vested in themselves? Since, as was before observed, no man can give more authority to another than he has himself: and that the people have this authority is plain from one of those very texts which he brings to support the contrary doctrine, Gen. ix. 6. *Whoso sheddeth man's blood, by man shall his blood be shed.* For this is not an authority given to magistrates, but a law given to Noah and his sons, and in them to all mankind. The people derive indeed the authority to punish with death, (as they do the right of self-defence and all other natural rights) from the immediate appointment of God; but he has left them to institute government, and to assign over to their governors whatever power is necessary for the safety of society . . . It is very evident that all the governments that are or have been in the world (excepting the particular case of the Israelites), were of human institution, whether established by force or by compact, and must be maintained either by the express or tacit consent of the people. And yet government is very properly said to be the ordinance of God, as he is the God of order, and author of that rational and social nature, of which government is a necessary consequence.

   I am, Sir,
      Yours etc. C C.

Remarks upon an Inquiry into the origins of human appetites and affections

The author of a late *Inquiry into the origin of the human appetites and affections Etc.* has attacked some remarks in the *History of the works of the learned* on the notes to Archbishop King's *Origin of Evil*, in so gentle a manner that one would think his chief design in it was to show the young gentlemen, for whose use his book is intended, the art of evading, or of raising a mist about arguments that will not bear answering. The first argument on which he has displayed his art is to this purpose: If there was no fitness or suitableness in *reverence* from a creature to his creator antecedent to the will of God, and the happiness he has annexed to it; then God might originally have annexed the happiness of his creatures to their *irreverence* towards him; and so made that their duty. If this appears an absurd supposition to those who deny any antecedent fitness or unfitness in things, it is a plain giving up their cause; for there can be no absurdity in that supposition, if the fitness or suitableness of reverence from the creature to the creator depends solely on the creator's will, and the happiness he has made consequent upon it; since in that case his willing the direct contrary would make irreverence as fit, or as suitable to the nature of both.

Now what does our author say upon this? Why truly he says a great deal about several matters, that have just as much to do with the argument as is necessary to make his readers lose sight of it; and then he comes to tell us 'That when a certain system is once resolved upon, to suppose the subjects of it might be under other and contrary obligations than to do what necessarily arise out of its establishment is to suppose the author of it unwilling what he had before willed. Irreverence therefore (says he) could never become a duty, even on our principle of deducing all duties from a consideration of the divine will.' This may pass for an answer through a mist of words, but the argument urges that upon their principles, who deny any antecedent fitness or unfitness in things, God might originally, that is before he had willed reverence to be a duty, have willed that irreverence should be so. And this sure is not supposing him to unwill what he had willed before; nor could this sense be easily mistaken; for the word *originally* is distinguished in this gentleman's quotation by a different character, as if it was thought to mean something; and if it had any meaning at all, it could be no other than what I have here explained. The argument speaks of what God might have willed before this system was created, and he answers with what the present constitution of things requires. However, if God enjoins reverence, because it promotes his designs of creation, and forbids irreverence, because it has a contrary tendency, as this writer afterwards tells us; what is this but that very antecedent fitness and unfitness we contend for? If there was no tendency in the nature of things to promote or to hinder God's designs in the creation, everything would be equally fit for him to command; which is the absurdity the argument was intended to expose; and there is no way to get clear of it, but by owning an antecedent fitness in the nature of things, as this writer has here done, even whilst he is denying it. For if God has enjoined reverence on account of its tendency or fitness to promote the designs of creation, it must have had that tendency antecedently to his willing it; nothing can be plainer than this.

The next passage our author attacks is this question, Whether reverence and gratitude to the creator would not be always the duty of a creature, though we should suppose him unalterably placed in a state of the utmost happiness he was capable of? a question put to some who had asserted that nothing can be our duty that is not in our interest into the bargain. In respect of this, our author makes a threefold observation. First, to suppose a creature unalterably placed in the same state is to suppose that creature in a state of independence on its creator, and, as such, is a self-destructive notion. Secondly, it is of the nature and condition of a rational dependent being, to be ever improving and advancing itself to greater degrees of perfection, by the exercise of those powers belonging to it. It is absurd and contradictory, therefore, to suppose a creature advanced to such a height as to be incapable of rising higher, or to be happy to that degree as not to have it ever in his power to become more so. Thirdly, which (says he) is the most material observation, but generally overlooked, the question is put, and the appeal made, to beings known to be under the influence of this association, who being so, are prejudiced, and in that view incompetent judges to be applied to in determining an affair of this nature. For in a system of beings constituted dependent on each other, and absolutely so on the great author of it, gratitude is the proper duty of those beings: it will necessarily be formed, or will grow out of the circumstances of such beings: the supposition therefore is such as destroys itself.

To the first of these observations I answer that it is certainly possible for God, by his free bounty, in reward of tried obedience, to place a creature unalterably in a state of happiness. There is no contradiction in it; the case may therefore be supposed, and cannot be a self-destructive notion.

To the second I answer that an eternal progression in degrees of perfection and happiness, how beautifully soever it may be imagined, is but an hypothesis: it has no foundation in Scripture, nor any strong enough from reason or analogy, to make a different supposition absurd or contradictory; especially since, on the contrary, it is the generally received opinion that after the resurrection, good men will be fixed in the utmost happiness they are capable of, which is ground enough to form a supposition upon.

As to the third, which is said to be the most material observation, I do not well see the importance of it, nor is it very clearly expressed; but I think the meaning is that mankind are prejudiced in favour of gratitude; for in such a system of beings, benefits will be always received, and always expected; so that gratitude must be ever the duty of those beings (he should have said, *and ever their interest too*, to make his sense complete, and his conclusions hold) therefore such beings are incompetent judges of what might be the case in other circumstances; and therefore the supposition is such as destroys itself. But this is all mere evasion. Numberless instances may be given where benefits have been received and no more to be expected; and I see not why mankind may not be unprejudiced judges whether gratitude would not be a duty in such cases, which was the design of the question. However, the gentlemen to whom the appeal was made are in no danger of being prejudiced in favour of any virtue that is not their interest into the bargain. But here let me tell this author that fair answerers, who sincerely seek truth, consider chiefly the *intention* of an argument or a question, distinct from the particular manner of proposing it; and he cannot be insensible that the question before us might have been put in lower instances, which may frequently occur in such a system as ours that would have left no room for cavils or evasions.

The third and last passage which this gentleman takes notice of is in these words: 'The very notion of reward and punishment implies an antecedent duty or obligation, the conforming, or not conforming, to which is the only ground of the reward or punishment.' These therefore cannot be the foundation of the obligation; though the translator supposes all obligation to arise solely from a prospect of them. And what does he say to this? Does he attempt to prove that rewards and punishments may be established where there is no antecedent duty or obligation? No such matter. He only says that whenever I desire it, he is ready to demonstrate that all obligation is founded on a view of obtaining pleasure or of avoiding pain. And that to talk of obligation without a motive, or a motive distinct from happiness is quite ridiculous. But instead of desiring it, I should be sorry to see a reasonable being attempting to demonstrate that to promote the good of others, or to do what is fit and right to be done are not proper motives of obligation to moral agents.

MARY WOLLSTONECRAFT (1759–97)

Though virtually uneducated because of the shifting and declining fortunes of her family, Mary Wollstonecraft was a rebel from her early years, and a forceful critic of the role in society imposed by convention upon women. In 1787 she wrote *Thoughts on the Education of Daughters*, followed by a novel and numerous reviews and translations (she was an enormously successful autodidact), and in 1792 she produced her most famous work, *A Vindication of the Rights of Woman*, from which the following extract is taken. In the same year she went to Paris, where she met an American writer called Gilbert Imlay, by whom she had a daughter. In 1794 she published her view of the French Revolution (*An Historical and Moral View of the Origin and Progress of the French Revolution*). In the next year she came back to London, and in 1797 she married the anarchic socialist philosopher William Godwin. She had a daughter, Mary, later to become Mary Shelley, and died shortly after the birth. Godwin published a memoir of her in 1798 and edited her posthumous works in the same year. *A Vindication of the Rights of Woman* was an instant best-seller and was talked about all over Europe. It had many fervent admirers, though Horace Walpole designated its author both a 'philosophizing serpent' and a 'hyena in petticoats'. It is perhaps from 1792 that one can date a specific feminist 'movement', with a determination among free-thinking women to unite to claim their rights.

Further Reading

Claire Tomalin, *The Life and Death of Mary Wollstonecraft* (London: Weidenfeld & Nicolson, 1974)

Jean-Jacques Rousseau, *Julie, ou La Nouvelle Héloïse* (1760; first London edition 1784), ed. R. Pomeau (Paris: Classiques Garnier, 1960)

Mary Wollstonecraft, *Mary: A Fiction* (London: J. Johnson, 1788)

(For a full bibliography, see Tomalin, and the Everyman edition edited by
Ashley Tauchert, 1995.)

From Mary Wollstonecraft, A Vindication of the Rights of Woman *(London: For J. Johnson, 1792)*

I have already animadverted on the bad habits which females
acquire when they are shut up together; and, I think, that the
observation may fairly be extended to the other sex, till the natural
inference is drawn which I have had in view throughout – that to
improve both sexes they ought, not only in private families, but in
public schools, to be educated together. If marriage be the cement
of society, mankind should all be educated after the same model,
or the intercourse of the sexes will never deserve the name of
fellowship, nor will women ever fulfil the peculiar duties of their
sex, till they become enlightened citizens, till they become free by
being enabled to earn their own subsistence, independent of men;
in the same manner, I mean, to prevent misconstruction, as one
man is independent of another. Nay, marriage will never be held
sacred till women, by being brought up with men, are prepared to
be their companions rather than their mistresses; for the mean
doublings of cunning will ever render them contemptible, whilst
oppression renders them timid. So convinced am I of this truth,
that I will venture to predict that virtue will never prevail in society
till the virtues of both sexes are founded on reason; and, till the
affections common to both are allowed to gain their due strength
by the discharge of mutual duties.

Were boys and girls permitted to pursue the same studies
together, those graceful decencies might early be inculcated which
produce modesty without those sexual distinctions that taint the
mind. Lessons of politeness, and that formulary of decorum,
which treads on the heels of falsehood, would be rendered useless
by habitual propriety of behaviour. Not indeed put on for visitors,
like the courtly robe of politeness, but the sober effect of
cleanliness of mind. Would not this simple elegance of sincerity be
a chaste homage paid to domestic affections, far surpassing the
meretricious compliments that shine with false lustre in the

heartless intercourse of fashionable life? But till more understanding preponderates in society, there will ever be a want of heart and taste, and the harlot's *rouge* will supply the place of that celestial suffusion which only virtuous affections can give to the face. Gallantry, and what is called love, may subsist without simplicity of character; but the main pillars of friendship are respect and confidence – esteem is never founded on it cannot tell what!

A taste for the fine arts requires great cultivation, but not more than a taste for the virtuous affections, and both suppose that enlargement of mind which opens so many sources of mental pleasure. Why do people hurry to noisy scenes and crowded circles? I should answer, because they want activity of mind, because they have not cherished the virtues of the heart. They only therefore see and feel in the gross, and continually pine after variety, finding everything that is simple insipid.

This argument may be carried further than philosophers are aware of, for if nature destined woman, in particular, for the discharge of domestic duties, she made her susceptible of the attached affections in a great degree. Now women are notoriously fond of pleasure, and naturally must be so according to my definition, because they cannot enter into the minutiae of domestic taste, lacking judgment, the foundation of all taste; for the understanding, in spite of sensual cavillers, reserves to itself the privilege of conveying pure joy to the heart.

With what a languid yawn have I seen an admirable poem thrown down that a man of true taste returns to again and again with rapture; and whilst melody has almost suspended respiration, a lady has asked me where I bought my gown. I have seen also an eye glanced coldly over a most exquisite picture rest, sparkling with pleasure, on a caricature rudely sketched; and whilst some terrific feature in nature has spread a sublime stillness through my soul, I have been desired to observe the pretty tricks of a lap-dog that my perverse fate forced me to travel with. Is it surprising that such a tasteless being should rather caress this dog than her children? Or that she should prefer the rant of flattery to the simple accents of sincerity?

To illustrate this remark I must be allowed to observe that men of the first genius and most cultivated minds have appeared to have the highest relish for the simple beauties of nature; and they must have forcibly felt, what they have so well described, the charm which natural affections and unsophisticated feelings spread round the human character. It is this power of looking into the heart, and responsively vibrating with each emotion, that enables the poet to personify each passion, and the painter to sketch with a pencil of fire.

True taste is ever the work of the understanding employed in observing natural effects; and till women have more understanding, it is vain to expect them to possess domestic taste. Their lively senses will ever be at work to harden their hearts, and the emotions struck out of them will continue to be vivid and transitory, unless a proper education store their mind with knowledge.

It is the want of domestic taste, and not the acquirement of knowledge, that takes women out of their families, and tears the smiling babe from the breast that ought to afford it nourishment. Women have been allowed to remain in ignorance and slavish dependence many, very many, years, and still we hear of nothing but their fondness of pleasure and sway, their preference of rakes and soldiers, their childish attachment to toys, and the vanity that makes them value accomplishments more than virtues.

History brings forward a fearful catalogue of the crimes which their cunning has produced, when the weak slaves have had sufficient address to overreach their masters. In France, and in how many other countries, have men been the luxurious despots, and women the crafty ministers? Does this prove that ignorance and dependence domesticate them? Is not their folly the byword of the libertines, who relax in their society? and do not men of sense continually lament that an immoderate fondness for dress and dissipation carries the mother of a family for ever from home? Their hearts have not been debauched by knowledge, or their minds led away by scientific pursuits, yet they do not fulfil the peculiar duties which, as women, they are called upon by Nature to fulfil. On the contrary, the state of warfare which subsists between the sexes makes them employ those wiles that often frustrate the more open designs of force.

When therefore I call women slaves, I mean in a political and civil sense; for indirectly they obtain too much power, and are debased by their exertions to obtain illicit sway.

Let an enlightened nation then try what effect reason would have to bring them back to nature, and their duty; and allowing them to share the advantages of education and government with man, see whether they will become better, as they grow wiser and become free. They cannot be injured by the experiment, for it is not in the power of man to render them more insignificant than they are at present.

To render this practicable, day-schools for particular ages should be established by Government, in which boys and girls might be educated together. The school for the younger children, from five to nine years of age, ought to be absolutely free and open to all classes. A sufficient number of masters should also be chosen by a select committee in each parish, to whom any complaint of negligence, etc., might be made, if signed by six of the children's parents.

Ushers would then be unnecessary; for I believe experience will ever prove that this kind of subordinate authority is particularly injurious to the morals of youth. What, indeed, can tend to deprave the character more than outward submission and inward contempt? Yet how can boys be expected to treat an usher with respect, when the master seems to consider him in the light of a servant, and almost to countenance the ridicule which becomes the chief amusement of the boys during the play hours?

But nothing of this kind could occur in an elementary day-school, where boys and girls, the rich and poor, should meet together. And to prevent any of the distinctions of vanity, they should be dressed alike, and all obliged to submit to the same discipline, or leave the school. The schoolroom ought to be surrounded by a large piece of ground, in which the children might be usefully exercised, for at this age they should not be confined to any sedentary employment for more than an hour at a time. But these relaxations might all be rendered a part of elementary education, for many things improve and amuse the senses, when introduced as a kind of show, to the principles of which, dryly laid down, children would turn a deaf ear. For instance, botany, mechanics, and astronomy; reading, writing, arithmetic, natural history, and some simple experiments in natural philosophy, might fill up the day; but these pursuits should never encroach on gymnastic plays in the open air. The elements of religion, history, the history of man, and politics, might also be taught by conversations in the Socratic form.

After the age of nine, girls and boys, intended for domestic employments, or mechanical trades, ought to be removed to other schools, and receive instruction in some measure appropriated to the destination of each individual, the two sexes being still together in the morning; but in the afternoon the girls should attend a school, where plain work, mantua-making, millinery, etc., would be their employment.

The young people of superior abilities, or fortune, might now be taught, in another school, the dead and living languages, the elements of science, and continue the study of history and politics, on a more extensive scale, which would not exclude polite literature.

Girls and boys still together? I hear some readers ask. Yes. And I should not fear any other consequence than that some early attachment might take place; which, whilst it had the best effect on the moral character of the young people, might not perfectly agree with the views of the parents, for it will be a long time, I fear, before the world will be so far enlightened that parents, only anxious to render their children virtuous, shall allow them to choose companions for life themselves.

Besides, this would be a sure way to promote early marriages, and from early marriages the most salutary physical and moral effects naturally flow. What a different character does a married citizen assume from the selfish coxcomb, who lives but for himself, and who is often afraid to marry lest he should not be able to live in a certain style. Great emergencies excepted, which would rarely occur in a society of which equality was the basis, a man can only be prepared to discharge the duties of public life, by the habitual practice of those inferior ones which form the man.

In this plan of education the constitution of boys would not be ruined by the early debaucheries, which now make men so selfish, or girls rendered weak and vain, by indolence, and frivolous pursuits. But, I presuppose, that such a degree of equality should be established between the sexes as would shut out gallantry and coquetry, yet allow friendship and love to temper the heart for the discharge of higher duties.

These would be schools of morality – and the happiness of man, allowed to flow from the pure springs of duty and affection, what advances might not the human mind make? Society can only be happy and free in proportion as it is virtuous; but the present distinctions, established in society, corrode all private, and blast all public virtue.

I have already inveighed against the custom of confining girls to their needle, and shutting them out from all political and civil employments; for by thus narrowing their minds they are rendered unfit to fulfil the peculiar duties which Nature has assigned them.

Only employed about the little incidents of the day, they necessarily grow up cunning. My very soul has often sickened at observing the sly tricks practised by women to gain some foolish thing on which their silly hearts were set. Not allowed to dispose of money, or call anything their own, they learn to turn the market penny; or, should a husband offend, by staying from home, or give rise to some emotions of jealousy – a new gown, or any pretty bauble, smooths Juno's angry brow.

But these *littlenesses* would not degrade their character, if women were led to respect themselves, if political and moral subjects were opened to them; and, I will venture to affirm, that this is the only way to make them properly attentive to their domestic duties. An active mind embraces the whole circle of its duties, and finds time enough for all. It is not, I assert, a bold attempt to emulate masculine virtues; it is not the enchantment of literary pursuits, or the steady investigation of scientific subjects, that leads women astray from duty. No, it is indolence and vanity – the love of pleasure and the love of sway, that will reign paramount in an empty mind. I say empty emphatically, because the education which women now receive scarcely deserves the name. For the little knowledge that they are led to acquire, during the important years of youth, is merely relative to accomplishments; and accomplishments without a bottom, for unless the understanding be cultivated, superficial and monotonous is every grace. Like the charms of a made-up face, they only strike the senses in a crowd; but at home, wanting mind, they want variety. The consequence is obvious; in gay scenes of dissipation we meet the artificial mind and face, for those who fly from solitude dread, next to solitude, the domestic circle; not having it in their power to amuse or interest, they feel their own insignificance, or find nothing to amuse or interest themselves.

Besides, what can be more indelicate than a girl's *coming out* in the fashionable world? Which, in other words, is to bring to market a marriageable miss, whose person is taken from one public place to another, richly caparisoned. Yet, mixing in the giddy circle under restraint, these butterflies long to flutter at large, for the first affection of their souls is their own persons, to which their attention has been called with the most sedulous care whilst they were preparing for the period that decides their fate for life. Instead of pursuing this idle routine, fighting for tasteless show, and heartless state, with what dignity would the youths of both sexes form attachments in the schools that I have cursorily pointed out; in which, as life advanced, dancing, music, and drawing, might be admitted as relaxations, for at these schools young people of fortune ought to remain, more or less, till they were of age. Those who were designed for particular professions might attend, three or four mornings in the week, the schools appropriated for their immediate instruction . . .

Humanity to animals should be particularly inculcated as a part of national education, for it is not at present one of our national virtues. Tenderness for their humble dumb domestics, amongst the lower class, is oftener to be found in a savage than a civilised state. For civilisation prevents that intercourse which creates affection in the rude hut, or mud hovel, and leads uncultivated minds who are only depraved by the refinements which prevail in the society, where they are trodden under foot by the rich, to domineer over them to revenge the insults that they are obliged to bear from their superiors.

This habitual cruelty is first caught at school, where it is one of the rare sports of the boys to torment the miserable brutes that fall in their way. The transition, as they grow up, from barbarity to brutes to domestic tyranny over wives, children, and servants, is very easy. Justice, or even benevolence, will not be a powerful spring of action unless it extend to the whole creation; nay, I believe that it may be delivered as an axiom, that those who can see pain, unmoved, will soon learn to inflict it.

The vulgar are swayed by present feelings, and the habits which they have accidentally acquired; but on partial feelings much dependence cannot be placed, though they be just; for, when they are not invigorated by reflection, custom weakens them, till they are scarcely perceptible. The sympathies of our nature are strengthened by pondering cogitations, and deadened by thoughtless use. Macbeth's heart smote him more for one murder, the first, than for a hundred subsequent ones, which were necessary to back it.

But, when I used the epithet vulgar, I did not mean to confine my remark to the poor, for partial humanity, founded on present sensations, or whim, is quite as conspicuous, if not more so, amongst the rich.

The lady who sheds tears for the bird starved in a snare, and execrates the devils in the shape of men, who goad to madness the poor ox, or whip the patient ass, tottering under a burden above its strength, will nevertheless keep her coachman and horses whole hours waiting for her, when the sharp frost bites, or the rain beats against the well-closed windows which do not admit a breath of air to tell her how roughly the wind blows without. And she who takes her dogs to bed, and nurses them with a parade of sensibility, when sick, will suffer her babes to grow up crooked in a nursery. This illustration of my argument is drawn from a matter of fact. The woman whom I allude to was handsome, reckoned very handsome, by those who do not miss the mind when the face is plump and fair; but her understanding had not been led from female duties by literature, nor her innocence debauched by knowledge. No, she was quite feminine, according to the masculine acceptation of the word; and, so far from loving these spoiled brutes that filled the place which her children ought to have occupied, she only lisped out a pretty mixture of French and English nonsense, to please the men who flocked round her. The wife, mother, and human creature, were all swallowed up by the factitious character which an improper education and the selfish vanity of beauty had produced . . .

This brood of folly shows how mistaken they are who, if they allow women to leave their harems, do not cultivate their understandings, in order to plant virtues in their hearts. For had they sense, they might acquire that domestic taste which would lead them to love with reasonable subordination their whole family, from their husband to the house dog; nor would they ever insult humanity in the person of the most menial servant by paying more attention to the comfort of a brute, than to that of a fellow-creature.

My observations on national education are obviously hints; but I principally wish to enforce the necessity of educating the sexes together to perfect both, and of making children sleep at home that they may learn to love home; yet to make private support, instead of smothering, public affections, they should be sent to school to mix with a number of equals, for only by the jostlings of equality can we form a just opinion of ourselves.

To render mankind more virtuous, and happier of course, both sexes must act from the same principle; but how can that be expected when only one is allowed to see the reasonableness of it? To render also the social compact truly equitable, and in order to spread those enlightening principles, which alone can ameliorate the fate of man, women must be allowed to found their virtue on knowledge, which is scarcely possible unless they be educated by the same pursuits as men. For they are now made so inferior by ignorance and low desires, as not to deserve to be ranked with them; or, by the serpentine wrigglings of cunning, they mount the tree of knowledge, and only acquire sufficient to lead men astray . . .

Let men take their choice. Man and woman were made for each other, though not to become one being; and if they will not improve women, they will deprave them.

I speak of the improvement and emancipation of the whole sex, for I know that the behaviour of a few women, who, by accident, or following a strong bent of nature, have acquired a portion of knowledge superior to that of the rest of their sex, has often been overbearing; but there have been instances of women who, attaining knowledge, have not discarded modesty, nor have they always pedantically appeared to despise the ignorance which they laboured to disperse in their own minds. The exclamations then which any advice respecting female learning commonly produces, especially from pretty women, often arise from envy. When they chance to see that even the lustre of their eyes, and the flippant sportiveness of refined coquetry, will not always secure them attention during a whole evening, should a woman of a more cultivated understanding endeavour to give a rational turn to the conversation, the common source of consolation is that such women seldom get husbands. What arts have I not seen silly women use to interrupt by *flirtation* – a very significant word to describe such a manoeuvre – a rational conversation, which made the men forget that they were pretty women.

But, allowing what is very natural to man, that the possession of rare abilities is really calculated to excite over-weening pride, disgusting in both men and women, in what a state of inferiority must the female faculties have rusted when such a small portion of knowledge as those women attained, who have sneeringly been termed learned women, could be singular? – sufficiently so to puff up the possessor, and excite envy in her contemporaries, and some of the other sex. Nay, has not a little rationality exposed many women to the severest censure? I advert to well-known facts, for I have frequently heard women ridiculed, and every little weakness exposed, only because they adopted the advice of some medical men, and deviated from the beaten track in their mode of treating their infants. I have actually heard this barbarous aversion to innovation carried still further, and a sensible woman stigmatised as an unnatural mother, who has thus been wisely solicitous to preserve the health of her children, when in the midst of her care she has lost one by some of the casualties of infancy, which no prudence can ward off. Her acquaintance have observed that this was the consequence of new-fangled notions – the new-fangled notions of ease and cleanliness. And those who pretending to experience, though they have long adhered to prejudices that have, according to the opinion of the most sagacious physicians, thinned the human race, almost rejoiced at the disaster that gave a kind of sanction to prescription.

Indeed, if it were only on this account, the national education of women is of the utmost consequence, for what a number of human sacrifices are made to that Moloch prejudice! And in how many ways are children destroyed by the lasciviousness of man? The want of natural affection in many women, who are drawn from their duty by the admiration of men, and the ignorance of others, render the infancy of man a much more perilous state than that of brutes; yet men are unwilling to place women in situations proper to enable them to acquire sufficient understanding to know how even to nurse their babes.

So forcibly does this truth strike me that I would rest the whole tendency of my reasoning upon it, for whatever tends to incapacitate the maternal character, takes woman out of her sphere.

But it is vain to expect the present race of weak mothers either to take that reasonable care of a child's body, which is necessary to lay the foundation of a good constitution, supposing that it do not suffer for the sins of its fathers; or to manage its temper so judiciously that the child will not have, as it grows up, to throw off all that its mother, its first instructor, directly or indirectly taught; and unless the mind have uncommon vigour, womanish follies will stick to the character throughout life. The weakness of the mother will be visited on the children. And whilst women are educated to rely on their husbands for judgment, this must ever be the consequence, for there is no improving an understanding by halves, nor can any being act wisely from imitation, because in every circumstance of life there is a kind of individuality, which requires an exertion of judgment to modify general rules. The being who can think justly in one track will soon extend its intellectual empire; and she who has sufficient judgment to manage her children will not submit, right or wrong, to her husband, or patiently to the social laws which make a nonentity of a wife.

In public schools women, to guard against the errors of ignorance, should be taught the elements of anatomy and medicine, not only to enable them to take proper care of their own health, but to make them rational nurses of their infants, parents, and husbands; for the bills of mortality are swelled by the blunders of self-willed old women, who give nostrums of their own without knowing anything of the human frame. It is likewise proper, only in a domestic view, to make women acquainted with the anatomy of the mind, by allowing the sexes to associate together in every pursuit, and by leading them to observe the progress of the human understanding in the improvement of the sciences and arts – never forgetting the science of morality, or the study of the political history of mankind.

A man has been termed a microcosm, and every family might also be called a state. States, it is true, have mostly been governed by arts that disgrace the character of man, and the want of a just constitution and equal laws have so perplexed the notions of the worldly wise, that they more than question the reasonableness of contending for the rights of humanity. Thus morality, polluted in the national reservoir, sends off streams of vice to corrupt the constituent parts of the body politic; but should more noble, or rather more just, principles regulate the laws, which ought to be the government of society, and not those who execute them, duty might become the rule of private conduct.

Besides, by the exercise of their bodies and minds women would acquire that mental activity so necessary in the maternal character, united with the fortitude that distinguishes steadiness of conduct from the obstinate perverseness of weakness. For it is dangerous to advise the indolent to be steady, because they instantly become rigorous, and to save themselves trouble, punish with severity faults that the patient fortitude of reason might have prevented.

But fortitude presupposes strength of mind, and is strength of mind to be acquired by indolent acquiescence? by asking advice instead of exerting the judgment? by obeying through fear, instead of practising the forbearance which we all stand in need of ourselves? The conclusion which I wish to draw is obvious. Make women rational creatures and free citizens, and they will quickly become good wives and mothers – that is, if men do not neglect the duties of husbands and fathers.

Discussing the advantages which a public and private education combined, as I have sketched, might rationally be expected to produce, I have dwelt most on such as are particularly relative to the female world, because I think the female world oppressed; yet the gangrene, which the vices engendered by oppression have produced, is not confined to the morbid part, but pervades society at large; so that when I wish to see my sex become more like moral agents, my heart bounds with the anticipation of the general diffusion of that sublime contentment which only morality can diffuse.

Harriet Martineau wrote and published continuously from the age of twenty-one. Born in Norwich, she had been brought up a Unitarian, and her first published work was strictly religious, entitled *Devotional Exercises* (1823). Her younger brother, James, became a Unitarian minister, and later Professor of Moral Philosophy at Manchester New College. Harriet had a strong interest in social reform and was much influenced by Jeremy Bentham and John Stuart Mill. She wrote novels and stories, some for children. She had many literary friends and in her early forties settled in the Lake District, where she became a friend of the Wordsworths. She wrote several guides to the Lake District.

She abandoned her religious faith when she was still quite young and, in the correspondence with Henry George Atkinson from which the extract below is taken, showed a remarkable open-mindedness and freedom in her pursuit of knowledge. Atkinson, who seems to have written nothing that was published separately, was an enthusiastic exponent of what has come to be called 'identity theory', according to which the mind and the brain are one thing, though experienced in different ways. Atkinson spoke of the mind as the 'appearance' or 'phenomenon' of the brain. In one of his letters he wrote: 'There are not two philosophies, one for Mind and the other for Matter. Nature is one, and to be studied as a whole.' Again, he wrote:

> Men have sought to make out a philosophy of mind, by studying effects apart from causes, and have even asserted that mind was entirely separate from body, and having some unintelligible rules of its own called free will, not subject to law or dependent on material conditions. Of course I need not say to you that these popular notions are mere delusions. I cannot tell you how odd it seems to me to have to assert such a self-evident fact.

In the nineteenth century this was a revolutionary and a shocking theory, because it appeared to undermine religion. Christian teaching, it was held, demanded that the soul and the body be two completely separable entities. And if the soul must be distinct from the body, then surely so must the higher consciousness, within which the soul must be thought to reside, or with which it should perhaps be identified. Thus it was part of Harriet Martineau's abandonment of religion that she should be so eager, as she shows herself in her correspondence with Mr Atkinson, to embrace a doctrine of identity between brain and mind. She herself, as she says in the preface to the letters, arranged for their publication by Chapman in 1851. They did not go into another edition.

Further Reading

G. J. Romanes, 'Mind and motion' (1885), in *Body and Mind: Readings*, ed. G. N. A. Vesey (London: George Allen & Unwin, 1964)

M. Warnock, *Imagination and Time* (Oxford: Blackwell, 1994), chapter 6

A. Desmond, *Huxley: The Devil's Disciple* (London: Michael Joseph, 1994)

from H. G. Atkinson and H. Martineau, Letters on the Laws of Man's Nature and Development *(London: John Chapman, 1851)*

I
H. M. TO H. G. A.

My dear Friend,

I rather think the reason why we have so much pleasure in talking over, and writing about, the powers and action of men, and the characters of individuals, is, that your observations proceed upon some basis of real science, and that I know that they do; and that thus we are talking to some purpose on those most interesting subjects, instead of theorizing without taking stock of our facts on the one hand, or merely amusing ourselves with desultory observations on the other. I want, however, to look closer into the matter. I want to know precisely what your scientific basis is, instead of merely profiting by your having one, and having a general notion how you came by it. I want you to tell me, with great particularity, (if you will,) how you would have one set about the study of the powers of Man, in order to understand his nature, and his place, business and pleasure in the universe.

For thirty years past I have been disposed to this kind of study; and it is strange to think how many books I have read, and how often over, and what an amount of hours I have spent in thinking, and how many hundreds of human beings I have watched and speculated upon, without being ever, for one moment, satisfied that I knew what I was about, – for want, I suppose, of some scientific basis for the inquiry, and of some laws manifesting themselves in its course; laws on which one might rest, and to which one might recur, when in perplexity how to proceed. I am sure I do not wonder at scientific men sneering at metaphysics, if the case be at all as I suppose it: – that Natural Philosophy and Mental Philosophy are arbitrarily separated; – that the one is in a regenerate state (thanks to Bacon), and the other in an unregenerate state; – and that we can no more get on in Mental Philosophy without an ascertainment of the true method of inquiry, than the men of the middle ages could get on with Natural Philosophy (except in departments of detail), till a man rose up to give us a *Novum Organon Scientiarum*. And why Mental Philosophy is not yet included among the sciences which are benefiting by the *Novum Organon* of Bacon is a thing that I am quite unsatisfied about. I do not mean that I at all wonder that the greater number of students have recourse to unsound methods; because we see that the fact is so with the greater number of physical inquirers, – the true followers of Bacon being few indeed among Natural philosophers, as they are called. My wonder is, – not that there are few so-called Mental philosophers who use or even advocate any experimental method of inquiry into the science of mind; but that there seem to me to be none. If I am wrong as to the fact, tell me; and pray point out where I may find such, if you know them to exist.

I am well aware what the answer of metaphysicians to this difficulty of mine would be. They would plead the totally different and incompatible nature of the two regions of inquiry, and therefore of the method of penetrating those regions. But this is exactly what I am not satisfied about. When I look at the course of metaphysical inquiry from the beginning to this day, I see something very much like the course of physical inquiry from the beginning to Bacon's day: and I am not sure that Bacon may not yet throw down the barrier between the two regions, and make them one. When I look back upon the two paths, it seems to me that I see the same Idols set up for worship on the way-side; and I hear the same excuses for wild theorizing in both departments, – that spiritual agencies are at work, which can be recognized only by each man for himself, by means of a special spiritual sense of which no one can give an account. Now, Science has disabused us of our blinding and perplexing notions of spiritual anti-types of material things, and of spiritual interference in material operations; and we have arrived at the notion of chance-excluding Law in the physical operations of the universe. I want to know why it is not possible for us to pursue the same process in regard to Mental Philosophy; – why we are to take for granted that the two regions of science are so unlike, that the same principle of inquiry is not applicable to both; – and if so, what we are to do next; for we cannot remain for ever as hopelessly adrift on the sea of conjecture about the truths of Mental Science as we are now. I do not ask you, however, to make an express reply to every thing I may put in the form of a question, – as above. If you will tell me how you would set to work to ascertain the powers of Man, in order to understand his position and destiny in the Universe, that will include an answer to my speculations on past methods of inquiry.

Your ideas will descend upon this locality in curious contrast with some which are to be found here. I like to talk with the gardener, and the cowherd's-wife, and any workman who may relish a bit of talk on Sundays, on their notions of how body and mind should be treated, and what they are living for, and what is wrong and right in morals. There is much amusement and instruction in hearing them lay down the law about health and duty. And then, when I meet a poet here, and a scholar there, and a Quaker or Swedenborgian religionist somewhere else, it seems to me that I have been carried back some thousands of years, to the time when science was composed of dreaming, and when men's instincts constituted the mythology under which they lived. It is all very interesting, however, and all worthy of respect. To us, who are in search of facts, there is no dream of any intellect, no dogmatic assurance, no stirring of any instinct, which is not full of interest and instruction. But I shall be glad of your answer to my question, as guidance in using the material furnished by my neighbours.

III
H. M. TO H. G. A.

Yes, – the reason why I want to understand your views is that which you assign; – that you have abjured idols, and come with a free mind to the study of a subject which is rarely entered upon from the beginning. It appears to me that men come to the subject with antecedent notions of 'dignity of origin' for man; with words upon their lips about man being made in the image of God; and then, in the fear of impiety, if this notion is invaded, they lose their freedom, and desire to find the truth lying in one direction, rather than another. Now, from the moment that a man desires to find the truth on one side rather than another, it is all over with him as a philosopher. I doubt whether I have ever met with any one but yourself who was perfectly free from such leaning. I have sometimes supposed that I had met with a truly impartial inquirer, – judging him by the sacrifices he had made for his convictions. But, sooner or later, out it comes! He lets out, in one connection or another, that he should be sorry to believe this or that, which he has not yet the means of fully comprehending. He may have gone further in free inquiry than his neighbours, and he rejoices in what he has attained; yet, not the less does he pity those who have outstripped him, as the brethren and friends whom he has outstripped are pitying him. He says that his brethren and ancient friends cannot judge for him, because they have never been in his state of mind, – have never looked from his point of view; and he straightway forgets that this is precisely his own position with regard to those by whom he is outstripped. This pitying, this mutual judging, is so wholly incompatible with an effectual pursuit of truth, that I am concerned to hear it going forward on every hand, – concerned to see that you are perhaps the only person of all my acquaintance that is altogether above it. I dare not say that I am. I can only say that I ought to be ashamed if I am not, for I have had some blessed lessons on this matter. Feeling, as I do, daily comfort in the knowledge of some things which I should once have shrunk from supposing, it would be weak, – as foolish as cowardly, – ever again to shrink from knowing anything that is true, or to have any preferences whatever among unascertained matters of speculation or fact.

As to the notion about dignity of origin that inquirers bring with them as their first misleading partiality, – it seems to me premature, in the first place. What we want to know is what our powers are, and how they work: and it would be vitiating the research at once to conclude, on moral grounds, against admitting evidence of physical fact. Such a kind of objection appears also to be worse than premature; even foolish. Surely it is the quality of the powers alone which can determine the quality of their origin: and if we set about objecting to the universal law, or to any of its applications, whereby great things invariably issue from small beginnings, we may safely conclude that it is our notion of dignity that is wrong, and not any one application of that universal law.

For me it is enough that I am what I am; – something far beyond my own power of analysis and comprehension. By what combination of elements, or action of forces, I came to be what I am, does not at all touch my personal complacency, or interfere with my awe of the universe. If, because I can at this moment think abstractedly and feel keenly, I abjure an origin in matter which cannot think, and forces which cannot feel, I cannot reasonably stop short of despising myself for having once been a babe, 'mewling and puking in the nurse's arms'. But it is enough to say that we are satisfied with the truism, – 'Here we are! We are what we are, however we came to be so.'

As to the great point of controversy between you and the holders of popular views and language, – the question whether there are two methods of access to knowledge of man's nature open to us, or one, – I think the *onus* rests with the holders that there are two, to prove their point against him who declares that one suffices. You are satisfied with observation of phenomena manifesting themselves through matter. Others insist that there is also an interior consciousness which teaches us things not only unattainable by other means, but bearing no relation to knowledge which comes by any other channel. We deny, for our part, having any interior consciousness which informs us of any spiritual existence antagonistic to, or apart from, matter. If we once fancied we had, we have learned that it was through an ignorant and irreverent misapprehension of the powers and functions of matter. We have a right to require evidence of their assertion from those who say that man is endowed with such a means of knowledge of his origin and constitution. Such evidence, however, can never be had. All declare it to be impossible; we, because we are confident that it does not exist; and its advocates because facts of consciousness are not provable. They pity us, as Mr Newman does, in his book on 'the Soul': and we are happy in having open before us (and in being free to follow it) a single path which will surely lead us to what we want: – happy and satisfied to agree with Bacon that 'all things are delivered in matter', and that 'we must bring men to particulars'.

We agree that we know only conditions. We agree that we will not go a step beyond what we know. We abjure dreams, whether inbred or caught by infection. We must be sure of the assent of our understanding at every step of the inquiry.

Thus is our ground agreed upon. You must now, if you please, do as Bacon bids you, and 'bring me to particulars'. You must exhibit to me some of those conditions which are all we know. We must try to put away that shadow of ourselves which we once took for a spirit, and which we now know we had no right so to pronounce upon. If we cannot set ourselves back to the beginning of our reflective existence, and trace the whole course of our ideas and experience, you can teach me much of that particular department of matter through which Mind is manifested.

At which end will you begin? Will you indicate to me what you conceive to be the powers of living beings, and trace them to their origin in the brain? Or will you lay open the brain before me first, and follow abroad the resulting mental actions, till we are stopped by the limitations of our knowledge, – however well aware that there is the infinite field of the unknown lying beyond?

I am not a whit alarmed at that declaration of yours, 'that all the systems of the whole world are wrong'. Sweeping as it appears, and presumptuous as many might pronounce it, it only shows you to have gone one step further than other people. Everybody thinks that all the systems but one of the whole world are wrong; that one being the system that he upholds. At the same time, I believe you are more modest than they, in as far as you have no system to propound, but only an inquiry to propose.

v

H. M. TO H. G. A.

We are coming to the pith of the matter now. When people speak of the brain as 'the instrument of the mind', I want them to tell me whether they think the dog, and the bee, and the ape, have each a mind which puts the brain in operation: and if so, whence it came, and whither it goes. You remember Scott's dog, which somehow attacked or alarmed a certain baker; and how this dog slunk into a corner whenever his master spoke of the adventure, whatever might be the tone of voice or the artifice with which the story was introduced; and how, when the upshot was told, – 'and the baker was not hurt after all', – the dog came out of his corner, frisking and joyful, and barking merrily. Now, this creature evidently felt shame and fear, and consciousness of self, relief and joy. And, again, when the monkey puts the wig into the boiler, and hides the plum-pudding, and then gets out of reach of punishment, as soon as any one goes near the boiler, – here is an exercise of several faculties, besides the most prominent ones of imitation and consciousness of self. Will any one say that these creatures have a separate mind, which uses the brain as a manifesting instrument? If so, what is the evidence? and how do we know that these animals are not of a nature equal to man, but furnished with a smaller apparatus of brain? If not, why suppose man to be of an essentially different make from them, while their powers are, as far as they can be traced, absolutely analogous?

In these instances, the point of most importance appears to me to be the consciousness of self indicated by the dog and the monkey. I am constantly told that this consciousness is an attribute of the human being alone; whereas I cannot see how the jealousies, the vindictiveness, the moral fear, the love of approbation, and the forecast of brute animals, can be exercised without a sense of the Ego. We know but little of the powers and experience of brutes, even as the dog knows little of the experience of the cat, or the bird of that of the frog: but what we do know indicates consciousness as clearly as sentience.

As for how any faculties exist at all, we are so absolutely ignorant, that we may fairly pass over any objections to Thought and Feeling being results of brain, from the impossibility of explaining the How. When we know how anything else is produced, it will be time enough to require explanations of this. In the old ages of Geology, before there was animal existence, there were electric lights, and aroma from vegetation, and solemn music from winds sounding through vast cane brakes, and among clattering or swinging palm and plantain leaves: but there was then no sentience to grasp and appropriate these products. When the sentience was provided, it probably only enjoyed. After more ages, consciousness followed upon the sentience; or, if consciousness came with the sentience, reflection followed, and the results of material action were naturally, but ignorantly, attributed to preternatural agency; as you observe of the rainbow. Is there more ground (in these days of our physiological ignorance) for our supposing mental results to be of a spiritual origin than there was for the first half-dozen men to suppose lightning to be a spirit, and the harp-music of the pine forest the voice of a spirit, and, in short, all intangible matter and material effects to be manifestations of spirit? I cannot see how we can be justified in falling into such assumptions, with so many ancient warnings, and such vast modern scientific discoveries before our eyes.

Show me, therefore, how we are to set about the study of the structure and functions of the brain, and what we really know of them. I have seen for myself, by the actual examination of the brains of the dead, how great was the folly of slicing them through, instead of tracing out their convolutions and compartments; a folly even greater than that of slicing through the muscles, if the view was to ascertain their whole structure and use. I have a distinct idea of the appearance and general form of the human brain. I now look to you for an account of – not what one may find arrogantly mapped out in every manual of phrenology, – but what you conceive to be clearly established, what conjectured, and what merely hinted, up to the present time. I hope to obtain much more satisfaction from you than I have ever got from all the metaphysicians I have read. As you say, they have regarded only effects, and the relation of those effects to each other, while the effects themselves can hardly appear alike to any two observers: and that the true philosophy that we want is the relation of these effects to their causes: an investigation which can never be made while men take for granted that the real agent is, in each of us, an intangible Mind or Spirit, whose nature and qualities are not knowable. It is really wearisome to read theories by the score, all unsupported by any thing that can be called evidence, and descriptions and so-called analyses of faculties whose nature and origin are not even looked for, and whose management and control cannot therefore be provided for. You will teach me better. You will open the matter to me as if you were going to treat of the eye, – showing me the structure of the ball and the nerve, and what share of the brain it appropriates; and then how the laws of optics bear upon it; and then, the mental facts of vision, – with some curious secrets that I know you hold thereupon. Now then, – what is our brain?

Yes, indeed, we feel reverently in regard to this research. The true ground of awe is in finding ourselves what we are; not in dreams of how we came to be what we are. I suppose all we know is, that every thing occurs and proceeds by immutable laws; and the more this fact strengthens our reliance, the more it must enhance our reverence. We are what we are, however we came to be: and what we are is too great for our present selves to know.

XXIII
H. M. TO H. G. A.

I do not like to say anything after your last letter. I do not like to touch it, or the state of mind it produces in me. Yet it is right to tell you that it does so work upon any one mind as it does upon mine. – What an emancipation it is, – to have escaped from the little enclosure of dogma, and to stand, – far indeed from being wise, – but free to learn! How I wonder at myself now for having held (and very confidently held forth upon it, I am ashamed to say) that at all events it was safe to believe dogma: that for instance, whether there was a future state or not, it was safe and comfortable to believe it: – that if, even, there was no God, serving as a model to Man, – the original of the image, – it was safe and tranquillizing to take for granted that there was. The enormity of this mistake was not fully apparent to me till last year, when a young man destined for the Church, but not satisfied about all its doctrines, and in a state of fluctuation about his duty altogether, laid down as the one certain thing in his own and every other case, that at all events it was safe to take for granted what the Church prescribed. The very first step he took from this position was to conclude that his difficulties about a leading doctrine arose from personal sinfulness, and must be resolutely put down. I found then how clear and strong had become my vision and grasp of the truth that the holding of error is an incapacitating condition: – an evil infinitely worse than the merely being occupied with what is untrue, – bad as that is. I saw clearly how enervating and depraving is the practice of harbouring, through timidity or indolence, what is suspected to be untrue. The mere exclusion of the truth, by presence of the error, is a prodigious evil: but far greater is the misfortune of the deterioration of all the powers, – from the lowest faculties of perception up to the highest of conscientiousness, reverence and benevolence, – which ensues upon all tampering with our own best nature. – And what a *feeling* it is, – that which grows up and pervades us when we have fairly returned to our obedience to Nature! What a healthful glow animates the faculties! what a serenity settles down upon the temper! One seems to have even a new set of nerves, when one has planted one's foot on the broad common of Nature, and clear daylight and bracing breezes are about one, and there are no more pit-falls and rolling vapours, – no more raptures and agonies of selfish hope and fear, – but sober certainty of reliance on the immutability of Nature's laws; and the lofty liberty that is found in obedience to them. – We are still, and our kind must long continue to be, injured in power and in peace by the operation of past ignorance, which has mournfully impaired the conditions of human life; but the emancipation which may be obtained, is already precious beyond all estimate. Ignorant as we yet are, – hardly able yet (even the wisest of men) to snatch a glimpse of the workings of Nature, or to form a conception of the existence of Law, – obvious as it is that our condition is merely that of infant-waking upon the world of existence, the privilege of freedom, as far as we are able to go, is quite inestimable: – perhaps indeed as great as it can ever be. It is hard to conceive that it can do more for individuals at any time than animate their intellects, renovate their consciences, elevate and refine their moral conceptions and conduct, and lift them out of the condition of passionate children into one of serene maturity of faculty, though not of knowledge.

I thank you for the indications you give in this last letter of yours of the immediate nature and immeasurable extent of our ignorance. What a field it opens! what a prospect of ever-growing enjoyment to succeeding generations, in the development of the universe under their contemplation! If we, – you with your habit of study, and I with my growing conception of what study is, – are daily sensible of the enjoyment of that 'perpetual spring of fresh ideas' which Mrs Barbauld so well holds out, what must be the privilege of future generations who shall at the same time be more naturally free to learn, and find themselves in a bright noon-day region and season of inquiry! It is truly cheering to think of. If we feel a contentment in our own lot which must be sound because it is derived from no special administration of our affairs, but from the impartial and necessary operations of Nature, we cannot but feel, for the same reasons, a new exhilaration on account of the unborn multitudes who will, ages hence, enter upon existence on better terms than those on which we hold it, – contented as we are with our share of the good and the evil of human life. – It is a pleasant thing to have a daily purpose of raising and disciplining ourselves for no end of selfish purchase or ransom, but from the instinctive tendency to mental and moral health. It is a pleasant thing to be free from all arbitrary restraint in ministering to the good – great or small, – of any who are about us. But what a thing it is to have, over and above all this, the conception of a future time, when all discipline will consist in a sweet and joyful surrender to Nature, and all the forces of the universe will combine to lift Man above his sorrows, to expand his old faculties, and elicit new, and to endow him at once with all the good obtained by former generations, together with new accessions far beyond the compass of our thought! – Nothing short of this seems to be the prospect of our race: and does it not shed back a light to our very feet, – not only on high occasions of intercourse or meditation, but every day?

THE HON. VICTORIA LADY WELBY (1837–1912)

Victoria Lady Welby was the daughter of the Hon. Charles and Lady Emmeline Stuart-Wortley. In 1863 she married Sir William Welby-Gregory, and she devoted much of her time thereafter to developing a theory of meaning, which she called 'significs', and which merited a long article contributed by her to the 1911 edition of the *Encyclopaedia Britannica*. It is not known how she became interested in philosophy. She was certainly a thoroughly independent thinker; but her theory of symbols bears considerable resemblance to that of the American pragmatist C. S. Peirce (1839–1914), with whom she had an extensive and important correspondence. In 1902 she published a book entitled *What is Meaning?* Peirce reviewed this at length in *The Nation*, 1903. In the review he introduced some of his many (and by no means always consistent) tripartite classifications of 'interpretants', that is objects symbolized, or emotions or actions caused by, particular symbols. It was in pursuit of refinement and agreement over these various ways in which a symbol can be interpreted that Victoria Welby and Peirce corresponded. She was as enthusiastic about divisions and subdivisions of her subject, classifying and subclassifying types of meaning, as was Peirce himself. In the first of her two *Mind* articles of 1898, reproduced below, all the main characteristics of her approach are to be found. Peirce may have made her change her mind in matters of detail, perhaps, or she may have changed his; it is certain that their long correspondence, still flourishing in 1909, contributed to the development of pragmatism as a kind of systematic epistemology.

Further Reading

Victoria Welby, *What is Meaning? Studies in the Development of Significance* (London: Macmillan, 1902)
A. J. Ayer, *The Origins of Pragmatism* (London: Macmillan, 1968)

From 'Sense, meaning and interpretation. (I)', Mind,
5 (1898), 24–37

The drawbacks and even dangers of linguistic ambiguity and
obscurity have always been more or less recognised and deplored,
and most of us have exhorted others and have been ourselves
exhorted to be clear and definite in statement and exposition, and
not to wander from the 'plain meaning' or the 'obvious sense' of
the words which we might have occasion to use. For it is
undeniable that obscurity or confusion in language, if it does not
betray the same defect in thought, at least tends to create it. The
clearest thinking in the world could hardly fail to suffer if *e.g.* an
Englishman could only express it in broken Chinese.

But when we ask what authority is to be appealed to in order to
settle such meaning or sense, and how we are to avoid ambiguity
and obscurity: when we ask how we are always to be 'clear' for all
hearers or readers alike under all circumstances: when we ask
where we may obtain some training not only in the difficult art of
conveying our own meaning, but also in that of interpreting the
meaning of others: when further we inquire into the genesis of
sign, symbol, mark, emblem, &c. and would learn how far their
'message' must always be ambiguous or may become more
adequately representative and more accurately suggestive, then
the only answers as yet obtainable are strangely meagre and
inconsistent. And they can hardly be otherwise so long as no
serious attention, still less study, is given to the important ideas
which we vaguely and almost at random convey by 'sense',
'meaning', and allied terms, or to that process of 'interpretation'
which might perhaps be held to include attention, discrimination,
perception, interest, inference and judgment, but is certainly both
distinct from, and as important as, any of these.

The question where the interpreting function begins: where any
stimulus may be said to suggest, indicate or signalise somewhat
other than itself, is already to some extent a question of Meaning,
– of the *sense* in which we use the very word. In one sense, the first
thing which the living organism has to do, – beginning even with
the plant – is to interpret an excitation and thus to discriminate
between the appeals *e.g.* of food and danger. The lack of this
power is avenged by elimination. From this point of view,
therefore, the problem which every root as well as the tentacle and

even the protozoic surface may be said to solve is that of 'meaning', which thus applies in unbroken gradation and in ever-rising scale of value, from the lowest moment of life to the highest moment of mind.

But 'meaning', one of the most important of our conceptions and indeed that on which the value of all thought necessarily depends, strangely remains for us a virtually unstudied subject. We are content to suppose it vaguely equivalent to 'significance' or to ideas expressed by a long list of so-called synonyms, never used with any attempt to utilise the distinctions of idea which they may embody, and which inquiry might show to be of real value in disentangling the intricacies and avoiding the pitfalls of philo-sophic thought. For example, for the purposes of such inquiry some of the main lines of thought might be tentatively correlated with the meaning-terms which seem more especially to belong to them; and this would at least help us to understand that we are not to demand of any one what more properly belongs to another.

The following attempt at such a classification is of course only a suggestion of what is here intended (*i.e.* meant): –

Philology and Signification		
Logic and Import		
Science and Sense		Meaning (or Intent?)
Philosophy		
Poetry	and Significance	
Religion		

It is evident that the questions here opened are too wide to be adequately dealt with in an Article; but it may be possible briefly to suggest the kind of advantage which might accrue from the direction of attention to this subject.

Signification here represents the value of language itself: it seems naturally concerned with words and phrases, and is generally confined to them, although the numerous exceptions show that the distinction is not clearly recognised.

Import, on the other hand, introduces us to the idea of 'importance' and marks the intellectual character of the logical process. When we speak of the import of propositions, we are thinking of more than bare linguistic value: and we may find that to master such 'import' has a real 'importance' with reference to the subtle dangers of fallacy.

In coupling *sense* with physical science, three main current senses of the word should be borne in mind. There must certainly be some 'sense' both as meaning and as judgment in observation and experiment to give them any value whatever, as our use of 'the senseless' testifies, while the word is perhaps freer from any speculative taint than even 'meaning'. But in another 'sense', Sense is the inevitable starting-point and ultimate test of scientific generalisation, and this suggests the question whether these divers senses of the word 'sense' are independent: whether the fact of the one word being used to convey what are now quite different ideas is merely accidental, or whether it points to a very close original connection between the ideas, if not to their actual identity. There seems at least a strong presumption in favour of the latter alternative: since the divergence of the senses of 'sense' has been a comparatively recent development and is thus possible to trace . . . If admitted, the fact is a pregnant one, as we may see when the subject can be treated more fully. Here we may perhaps note that the word seems to give us the link between the sensory, the sensible and the significant: there is apparently a real connection between the 'sense' – say of sight – in which we react to stimulus, and the 'sense' in which we speak or act.

Meanwhile the idea of *significance* stands on a different footing from the other meaning-terms. It will hardly be denied that it has or may have an implication both of importance and special interest or value which is completely lacking not only to 'signification', but also to 'import', in spite of the verbal connection of this last with 'importance'; and to 'sense' in spite of its wider application. We naturally lay stress on the significance of some fact or event like the French Revolution or the Chino-Japanese war, when we feel that its 'import', its 'sense', – even its 'meaning' – are quite inadequate to express its effect on our minds, while it would not occur to any one to speak of its 'signification'. It has 'significance', it is 'significant', because it indicates, implies, involves, (or may entail) great changes or momentous issues: because it demands serious attention and, it may be, decisive action: or because it must modify more or less profoundly our mental attitude towards the nations or races affected by it, and towards the problems called social.

This applies still more in the case of the great provinces of thought we call philosophy, poetry and religion, as the ideas belonging to these pre-eminently possess that kind of value best expressed by 'significance'. And if we say that philology or logic or physical science may also claim significance, it is in virtue of these 'knowledges' possessing some at least of the higher value which the word has come to imply: it is in virtue of their special emotional or moral interest either for all intelligent minds or for special groups of these.

Besides the sense-terms already instanced, there are of course many others. We have purport, reference, acceptation, bearing, indication, implication: we speak of expressing, symbolising, standing for, marking out, signalising, designating, suggesting, betokening, portending: words or phrases (and also gestures or actions) are intelligible, descriptive, definitive, emblematic: they are used to this 'effect', to that 'purpose', in this 'sense', or in that 'intent'. All these and many others come in ordinary usage under the general term 'meaning': it remains to consider the claim of Meaning to cover more ground than Sense, and to stand therefore for all those conceptions which are expressed by the words commonly used as its synonyms. In the first place we must not forget that import (or purport) is really the secondary sense of the word Meaning: and that when we say we 'mean' to do this and that (*i.e.* we intend to do it) we are using it in its primary sense. It therefore becomes, like the various senses of 'sense', an interesting subject for inquiry how the idea of intention has here given way to the idea of sense; because there certainly does not seem at first sight to be any close connection between the 'intention' which implies volition and looks to the future, and the 'meaning' which has no direct reference to either. On the other hand, when we say 'it is my intention to do this or that' we may use as an alternative 'it is my purpose to do it': and does not that bring us to a teleological value? If so, may the link be found in the idea of End? If we organise some expedition and charter means of transport and supplies, our meaning in all this is the furtherance of the object of such expedition: all our actions have reference to this end, which is the point and only 'sense' of our exertions.

We have thus linked Intention, Meaning and End. The fact that Meaning includes Intention and End seems to indicate that it is the most general term we have for the value of a sign, symbol, or mark. And yet it is precisely Meaning which has given rise to the denotative *v.* connotative controversy and which some logicians would deny to the 'proper name'. Of this it need only at present be remarked that if the latter view is to prevail, the logical use in narrowing the sense of 'meaning' will traverse the popular one, thus tending to create confusion unless we can bring another term into use in its place; while it would seem that all needed purpose would be served by admitting that the proper name, being a sign, is *literally* significant, *i.e.* has meaning, but is neither descriptive nor definable.

What exactly then is the point to which I am venturing to call the attention of scholars, thinkers, teachers? The very fact of the need and the lack of this attention makes a succinct answer which shall really be an answer, difficult if not even impossible. But we may provisionally express it as being, in the first place, the universal and strange neglect to master and teach the conditions of what is called, as vaguely in scientific as in philosophical writing, Sense, Meaning, Import, Significance, etc. with the conditions of its Interpretation, and in the second place the advantages, direct and indirect, present and future, of a systematic inquiry into the subject, and of its introduction from the first into all mental training.

This is emphatically more than a merely linguistic question, and it has more than even a logical or psychological value. But even if this were doubted, no one would deny that modes of expression tend both to reveal and to modify modes of thought; and this must be especially true in any attempt to make language express more perfectly, and thus enable thought to signify more and to interpret more. From this point of view we ought properly therefore to begin our quest from the linguistic stand-point, since a word *quâ* word is a meaning-sign, and thus the so-called question of words is really a question of sense. It is not too much to say, though the fact seems little realised, that it is largely through the very instinct which prompts even the most futile 'verbal' dispute that language has gained that degree of efficiency which it already possesses. But it seems impossible here to enter satisfactorily upon this side of the question, which must thus wait for a more general recognition of the importance of the whole subject.

To take an instance of the increased power of discrimination which we might hope to gain if attention could be effectually roused on this subject, we may point to the many derivative forms of (bodily) sense, all of which are in fact used with consistency and clearness. We have *e.g.* the sensory, the sensible, the sensuous, the sensual, the sensitive; but all these have exclusive reference to the *feeling*-sense of sense. Again, we have a different set of words for each special sense. We listen and hear, we glance, behold and stare, gaze and see; we touch and feel, etc. Now suppose that our sense-words were all used indifferently, and that we made no effort to remedy this, insisting when complaint was made that context determined quite well enough whether we meant sight or hearing or touch. In both these cases the loss of distinction would be a serious one. Yet in its meaning as significance, Sense is in fact credited with a number of synonyms, which we use simply at pleasure and only with reference to literary considerations instead of as valuable discriminatives, while no derivatives at all comparable with those from sense exist, from any word which stands for meaning. What is the consequence? That our speech is so far less significant than it might be: we fail to recognise what a wealth of significance lies in the idea of meaning itself, or how much depends upon the development of its applications. What after all is the moral basis of speech-life, – of articulate communion? Significance and lucidity. These are not merely accomplishments, they are ethically valuable. We owe it to our fellows to assimilate truth and to convey it to them unalloyed by needless rubbish of the senseless, the meaningless, the confused and the contradictory. It is our distinct duty to study the causes, to provide against the dangers, and to realise the true significance of ambiguity, – a point to which I shall hope to return later. But we find in serious discussion only too much witness to the absence of any cultivated sense either of the urgent need of conscientious, even scrupulous consistency in expression or of the importance of preserving the plasticity of language. Such a sense ought to be as delicate and as imperative as that of honour and honesty. We recognise that it is essential to good poetry that epithet and metaphor should be exquisitely chosen, should be delicately apposite, bringing us faithfully the picture or the emotion the poet wished for. But this is even more important when the result is to be not merely the highest delight but the most far-reaching and radical effect on knowledge. It is but seldom that a poet's metaphor or epithet can affect the whole outlook of generations to come, or will introduce permanent intellectual confusion. But when a philosophical or scientific writer uses metaphors or special epithets, they are intended to enforce some supposed truth or to convey fact often of crucial importance. It is therefore hardly far-fetched to appeal to the moral aspect of the question and to speak of developing a linguistic conscience. As it is, school-books abound with instances of the vagueness of our ideas of sense or meaning. We find, *e.g.* in an elementary text-book of Algebra: what is the meaning = what is indicated = what is denoted; and are indiscriminately told to interpret, translate and express, apparently only with the object of avoiding tautology.

One difficulty with which we are thus brought face to face is this: how are we to secure a word for the act or process which has been so much overlooked that we have not yet even acquired a means of expressing it? A given excitation suggests what is not itself and thus becomes a Sign and acquires Sense. What are we to call the act of ascribing, attributing, assigning to, bestowing or imposing upon, the sensation or impression or object, the sense – or meaning, which constitutes its 'sign-hood'? Is the process a 'referential' one? Though Signification as the 'signifying act' would bear the sense above proposed for it, it has the serious disadvantage of being already appropriated to another use. In the absence of anything better I would therefore venture here to speak of the act or process of *sensifying*. It is true that 'to sensify' must share the uncertainty of reference which belongs to sense itself. It might mean *e.g.* the attributing of our 'senses' to a tree or rock, which we suppose to hear, feel, see, etc. like ourselves. But as there is apparently no word which is free from all established associations, we may perhaps be allowed to use 'sensification' for that fundamental tendency to 'assign sense' and 'give meaning' without which Attention, Imitation and even Adaptation itself would either not exist or would be deprived of all their practical value. For the lowest forms of response to excitation or reaction to stimulus only become useful, only become means of physical and mental rise in scale, in so far as they attach some 'meaning' to that which affects them, and thus foster the development of the discriminating function.

It must however be obvious by now that what we are considering is the need not merely of substituting one word for another, not merely of more precise definition or even of more accurate or consistent usage in expression, but of a profound change in mental perspective which must affect every form of thought and may indeed in time add indefinitely to its capacity. If we get this increased power both of signifying and of apprehending or understanding Significance, we might hope for a general agreement as to the possibility of expanding the present limits of valid speculation. Thought might well attain the power to overpass these boundaries with the most indisputably profitable result. There would be less danger of wasting thought and time on plausible but fruitless inquiry.

Indeed one is almost tempted to ask whether the peremptory stress laid by modern science on the futility of attempts to overleap assumed mental barriers, may not be fully justified as in fact owing to an obscure instinctive sense that as yet thought is only reliable within these frontiers, as the lack of philosophical consensus seems to indicate; while on the other hand the tendency of the speculative mind to explore outlying regions, is in its turn due to an obscure impulse which is equally justified as really predictive. At present, it is true, such regions cannot be opened up for full colonization. Before the pioneer can hope to bring back the necessary information for the future colonist, he needs to be specially equipped for his task, and to have gone through a training which shall tend to heighten his natural powers of observation and inference. And we must not be misled by the popular notion that only a few of us can or may take up the vocation of a pioneer. As a matter of fact every one of us is in one sense a born explorer: our only choice is what world we will explore, our only doubt whether our exploration will be worth the trouble. From our earliest infancy we obey this law. And the idlest of us wonders: the stupidest of us stares: the most ignorant of us feels curiosity: while the thief actively explores his neighbour's pocket or breaks into the 'world' of his neighbour's house and plate-closet.

But the mental pioneer needs equipment, and it must be adequately provided in his training. The child's natural demand for the meaning of, as well as the reason for everything that he sees or that happens, is the best of all materials to work upon. He at least wants all that the richest vocabulary of meaning can give us. Just as every fresh acquirement of feeling-sense interests and excites him: just as he runs to us with the eager account of what he now finds he can detect by his eye or his ear or his finger: just as the exploring instinct develops in forms even sometimes trying to his elders, so it would be if the growth of the meaning-sense were stimulated and cultivated. And the thirst for exploring the inside of our watches might be diverted into the useful channel of exploring their 'meaning', – or rather the different kinds of value they had, or the different senses in which they were valuable. Thus he would arrive at the *meaning* of one objection to their dissection, and everywhere would acquire fresh occasions for triumphant appeals to our admiration of his discoveries.

Beginning in the simplest and most graphic form: taking advantage of the child's sense of fun as well as of his endless store of interest and curiosity, it ought to be easy to make 'significs' or 'sensifics' the most attractive of studies. Following the physiological order, it would become the natural introduction to all other studies, while it would accompany them into their highest developments; clearing and illuminating everything it touched, giving us a self-acting consensus where as yet that seems most hopeless, and suggesting, if not providing, solutions to some of the most apparently insoluble of problems.

Here then, if I am right, would be the gain. The area of confusion, misunderstanding and dispute would be continually shrinking, and the area of really significant expression and intelligent assent constantly expanding, the limits of consensus enlarging with it. The adaptation of language to growing complexity of experience and to continually developing need would become, like that of the organism, more and more adequate: while correspondence – or at least mutual recognition – in usage, would become compatible with endless variety in application and implication: a variety all the more possible because we had at last begun to realise in earnest the lesson which in one form begins with life and in another ends only with experience, – the lesson of Interpretation.

In his *Essentials of Logic* – lectures expressly intended for the elementary student – Mr Bosanquet complains (p. 99) that the commonest mistakes in the work of beginners within his experience as a teacher 'consist in failure to interpret rightly the sentences given for analysis'. A much wider bearing, it seems to me, might be given to this remark. It surely applies to the whole field of mental activity. But can we wonder at any kind of failure to interpret, when we realise that the unhappy 'beginner' has never, unless incidentally or indirectly, been trained to interpret at all, or even to understand clearly what interpretation – as distinguished *e.g.* from judgment or inference or bare perception – really is?

Various objections may here suggest themselves. The principal ones may perhaps be summed up as (1) that there is no need for such a study as we are pleading for, since the subject is already dealt with in various connections and is implied in all sound educational methods: and (2) that its introduction would be impossible, and even if not impossible would be undesirable, as tending to foster pedantry and shackle thought.

The answer to the first of these objections is of course largely a matter of evidence, and of inference from admitted facts. The unexpected and startling conclusions to which a careful investigation of the present state of things has led me, require, I am well aware, the most irrefragable witness to sustain them. Before attempting to deal with this evidence even in the too brief form alone possible within our present limits – and thus at least to indicate the answer required – I would lay stress upon two points: first that the ablest of thinkers, speakers and writers is now at the mercy of students, hearers, and readers, who have never been definitely trained to be significant or lucid or interpretative, and who are therefore liable to read their own confusion of mind on the subject of meaning into the clearest exposition: and, secondly, that where inconsistency or ambiguity may seem to occur even in first-rate writing, it goes to prove that the highest and most thoroughly trained ability does not escape the disastrous effects of comparative indifference to questions of meaning from which all alike inevitably suffer, and for which I am venturing to bespeak special attention.

MARY WHITON CALKINS (1863–1930)

Mary Whiton Calkins studied for a doctorate at Harvard, under Josiah Royce and William James, both of whom recommended her warmly for a doctorate. Harvard did not yet admit women to degrees, and Mary Calkins was offered a degree from Radcliffe, the women's college in Cambridge, Massachusetts, and the neighbour of Harvard. She refused this, as a matter of principle. However, she soon started teaching philosophy at Wellesley, another women's college (in Massachusetts), and she taught there for the whole of her professional life. Her book *The Persistent Problems of Philosophy*, from which the following extract is taken, was published in 1907 and represents her introduction to philosophy for her students. She was what she called a 'personalist'. This meant that she distinguished between the traditional doctrine (characteristic of seventeeth- and eighteenth-century thought) of the soul, described mostly negatively, as not having the properties of body or matter, and the contemporary doctrine of the self as the subject of psychology, but as also the foundation of all experience, and so an essential element in any epistemology. She was also interested in moral philosophy, and believed that the fundamental concept of morality was of a great society of which all are members. There could be no such thing as a purely individual morality. Mary Calkins was not, perhaps, a very original thinker, but she was probably the first devoted female professional, a true academic and a teacher, and as such she deserves her place in this collection.

Further Reading

Mary Whiton Calkins, 'The philosophical "credo" of an absolutist personalist', in *Contemporary American Philosophy*, ed. G. P. Adams, Volume I (London: George Allen & Unwin; New York: Macmillan Co., 1930)

—— *The Good Man and the Good: An Introduction to Ethics* (New
   York: Macmillan Co., 1918)
American Women Philosophers 1650–1930: Six Exemplary Thinkers,
   ed. Therese Boos Dykeman (Lewiston and Lampeter: Edwin Mellen
   Press, 1993)

From Mary Whiton Calkins, The Persistent Problems of Philosophy *(New York: Macmillan Co., 1907)*, *chapters 1 and 10*

The Nature of Philosophy

When Socrates, in the immortal conversation at the house of
Cephalus, defined the philosopher as lover of the vision of the
truth, he was describing, not the metaphysician, but the seer. For
philosophy, in the more technical sense, differs from the mere love
of wisdom; it is reasoned knowledge, not pure insight, and the
philosophic lover of the vision must work out the blessed way to
realized truth. With philosophy in this more restricted meaning of
the term, a meaning which Plato and Aristotle fixed by adopting it,
this chapter and this book will principally deal.

Philosophy, once conceived as reasoning discipline, is not,
however, completely defined. Thus regarded, philosophy is indeed
distinguished, as reflective, from everyday experience which
accepts or rejects but does not reflect on its object; and is
distinguished, as theoretical, from art which creates but does not
reason. In both these contrasts, however, philosophy resembles
natural science, for that also reflects and reasons. The really
important problem of the definition of philosophy is consequently
this: to distinguish philosophy from natural science. Evidently,
philosophy differs from science negatively in so far as, unlike
science, it does not seek and classify facts, but rather takes its
materials ready-made from the sciences, simply reasoning about
them and from them. But if this constituted the only contrast, then
philosophy would be a part, merely, of science, not a distinct
discipline. For science does not stop at observation, though it
begins with it; in truth, science as well as philosophy reasons and
explains. Philosophy, therefore, if conceived simply as the process

of reasoning about scientific phenomena, would be merely the explanatory side of science. There are, however, in the view of most students, two important contrasts which hold between science and philosophy: philosophy *must* take as its object the utterly irreducible nature of some reality; and philosophy *may* take as its object the ultimate nature not only of a single fact or group of facts, but of all-that-there-is, 'the ultimate reality into which all else can be resolved and which cannot itself be resolved into anything beyond, that in terms of which all else can be expressed and which cannot itself be expressed in terms of anything outside itself.'[1] In both respects a natural science differs from philosophy. To begin with the character last named: philosophy, as has been said, may concern itself with the all-of-reality – and an adequate philosophy will certainly seek to discover the nature of the all-of-reality; a science, on the other hand, studies facts of one order only, that is, it analyzes merely a limited group of phenomena. Again, philosophy, whatever its scope, always concerns itself with the irreducible nature of some reality; whereas a science does not properly raise the question whether these, its phenomena, are in the end reducible to those of another order.

These distinctions may be readily illustrated. The physiologist, for example, does not inquire whether or not the limited object of his study, the living cell, is in its fundamental nature a physical or a psychical phenomenon – whether, in other words, protoplasm reduces, on the one hand, to physical energy, or, on the other hand, to consciousness. On the contrary the physiologist, properly unconcerned about the completeness or about the utter irreducibleness of his object, confines himself to analysis within arbitrary limits of his living cells, leaving to the philosopher the questions: What is the real nature of these psychical and these physical processes? Is reality ultimately split up into psychical and physical? Is the division a final one, or is the psychical reducible to the physical? Is thought a function of brain activity? Or, finally, is the physical itself reducible to the psychical; that is, is matter a manifestation of conscious spirit? More than this, the physicist links fact with fact, the rising temperature with the increased friction, the spark with the electric contact. The philosopher, on the other hand, if he take the largest view of his calling, seeks the

[1] R. B. Haldane, 'The Pathway to Reality,' I, p. 19.

connection of each fact or group of facts – each limited portion of reality – with the adequate and complete reality. His question is not, how does one fact explain another fact? but, how does each fact fit into the scheme as a whole?

Both characters of the object of philosophy are indicated by the epithet 'ultimate,' of which frequent use is made in this book. Because the object of philosophy is entirely irreducible and because the object of philosophy may be the all-of-reality – for both these reasons, it is often called ultimate and is contrasted with the proximate realities of natural science. It is ultimate because it is utterly irreducible and is not a mere manifestation of a deeper reality; it is ultimate, also, in so far as there is nothing beyond it, in so far, that is, as it includes all that exists. It follows, from the utter irreducibleness and from the absolute completeness which an adequate philosophy sets before itself, that philosophy is rather a search, a pursuit, an endeavor, than an achievement. This character is widely recognized. Stumpf, for example, conceives philosophy as the question-science; James defines metaphysics as the unusually obstinate effort to ask questions; and Paulsen says that philosophy is no 'closed theory' but a 'problem.' All these characters assigned to philosophy may finally be gathered up into one definition: Philosophy is the attempt to discover by reasoning the utterly irreducible nature of anything; and philosophy, in its most adequate form, seeks the ultimate nature of all-that-there-is.

The Approach to Philosophy

The preceding discussion, brief as it is, of the nature of philosophy, has disclosed certain perils which menace the student of philosophy. Because the systematic observation of phenomena is the peculiar province not of philosophy but of science, the student of philosophy is tempted to deal in vague abstractions, in lifeless generalities, often, alas, in mere bloodless words and phrases. And because he admits that his own study is, at the beginning, a setting of problems, a questioning, not a dogmatic formulation, he is tempted not to press for a solution of his problems, to cherish his questions for their own sake.

The only way of avoiding both these pitfalls is to approach the philosophical problems by the avenue of scientific investigation, and from time immemorial, the great philosophers have emphasized this truth. Hegel heaped scorn upon the common view that philosophy consists in the lack of scientific information, and had no condemnation too severe for the 'arm-chair philosophy' which makes of metaphysic a 'rhetoric of trivial truths'; and, in the same spirit, Paulsen recently writes, 'A true philosopher attacks things (*ein rechtschaffener Philosoph macht sich an die Dinge selbst*).' The philosopher, Paulsen continues, 'must at some point, touch bottom with his feet. . . . He may freely choose his subject from the psychological or from the physical sciences; for as all roads lead to Rome, so among the sciences, all paths lead to philosophy, but there are no paths through the air.'

Paulsen's assertion that philosophy may be reached by way of any one of the sciences is confirmed by the experience of the great philosophers. Descartes and Leibniz and Kant were mathematicians and physical scientists as well as philosophers; and Locke, Berkeley, and Hume were psychologists. But though metaphysics may be approached from any point on the circumference of the sciences, it is not to be denied that certain inconsistencies and even fallacies have often characterized the systems of mathematicians and natural scientists who turn to philosophy. It is equally certain that these defects have been due to a confusion of scientific with philosophical ideals, of scientific with metaphysical standards. Indirectly, these confusions suggest the value of still another entrance to philosophy, the approach by way of what is ordinarily called the history of philosophy.

Such a study has two definite advantages, and one of these is distinctive. In common with the natural sciences, this study of philosophical texts shares the advantage of being a study of facts. Its facts, to be sure, are second-hand transcripts of reality, not direct experiences (and herein lies the disadvantage of the method); but nobody who hammers out the meaning of Spinoza, of Kant, or of Aristotle, who compares passages to get at their common significance or divergence, who estimates the different statements of a philosopher with reference to the date of their formulation – no student of texts, in a word, can be accused of floating about vaguely in a sea of abstractions. The more characteristic advantage of this approach to philosophy is the fact that it forces the student to take different points of view. Spinoza's monism challenges the dualism of Descartes, and Leibniz's emphasis on individuality throws into relief the problem neglected by Spinoza. The student of pre-Kantian philosophy may turn out dualist or monist or pluralist, but he cannot accept any one hypothesis in a wholly uncritical and dogmatic way, as if no other alternative could be seriously considered. Even the scrupulous and rigorous study of any one great philosophical system must reveal the means for the correction of its own inconsistencies . . .

All this suggests the requirements of an adequate study of philosophical texts. It is, first and foremost, the duty of the student to find out what the philosopher whom he studies says and means. This is not always an easy task. If, for example, one is studying Kant or Hegel, one has virtually to learn a new language. It makes no difference how much German one knows, Kant and Hegel do not always speak in German, and Kant does not even always use the same language for two consecutive sections. This bare text criticism, indispensable as it is, is however a mere preliminary to the real expository process, the re-thinking of a philosopher's argument, the sympathetic apprehension of his thought. This means, of course, that one reads and re-reads his text, that one outlines his argument and supplies the links that are evidently implied but verbally lacking, and that one combines the arguments of his different philosophical works. Only when this task of interpretation is completed can one fairly enter upon the criticism of a metaphysical system. But the criticism, though chronologically later, is a necessary feature of the study. We do not read philosophy in order to become disciples or to adopt, wholesale, anybody's views. We must, therefore, challenge a philosopher's conclusions and probe his arguments. The only danger in the process is that it will be premature; in other words, that we oppose what we do not fully understand. Both interpretation and criticism, to be of value, must be primarily first-hand. The curse of the study of literature and of philosophy alike is the pernicious habit of reading books about books, without reading the books themselves. Interpretation and criticism, finally, have for their main purpose the development of one's own capacity to think constructively, or at any rate, independently. One's first object in reading philosophy is, to be sure, the discovery of what philosophers mean, but this is not one's main purpose. For of the great teacher of philosophy that must be true which Herder said of Kant in the early years of his teaching, 'He obliged me to think for myself; for tyranny was foreign to his soul.' Independent thought about the problems of ultimate reality is, thus, the goal of philosophical study. Independent criticism is the first stage of this spontaneous and original thinking, but it reaches its completion only in the attainment of a metaphysical system which one has adopted or created for oneself.

The Nature of the Absolute Self: Monistic Personalism

Fundamental to the study of other problems of monistic personalism is the analysis of the conception of the absolute self. Here it is of capital importance to remember that the term 'self,' as applied to the Absolute, must mean, qualitatively, precisely what it means in its application to human selves. To call the absolute reality self is meaningless, unless there is then attributed to the absolute self a consciousness which is like that of finite selves. From finite selves the absolute self must, it is true, differ; but it differs by virtue of its absoluteness, not by virtue of its selfhood. One may be guided, therefore, in the study of the nature of the absolute self by the following principle: to attribute to the absolute self all experiences and characters of the finite self which are essential to selfhood, but not to attribute to it any qualities which are inconsistent with absoluteness. If this prove impossible, – if it be shown, in other words, that a self is necessarily hampered by relativity, that is, by limitation from without, or conversely, if it be shown that an absolute reality necessarily lacks some of the essential characters of a self, – then the concept of absolute self will perish, as it were, by its own hands in disclosing its inner contradictoriness. It is, however, the belief of the monistic personal idealist that the two characters, selfhood and absoluteness, are compatible. In what follows the effort will be made to exhibit this compatibility. Negatively it will be pointed out that the absoluteness of the Self prevents our conceiving it as primarily or exclusively temporal. This follows from the evident incompleteness and contradiction of time. An absolute self is at least a complete self, and the very essence of time is its incompleteness. Thus, the Absolute must be conceived as supra-temporal, as immediately conscious of what appears to finite selves as present, past, or future. This character of the absolute self will be later considered in the discussion of the relation of absolute to partial self.

The immediate problem of this study of the absolute self is the discovery of those experiences and characters of the partial self which may be attributed to the absolute. For the purposes of a rough analysis, these may be grouped as, on the one hand, forms of consciousness: (1) perceiving and imagining, (2) thinking, (3) feeling (emotion), (4) affirming (willing and believing); and in the second place moral quality (goodness and badness).

(1) To begin with the form of consciousness first named: perception has four noticeable features. It includes a peculiar group of elemental, conscious experiences – sensations, as they are usually called; it involves the passive acceptance by the human self of these sensational experiences; it is a direct, an unmediated, consciousness; and finally, perception is an experience regarded as shared: the actual or possible consciousness of oneself as experiencing what one feels that any number of other selves do or may experience. Now it is necessary to attribute to the absolute self the first and third of these factors of experience, sensuousness and immediateness. All the consciousness of the absolute self, in its absoluteness, is immediate, since mediation requires time, whereas the absolute must be supra-temporal. It is equally evident that the absolute self must have sensational consciousness, since he must experience every sort and variety of consciousness which is experienced by human selves – otherwise, of course, the absolute self would miss what the finite self possesses. In Royce's words: 'Unless the Absolute knows what we know when we endure and wait, when we love and struggle, when we long and suffer, the Absolute in so far is less and not more than we are.' The old rationalistic view which denied sense experience to God, which thought it impious to conceive of God as smelling or tasting, really derogates from the infiniteness, the completeness, of God's consciousness. But though the sensuousness and the immediacy of perception are rightly attributed to the absolute self, it is impossible for him to experience its passivity. For passivity is evidently a consequence of the limitation, the partialness of the human self. To the Absolute, whose being constitutes reality, there can be nothing unavoidable, inevitable. We see and hear what we must see and hear, but the absolute self must be free and uncompelled, in his seeing and hearing, as in all his experiences. There remains the question whether the absolute self may be said to perceive in the sense of sharing his sense consciousness with other selves. An affirmative answer to this question is at least possible. For, as the next section will show in more detail, the existence of the absolute self cannot be taken as denying the existence of the finite and perceiving selves. The perception (if the term be allowed) of the absolute self may well, then, be

defined as the sense consciousness which he shares with the finite selves, included within him.

At this point emerges the following question: does the absolute self not only perceive, but imagine? For imagination, as possessed by human beings, is distinguished from perception precisely herein that imagination is regarded as a primarily private unshared experience, whereas in perception one regards other selves as sharing one's sensational consciousness. Now imagination, in at least one allied meaning of the term, may be attributed to the absolute self. Human selves imagine possibilities contrary to fact. I may, for instance, imagine that Columbus did not discover America; but my imagination must be object of the consciousness of the absolute self – else there were, *per impossibile*, conscious experience outside him; and the Absolute's consciousness of this idea of mine as relatively unshared may, not unfairly, be called imagination.

It is necessary, then, to conclude that the absolute self must have, like the finite selves, all varieties of elemental sense experience; that he may share it with conscious finite selves; but that the passivity which belongs to all human perception is incompatible with the experience of the Self who inhabits eternity and beyond whom is no reality.

(2) The second of the definite questions proposed in this section is the following: may the absolute self be said to think? Tradition, which has almost uniformly denied the perceptual nature of the supra-human consciousness, has here no objection to offer. Thought, like perception, is realized as a shared consciousness; it is contrasted with perception in the following ways: it is characterized by relational not by sensational elements; it is, in general, more complete, less fragmentary, than perception; it is a more indirect or mediate consciousness; finally, a certain necessity is attributed to it. In the first of these aspects, thought must evidently be attributed to the absolute self. Absoluteness involves inclusiveness of experience and the absolute self must be conscious of every shade and variety of likeness, difference, union, and opposition, no less than of every hue, tint, odor, and form. It is equally evident that the absolute self-consciousness must be characterized by a necessity deeper than that of any partial self's consciousness, and by a completeness which human experience approximates only in the form of thought. Between our fragmentary, relatively uncon- nected, perceptions and the systems of thought in which percepts

and images are linked in well-ordered dependence, one on the other, there is indeed a marked contrast. The absolute self, also, is conscious of well-ordered wholes; but his whole is the complete sphere of reality, and he has not to attain this completeness of insight in a slow and mediated way. Thus, the mediacy and the indirectness of thinking – evidenced especially in the slow process of syllogistic reasoning – must be foreign to the absolute consciousness. The Self, which knows and is all, does not gain truth by degrees, or see it bit by bit. To borrow a term from traditional metaphysics, the absolute self has *intellektuale Anschauung*, thought-in-tuition; he unites the directness of human perception with more than the completeness of human thought. Thus, to recapitulate and complete this section of the discussion: the absolute self must contain all the characteristic elements of the thought consciousness; his must be indeed the only really necessary and complete consciousness. The absolute self may, furthermore, share his thoughts, no less than his percepts, with finite selves. The mediacy and indirectness of human thought is, however, incompatible with his absoluteness.

(3) Emotions constitute the next great group of human experiences, and accordingly the next problem of the present discussion is the question whether emotional consciousness may be attributed to the absolute self. The answer to the question, of course, requires a preliminary analysis. In the opinion of the present writer, emotion is a doubly individualizing, passive, and affective experience. That is to say, in emotion I am profoundly conscious of myself as affected, happily or unhappily, by selves or objects which I individualize, differentiate from the mass of selves or things, in being emotionally conscious of them. These characters are best considered in reverse order. To begin with, since the absolute self is utterly complete, it must have every sort of experience, and therefore the affective experience in both its phases, pleasure and pain.[2] Here, again, we do violence to traditional philosophy. For centuries past, expositors of the nature of the supra-human self, Greek mythologists and Christian theologians alike, have denied the possibility of his suffering –

[2] The word 'pain' is here used, for want of an exact opposite to 'pleasure,' in a psychologically inaccurate sense, not to designate the dermal sense consciousness due to laceration, but to mean 'consciousness of the unpleasant.'

have represented him as secure from the human lot of misery and sorrow. Philosophical upholders of this doctrine have, it is true, admitted the necessity of reconciling it with that of the completeness of the divine consciousness; and they have attempted this reconciliation by distinguishing divine, or supra-human, knowledge from feeling, and by the teaching that the supra-human self knows pain without feeling it.[3] In the opinion of the present writer, this distinction is psychologically unjustifiable. One can no more know pain without feeling it, than one can know color without seeing it. And, more than this, the doctrine buttressed by this shaky psychology is, after all, incompatible with the conception of the absolute self's completeness and all-inclusiveness of experience. Pain, as felt, is as distinct and elemental a kind of consciousness as color or form or pleasure; it must, therefore, constitute an element of the absolute experience.

It is thus evident that the absolute self must be affectively conscious. But affection is one aspect only of emotion. A second aspect, passivity, belongs, of course, to the limited experience only, not to the absolute. On this character, not universally attributed to emotion, it is, however, unimportant to lay much stress. But the final factor of emotion, its doubly individualizing tendency, is of the greatest significance. In feeling, my own central personality is the object of my individualizing attention, always as related to some special other self, or special object. In perception and in thought also, I am, it is true, conscious of other selves as sharing my experience, but these are 'any' or 'all' selves, whereas in loving or in hating it is a particular self of whom I am conscious. Such an individualizing consciousness must, now, be attributed to the absolute self if any human individual is in any sense admitted to exist. For the absolute self, with his perfect knowledge, could know such limited individual self only as particular and unique. Now introspection testifies that I, at least, exist; and evidently, therefore, since the absolute self is affectively conscious, he must be able affectively to individualize me – and, therefore, to entertain toward me an emotional consciousness, so far as passivity is not an essential factor of emotion.

(4) In attributing to the absolute self the active experience of will, we are once more in accord with much of traditional

---

[3] Cf. Berkeley, 'Dialogues between Hylas and Philonous,' III., Open Court edition, p. 105.

philosophy. By will is meant the active, dominating relation of a self to other selves or to things; and it is plain that the Self of which all other real beings, selves or not-selves, are the expressions, must be actively, assertively related to them. It should be noted with the utmost care that this conception of the absolute self as Will does not involve two conclusions which are sometimes drawn from it. On the one hand, it is often thought that the conception of the supra-human self as Will is practically identical with the doctrine of God as creator of the universe; and the conception of creation – bringing the utterly non-existent into existence – is then challenged as unthinkable. In answer to this objection it must be urged that willing is not creating; that, in willing, one does not necessarily 'do' anything; that willing may indeed, but need not, be followed by a physical change. Will is, on the other hand, inherently an attitude of self to selves – the supreme, the assertive attitude of the dominating self; will is, therefore, a necessary relation of the all-including, the absolute, self toward the manifestations of itself. Again, it is sometimes assumed that the absolute self, if a willing self, has a consciousness necessarily bound down to the temporal order, since the will – it is asserted – has always a reference to the future. This assertion, again, must be denied. Volitions, in the phenomenalistic sense of the word are, it is true, anticipatory images of acts-to-be-done; and even the willing, dominating attitude of a self may be directed toward the future. But will does not necessarily look toward the future; it is, primarily, an active, subordinating attitude of one self to another, in which time may be left out of account.

This attempted analysis of the absolute self-consciousness would be culpably incomplete if it halted here. For, besides the predicates, 'knowing,' 'feeling,' and 'willing,' by which we characterize human selves, there are the so-called moral attributes, 'good' and 'bad.' And one of the peculiarities of these attributes is their opposition: a self is a knowing, feeling, and willing self; but it is not, either once for all or at one and the same time, both a good and a bad self. The present problem is, therefore, whether either goodness or badness, or both goodness and badness, or neither, should be predicated of the absolute self. It must be remembered that this question is asked of the absolute self, in its absoluteness. That the absolute self includes what we know as goodness and badness is as certain as the existence of good and evil finite selves, or even as the existence of a single self, alternately good and bad.

But this inquiry concerns the individuality of the Absolute, *as absolute*, the individuality which is manifested in, and not made up by, that of the human selves. Is the one real Self, the self whose selfhood is unshared with any partial self, good or bad, both, or neither?

To one of these questions, a negative answer may at once be given. An absolute self is a complete, a consistent, not a self-contradictory consciousness. Therefore, since 'good' and 'bad' are antithetical, an absolute self-consciousness is not, as absolute, both good and bad. And it will furthermore appear, if one follow the clue of human analogy, that an absolute self-consciousness is not itself bad. For observation indicates that moral badness is a function of partialness. It is a commonplace of practical ethics that the more closely self-centred or selfish I – the single self – become, the more morally defective I grow. In other words: the greater my emphasis on myself, as distinguished from other selves, the greater my sin. And the converse is true: the self who sees others as belonging within the confines of his own true self will do justice and love mercy and fulfil all the ideals of moral goodness. It will follow, if this analogy may properly be extended, that the Absolute who recognizes all finite selves as parts of himself, the Self whose selfhood is complete and all-extensive, will rightly be named 'good.'

A real difficulty is, however, involved in the reconciliation of the possible or probable goodness of the absolute self with the actually experienced evils of the universe. How, if the absolute self be inherently good, can the universe contain the evil which we directly know? Anti-theistic, pluralist idealism does not, of course, encounter this problem, for it finds no difficulty in attributing evil to any limited self. Even theistic personalism may avoid the difficulty if it frankly conceive God, after F. C. S. Schiller's fashion, as a finite, though greater-than-human, self. The prevailing religious consciousness, on the other hand, acutely feels this difficulty of monistic personalism. For the religious consciousness has inherited the conviction of God's power, and believes itself to experience his goodness: it consequently realizes the difficulty of proving this goodness in the face of the shattering and devastating evils of human experience. It is primarily of importance not to belittle the problem. A shallow optimism, which neglects the evil either from selfish preoccupation with personal good fortune, or from an arbitrarily limited observation of nature-adaptations, offers no foundation for the doctrine that the absolute self is not merely all-real, all-powerful, and all-knowing, but all-good. The goodness of the absolute self, if it be not compatible with the existence of actual suffering and real sin, is a baseless fiction, not a sober metaphysical doctrine.

The abstract requirements of a conception of the absolute self as good are readily outlined. If the absolute self, in its absoluteness, is to be good, not bad, and if yet the evil must be regarded as actual, then evil must be a subordinate factor, or element, of the good: it must be evil, in isolation, yet capable of forming part of a total good, somewhat as a chord which, taken by itself, is a discord, may yet form a part of a larger harmony. Two considerations ably set forth, years ago, by Professor Royce,[4] establish, in the writer's opinion, the possibility – nay, the probability – of this view of evil as a transcended factor in the experience of the absolute self. The first of these is an undoubted fact of human consciousness: the experience that suffering nobly borne and temptation vanquished enrich the life and strengthen the character – in a word, that they are elements of a wider good. Every human self which knows, however intermittently, the strength developed by resistance of moral seductions and the rich fruits of sorrow patiently endured, knows that the 'hours of mental moral strife, alone aright reveal' the deepest goodness of the soul. From this point of view, the evils of our human existence are the elements of an experience which, regarded in its totality, is good, not evil. And the absolute self's consciousness of these evils, as in themselves bad, is such a consciousness as the good man's experience of temptation: he is aware of the luring thought, of the enticing evil, but he is not morally defiled by this awareness of evil, for he is conscious of the bad only to hate it; he recognizes evil only to vanquish it. So the Absolute, which is the complete self, must indeed be conscious of sorrow and of sin, but is conscious of them only in conquering them, and is not, therefore, evil by the fact of including evil.

To this conception of the goodness of the absolute self, the following objection may be made: It has indeed – it may be admitted – been shown how evil, granted its existence, may be a subordinate part of the absolute self. But why, it may be urged, does evil exist at all, if all that exists is willed, assented to, or chosen, by an absolute and yet a good self? It is easy to see how

[4] 'Spirit of Modern Philosophy,' Lecture XIII., pp. 440 seq.

suffering greatly borne and temptation fiercely fought may be the self-assertions of an absolutely good self. But there is sin and sorrow which cannot, it is insisted, be regarded as the objects of the will of a good and yet an absolute self – in terms of theology, of a God who permits them. Griefs which narrow and belittle the mind, unresisted temptations which work the ruin of the soul, contaminating vice with its entail of hopeless misery and multiplying sin, – all these, it is urged, are evils of so positive a nature that they must taint the goodness of the self which, by virtue of its absoluteness, actually must have willed them, inasmuch as they exist.

Only one reply can be made to this objection. The absolute self, because complete, includes – it has been shown – all human experience as integral part of himself. It follows that the absolute self has all the experience that the human selves have. In a real sense, therefore, he shares our sorrow, is afflicted in our affliction, knows our grief. No anguish can wring the human heart but is felt by the absolute self; no self-contempt can flame up within the human spirit but is experienced by the all-including self. In other words, the absolute self is no God afar off, no supreme Being who decrees misery that he does not share, no divinity who feasts and delights in a distant Olympus, while below him his human subjects toil and sin and suffer. But it is not conceivable that a self whose will constitutes reality should will his own evil, if that evil be positive and unconquered. The fact that the absolute self shares in human suffering is, thus, a guarantee that the sorrow is neither final nor ultimate, that sin and misery, to human view irreconcilable with goodness, are none the less the elements – but the transcended elements – of the experience of an absolute and good self. It must be conceded that this reply to the objection of those who hold that the absolute self, because he wills and asserts the evil, cannot be good, offers no explanation of the existence of the deepest human suffering. No finite self, indeed, has ever probed this tragic mystery. What has been insisted on is simply this: that the existence of evil is reconcilable, though not by us at this stage of our development, with the goodness of the absolute self. And the grounds of this conclusion are simply these: the absolute self has willed his own evil, as well as ours; and would not have affirmed it save as subordinated to a wider good.

This analysis of the consciousness to be attributed to an absolute

self gives the following results: it has been found that the absolute
self has all the elemental experiences – sensational, affective,
relational – of human selves; that he is conscious of himself as
actively related to the finite selves, included within himself; that his
experience is utterly complete. Because of this completeness,
however, the absolute experience, as absolute, lacks the essential
temporality, the mediacy, and the passivity of the human consciousness. The more general conclusions from the discussion
are, first, a conviction of the richness of this absolute self-
consciousness and of the consequent impossibility of defining it in
terms of any one of its aspects – whether Thought, or Will, or
Love. Only when thought (for example) is taken, after Hegel's
fashion, to mean self-consciousness can it be rightly used as
synonym for the absolute, and consequently complete, experience.
It is observable, in the second place, that the attempt to classify the
absolute self-consciousness has broken certain lines of division
necessary to a purely human psychology; and that it is indeed,
therefore, impossible to conceive the absolute self as perceiving,
thinking, or feeling, in the precise sense which psychology gives to
these terms. Perception and thought merge the one into the other,
when perception has lost its passivity and thought its mediateness.
Similarly, emotion approaches will when it is conceived as an
active form of consciousness. The main distinction in the absolute
self's consciousness really – it appears – lies between his unparticu-
larizing consciousness (roughly coordinate, but not identical, with
human perception and thought), and his strongly individualizing
consciousness (coordinate with emotion and will), the aspects of
his experience which demand the existence of sharply differentiated, unique, partial selves. The problems involved in the conception of these partial selves must now be discussed. These problems
are the nature of the individuality attributed to these human
selves; the reasons for attributing to human selves, which are
expressions of an absolute self, any individuality; and the
reconciliation of human with absolute individuality.

Human Individuality

The issue between pluralistic personal idealism and the monistic
personalism, which this chapter outlines and defends, is simply
this: Pluralist and monist alike are immediately certain of human
individuality, 'the essentially unique being' of the human self. The

monist, however, reasons that ultimate reality must consist in absolute self. To this doctrine the pluralist offers two significant objections. He urges, first, that the conception of a self as including selves involves an impossibility, second, that the existence of the human selves merely as manifestations of an including absolute self would make human individuality impossible. The monist has, thus, the alternative of meeting these objections or of abandoning either the immediate certainty that human selves exist or the inferred doctrine that the universe is absolute self. In defence of his first objection, the pluralist insists: The monist conceives what is directly contrary to human experience. Misled by a spatial metaphor, he talks of minds as if they were 'Chinese boxes which can be put inside of each other,' whereas one self simply cannot include another self. Now it is open to the monist to retort: Pluralism involves the reality of an experience at least equally inconceivable, in that it conceives of essentially distinct selves as aware of each other. The reality of my experience of other selves involves, the monist well may insist, the only sort of 'inclusion' of selves within an absolute self which monism claims. But to meet charge with counter charge is an unsatisfying argument, even when, as here, one believes that one's opponent's inconsistency implies the truth that he criticizes. The monist has, in fact, a reply far better than a *tu quoque* to the pluralist's charge. For he can show that the private experience of each one of us furnishes the example of a self inclusive of selves. How sharply, for example, I distinguish my childhood self, the self of one jubilant year of youth, the self of a period of philosophic vagaries, from what I know as my whole self, myself *par excellence*. Even without the distinction by temporal periods, I am conscious of well-differentiated partial selves within myself – of a radical and a conservative self, a frivolous and a strenuous self, for example. Such self-differentiation of the finite self makes it impossible to deny *a priori* the inclusion of partial selves within the absolute self.

At this point the pluralist may suggest the following difficulties. The conception of absolute monism supposes, he will urge, the existence of an Absolute which is not only includer but also self. And this unique personality must be regarded, the pluralist says, as indivisible. Hence, he proceeds, if the absolute self is *in* any partial self, it must be all in that self. But this is impossible, for it would make such a partial self absolute; and it follows that the absolute self cannot be in any partial self. Otherwise put, the pluralist continues, the aspect or character that constitutes the Absolute a person is just the aspect in which he is contrasted with any partial self – with you or me. On this side, he doesn't include us; hence it is not as unique self that he is absolute; hence his personality as such is limited personality – limited by what is not it. Hence *as person* he is not absolute. The appeal of this objection (which recalls a famous passage of the 'Parmenides') is due partly to the spatial metaphor illicitly suggested by the word 'indivisible'; and partly to the assumption that personality is a mere aspect of the Absolute. In reply the monist insists that the Absolute, and not a mere character of the Absolute, is personality or self; and he energetically denies that the Absolute is indivisible in the sense which this argument requires: only a spatial unit, he holds, is in this sense either divisible or indivisible. Just as I, John Smith, know myself as constituting both my childhood and my adult self, and therefore as opposed or limited by neither of them, and just as I know myself, also, as more than any sum of partial selves or experiences so the absolute person includes us, the partial selves, and yet his personality is neither exhausted nor limited by that of any partial self.

But the pluralist, it will be remembered, has another objection to the doctrine of an absolute self. Even if finite selves were 'included,' in some sense, within the absolute self, they would lack, the pluralist insists, all that we call individuality; they would be unparticularized selves, each distinguished only by numerical position, from all the others, since each would be merely the expression of the one and same absolute self. In meeting this objection, it is necessary, first, to undertake a close scrutiny of the nature of individuality. The results of such a scrutiny have been suggested in the preceding section of this chapter. The individual is the unique, and since all reality is conscious self, an individual is such through and for the individualizing consciousness. But, as has appeared, one individualizes when one feels or wills. There is nothing individualizing in the merely perceiving or thinking consciousness. The objects of perception or of thought are members of a group and replaceable one by the other. I see things common to every man's vision, I think thoughts sharable with any minds. But with the objects of my feeling, as with those of my will, it is different. The object of my love or of my hate is unique, and not to be replaced by any one, however similar. I envy or pity this man, this child; I am thrilled with the beauty of this sunset; I feel myself as individual in relation to this other individual. In a word, no one – however similar – can take the place of the particular and unique object of my emotion or will. The essence of individuality is evidently, then, uniqueness, the character of being irreplaceable. And the problem of the compatibility of human personality with the absoluteness of the One Self reduces to this: does the existence of the absolute self permit or preclude the existence of unique partial selves?

The monist undertakes to show that the existence of the absolute self not merely permits, but requires, the existence of unique, included, human selves. The proof is the following: It has been shown already that the absolute self, if he exist, must be like human selves. Therefore, the absolute self must possess the individualizing consciousness, and his absoluteness must not thereby be lessened. Now the absoluteness of the self is not derogated from, the monist insists, by the existence of lesser selves within himself. In fact, the absolute self-consciousness would be less rich and complete – which is impossible – than the human consciousness, if the absolute self were incapable of individualizing, of distinguishing through personal feeling and will, the mutually exclusive parts of himself. Thus viewed, the existence of distinct individuals, each representing a different emotion or purpose of the absolute self, is not merely reconcilable with his existence, but essential to the completeness and fulness of his experience. And not only is the multiplicity of individuals essential to the Absolute, but the existence of the Absolute is necessary to insure to each partial self its individuality. For individuality, on which the pluralist lays such stress, is a shifting, contradictory affair unless defined from the standpoint of the absolute self. A given human being is *this* to one of his friends and *this* to another and still a third *this* to himself. He would possess no one individuality were he not, fundamentally, the expression of the unique individualizing consciousness of the absolute self. Thus, this monistic personalism does not involve, as its opponents assert, the loss of human individuality. You and I, so far from being swallowed up in the absolute self, so far from being lost or engulfed in the ultimate I, find the guarantee of our individual reality precisely herein that we are essential and unique expressions of this absolute self. It is idle to raise the question, might the absolute self have existed without me – you – him? For as a matter of direct observation, I at least exist in relation to other-than-myself. Hence the absolute self is a self which includes this precise, finite self. But since his reality is absolute, it follows that whatever exists is expression of him. Thus, because the Absolute is as he is, I am what I am.

In the end, therefore, we reassert the monistic, and yet personalistic, doctrine. Ultimate reality is absolute self, not a totality of related conscious selves, but a Self, inclusive of the many selves, yet characterized by a single personality.

L. SUSAN STEBBING (1885–1943)

Susan Stebbing went up to Girton College, Cambridge, to read history but by chance, in 1907, she picked up F. H. Bradley's *Appearance and Reality*, started to read it and immediately realized that philosophy was what she wanted to study. She was first fascinated by the new formal logic; Bertrand Russell and A. N. Whitehead were both in Cambridge at this time. She became sufficiently expert in the subject to write, twenty years later, an interesting and original textbook for students called *A Modern Introduction to Logic*, in which the ideas of Russell and Whitehead's *Principia Mathematica* were introduced, as well as traditional or Aristotelian logic. She wrote a number of other books on logic, including an early Penguin book, *Thinking to Some Purpose* (1939).

But by far the greatest Cambridge influence on her, both as an undergraduate and when she went back to teach at Girton in 1923, was G. E. Moore. Moore was the guru of the Bloomsbury set, who especially revered his pronouncements on values. It was his epistemology, however, that influenced Susan Stebbing. Moore's 'A Defence of Common Sense' (1925) and 'Proof of an External World' (1930) were wholly original in their insistence that words in common use must be understood as they are really used; and that the answer to the persistent philosophical question 'Is there anything that we can be truly said to know?' is 'Yes'. The determination to find in language both the source and sometimes the solution of traditional philosophical puzzles was later at the centre of the work of J. L. Austin and Ludwig Wittgenstein. Susan Stebbing's understanding of the philosophical significance of this approach, which can properly be described as revolutionary, and the wit and good humour of her style, are best illustrated in *Philosophy and the Physicists* (1937), from which the extract below is taken.

The physicists in question were Sir Arthur Eddington and Sir James Jeans, both Cambridge scientists, whose writing had a vast popular following in the 1930s on account of the excitable mysticism of their style. Non-scientists felt a *frisson* of amazement at the vision of reality presented in Jeans's book *The Mysterious Universe* and in Eddington's *Science and the Unseen World*. Susan Stebbing's book was a precursor of the wonderful debunking spirit of the post-war world, and undergraduates of the 1950s read it as eagerly as those for whom it had been written fifteen years earlier.

Susan Stebbing became Professor of Philosophy at Bedford College in the University of London in 1933. She was the first woman professor of philosophy in Britain. She was successively President of the Aristotelian Society and of the Mind Association. There is no doubt that she was a supreme professional, and a highly successful writer.

Further Reading

Gilbert Ryle *et al.*, *The Revolution in Philosophy* (London: Macmillan, 1956), especially chapter 4 on G. E. Moore by G. A. Paul

L. Susan Stebbing, *Ideals and Illusions* (Cambridge: Cambridge University Press, 1941)

From L. Susan Stebbing, Philosophy and the Physicists *(London: Methuen & Co., 1937), chapter 3: ' "Furniture of the earth" '*[1]

'Furniture of the earth'

Roused by the shock he started from his trance –
The cold white light of morning, the blue moon
Low in the west, the clear and garish hills,
The distant valley and the vacant woods,

[1] The chapter title is a quotation from Berkeley's *Principles of Human Knowledge*, Part I, section VI.

Spread round him where he stood. Whither have fled
The hues of heaven that canopied his bower
Of yesternight? The sounds that soothed his sleep,
The mystery and the majesty of Earth,
The joy, the exultation?

Wordsworth

I enter my study and see the blue curtains fluttering in the breeze, for the windows are open. I notice a bowl of roses on the table; it was not there when I went out. Clumsily I stumble against the table, bruising my leg against its hard edge; it is a heavy table and scarcely moves under the impact of my weight. I take a rose from the bowl, press it to my face, feel the softness of the petals, and smell its characteristic scent. I rejoice in the beauty of the graded shading of the crimson petals. In short – I am in a familiar room, seeing, touching, smelling familiar things, thinking familiar thoughts, experiencing familiar emotions.

In some such way might any common reader describe his experiences in the familiar world that he inhabits. With his eyes shut he may recognize a rose from its perfume, stumble against a solid obstacle and recognize it to be a table, and feel the pain from its contact with his comparatively yielding flesh. You, who are reading this chapter, may pause and look around you. Perhaps you are in your study, perhaps seated on the seashore, or in a cornfield, or on board ship. Wherever you may be, you will see objects distinguishable one from another, differing in colour and in shape; probably you are hearing various sounds. You can see the printed marks on this page, and notice that they are black marks on a whitish background. That you are perceiving something coloured and shaped you will not deny; that your body presses against something solid you are convinced; that, if you wish, you can stop reading this book, you know quite well. It may be assumed that you have some interest in philosophy; otherwise you would not be reading *this*. Perhaps you have allowed yourself to be persuaded that the page is not 'really coloured', that the seat upon which you are sitting is not 'really solid'; that you hear only 'illusory sounds'. If so, it is for such as you that this chapter is written.

Imagine the following scene. You are handed a dish containing some apples – rosy-cheeked, green apples. You take the one nearest to you, and realize that you have been 'had'. The 'apple' is too hard and not heavy enough to be really an apple; as you tap it with your finger-nail it gives out a sound such as never came from tapping a 'real' apple. You admire the neatness of the imitation. To sight the illusion is perfect. It is quite sensible to contrast this ingenious fake with a 'real' apple, for a 'real' apple just is an object that *really* is an apple, and not only *seems* to be one. This fake is an object that looks to your eyes to be an apple, but neither feels nor tastes as an apple does. As soon as you pick it up you know that it is not an apple; there is no need to taste it. We should be speaking in conformity with the rules of good English if we were to say that the dish contained real apples and imitation apples. But this mode of speaking does not lead us to suppose that there are two varieties of *apples*, namely real and imitation apples, as there are Bramley Seedlings and Blenheim Pippins. Again, a shadow may be thrown on a wall, or an image may be thrown through a lantern on to a screen. We distinguish the shadow from the object of which it is the shadow, the image from that of which it is the image. Shadow and image are apprehensible only by sight; they really are visual, i.e. *seeable*, entities. I can see a man, and I can see his shadow; but there is not both a *real* man and a *shadow* man; there is just the shadow of the man.

This point may seem to have been unduly laboured. It is, however, of great importance. The words 'real' and 'really' are familiar words; they are variously used in every-day speech, and are not, as a rule, used ambiguously. The opposition between a *real* object and an *imitation* of a real object is clear. So, too, is the opposition between 'really seeing a man' and having an illusion. We can speak sensibly of the distinction between 'the real size' and 'the apparent size' of the moon, but we know that both these expressions are extremely elliptical. The significance of the words 'real' and 'really' can be determined only by reference to the context in which they are used. Nothing but confusion can result if, in one and the same sentence, we mix up language used appropriately for the furniture of earth and our daily dealings with it with language used for the purpose of philosophical and scientific discussion.

A peculiarly gross example of such a linguistic mixture is provided by one of Eddington's most picturesque passages [Sir Arthur Eddington, *The Nature of the Physical World*, Gifford Lectures 1927 (Cambridge: Cambridge University Press, 1928)]:

I am standing on a threshold about to enter a room. It is a complicated business. In the first place I must shove against an atmosphere pressing with a force of fourteen pounds on every square inch of my body. I must make sure of landing on a plank travelling at twenty miles a second round the sun – a fraction of a second too early or too late, the plank would be miles away. I must do this whilst hanging from a round planet head outward into space, and with a wind of aether blowing at no one knows how many miles a second through every interstice of my body. The plank has no solidity of substance. To step on it is like stepping on a swarm of flies. Shall I not slip through? No, if I make the venture one of the flies hits me and gives me a boost up again; I fall again and am knocked upwards by another fly; and so on. I may hope that the net result will be that I remain steady; but if unfortunately I should slip through the floor or be boosted too violently up to the ceiling the occurrence would be, not a violation of the laws of Nature, but a rare coincidence.

(N.Ph.W. 342.)

Whatever we may think of Eddington's chances of slipping through the floor, we must regard his usage of language in this statement as gravely misleading to the common reader. I cannot doubt that it reveals serious confusion in Eddington's own thinking about 'the nature of the physical world'. Stepping on a plank is not in the least like 'stepping on a swarm of flies'. This language is drawn from, and is appropriate to, our daily intercourse with the familiar furniture of earth. We understand well what it is like to step on to a solid plank; we can also imagine what it would be like to step on to a swarm of flies. We know that two such experiences would be quite different. The plank is solid. If it be securely fixed, it will support our weight. What, then, are we to make of the comparison of stepping on to a plank with stepping on to a swarm of flies? What can be meant by saying that 'the plank has no solidity of substance'?

Again, we are familiar with the experience of shoving against an obstacle, and with the experience of struggling against a strong head-wind. We know that we do not have 'to shove against an atmosphere' as we cross the threshold of a room. We can imagine what it would be like to jump on to a moving plank. We may have seen in a circus an equestrian acrobat jump from the back of a swiftly moving horse on to the back of another horse moving with approximately the same speed. We know that no such acrobatic feat is required to cross the threshold of a room.[2]

I may seem too heavy-handed in my treatment of a picturesque passage, and thus to fall under the condemnation of the man who cannot see a joke and needs to be 'in contact with merry-minded companions' in order that he may develop a sense of humour. But the picturesqueness is deceptive; the passage needs serious criticism since Eddington draws from it a conclusion that is important. 'Verily', he says, 'it is easier for a camel to pass through the eye of a needle than for a scientific man to pass through a door. And whether the door be barn door or church door it might be wiser that he should consent to be an ordinary man and walk in rather than wait until all the difficulties involved in a really scientific ingress are resolved.' It is, then, suggested that an ordinary man has no difficulty in crossing the threshold of a room but that 'a really scientific ingress' presents difficulties. The suggested contrast is as absurd as the use of the adjective 'scientific' prefixed to 'ingress', in this context, is perverse. Whatever difficulties a scientist, by reason of his scientific knowledge, may encounter in becoming a member of a spiritual church, these difficulties bear no comparison with the difficulties of the imagined acrobatic feat. Consequently, they are not solved by the consideration that Eddington, no less than the ordinary man, need not hesitate to cross the threshold of his room . . .

If Eddington had drawn this picture for purely expository purposes, it might be unobjectionable. The scientist who sets out to give a popular exposition of a difficult and highly technical subject must use what means he can devise to convey to his readers what it is all about. At the same time, if he wishes to avoid being misunderstood, he must surely warn his readers that, in the present stage of physics, very little can be conveyed to a reader who lacks the mathematical equipment required to understand the methods by which results are obtained and the language in which these results can alone find adequate expression. Eddington's picture seems to me to be open to the objection that the image of a

[2] Eddington's words suggest that he is standing on a stationary plank and has to land on to another plank that is moving, relatively to himself, with a speed of twenty miles a second. It would be charitable to regard this as a slip, were it not that its rectification would spoil this part of his picture. There is an equally gross absurdity in the statement that he is 'hanging head outward into space'.

swarm of flies used to explain the electronic structure of matter is more appropriate to the old-fashioned classical conceptions that found expression in a model than to the conceptions he is trying to explain. Consequently, the reader may be misled unless he is warned that nothing resembling the spatial relations of flies in a swarm can be found in the collection of electrons. No concepts drawn from the level of common-sense thinking are appropriate to sub-atomic, i.e. microphysical, phenomena. Consequently, the language of common sense is not appropriate to the description of such phenomena. Since, however, the man in the street tends to think in pictures and may desire to know something about the latest developments of physics, it is no doubt useful to provide him with some rough picture. The danger arises when the scientist uses the picture for the purpose of making explicit denials, and expresses these denials in common-sense language used in such a way as to be devoid of sense. This, unfortunately, is exactly what Eddington has done in the passage we are considering, and indeed, in many other passages as well.

It is worth while to examine with some care what exactly it is that Eddington is denying when he asserts that 'the plank has no solidity of substance'. What are we to understand by 'solidity'? Unless we do understand it we cannot understand what the denial of solidity to the plank amounts to. But we can understand 'solidity' only if we can truly say that the plank is solid. For 'solid' just is the word we use to describe a certain respect in which a plank of wood resembles a block of marble, a piece of paper, and a cricket ball, and in which each of these differs from a sponge, from the interior of a soap-bubble, and from the holes in a net. We use the word 'solid' sometimes as the opposite of 'empty', sometimes as the opposite of 'hollow', sometimes as the opposite of 'porous'. We may also, in a very slightly technical usage, contrast 'solid' with 'liquid' or with 'gaseous'. There is, no doubt, considerable variation in the precise significance of the word 'solid' in various contexts. Further, as is the case with all words, 'solid' may be misused, and may also be used figuratively. But there could not be a *misuse*, nor a *figurative* use, unless there were some correct and literal usages. The point is that the common usage of language enables us to attribute a meaning to the phrase 'a solid plank'; but there is no common usage of language that provides a meaning for the word 'solid' that would make sense to say that the plank on which I stand is not *solid*. We oppose the solidity of the walls of a house to the emptiness of its unfurnished rooms; we oppose the solidity of a piece of pumice-stone to the porous loofah sponge. We do not deny that the pumice-stone is to some degree porous, that the bricks of the wall have chinks and crevices. But we do not know how to use a word that has no sensible opposite. If the plank is non-solid, then what does 'solid' *mean*? In the companion passage to the one quoted above ... Eddington depicts the physicist, about to enter a room, as reflecting that 'the plank is not what it appears to be – a continuous support for his weight'. This remark is absurd. The plank appears to be capable of supporting his weight, and, as his subsequent entry into the room showed, it *was* capable of supporting his weight. If it be objected that the plank is 'a support for his weight' but not 'a *continuous* support', I would reply that the word 'continuous' is here used without any assigned meaning. The plank appears *solid* in that sense of the word 'solid' in which the plank is, in fact, solid. It is of the utmost importance to press the question: If the plank appears to be *solid*, but is really *non-solid*, what does 'solid' mean? If 'solid' has no assignable meaning, then 'non-solid' is also without sense. If the plank is non-solid, then where can we find an example to show us what 'solid' means? The pairs of words, 'solid' – 'empty', 'solid' – 'hollow', 'solid' – 'porous', belong to the vocabulary of common-sense language; in the case of each pair, if one of the two is without sense, so is the other.

This nonsensical denial of solidity is very common in popular expositions of the physicist's conception of material objects. The author of a recently published book says: 'A table, a piece of paper, no longer possess that solid reality which they appear to possess; they are both of them porous, and consist of very small electrically charged particles, which are arranged in a peculiar way.'[3] How are we to understand the statement that the table *no longer* possesses 'the solid reality' which it appears to possess? The context of the statement must be taken into account. The sentence quoted occurs in a summary of the view of the physical world according to classical physics. It immediately follows the statement: 'This picture formed by the physicists has one great drawback as compared with the picture formed by the non-scientific man in the street. It is much more abstract.' In a later chapter we shall find

[3] Ernst Zimmer, *The Revolution of Physics*, trans. by H. Stafford Hatfield, 1936, p. 51.

reason to consider carefully what is meant by 'more abstract'. Here we are concerned only with the suggestion that the non-scientific man forms one 'picture' of the material world and the scientist another. There are, then, two pictures. Of what, we must ask, are they pictures? Where are we to find application for the words 'solid reality', which we may not use with reference to the table? Again we must ask: If the table is non-solid, what does 'solid' mean?

No doubt the author had in mind the nineteenth-century view of the ultra-microscopic world as consisting of solid, absolutely hard, indivisible billiard-ball-like atoms, which were assumed to be solid and hard in a perfectly straightforward sense of the words 'solid' and 'hard'. If so, it would be more appropriate to say that the modern physicist no longer believes that the table *consists* of solid atomic balls, than to say that 'the table no longer possesses solid reality'. There is, indeed, a danger in talking about *the table* at all, for the physicist is not, in fact, concerned with tables. The recent habit of talking as though he were is responsible for much confusion of thought. It leads Eddington into the preposterous nonsense of the 'two tables'. This view will be familiar to every one who is interested in the philosophy of the physicists. Nevertheless, it is desirable to quote a considerable part of Eddington's statement, since it is important to examine his view in some detail.

I have settled down to the task of writing these lectures and have drawn up my chairs to my two tables. Two tables! Yes; there are duplicates of every object about me – two tables, two chairs, two pens . . . One of them has been familiar to me from earliest years. It is a commonplace object of that environment which I call the world. How shall I describe it? It has extension; it is comparatively permanent; it is coloured; above all, it is *substantial* . . . Table No. 2 is my scientific table. It is a more recent acquaintance and I do not feel so familiar with it . . . My scientific table is mostly emptiness. Sparsely scattered in that emptiness are numerous electric charges rushing about with great speed; but their combined bulk amounts to less than a billionth of the bulk of the table itself. Notwithstanding its strange construction it turns out to be an entirely efficient table. It supports my writing paper as satisfactorily as table No. 1; for when I lay the paper on it the little electric particles with their headlong speed keep on hitting the underside, so that the paper is maintained in shuttlecock fashion at a nearly steady level. If I lean upon this table I shall not go through; or, to be strictly accurate, the chance of my scientific elbow going through my scientific table is so excessively small that it can be neglected in practical life . . . There is nothing *substantial* about my second table. It is nearly all empty space – space pervaded it is true by fields of force, but these are assigned to the categories of 'influences', not of 'things'.[4]

There is so much to criticize in this passage that it is difficult to know where to begin. Probably Eddington's defence against any criticism would be that this is one of the passages in which he 'was leading the reader on' (presumably – to put it vulgarly – 'up the garden path'), and that consequently it must not be taken as giving 'explicit statements' of his philosophical ideas. But he has nowhere expounded his philosophical ideas in non-popular language. Moreover, the mistakes are so frequently repeated in his writings and seem to be so inextricably bound up with his philosophical conclusions, that it is inevitable that these mistakes should be submitted to detailed criticism.

Perhaps the first comment that should be made is that Eddington takes quite seriously the view that there are *two tables*; one belongs to 'the external world of physics', the other to 'a world of familiar acquaintance in human consciousness'. Eddington's philosophy may be regarded as the outcome of a sustained attempt to answer the question: How are the two tables related to one another? It never seems to occur to him that the form of the question is absurd. In answering the question he is hampered from the start by his initial assumption that the tables are *duplicates* of each other, i.e. that it really isn't nonsensical to speak of two *tables*. I hazard the conjecture that Eddington is an inveterate visualizer, and that once he has committed himself to the language of 'two tables' he cannot avoid thinking of one as the shadow and of the other as the substance. (In this sentence, I have used the word 'substance' simply as the correlative of 'shadow'. This usage has undoubtedly influenced Eddington's thinking on this topic.) It is evident that the scientific table is to be regarded as the shadow. There are statements that conflict with this interpretation, but Eddington does not leave us in doubt that, whenever he is using the language of *shadowing*, it is the scientific table that is a shadow of the familiar table. It is true that he says, 'I need not tell you that modern physics has by delicate test and remorseless logic assured me that my second scientific table is the only one which is really there – wherever "there" may be.' Elsewhere he says, 'Our conception of the familiar table was an illusion' (*N.Ph.W.* 323). These discrepancies result from the deep-seated confusions out of which his philosophy springs; they will be examined in the following chapters. At present we are concerned with the view – in conflict with the statements just quoted – that the scientific table is a shadow. 'In the world of physics', he says, 'we watch a shadowgraph performance of the drama of familiar life. The shadow of my elbow rests on the shadow table as the shadow ink flows over the shadow paper. It is all symbolic, and as a symbol the physicist leaves it' (xvi). Elsewhere he suggests that physicists would generally say that 'the matter of this familiar table is *really* a curvature of space', but that is a view difficult to reconcile with either of the statements we are considering now.

Certainly there is much in the passage about the two tables that seems to conflict with the view of the scientific table as a shadow. It is said to be 'mostly emptiness', but scattered in the emptiness are numerous electric charges whose 'combined bulk' is compared in amount with 'the bulk of the table itself'. Is 'the table itself' the familiar table? I think it must be. But the comparison of the *two* bulks is surely nonsensical. Moreover, a shadow can hardly be said to have *bulk*. Yet Eddington insists that the two tables are 'parallel' – an odd synonym, no doubt, for a 'shadow'. He contrasts the scientific *table*, which has a familiar *table* parallel to it, with the scientific electron, quantum, or potential, which have no familiars that are parallel. Of the latter he says that the physicist is scrupulously careful to guard them 'from contamination by conceptions borrowed from the other [i.e. the familiar] world'. But if electrons, belonging to world No. 2, are to be scrupulously guarded from contamination by world No. 1, how can it make sense to say that they 'keep on hitting the underside' of a sheet of paper that, indubitably, is part of the familiar furniture of earth? It is Eddington who reintroduces contamination when he talks in this fashion, and he does so because he supposes that there is a scientific table parallel to the familiar table. I venture to suggest that it is as absurd to say that there is a scientific table as to say that there is a familiar electron or a familiar quantum, or a familiar potential. Eddington insists upon the lack of familiar parallels in the latter cases; surely he is justified in doing so. What is puzzling is his view that there are parallel *tables*. It suggests a return to the days when physicists demanded a model; 'the physicist', says

Eddington, 'used to borrow the raw material of his world from the familiar world, but he does so no longer' (xv). But if the 'scientific table' is to be regarded as the product of the 'raw material of the scientific world', how can it be regarded as parallel to the familiar table? Eddington seems unable to free himself from the conviction that the physicist is concerned with things of the same nature as the things of the familiar world; hence, *tables* are to be found in both world No. 1 and world No. 2. There is a statement in his exposition of 'The Downfall of Classical Physics' that shows how deep-rooted this conviction is. 'The atom', he says, 'is as porous as the solar system. If we eliminated all the unfilled space in a man's body and collected his protons and electrons into one mass, the man would be reduced to a speck just visible with a magnifying glass' (*N.Ph.W.* 1–2). The comparison is useful enough; the absurdity comes from speaking of the speck as a *man*. If this statement stood alone, it might well be regarded as an expository device. But the constant cropping up of the parallel tables shows that Eddington does not regard it as absurd to think of the reduction as still leaving a *man*. When, later in the book, he is expounding the conception of space required by relativity theory, he points out that our difficulty in conceiving it is due to the fact that we are 'using a conception of space which must have originated many millions of years ago and has become rather firmly embedded in human thought' (81). He adds: 'But the space of physics ought not to be dominated by this creation of the dawning mind of an enterprising ape.' It seems to me that in allowing himself to speak of the speck as a man, Eddington is allowing himself to be thus dominated. It is true that, in the statement just quoted, Eddington was speaking of relativity physics, but I do not think that 'the creation of the dawning mind of an enterprising ape' is any more appropriate to the conception of space in atomic physics. To this point we must return later. It must suffice at the moment to insist that a *man* is an object belonging to the familiar world, and has no duplicate in 'the scientific world'.

Perhaps we may be convinced of the absurdity of the notion that there are 'duplicates of every object' in the familiar world, if we return to the consideration of the description of a familiar scene with which this chapter opened. I spoke there of 'blue curtains', of a crimson and scented rose, of a bruised leg. Neglecting at present the consideration of the bruised leg, which – judging by Eddington's account of the adventures of an elephant – is beneath the notice of a scientist, we may ask what duplicate of *blue* is to be found in the scientific world. The answer is that there is no duplicate. True that it has a 'counterpart', but that is a very different matter. The counterpart of colour is 'its scientific equivalent electromagnetic wave-length' (88). 'The wave', says Eddington, 'is the reality – or the nearest we can get to a description of reality; the colour is mere mind-spinning. The beautiful hues which flood our consciousness under stimulation of the waves have no relevance to the objective reality.' It is obvious that here Eddington is regarding the scientific world as 'the objective reality'; the familiar world is subjective. This does not square with the view that the scientific world is the shadow of the familiar world, but it is hopeless to attempt to extract from Eddington any consistent view of their relation. With this difficulty, however, we are not at the moment concerned. The point is that Eddington firmly extrudes *colour* from the scientific world, and rightly so. But the *rose* is coloured, the *table* is coloured, the *curtains* are coloured. How, then, can that which is not coloured duplicate the rose, the curtains, the table? To say that an electromagnetic wave-length is coloured would be as nonsensical as to say that symmetry is coloured. Eddington does not say so. But he has failed to realize that a coloured object could be *duplicated* only by something with regard to which it would not be meaningless to say that it was coloured.

It seems to me that in his theory of the duplicate worlds Eddington has fallen into the error of which Berkeley accused the Newtonians. Berkeley was strongly convinced that the sensible world[5] was pre-eminently a *seeable* world. No doubt he overstressed the sense of sight at the expense of the other senses, but in the climate of opinion in which he was living this over-emphasis served a useful purpose. Consider the following passage:

> How vivid and radiant is the lustre of the fixed stars! how magnificent and rich that negligent profusion, with which they appear to be scattered throughout the whole azure vault! Yet if you take the telescope, it brings into your sight a new host of stars that escape the naked eye . . . Is not the whole system immense, beautiful, glorious

[5] I use the phrase 'sensible world' here with the same denotative reference as Eddington's phrase 'familiar world'.

beyond expression and beyond thought? What treatment then do those philosophers deserve, who would deprive these noble and delightful scenes of all reality? How should those principles be entertained, that lead us to think all the visible beauty of the creation a false imaginary glare?[6]

It seemed to Berkeley that the metaphysics of Descartes and Newton resulted in the description of a 'real world' that had all the properties of the sensible world except the vital property of being seeable. 'Ask a Cartesian', he said,[7] 'whether he is wont to imagine his globules without colour. Pellucidness is a colour. The colour of ordinary light of the sun is white. Newton is in the right in assigning colour to the rays of light.[8] A man born blind would not imagine Space as we do. We give it always some dilute, or duskish, or dark colour – in short, we imagine it as visible, or intromitted by the eye, which he would not do.' *Black* also is, in the sense required, a *colour*; a 'dark world' is no less a world apprehensible only by sight than a 'bright world' is. But the pure mathematician cannot take note of colour. Hence, under the influence of the *Mathematical Principles of Natural Philosophy* and of the rapidly developing science of optics, Berkeley's contemporaries looked to the principles of optics to account for the *seeability* of things. It is Berkeley's merit to have realized that the Cartesian–Newtonian philosophers, seeking to account for a *seeable* world, succeeded only in substituting a world that could in no sense be *seen*. He realized that they had substituted a theory of optics for a theory of visual perception. The outcome of this mistake is a duplication of worlds – the Image-World, sensibly perceived by men, the Real-World apprehended only by God. Newton is quite explicit on this point:

> Was the Eye contrived without Skill in Opticks, and the Ear without Knowledge of Sounds? . . . Is not the sensory of Animals that place to which the sensitive Substance is present, and into which the sensible Species of Things are carried through the Nerves and Brain, that there they may be perceived by their immediate presence to that Substance? And these things being rightly dispatch'd, does it not appear from Phaenomena that there is a Being incorporeal, living, intelligent,

[6] *Three Dialogues between Hylas and Philonous* (Second Dialogue).
[7] *Commonplace Book*, ed. by G. A. Johnston, p. 50.
[8] But see below, pp. 107–8.

omnipresent, who in infinite Space, as it were in his Sensory, sees the things themselves intimately, and thoroughly perceives them, and comprehends them wholly by their immediate presence to himself: Of which things the Images only carried through the Organs of Sense into our little Sensoriums, are there seen and beheld by that which in us perceives and thinks.[9]

Berkeley saw the absurdity of this duplication; he failed to realize that it was rendered necessary only by the confusion of the theory of optics with the theory of vision. He saw that the question – How is perception possible? – is devoid of sense; he saw that it is no less absurd to look to physics for an answer to the question. Unfortunately he accepted the account of objects of sight that was provided by the Optical Theory, and thus abolished the duplication of worlds only by locating (however indirectly) 'the things by me perceived' in the Mind of the Infinite Spirit. Newton had transferred colours from *things seen* into 'our little Sensoriums'; he conceived them as optical Images; accordingly, there were still required the things in themselves *of which* they were Images. These things must be found in the Sensory of God. Berkeley abolished the Images but only by carrying to a conclusion the absurdities initiated by the use of the language of Optics.

The achievement of Newton in the theory of Optics was that by his discovery of differently refrangible rays he discovered *measurable correlates of colour*; he thereby made the use of quantitative methods possible in a domain which would otherwise be excluded from the scope of physics. His extremely confused metaphysics is the result of his refusal to admit that there is anything in the perceived world except the measurable correlates, which ought, accordingly, to be regarded as the correlates of nothing. Newton saved himself from this manifest contradiction by having resort to a transmissive theory of Nature, and thus to a causal theory of perception. Allowing for the difference of phraseology we may surely see in the following quotation from Newton an anticipation of Eddington's theory of the sensible world.

The homogeneal Light and Rays which appear red, or rather make Objects appear so, I call Rubrifick or Red-making; those which make Objects appear yellow, green, blue, and violet, I call Yellow-making, Green-making, Blue-making, Violet-making, and so of the rest. And if

[9] *Opticks*, Query 28. (Edition reprinted 1931, p. 370.)

at any time I speak of Light and Rays as coloured or endued with Colours, I would be understood to speak not philosophically and properly, but grossly, and accordingly to such Conceptions as vulgar People in seeing all these experiments would be apt to frame. For the Rays to speak properly are not coloured. In them there is nothing else than a certain Power and Disposition to stir up a Sensation of this or that Colour. For as Sound in a Bell or musical String, or other sounding Body, is nothing but a trembling Motion, and in the Air nothing but that motion propagated from the Object, and in the Sensorium 'tis a Sense of that Motion under the Form of Sound; so Colours in the Object are nothing but a Disposition to reflect this or that sort of Rays more copiously than the Rest; in the Rays they are nothing but their Dispositions to propagate this or that Motion into the Sensorium, and in the Sensorium they are Sensations of those Motions under the Forms of Colours.[10]

This wholly fallacious argument has been strangely persuasive to physicists. Sensible qualities have no place in the world; they are *nothing but* 'dispositions to propagate this or that motion into the Sensorium'. There they undergo a transformation, not in the mathematical sense of that word, but a strange transformation indeed – a metamorphosis of 'the external world of physics' into 'a world of familiar acquaintance in human consciousness'.[11] The transformation remains inexplicable. Small wonder that Mr. Joad, reflecting upon the philosophical consequences of 'modern physics', exclaimed in perplexity, 'But, if I never know directly events in the external world, but only their alleged effects on my brain, and if I never know my brain except in terms of its alleged effects on my brain, I can only reiterate in bewilderment my original questions: "What sort of thing is it that I know?" and "Where is it?" '[12] Such perplexity can be resolved only by reconsidering the assumptions that led to the asking of these unanswerable questions. We shall find that the problem of perception, in this form, arose only because we have allowed the physicists to speak of a 'real world' that does not contain any of the qualities relevant to perception. To adopt the striking phrase of Professor E. A. Burtt, we have allowed the physicists 'to make a metaphysic out of a method'. In so doing they have forgotten, and

[10] *Opticks*, Bk. I, Pt. II (1931 ed., pp. 124–5).
[11] See N.Ph.W. xiv.
[12] *Aristotelian Society*: Supp. Vol. IX, p. 137.

philosophers do not seem to remember, that their method has been designed to facilitate investigations originating from a study of 'the furniture of the earth'.

SUSANNE K. LANGER (1895–1985)

Susanne Langer was a pupil of Alfred North Whitehead and was much impressed and excited by the new symbolic logic. She spent all her working life teaching in American universities, first at Columbia, then at Connecticut College. In her book *Philosophy in a New Key: A Study in the Symbolism of Reason, Rite and Art*, from which the following extract is taken, she attempted to show that art can be considered to be meaningful insofar as it is a symbolic form of expression, capable of being interpreted. She argued that the concept of the symbol was that which was at the source of all new, that is post-Kantian, philosophy. *Philosophy in a New Key* went into many editions and was a highly original venture into the philosophy of art. Susanne Langer's work is also original in that she, unlike most aestheticians, was primarily concerned not with the visual arts but with music. In her later book *Feeling and Form* she argued that unlike the discursive symbols of scientific language, the symbols of music are highly articulated and express what cannot be expressed in language, namely emotion, motion and sensation. Such non-linguistically expressible elements were, she held, the fundamental elements of mind.

Further Reading

Susanne Langer, *Mind: An Essay on Human Feeling* (Baltimore, Md: Johns Hopkins University Press, 1974)
The Symbolic Order, ed. Peter Abbs (Brighton: Falmer Press, 1989)

From Susanne K. Langer, Philosophy in a New Key *(Cambridge, Mass.: Harvard University Press, 1942), chapter 1: 'The new key'*

Every age in the history of philosophy has its own preoccupation. Its problems are peculiar to it, not for obvious practical reasons – political or social – but for deeper reasons of intellectual growth. If we look back on the slow formation and accumulation of doctrines which mark that history, we may see certain *groupings* of ideas within it, not by subject-matter, but by a subtler common factor which may be called their 'technique.' It is the mode of handling problems, rather than what they are about, that assigns them to an age. Their subject-matter may be fortuitous, and depend on conquests, discoveries, plagues, or governments; their treatment derives from a steadier source.

The 'technique,' or treatment, of a problem begins with its first expression as a question. The way a question is asked limits and disposes the ways in which any answer to it – right or wrong – may be given. If we are asked: 'Who made the world?' we may answer: 'God made it,' 'Chance made it,' 'Love and hate made it,' or what you will. We may be right or we may be wrong. But if we reply: 'Nobody made it,' we will be accused of trying to be cryptic, smart, or 'unsympathetic.' For in this last instance, we have only seemingly given an answer; in reality we have *rejected the question.* The questioner feels called upon to repeat his problem. 'Then how did the world become as it is?' If now we answer: 'It has not "become" at all,' he will be really disturbed. This 'answer' clearly repudiates the very framework of his thinking, the orientation of his mind, the basic assumptions he has always entertained as common-sense notions about things in general. Everything has become what it is; everything has a cause; every change must be to some end; the world is a thing, and must have been made by some agency, out of some original stuff, for some reason. These are natural ways of thinking. Such implicit 'ways' are not avowed by the average man, but simply followed. He is not conscious of assuming any basic principles. They are what a German would call his 'Weltanschauung,' his attitude of mind, rather than specific articles of faith. They constitute his outlook; they are deeper than facts he may note or propositions he may moot.

But, though they are not stated, they find expression in the *forms of his questions*. A question is really an ambiguous proposition; the answer is its determination. There can be only a certain number of alternatives that will complete its sense. In this way the intellectual treatment of any datum, any experience, any subject, is determined by the nature of our questions, and only carried out in the answers.

In philosophy this disposition of problems is the most important thing that a school, a movement, or an age contributes. This is the 'genius' of a great philosophy; in its light, systems arise and rule and die. Therefore a philosophy is characterized more by the *formulation* of its problems than by its solution of them. Its answers establish an edifice of facts; but its questions make the frame in which its picture of facts is plotted. They make more than the frame; they give the angle of perspective, the palette, the style in which the picture is drawn – everything except the subject. In our questions lie our *principles of analysis*, and our answers may express whatever those principles are able to yield.

There is a passage in Whitehead's *Science and the Modern World*, setting forth this predetermination of thought, which is at once its scaffolding and its limit. 'When you are criticizing the philosophy of an epoch,' Professor Whitehead says, 'do not chiefly direct your attention to those intellectual positions which its exponents feel it necessary explicitly to defend. There will be some fundamental assumptions which adherents of all the variant systems within the epoch unconsciously presuppose. Such assumptions appear so obvious that people do not know what they are assuming because no other way of putting things has ever occurred to them. With these assumptions a certain limited number of types of philosophic systems are possible, and this group of systems constitutes the philosophy of the epoch.'[1]

Some years ago, Professor C. D. Burns published an excellent little article called 'The Sense of the Horizon,' in which he made a somewhat wider application of the same principle; for here he pointed out that every civilization has its limits of knowledge – of perceptions, reactions, feelings, and ideas. To quote his own words, 'The experience of any moment has its horizon. Today's experience, which is not tomorrow's, has in it some hints and implications which are tomorrow on the horizon of today. Each man's experience may be added to by the experience of other men, who are living in his day or have lived before; and so a common world of experience, larger than that of his own observation, can

[1] From Chapter III: The Century of Genius. By permission of The Macmillan Company, publishers.

be lived in by each man. But however wide it may be, that common world also has its horizon; and on that horizon new experience is always appearing . . ."[2]

The formulation of experience which is contained within the intellectual horizon of an age and a society is determined, I believe, not so much by events and desires, as by the *basic concepts* at people's disposal for analyzing and describing their adventures to their own understanding. Of course, such concepts arise as they are needed, to deal with political or domestic experience; but the same experiences could be seen in many different lights, so the light in which they do appear depends on the genius of a people as well as on the demands of the external occasion. Different minds will take the same events in very different ways. A tribe of Congo negroes will react quite differently to (say) its first introduction to the story of Christ's passion, than did the equally untutored descendants of Norsemen, or the American Indians. Every society meets a new idea with its own concepts, its own tacit, fundamental way of seeing things; that is to say, *with its own questions*, its peculiar curiosity.

The horizon to which Professor Burns makes reference is the limit of clear and sensible questions that we can ask. When the Ionian philosophers, whom he cites as the innovators of Greek thought, asked what 'all' was made of, or how 'all' matter behaved, they were assuming a general notion, namely that of a parent substance, a final, universal *matter* to which all sorts of accidents could happen. This notion dictated the terms of their inquiries: what things were, and how they changed . . .

Between Thales and the Academy there is at least one further shift of the horizon, namely with the advent of the Sophists. The questions Socrates asked were as new to Greek thought in his day as those of Thales and Anaximenes had been to their earlier age. Socrates did not continue and complete Ionian thought; he cared very little about the speculative physics that was the very breath of life to the nature-philosophers, and his lifework did not further that ancient enterprise by even a step. He had not new answers, but new questions, and therewith he brought a new conceptual framework, an entirely different perspective, into Greek philosophy. His problems had arisen in the law-courts and the Sophists'

[2] *Philosophy*, VIII (1933), 31: 301–17. This preliminary essay was followed by his book, *The Horizon of Experience* (1934). See p. 301.

courses of oratory; they were, in the main, and in their significant features, irrelevant to the academic tradition. The validity of knowledge was only one of his new puzzles; the *value* of knowing, the *purpose* of science, of political life, practical arts, and finally of the course of nature, all became problematical to him. For he was operating with a new idea. Not prime matter and its disguises, its virtual products, its laws of change and its ultimate identity, constituted the terms of his discourse, but the notion of *value*. That everything had a value was too obvious to require statement. It was so obvious that the Ionians had not even given it one thought, and Socrates did not bother to state it; but his questions centered on what values things had – whether they were good or evil, in themselves or in their relations to other things, for all men or for few, or for the gods alone. In the light of that newly-enlisted old concept, *value*, a whole world of new questions opened up. The philosophical horizon widened in all directions at once, as horizons do with every upward step.

The limits of thought are not so much set from outside, by the fulness or poverty of experiences that meet the mind, as from within, by the power of conception, the wealth of formulative notions with which the mind meets experiences. Most new discoveries are suddenly-seen things that were always there. A new idea is a light that illuminates presences which simply had no form for us before the light fell on them. We turn the light here, there, and everywhere, and the limits of thought recede before it. A new science, a new art, or a young and vigorous system of philosophy, is generated by such a basic innovation. Such ideas as identity of matter and change of form, or as value, validity, virtue, or as outer world and inner consciousness, are not theories; they are the terms in which theories are conceived; they give rise to specific questions, and are articulated only in the form of these questions. Therefore one may call them *generative ideas* in the history of thought.

A tremendous philosophical vista opened when Thales, or perhaps one of his predecessors not known to us, asked: 'What is the world made of?' For centuries men turned their eyes upon the changes of matter, the problem of growth and decay, the laws of transformation in nature. When the possibilities of that primitive science were exhausted, speculations deadlocked, and the many alternative answers were stored in every learned mind to its confusion, Socrates propounded his simple and disconcerting questions – not, 'Which answer is true?' but: 'What is Truth?' 'What is Knowledge, and why do we want to acquire it?' His questions were disconcerting because they contained the new principle of explanation, the notion of value. Not to describe the motion and matter of a thing, but to see its purpose, is to understand it. From this conception a host of new inquiries were born. What is the highest good of man? Of the universe? What are the proper principles of art, education, government, medicine? To what purpose do planets and heavens revolve, animals procreate, empires rise? Wherefore does man have hands and eyes and the gift of language?

To the physicists, eyes and hands were no more interesting than sticks and stones. They were all just varieties of Prime Matter. The Socratic conception of *purpose* went beyond the old physical notions in that *it gave importance to the differences* between men's hands and other 'mixtures of elements.' Socrates was ready to accept tradition on the subject of elements, but asked in his turn: '*Why* are we made of fire and water, earth and air? Why have we passions, and a dream of Truth? Why do we live? Why do we die?' – Plato's ideal commonwealth and Aristotle's science rose in reply. But no one stopped to explain what 'ultimate good' or 'purpose' *meant*; these were the generative ideas of all the new, vital, philosophical problems, the measures of explanation, and belonged to common sense.

The end of a philosophical epoch comes with the exhaustion of its motive concepts. When all answerable questions that can be formulated in its terms have been exploited, we are left with only those problems that are sometimes called 'metaphysical' in a slurring sense – insoluble problems whose very statement harbors a paradox. The peculiarity of such pseudo-questions is that they are capable of two or more equally good answers, which defeat each other. An answer once propounded wins a certain number of adherents who subscribe to it despite the fact that other people have shown conclusively how wrong or inadequate it is; since its rival solutions suffer from the same defect, a choice among them really rests on temperamental grounds. They are not intellectual discoveries, like good answers to appropriate questions, but *doctrines*. At this point philosophy becomes academic; its watchword henceforth is Refutation, its life is argument rather than private thinking, fair-mindedness is deemed more important than single-mindedness, and the whole center of gravity shifts from actual philosophical issues to peripheral subjects – methodology, mental progress, the philosopher's place in society, and apologetics.

The eclectic period in Greco-Roman philosophy was just such a tag-end of an inspired epoch. People took sides on old questions instead of carrying suggested ideas on to their further implications. They sought a *reasoned belief*, not new things to think about. Doctrines seemed to lie around all ready-made, waiting to be adopted or rejected, or perhaps dissected and recombined in novel aggregates. The consolations of philosophy were more in the spirit of that time than the disturbing whispers of a Socratic daemon.

Yet the human mind is always active. When philosophy lies fallow, other fields bring abundance of fruit. The end of Hellenism was the beginning of Christianity, a period of deep emotional life, military and political enterprise, rapid civilization of barbarous hordes, possession of new lands. Wild northern Europe was opened to the Mediterranean world. Of course the old cultural interests flagged, and old concepts paled, in the face of such activity, novelty, and bewildering challenge. A footloose, capricious modernity took the place of deep-rooted philosophical thought. All the strength of good minds was consumed by the practical and moral problems of the day, and metaphysics seemed a venerable but bootless refinement of rather sheltered, educated people, a peculiar and lonely amusement of old-fashioned scholars. It took several centuries before the great novelties became an established order, the emotional fires burned themselves out, the modern notions matured to something like permanent principles; then natural curiosity turned once more toward these principles of life, and sought their essence, their inward ramifications, and the grounds of their security. *Interpretations* of doctrines and commandments became more and more urgent. But interpretation of general propositions is nothing more nor less than philosophy; and so another vital age of Reason began.

The wonderful flights of imagination and feeling inspired by the rise and triumph of Christianity, the questions to which its profound revolutionary attitude gave rise, provided for nearly a thousand years of philosophical growth, beginning with the early Church Fathers and culminating in the great Scholastics. But, at last, its generative ideas – sin and salvation, nature and grace, unity, infinity, and kingdom – had done their work. Vast systems of thought had been formulated, and all relevant problems had been mooted. Then came the unanswerable puzzles, the paradoxes that always mark the limit of what a generative idea, an intellectual vision, will do. The exhausted Christian mind rested its case, and philosophy became a reiteration and ever-weakening justification of faith.

Again 'pure thought' appeared as a jejune and academic business. History teachers like to tell us that learned men in the Middle Ages would solemnly discuss how many angels could dance on the point of a needle. Of course that question, and others like it, had perfectly respectable deeper meanings – in this case the answer hinged on the material or immaterial nature of angels (if they were incorporeal, then an infinite number of them could occupy a dimensionless point). Yet such problems, ignorantly or maliciously misunderstood, undoubtedly furnished jokes in the banquet hall when they were still seriously propounded in the classroom. The fact that the average person who heard them did not try to understand them but regarded them as cryptic inventions of an academic class – 'too deep for us,' as our Man in the Street would say – shows that the issues of metaphysical speculation were no longer vital to the general literate public. Scholastic thought was gradually suffocating under the pressure of new interests, new emotions – the crowding modern ideas and artistic inspiration we call the Renaissance.

After several centuries of sterile tradition, logic-chopping, and partisanship in philosophy, the wealth of nameless, heretical, often inconsistent notions born of the Renaissance crystallized into general and ultimate problems. A new outlook on life challenged the human mind to make sense out of its bewildering world; and the Cartesian age of 'natural and mental philosophy' succeeded to the realm.

This new epoch had a mighty and revolutionary generative idea: the dichotomy of all reality into *inner experience and outer world*, subject and object, private reality and public truth. The very language of what is now traditional epistemology betrays this basic notion; when we speak of the 'given,' of 'sense-data,' 'the phenomenon,' or 'other selves,' we take for granted the immediacy of an internal experience and the continuity of the external world. Our fundamental questions are framed in these terms: What is actually given to the mind? What guarantees the truth of sense-data? What lies behind the observable order of phenomena? What is the relation of the mind to the brain? How can we know other selves? – All these are familiar problems of today. Their answers have been elaborated into whole systems of thought: empiricism, idealism, realism, phenomenology, *Existenz-Philosophie*, and logical positivism. The most complete and characteristic of all these doctrines are the earliest ones: empiricism and idealism. They are the full, unguarded, vigorous formulations of the new generative notion, *Experience*; their proponents were the enthusiasts inspired by the Cartesian method, and their doctrines are the obvious implications derived by that principle, from such a starting-point. Each school in its turn took the intellectual world by storm. Not only the universities, but all literary circles, felt the liberation from time-worn, oppressive concepts, from baffling limits of inquiry, and hailed the new world-picture with a hope of truer orientation in life, art, and action.

After a while the confusions and shadows inherent in the new vision became apparent, and subsequent doctrines sought in various ways to escape between the horns of the dilemma created by the subject–object dichotomy, which Professor Whitehead has called 'the bifurcation of nature.' Since then, our theories have become more and more refined, circumspect, and clever; no one can be quite frankly an idealist, or go the whole way with empiricism; the early forms of realism are now known as the 'naive' varieties, and have been superseded by 'critical' or 'new' realisms. Many philosophers vehemently deny any systematic *Weltanschauung*, and repudiate metaphysics in principle.

The springs of philosophical thought have run dry once more. For fifty years at least, we have witnessed all the characteristic symptoms that mark the end of an epoch – the incorporation of thought in more and more variegated 'isms,' the clamor of their respective adherents to be heard and judged side by side, the defense of philosophy as a respectable and important pursuit, the increase of congresses and symposia, and a flood of text-criticism, surveys, popularizations, and collaborative studies. The educated layman does not pounce upon a new philosophy book as people pounced upon *Leviathan* or the great *Critiques* or even *The World as Will and Idea*. He does not expect enough intellectual news from a college professor. What he expects is, rather, to be argued into accepting idealism or realism, pragmatism or irrationalism, as his own belief. We have arrived once more at that counsel of despair, to find a reasoned faith.

But the average person who has any faith does not really care whether it is reasoned or not. He uses reason only to satisfy his curiosity – and philosophy, at present, does not even arouse, let alone satisfy, his curiosity. It only confuses him with impractical puzzles. The reason is not that he is dull, or really too busy (as he says he is) to enjoy philosophy. It is simply that the generative ideas of the seventeenth century – 'the century of genius,' Professor Whitehead calls it – have served their term. The difficulties inherent in their constitutive concepts balk us now; their paradoxes clog our thinking. If we would have new knowledge, we must get us a whole world of new questions.

Meanwhile, the dying philosophical epoch is eclipsed by a tremendously active age of science and technology. The roots of our scientific thinking reach far back, through the whole period of subjective philosophy, further back than any explicit empiricism, to the brilliant, extravert genius of the Renaissance. Modern science is often said to have sprung from empiricism; but Hobbes and Locke have given us no physics, and Bacon, who expressed the scientists' creed to perfection, was neither an active philosopher nor a scientist; he was essentially a man of letters and a critic of current thought. The only philosophy that rose directly out of a contemplation of science is positivism, and it is probably the least interesting of all doctrines, an appeal to common sense against the difficulties of establishing metaphysical or logical 'first principles.'

Genuine empiricism is above all a reflection on the validity of sense-knowledge, a speculation on the ways our concepts and beliefs are built up out of the fleeting and disconnected reports our eyes and ears actually make to the mind. Positivism, the scientists' metaphysic, entertains no such doubts, and raises no epistemological problems; its belief in the veracity of sense is implicit and dogmatic. Therefore it is really out of the running with post-Cartesian philosophy. It repudiates the basic problems of epistemology, and creates nothing but elbow-room for laboratory work. The very fact that it rejects *problems*, not answers, shows that the growing physical sciences were geared to an entirely different outlook on reality. They had their own so-called 'working notions'; and the strongest of these was the concept of *fact*.

This central concept effected the *rapprochement* between science and empiricism, despite the latter's subjective tendencies. No matter what problems may lurk in vision and hearing, there is something final about the guarantees of sense. Sheer observation is hard to contradict, for sense-data have an inalienable semblance of 'fact.' And such a court of last appeal, where verdicts are quick and ultimate, was exactly what scientists needed if their vast and complicated work was to go forward. Epistemology might produce intriguing puzzles, but it could never furnish facts for conviction to rest upon. A naive faith in sense-evidence, on the other hand, provided just such terminals to thought. Facts are something we can all observe, identify, and hold in common; in the last resort, seeing is believing. And science, as against philosophy even in that eager and active philosophical age, professed to look exclusively to the visible world for its unquestioned postulates.

The results were astounding enough to lend the new attitude full force. Despite the objections of philosophical thinkers, despite the outcry of moralists and theologians against the 'crass materialism' and 'sensationalism' of the scientists, physical science grew like Jack's beanstalk, and overshadowed everything else that human thought produced to rival it. A passion for observation displaced the scholarly love of learned dispute, and quickly developed the experimental technique that kept humanity supplied thrice over with facts. Practical applications of the new mechanical knowledge soon popularized and established it beyond the universities. Here the traditional interests of philosophy could not follow it any more; for they had become definitely relegated to that haven of unpopular lore, the schoolroom. No one really cared much about consistency or definition of terms, about precise conceptions, or formal deduction. The senses, long despised and attributed to the interesting but improper domain of the devil, were recognized as man's most valuable servants, and were rescued from their classical disgrace to wait on him in his new venture. They were so efficient that they not only supplied the human mind with an incredible amount of food for thought, but seemed presently to have most of its cognitive business in hand. Knowledge from sensory experience was deemed the only knowledge that carried any affidavit of truth; for truth became identified, for all vigorous modern minds, with empirical fact.

And so, a scientific culture succeeded to the exhausted philosophical vision. An undisputed and uncritical empiricism – not skeptical, but positivistic – became its official metaphysical creed, experiment its avowed method, a vast hoard of 'data' its capital, and correct prediction of future occurrences its proof. The programmatic account of this great adventure, beautifully put forth in Bacon's *Novum Organum*, was followed only a few centuries later by the complete, triumphant summary of all that was scientifically respectable, in J. S. Mill's Canons of Induction – a sort of methodological manifesto.

As the physical world-picture grew and technology advanced, those disciplines which rested squarely on 'rational' instead of 'empirical' principles were threatened with complete extinction, and were soon denied even the honorable name of science. Logic and metaphysics, aesthetics and ethics, seemed to have seen their day. One by one the various branches of philosophy – natural, mental, social, or religious – set up as autonomous sciences; the natural ones with miraculous success, the humanistic ones with more hope and fanfare than actual achievement. The physical sciences found their stride without much hesitation; psychology and sociology tried hard and seriously to 'catch the tune and keep the step,' but with mathematical laws they were never really handy . . .

Theology, which could not possibly submit to scientific methods, has simply been crowded out of the intellectual arena and gone into retreat in the cloistered libraries of its seminaries. As for logic, once the very model and norm of science, its only salvation seemed to lie in repudiating its most precious stock-in-trade, the 'clear and distinct ideas,' and professing to argue only from empirical facts to equally factual implications. The logician, once an investor in the greatest enterprise of human thought, found himself reduced to a sort of railroad linesman, charged with the task of keeping the tracks and switches of scientific reasoning clear for sensory reports to make their proper connections. Logic, it seemed, could never have a life of its own; for it had no foundation of facts, except the psychological fact that we do think thus and so, that such-and-such forms of argument lead to correct or incorrect predictions of further experience, and so forth. Logic became a mere reflection on tried and useful methods of fact-finding, and an official warrant for that technically fallacious process of generalizing known as 'induction.'

Yes, the heyday of science has stifled and killed our rather worn-out philosophical interests, born three and a half centuries ago from that great generative idea, the bifurcation of nature into an inner and an outer world. To the generations of Comte, Mill, and Spencer, it certainly seemed as though all human knowledge could be cast in the new mold; certainly as though nothing in any other mold could hope to jell. And indeed, nothing much *has* jelled in any other mold; but neither have the non-physical disciplines been able to adopt and thrive on the scientific methods that did such wonders for physics and its obvious derivatives. The truth is that science has not really fructified and activated *all* human thought. If humanity has really passed the philosophical stage of learning, as Comte hopefully declared, and is evolving no more fantastic ideas, then we have certainly left many interesting brain-children stillborn along the way.

But the mind of man is always fertile, ever creating and discarding, like the earth. There is always new life under old decay. Last year's dead leaves hide not merely the seeds, but the full-fledged green plants of this year's spring, ready to bloom almost as soon as they are uncovered. It is the same with the seasons of civilization: under cover of a weary Greco-Roman eclecticism, a baffled cynicism, Christianity grew to its conquering force of conception and its clear interpretation of life; obscured by creed, canon, and curriculum, by learned disputation and demonstration, was born the great ideal of *personal experience*, the 'rediscovery of the inner life,' as Rudolph Eucken termed it, that was to inspire philosophy from Descartes's day to the end of German idealism. And beneath our rival 'isms,' our methodologies, conferences, and symposia, of course there is something brewing, too.

No one observed, amid the first passion of empirical fact-finding, that the ancient science of mathematics still went its undisturbed way of pure reason. It fell in so nicely with the needs of scientific thought, it fitted the observed world of fact so neatly, that those who learned and used it never stopped to accuse those who had invented and evolved it of being mere reasoners, and lacking tangible data. Yet the few conscientious empiricists who thought that *factual* bases must be established for mathematics made a notoriously poor job of it. Few mathematicians have really held that numbers were discovered by observation, or even that geometrical relationships are known to us by inductive reasoning from many observed instances. Physicists may think of certain facts in place of constants and variables, but the same constants and variables will serve somewhere else to calculate other facts, and the mathematicians themselves give no set of data their preference. They deal only with items whose sensory qualities are quite irrelevant: their 'data' are arbitrary sounds or marks called *symbols*.

Behind these symbols lie the boldest, purest, coolest abstractions mankind has ever made. No schoolman speculating on essences and attributes ever approached anything like the abstractness of algebra. Yet those same scientists who prided themselves on their concrete factual knowledge, who claimed to reject every proof except empirical evidence, never hesitated to accept the demonstrations and calculations, the bodiless, sometimes avowedly 'fictitious' entities of the mathematicians. Zero and infinity, square roots of negative numbers, incommensurable lengths and fourth dimensions, all found unquestioned welcome in the laboratory, when the average thoughtful layman, who could still take an invisible soul-substance on faith, doubted their logical respectability.

What is the secret power of mathematics, to win hardheaded empiricists, against their most ardent beliefs, to its purely rational speculations and intangible 'facts'? . . .

The secret lies in the fact that a mathematician does not profess to say anything about the existence, reality, or efficacy of *things* at all. His concern is the possibility of *symbolizing things*, and of symbolizing the relations into which they might enter with each other. His 'entities' are not 'data,' but *concepts*. That is why such elements as 'imaginary numbers' and 'infinite decimals' are tolerated by scientists to whom invisible agents, powers, and 'principles' are anathema. Mathematical constructions are only symbols; they have meanings in terms of relationships, not of substance; something in reality answers to them, but they are not supposed to be items in that reality. To the true mathematician, numbers do not 'inhere in' denumerable things, nor do circular objects 'contain' degrees. Numbers and degrees and all their ilk only *mean* the real properties of real objects. It is entirely at the discretion of the scientist to say, 'Let x mean this, let y mean that.' All that mathematics determines is that *then* x and y must be related thus and thus. If experience belies the conclusion, then the formula does not express the relation of *this* x and *that* y; then x and y may not mean this thing and that. But no mathematician in his professional capacity will ever tell us that *this is x*, and has therefore such and such properties.

The faith of scientists in the power and truth of mathematics is so implicit that their work has gradually become less and less observation, and more and more calculation. The promiscuous collection and tabulation of data have given way to a process of assigning possible meanings, merely supposed real entities, to mathematical terms, working out the logical results, and then staging certain crucial experiments to check the hypothesis against the actual, empirical results. But the facts which are accepted by virtue of these tests are not actually *observed* at all. With the advance of mathematical technique in physics, the tangible results of experiment have become less and less spectacular; on the other hand, their *significance* has grown in inverse proportion. The men in the laboratory have departed so far from the old forms of experimentation – typified by Galileo's weights and Franklin's kite – that they cannot be said to observe the actual objects of their curiosity at all; instead, they are watching index needles, revolving drums, and sensitive plates. No psychology of 'association' of sense-experiences can relate these data to the objects they signify, for in most cases the objects have never been experienced. Observation has become almost entirely indirect; and *readings* take the place of genuine witness. The sense-data on which the propositions of modern science rest are, for the most part, little photographic spots and blurs, or inky curved lines on paper. These data are empirical enough, but of course they are not themselves the phenomena in question; the actual phenomena stand behind them as their supposed causes. Instead of watching the process that interests us, that is to be verified – say, a course of celestial events, or the behavior of such objects as molecules and ether-waves – we really see only the fluctuations of a tiny arrow, the trailing path of a stylus, or the appearance of a speck of light, and *calculate to the 'facts' of our science*. What is directly observable is only a sign of the 'physical fact'; it requires interpretation to yield scientific propositions. Not simply seeing is believing, but *seeing and calculating, seeing and translating*.

This is bad, of course, for a thoroughgoing empiricism. Sense-data certainly do not make up the whole, or even the major part, of a scientist's material. The events that are given for his inspection could be 'faked' in a dozen ways – that is, the same visible events could be made to occur, but with a different significance. We may at any time be wrong about their significance, even where no one is duping us; we may be nature's fools. Yet if we did not attribute an elaborate, purely reasoned, and hypothetical history of causes to the little shivers and wiggles of our apparatus, we really could not record them as momentous results of experiment. The problem of observation is all but eclipsed by the problem of *meaning*. And the triumph of empiricism in science is jeopardized by the surprising truth that *our sense-data are primarily symbols*.

Here, suddenly, it becomes apparent that the age of science has begotten a new philosophical issue, inestimably more profound than its original empiricism: for in all quietness, along purely rational lines, mathematics has developed just as brilliantly and vitally as any experimental technique, and, step by step, has kept abreast of discovery and observation; and all at once, the edifice of human knowledge stands before us, not as a vast collection of sense reports, but as a structure of *facts that are symbols* and *laws that are their meanings*. A new philosophical theme has been set forth to a coming age: an epistemological theme, the comprehension of science. The power of symbolism is its cue, as the finality of sense-data was the cue of a former epoch . . .

But it is not only in philosophy proper that the new keynote has been struck. There are at least two limited and technical fields, which have suddenly been developed beyond all prediction, by the discovery of the all-importance of symbol-using or symbol-reading. They are widely separate fields, and their problems and procedures do not seem to belong together in any way at all: one is modern psychology, the other modern logic.

In the former we are disturbed – thrilled or irritated, according to our temperaments – by the advent of psychoanalysis. In the latter we witness the rise of a new technique known as symbolic logic. The coincidence of these two pursuits seems entirely fortuitous; one stems from medicine and the other from mathematics, and there is nothing whatever on which they would care to compare notes or hold debate. Yet I believe they both embody the same generative idea, which is to preoccupy and inspire our philosophical age: for each in its own fashion has discovered the power of symbolization.

They have different conceptions of symbolism and its functions. Symbolic logic is not 'symbolic' in the sense of Freudian psychology, and *The Analysis of Dreams* makes no contribution to logical syntax. The emphasis on symbolism derives from entirely different interests, in their respective contexts. As yet, the cautious critic may well regard the one as a fantastic experiment of 'mental philosophy,' and the other as a mere fashion in logic and epistemology.

When we speak of fashions in thought, we are treating philosophy lightly. There is disparagement in the phrases, 'a fashionable problem,' 'a fashionable term.' Yet it is the most natural and appropriate thing in the world for a new problem or a new terminology to have a vogue that crowds out everything else for a little while. A word that everyone snaps up, or a question that has everybody excited, probably carries a generative idea – the germ of a complete reorientation in metaphysics, or at least the 'Open Sesame' of some new positive science. The sudden vogue of such a key-idea is due to the fact that all sensitive and active minds turn at once to exploiting it; we try it in every connection, for every purpose, experiment with possible stretches of its strict meaning, with generalizations and derivatives. When we become familiar with the new idea our expectations do not outrun its actual uses quite so far, and then its unbalanced popularity is over. We settle down to the problems that it has really generated, and these become the characteristic issues of our time.

The rise of technology is the best possible proof that the basic concepts of physical science, which have ruled our thinking for nearly two centuries, are essentially sound. They have begotten knowledge, practice, and systematic understanding; no wonder they have given us a very confident and definite *Weltanschauung*. They have delivered all physical nature into our hands. But strangely enough, the so-called 'mental sciences' have gained very little from the great adventure. One attempt after another has failed to apply the concept of causality to logic and aesthetics, or even sociology and psychology. Causes and effects could be found, of course, and could be correlated, tabulated, and studied; but even in psychology, where the study of stimulus and reaction has been carried to elaborate lengths, no true science has resulted. No prospects of really great achievement have opened before us in the laboratory. If we follow the methods of natural science our psychology tends to run into physiology, histology, and genetics; we move further and further away from those problems which we ought to be approaching. That signifies that the generative idea which gave rise to physics and chemistry and all their progeny – technology, medicine, biology – does not contain any vivifying concept for the humanistic sciences. The physicist's scheme, so faithfully emulated by generations of psychologists, epistemologists, and aestheticians, is probably blocking their progress, defeating possible insights by its prejudicial force. The scheme is not false – it is perfectly reasonable – but it is bootless for the study of mental phenomena. It does not engender leading questions and excite a constructive imagination, as it does in physical researches. Instead of a method, it inspires a militant methodology.

Now, in those very regions of human interest where the age of empiricism has caused no revolution, the preoccupation with symbols has come into fashion. It has not sprung directly from any canon of science. It runs at least two distinct and apparently incompatible courses. Yet each course is a river of life in its own field, each fructifies its own harvest; and instead of finding mere contradiction in the wide difference of forms and uses to which this new generative idea is put, I see in it a promise of power and versatility, and a commanding philosophical problem. One conception of symbolism leads to logic, and meets the new problems in theory of knowledge; and so it inspires an evaluation of science and a quest for certainty. The other takes us in the opposite direction – to psychiatry, the study of emotions, religion, fantasy, and everything but knowledge. Yet in both we have a central theme: the *human response*, as a constructive, not a passive thing. Epistemologists and psychologists agree that symbolization is the key to that constructive process, though they may be ready to kill each other over the issue of what a symbol is and how it functions. One studies the structure of science, the other of dreams; each has his own assumptions – that is all they are – regarding the nature of symbolism itself. Assumptions, generative ideas, are what we fight for. Our conclusions we are usually content to demonstrate by peaceable means. Yet the assumptions are philosophically our most interesting stock-in-trade.

In the fundamental notion of symbolization – mystical, practical, or mathematical, it makes no difference – we have the keynote of all humanistic problems. In it lies a new conception of 'mentality,' that may illumine questions of life and consciousness, instead of obscuring them as traditional 'scientific methods' have done. If it is indeed a generative idea, it will beget tangible methods of its own, to free the deadlocked paradoxes of mind and body, reason and impulse, autonomy and law, and will overcome the checkmated arguments of an earlier age by discarding their very idiom and shaping their equivalents in more significant phrase. The philosophical study of symbols is not a technique borrowed from other disciplines, not even from mathematics; it has arisen in the fields that the great advance of learning has left fallow. Perhaps

it holds the seed of a new intellectual harvest, to be reaped in the
next season of the human understanding.

HANNAH ARENDT (1906–75)

Hannah Arendt was born in Germany. She was a pupil of Husserl, the phenomenological philosopher who exercised a great influence on Jean-Paul Sartre. Then for a considerable time Karl Jaspers, an existentialist philosopher who later became a clinical psychiatrist, was both her teacher and her lover. When Hitler came into power in 1933, Hannah Arendt, along with many Jews, moved to Paris. She escaped to America in 1941 and became an American citizen in 1950. In 1951 she published *The Origins of Totalitarianism*, which explored the nature of Nazism and Soviet Communism. In this book she established her reputation for building general explanatory systems out of her own political experience. However, her systematizing became increasingly ambitious and proportionately less convincing. In 1958 she published *The Human Condition*, a study of the related concepts of labour, work and action. In 1961 she published a report on the Eichmann war-criminal trial in Jerusalem, in which she presented Eichmann as a mindless bureaucrat rather than a powerful and evil man; and she controversially argued that European Jews had been accomplices in the Holocaust. After her death her unfinished *magnum opus*, *The Life of the Mind*, was published (1978). This was the most grandiose and would-be systematic of all her projects, but it is now virtually forgotten. She was at her best in the analysis of contemporary political concepts; and it is for this reason that I have chosen to reproduce part of her essay *On Violence*, written in 1970.

Further Reading

J-P. Sartre, *Anti-Semite and Jew*, trans. George J. Becker (New York: Grove Press, 1960)

Leonard Schapiro, *Totalitarianism* (New York: Praeger, 1972)

Helen Silving, 'In re Eichmann: a dilemma of law and morality', *American Journal of International Law*, 55 (1961), 307–58

Hannah Arendt, *Between Past and Future: Eight Exercises in Political Thought* (New York: Viking Press, 1968)

From Hannah Arendt, On Violence *(New York: Harcourt, Brace & World, 1970), part 2*

There exists a consensus among political theorists from Left to Right to the effect that violence is nothing more than the most flagrant manifestation of power. 'All politics is a struggle for power; the ultimate kind of power is violence,' said C. Wright Mills, echoing, as it were, Max Weber's definition of the state as 'the rule of men over men based on the means of legitimate, that is allegedly legitimate, violence.'[1] The consensus is very strange; for to equate political power with 'the organization of violence' makes sense only if one follows Marx's estimate of the state as an instrument of oppression in the hands of the ruling class. Let us therefore turn to authors who do not believe that the body politic and its laws and institutions are merely coercive superstructures, secondary manifestations of some underlying forces. Let us turn, for instance, to Bertrand de Jouvenel, whose book *Power* is perhaps the most prestigious and, anyway, the most interesting recent treatise on the subject. 'To him,' he writes, 'who contemplates the unfolding of the ages war presents itself as an activity of States *which pertains to their essence*.'[2] This may prompt us to ask whether the end of warfare, then, would mean the end of states. Would the disappearance of violence in relationships between states spell the end of power?

The answer, it seems, will depend on what we understand by power. And power, it turns out, is an instrument of rule, while rule, we are told, owes its existence to 'the instinct of domination.' We are immediately reminded of what Sartre said about violence

[1] *The Power Elite*, New York, 1956, p. 171; Max Weber in the first paragraphs of *Politics as a Vocation* (1921). Weber seems to have been aware of his agreement with the Left. He quotes in the context Trotsky's remark in Brest-Litovsk, 'Every state is based on violence,' and adds, 'This is indeed true.'

[2] *Power: The Natural History of Its Growth* (1945), London, 1952, p. 122.

when we read in Jouvenel that 'a man feels himself more of a man when he is imposing himself and making others the instruments of his will,' which gives him 'incomparable pleasure.' 'Power,' said Voltaire, 'consists in making others act as I choose'; it is present wherever I have the chance 'to assert my own will against the resistance' of others, said Max Weber, reminding us of Clausewitz's definition of war as 'an act of violence to compel the opponent to do as we wish.' The word, we are told by Strausz-Hupé, signifies 'the power of man over man.' To go back to Jouvenel: 'To command and to be obeyed: without that, there is no Power – with it no other attribute is needed for it to be . . . The thing without which it cannot be: that essence is command.' If the essence of power is the effectiveness of command, then there is no greater power than that which grows out of the barrel of a gun, and it would be difficult to say in 'which way the order given by a policeman is different from that given by a gunman.' (I am quoting from the important book *The Notion of the State*, by Alexander Passerin d'Entrèves, the only author I know who is aware of the importance of distinguishing between violence and power.) 'We have to decide whether and in what sense "power" can be distinguished from "force", to ascertain how the fact of using force according to law changes the quality of force itself and presents us with an entirely different picture of human relations,' since 'force, by the very fact of being qualified, ceases to be force.' But even this distinction, by far the most sophisticated and thoughtful one in the literature, does not go to the root of the matter. Power in Passerin d'Entrèves's understanding is 'qualified' or 'institutionalized force.'[3] . . . Should everybody from Right to Left, from Bertrand de Jouvenel to Mao Tse-tung agree on so basic a point in political philosophy as the nature of power?

In terms of our traditions of political thought, these definitions have much to recommend them. Not only do they derive from the old notion of absolute power that accompanied the rise of the sovereign European nation-state, whose earliest and still greatest spokesmen were Jean Bodin, in sixteenth-century France, and Thomas Hobbes, in seventeenth-century England; they also coincide with the terms used since Greek antiquity to define the forms of government as the rule of man over man – of one or the

[3] *The Notion of the State, An Introduction to Political Theory* was first published in Italian in 1962.

few in monarchy and oligarchy, of the best or the many in aristocracy and democracy. Today we ought to add the latest and perhaps most formidable form of such dominion: bureaucracy or the rule of an intricate system of bureaus in which no men, neither one nor the best, neither the few nor the many, can be held responsible, and which could be properly called rule by Nobody. (If, in accord with traditional political thought, we identify tyranny as government that is not held to give account of itself, rule by Nobody is clearly the most tyrannical of all, since there is no one left who could even be asked to answer for what is being done. It is this state of affairs, making it impossible to localize responsibility and to identify the enemy, that is among the most potent causes of the current worldwide rebellious unrest, its chaotic nature, and its dangerous tendency to get out of control and to run amuck.)

Moreover, this ancient vocabulary was strangely confirmed and fortified by the addition of the Hebrew–Christian tradition and its 'imperative conception of law.' This concept was not invented by the 'political realists' but was, rather, the result of a much earlier, almost automatic generalization of God's 'Commandments,' according to which 'the simple relation of command and obedience' indeed sufficed to identify the essence of law.[4] Finally, more modern scientific and philosophical convictions concerning man's nature have further strengthened these legal and political traditions. The many recent discoveries of an inborn instinct of domination and an innate aggressiveness in the human animal were preceded by very similar philosophic statements. According to John Stuart Mill, 'the first lesson of civilization [is] that of obedience,' and he speaks of 'the two states of the inclinations . . . one the desire to exercise power over others; the other . . . disinclination to have power exercised over themselves.'[5] If we would trust our own experiences in these matters, we should know that the instinct of submission, an ardent desire to obey and be ruled by some strong man, is at least as prominent in human psychology as the will to power, and, politically, perhaps more relevant. The old adage 'How fit he is to sway / That can so well obey,' some version of which seems to have been known to all

[4] *Ibidem*, p. 129.
[5] *Considerations on Representative Government* (1861), Liberal Arts Library, pp. 59 and 65.

centuries and all nations,[6] may point to a psychological truth: namely, that the will to power and the will to submission are interconnected. 'Ready submission to tyranny,' to use Mill once more, is by no means always caused by 'extreme passiveness.' Conversely, a strong disinclination to obey is often accompanied by an equally strong disinclination to dominate and command. Historically speaking, the ancient institution of slave economy would be inexplicable on the grounds of Mill's psychology. Its express purpose was to liberate citizens from the burden of household affairs and to permit them to enter the public life of the community, where all were equals; if it were true that nothing is sweeter than to give commands and to rule others, the master would never have left his household.

However, there exists another tradition and another vocabulary no less old and time-honored. When the Athenian city-state called its constitution an isonomy, or the Romans spoke of the *civitas* as their form of government, they had in mind a concept of power and law whose essence did not rely on the command–obedience relationship and which did not identify power and rule or law and command. It was to these examples that the men of the eighteenth-century revolutions turned when they ransacked the archives of antiquity and constituted a form of government, a republic, where the rule of law, resting on the power of the people, would put an end to the rule of man over man, which they thought was a 'government fit for slaves.' They too, unhappily, still talked about obedience – obedience to laws instead of men; but what they actually meant was support of the laws to which the citizenry had given its consent. Such support is never unquestioning, and as far as reliability is concerned it cannot match the indeed 'unquestioning obedience' that an act of violence can exact – the obedience every criminal can count on when he snatches my pocketbook with the help of a knife or robs a bank with the help of a gun. It is the people's support that lends power to the institutions of a country, and this support is but the continuation of the consent that brought the laws into existence to begin with. Under conditions of representative government the people are supposed to rule those who govern them. All political institutions are manifestations and materializations of power; they petrify and

[6] John M. Wallace, *Destiny His Choice: The Loyalism of Andrew Marvell*, Cambridge, 1968, pp. 88–9.

decay as soon as the living power of the people ceases to uphold them. This is what Madison meant when he said 'all governments rest on opinion,' a word no less true for the various forms of monarchy than for democracies. ('To suppose that majority rule functions only in democracy is a fantastic illusion,' as Jouvenel points out: 'The king, who is but one solitary individual, stands far more in need of the general support of Society than any other form of government.'[7] Even the tyrant, the One who rules against all, needs helpers in the business of violence, though their number may be rather restricted.) However, the strength of opinion, that is, the power of the government, depends on numbers; it is 'in proportion to the number with which it is associated,'[8] and tyranny, as Montesquieu discovered, is therefore the most violent and least powerful of forms of government. Indeed one of the most obvious distinctions between power and violence is that power always stands in need of numbers, whereas violence up to a point can manage without them because it relies on implements. A legally unrestricted majority rule, that is, a democracy without a constitution, can be very formidable in the suppression of the rights of minorities and very effective in the suffocation of dissent without any use of violence. But that does not mean that violence and power are the same.

The extreme form of power is All against One, the extreme form of violence is One against All. And this latter is never possible without instruments. To claim, as is often done, that a tiny unarmed minority has successfully, by means of violence – shouting, kicking up a row, et cetera – disrupted large lecture classes whose overwhelming majority had voted for normal instruction procedures is therefore very misleading. (In a recent case at some German university there was even one lonely 'dissenter' among several hundred students who could claim such a strange victory.) What actually happens in such cases is something much more serious: the majority clearly refuses to use its power and overpower the disrupters; the academic processes break down because no one is willing to raise more than a voting finger for the *status quo*. What the universities are up against is the 'immense negative unity' of which Stephen Spender speaks in another context. All of which proves only that a minority can have

[7] *Op. cit.*, p. 98.
[8] *The Federalist*. No. 49.

a much greater potential power than one would expect by counting noses in public-opinion polls. The merely onlooking majority, amused by the spectacle of a shouting match between student and professor, is in fact already the latent ally of the minority. (One need only imagine what would have happened had one or a few unarmed Jews in pre-Hitler Germany tried to disrupt the lecture of an anti-Semitic professor in order to understand the absurdity of the talk about the small 'minorities of militants.')

It is, I think, a rather sad reflection on the present state of political science that our terminology does not distinguish among such key words as 'power,' 'strength,' 'force,' 'authority,' and, finally, 'violence' – all of which refer to distinct, different phenomena and would hardly exist unless they did. (In the words of d'Entrèves, 'might, power, authority: these are all words to whose exact implications no great weight is attached in current speech; even the greatest thinkers sometimes use them at random. Yet it is fair to presume that they refer to different properties, and their meaning should therefore be carefully assessed and examined . . . The correct use of these words is a question not only of logical grammar, but of historical perspective.')[9] To use them as synonyms not only indicates a certain deafness to linguistic meanings, which would be serious enough, but it has also resulted in a kind of blindness to the realities they correspond to. In such a situation it is always tempting to introduce new definitions, but – though I shall briefly yield to temptation – what is involved is not simply a matter of careless speech. Behind the apparent confusion is a firm conviction in whose light all distinctions would be, at best, of minor importance: the conviction that the most crucial political issue is, and always has been, the question of Who rules Whom? Power, strength, force, authority, violence – these are but words to indicate the means by which man rules over man; they are held to be synonyms because they have the same function. It is only after one ceases to reduce public affairs to the business of dominion that the original data in the realm of human affairs will appear, or, rather, reappear, in their authentic diversity.

[9] *Op. cit.*, p. 7. Cf. also p. 171, where, discussing the exact meaning of the words 'nation' and 'nationality,' he rightly insists that 'the only competent guides in the jungle of so many different meanings are the linguists and the historians. It is to them that we must turn for help.' And in distinguishing authority and power, he turns to Cicero's *potestas in populo, auctoritas in senatu*.

These data, in our context, may be enumerated as follows:

Power corresponds to the human ability not just to act but to act in concert. Power is never the property of an individual; it belongs to a group and remains in existence only so long as the group keeps together. When we say of somebody that he is 'in power' we actually refer to his being empowered by a certain number of people to act in their name. The moment the group, from which the power originated to begin with (*potestas in populo*, without a people or group there is no power), disappears, 'his power' also vanishes. In current usage, when we speak of a 'powerful man' or a 'powerful personality,' we already use the word 'power' metaphorically; what we refer to without metaphor is 'strength.'

Strength unequivocally designates something in the singular, an individual entity; it is the property inherent in an object or person and belongs to its character, which may prove itself in relation to other things or persons, but is essentially independent of them. The strength of even the strongest individual can always be overpowered by the many, who often will combine for no other purpose than to ruin strength precisely because of its peculiar independence. The almost instinctive hostility of the many toward the one has always, from Plato to Nietzsche, been ascribed to resentment, to the envy of the weak for the strong, but this psychological interpretation misses the point. It is in the nature of a group and its power to turn against independence, the property of individual strength.

Force, which we often use in daily speech as a synonym for violence, especially if violence serves as a means of coercion, should be reserved, in terminological language, for the 'forces of nature' or the 'force of circumstances' (*la force des choses*), that is, to indicate the energy released by physical or social movements.

Authority, relating to the most elusive of these phenomena and therefore, as a term, most frequently abused, can be vested in persons – there is such a thing as personal authority, as, for instance, in the relation between parent and child, between teacher and pupil – or it can be vested in offices, as, for instance, in the Roman senate (*auctoritas in senatu*) or in the hierarchical offices of the Church (a priest can grant valid absolution even though he is drunk). Its hallmark is unquestioning recognition by those who are asked to obey; neither coercion nor persuasion is needed. (A father can lose his authority either by beating his child or by starting to argue with him, that is, either by behaving to him like a tyrant or by treating him as an equal.) To remain in authority requires respect for the person or the office. The greatest enemy of authority, therefore, is contempt, and the surest way to undermine it is laughter.

Violence, finally, as I have said, is distinguished by its instrumental character. Phenomenologically, it is close to strength, since the implements of violence, like all other tools, are designed and used for the purpose of multiplying natural strength until, in the last stage of their development, they can substitute for it.

It is perhaps not superfluous to add that these distinctions, though by no means arbitrary, hardly ever correspond to water-tight compartments in the real world, from which nevertheless they are drawn. Thus institutionalized power in organized communities often appears in the guise of authority, demanding instant, unquestioning recognition; no society could function without it. (A small, and still isolated, incident in New York shows what can happen if authentic authority in social relations has broken down to the point where it cannot work any longer even in its derivative, purely functional form. A minor mishap in the subway system – the doors on a train failed to operate – turned into a serious shutdown on the line lasting four hours and involving more than fifty thousand passengers, because when the transit authorities asked the passengers to leave the defective train, they simply refused.) Moreover, nothing, as we shall see, is more common than the combination of violence and power, nothing less frequent than to find them in their pure and therefore extreme form. From this, it does not follow that authority, power, and violence are all the same.

Still it must be admitted that it is particularly tempting to think of power in terms of command and obedience, and hence to equate power with violence, in a discussion of what actually is only one of power's special cases – namely, the power of government. Since in foreign relations as well as domestic affairs violence appears as a last resort to keep the power structure intact against individual challengers – the foreign enemy, the native criminal – it looks indeed as though violence were the prerequisite of power and power nothing but a façade, the velvet glove which either conceals the iron hand or will turn out to belong to a paper tiger. On closer inspection, though, this notion loses much of its plausibility. For our purpose, the gap between theory and reality is perhaps best illustrated by the phenomenon of revolution.

Since the beginning of the century theoreticians of revolution have told us that the chances of revolution have significantly decreased in proportion to the increased destructive capacities of weapons at the unique disposition of governments.[10] The history of the last seventy years, with its extraordinary record of successful and unsuccessful revolutions, tells a different story. Were people mad who even tried against such overwhelming odds? And, leaving out instances of full success, how can even a temporary success be explained? The fact is that the gap between state-owned means of violence and what people can muster by themselves – from beer bottles to Molotov cocktails and guns – has always been so enormous that technical improvements make hardly any difference. Textbook instructions on 'how to make a revolution' in a step-by-step progression from dissent to conspiracy, from resistance to armed uprising, are all based on the mistaken notion that revolutions are 'made.' In a contest of violence against violence the superiority of the government has always been absolute; but this superiority lasts only as long as the power structure of the government is intact – that is, as long as commands are obeyed and the army or police forces are prepared to use their weapons. When this is no longer the case, the situation changes abruptly. Not only is the rebellion not put down, but the arms themselves change hands – sometimes, as in the Hungarian revolution, within a few hours . . . Only after this has happened, when the disintegration of the government in power has permitted the rebels to arm themselves, can one speak of an 'armed uprising,' which often does not take place at all or occurs when it is no longer necessary. Where commands are no longer obeyed, the means of

[10] Thus Franz Borkenau, reflecting on the defeat of the Spanish revolution, states: 'In this tremendous contrast with previous revolutions one fact is reflected. Before these latter years, counter-revolution usually depended upon the support of reactionary powers, which were technically and intellectually inferior to the forces of revolution. This has changed with the advent of fascism. Now, every revolution is likely to meet the attack of the most modern, most efficient, most ruthless machinery yet in existence. It means that the age of revolutions free to evolve according to their own laws is over.' This was written more than thirty years ago (The Spanish Cockpit, London, 1937; Ann Arbor, 1963, pp. 288–9) and is now quoted with approval by Chomsky (op cit., p. 310). He believes that American and French intervention in the civil war in Vietnam proves Borkenau's prediction accurate, 'with substitution of "liberal imperialism" for "fascism." ' I think that this example is rather apt to prove the opposite.

violence are of no use; and the question of this obedience is not decided by the command–obedience relation but by opinion, and, of course, by the number of those who share it. Everything depends on the power behind the violence. The sudden dramatic breakdown of power that ushers in revolutions reveals in a flash how civil obedience – to laws, to rulers, to institutions – is but the outward manifestation of support and consent.

Where power has disintegrated, revolutions are possible but not necessary. We know of many instances when utterly impotent regimes were permitted to continue in existence for long periods of time – either because there was no one to test their strength and reveal their weakness or because they were lucky enough not to be engaged in war and suffer defeat. Disintegration often becomes manifest only in direct confrontation; and even then, when power is already in the street, some group of men prepared for such an eventuality is needed to pick it up and assume responsibility. We have recently witnessed how it did not take more than the relatively harmless, essentially nonviolent French students' rebellion to reveal the vulnerability of the whole political system, which rapidly disintegrated before the astonished eyes of the young rebels. Unknowingly they had tested it; they intended only to challenge the ossified university system, and down came the system of governmental power, together with that of the huge party bureaucracies – *'une sorte de désintégration de toutes les hiérarchies.'*[11] It was a textbook case of a revolutionary situation that did not develop into a revolution because there was nobody, least of all the students, prepared to seize power and the responsibility that goes with it. Nobody except, of course, de Gaulle. Nothing was more characteristic of the seriousness of the situation than his appeal to the army, his journey to see Massu and the generals in Germany, a walk to Canossa, if there ever was one, in view of what had happened only a few years before. But what he sought and received was support, not obedience, and the means were not commands but concessions. If commands had been enough, he would never have had to leave Paris.

No government exclusively based on the means of violence has ever existed. Even the totalitarian ruler, whose chief instrument of rule is torture, needs a power basis – the secret police and its net of informers. Only the development of robot soldiers, which, as

[11] Raymond Aron, *La Révolution Introuvable*, 1968, p. 41.

previously mentioned, would eliminate the human factor completely and, conceivably, permit one man with a push button to destroy whomever he pleased, could change this fundamental ascendancy of power over violence. Even the most despotic domination we know of, the rule of master over slaves, who always outnumbered him, did not rest on superior means of coercion as such, but on a superior organization of power – that is, on the organized solidarity of the masters.[12] Single men without others to support them never have enough power to use violence successfully. Hence, in domestic affairs, violence functions as the last resort of power against criminals or rebels – that is, against single individuals who, as it were, refuse to be overpowered by the consensus of the majority. And as for actual warfare, we have seen in Vietnam how an enormous superiority in the means of violence can become helpless if confronted with an ill-equipped but well-organized opponent who is much more powerful. This lesson, to be sure, was there to be learned from the history of guerrilla warfare, which is at least as old as the defeat in Spain of Napoleon's still-unvanquished army.

To switch for a moment to conceptual language: Power is indeed of the essence of all government, but violence is not. Violence is by nature instrumental; like all means, it always stands in need of guidance and justification through the end it pursues. And what needs justification by something else cannot be the essence of anything. The end of war – end taken in its twofold meaning – is peace or victory; but to the question And what is the end of peace? there is no answer. Peace is an absolute, even though in recorded history periods of warfare have nearly always outlasted periods of peace. Power is in the same category; it is, as they say, 'an end in itself.' (This, of course, is not to deny that governments pursue policies and employ their power to achieve prescribed goals. But the power structure itself precedes and outlasts all aims, so that power, far from being the means to an end, is actually the very condition enabling a group of people to think and act in terms of the means–end category.) And since government is essentially organized and institutionalized power,

[12] In ancient Greece, such an organization of power was the polis, whose chief merit, according to Xenophon, was that it permitted the 'citizens to act as bodyguards to one another against slaves and criminals so that none of the citizens may die a violent death.' (*Hiero*, IV, 3.)

the current question What is the end of government? does not make much sense either. The answer will be either question-begging – to enable men to live together – or dangerously utopian – to promote happiness or to realize a classless society or some other nonpolitical ideal, which if tried out in earnest cannot but end in some kind of tyranny.

Power needs no justification, being inherent in the very existence of political communities; what it does need is legitimacy. The common treatment of these two words as synonyms is no less misleading and confusing than the current equation of obedience and support. Power springs up whenever people get together and act in concert, but it derives its legitimacy from the initial getting together rather than from any action that then may follow. Legitimacy, when challenged, bases itself on an appeal to the past, while justification relates to an end that lies in the future. Violence can be justifiable, but it never will be legitimate. Its justification loses in plausibility the farther its intended end recedes into the future. No one questions the use of violence in self-defense, because the danger is not only clear but also present, and the end justifying the means is immediate.

Power and violence, though they are distinct phenomena, usually appear together. Wherever they are combined, power, we have found, is the primary and predominant factor. The situation, however, is entirely different when we deal with them in their pure states – as, for instance, with foreign invasion and occupation. We saw that the current equation of violence with power rests on government's being understood as domination of man over man by means of violence. If a foreign conqueror is confronted by an impotent government and by a nation unused to the exercise of political power, it is easy for him to achieve such domination. In all other cases the difficulties are great indeed, and the occupying invader will try immediately to establish Quisling governments, that is, to find a native power base to support his dominion. The head-on clash between Russian tanks and the entirely nonviolent resistance of the Czechoslovak people is a textbook case of a confrontation between violence and power in their pure states. But while domination in such an instance is difficult to achieve, it is not impossible. Violence, we must remember, does not depend on numbers or opinions, but on implements, and the implements of violence, as I mentioned before, like all other tools, increase and multiply human strength. Those who oppose violence with mere power will soon find that they are confronted not by men but by men's artifacts, whose inhumanity and destructive effectiveness increase in proportion to the distance separating the opponents. Violence can always destroy power; out of the barrel of a gun grows the most effective command, resulting in the most instant and perfect obedience. What never can grow out of it is power.

In a head-on clash between violence and power, the outcome is hardly in doubt. If Gandhi's enormously powerful and successful strategy of nonviolent resistance had met with a different enemy – Stalin's Russia, Hitler's Germany, even prewar Japan, instead of England – the outcome would not have been decolonization, but massacre and submission. However, England in India and France in Algeria had good reasons for their restraint. Rule by sheer violence comes into play where power is being lost; it is precisely the shrinking power of the Russian government, internally and externally, that became manifest in its 'solution' of the Czechoslovak problem – just as it was the shrinking power of European imperialism that became manifest in the alternative between decolonization and massacre. To substitute violence for power can bring victory, but the price is very high; for it is not only paid by the vanquished, it is also paid by the victor in terms of his own power. This is especially true when the victor happens to enjoy domestically the blessings of constitutional government. Henry Steele Commager is entirely right: 'If we subvert world order and destroy world peace we must inevitably subvert and destroy our own political institutions first.'[13] The much-feared boomerang effect of the 'government of subject races' (Lord Cromer) on the home government during the imperialist era meant that rule by violence in faraway lands would end by affecting the government of England, that the last 'subject race' would be the English themselves. The recent gas attack on the campus at Berkeley, where not just tear gas but also another gas, 'outlawed by the Geneva Convention and used by the Army to flush out guerrillas in Vietnam,' was laid down while gas-masked Guardsmen stopped anybody and everybody 'from fleeing the gassed area,' is an excellent example of this 'backlash' phenomenon. It has often been said that impotence breeds violence, and psychologically this is quite true, at least of persons possessing natural strength, moral or physical. Politically speaking, the point is that loss of power

[13] 'Can We Limit Presidential Power?' in *The New Republic*, April 6, 1968.

becomes a temptation to substitute violence for power – in 1968 during the Democratic convention in Chicago we could watch this process on television – and that violence itself results in impotence. Where violence is no longer backed and restrained by power, the well-known reversal in reckoning with means and ends has taken place. The means, the means of destruction, now determine the end – with the consequence that the end will be the destruction of all power.

Nowhere is the self-defeating factor in the victory of violence over power more evident than in the use of terror to maintain domination, about whose weird successes and eventual failures we know perhaps more than any generation before us. Terror is not the same as violence; it is, rather, the form of government that comes into being when violence, having destroyed all power, does not abdicate but, on the contrary, remains in full control. It has often been noticed that the effectiveness of terror depends almost entirely on the degree of social atomization. Every kind of organized opposition must disappear before the full force of terror can be let loose. This atomization – an outrageously pale, academic word for the horror it implies – is maintained and intensified through the ubiquity of the informer, who can be literally omnipresent because he no longer is merely a professional agent in the pay of the police but potentially every person one comes into contact with. How such a fully developed police state is established and how it works – or, rather, how nothing works where it holds sway – can now be learned in Aleksandr I. Solzhenitsyn's *The First Circle*, which will probably remain one of the masterpieces of twentieth-century literature and certainly contains the best documentation on Stalin's regime in existence. The decisive difference between totalitarian domination, based on terror, and tyrannies and dictatorships, established by violence, is that the former turns not only against its enemies but against its friends and supporters as well, being afraid of all power, even the power of its friends. The climax of terror is reached when the police state begins to devour its own children, when yesterday's executioner becomes today's victim. And this is also the moment when power disappears entirely. There exist now a great many plausible explanations for the de-Stalinization of Russia – none, I believe, so compelling as the realization by the Stalinist function-aries themselves that a continuation of the regime would lead, not to an insurrection, against which terror is indeed the best safeguard, but to paralysis of the whole country.

To sum up: politically speaking, it is insufficient to say that power and violence are not the same. Power and violence are opposites; where the one rules absolutely, the other is absent. Violence appears where power is in jeopardy, but left to its own course it ends in power's disappearance. This implies that it is not correct to think of the opposite of violence as nonviolence; to speak of nonviolent power is actually redundant. Violence can destroy power; it is utterly incapable of creating it. Hegel's and Marx's great trust in the dialectical 'power of negation,' by virtue of which opposites do not destroy but smoothly develop into each other because contradictions promote and do not paralyze development, rests on a much older philosophical prejudice: that evil is no more than a privative *modus* of the good, that good can come out of evil; that, in short, evil is but a temporary manifestation of a still-hidden good. Such time honored opinions have become dangerous. They are shared by many who have never heard of Hegel or Marx, for the simple reason that they inspire hope and dispel fear – a treacherous hope used to dispel legitimate fear. By this, I do not mean to equate violence with evil; I only want to stress that violence cannot be derived from its opposite, which is power, and that in order to understand it for what it is, we shall have to examine its roots and nature.

SIMONE DE BEAUVOIR (1908–86)

Simone de Beauvoir was one of the best-known women of the twentieth century, a novelist, essayist and feminist. Her book *The Second Sex* was published in 1949 and caused scandal and acclaim in equal degree. It was genuinely original, though enormously long and rambling in construction. Her life itself was a part of the history of philosophy; she was Jean-Paul Sartre's constant intellectual companion and supporter, with whom he shared all his philosophical ideas; and when he became more and more involved in politics she remained at his side, though never herself particularly political. She wrote only two philosophical works: an essay on freedom entitled *Pyrrhus et Cineas* (1944), and *Pour une morale de l'ambiguité* (1947). Even these short works were more comments on aspects of Sartre's work than arguments in their own right. Yet in another sense all her written works were philosophical, even her memoirs and her novels. The book on old age from which the extract below is taken is, in form, comparable with *The Second Sex*: general conclusions about the experience of being a woman, or, in this case, of being old, are loosely based on literary descriptions and on interviews. *Old Age*, though obviously not as dramatic or appealing as *The Second Sex* (and lacking the catchy title, thought up by Sartre and Simone de Beauvoir together), is nevertheless a serious and original study, with a strong commitment to social change.

Further Reading

Deirdre Bair, *Simone de Beauvoir: A Biography* (London: Jonathan Cape, 1990). (This, besides being an excellent analytic biography, contains a full bibliography.)

From Simone de Beauvoir, Old Age, *trans. Patrick O'Brian (Harmondsworth: Penguin, 1977), chapter 6*

For human reality, existing means existing in time: in the present we look towards the future by means of plans that go beyond our past, in which our activities fall lifeless ... Age changes our relationship with time: as the years go by our future shortens, while our past grows heavier ... The consequences of these changes influence one another and bring into being a situation that varies according to the individual's earlier history but whose constant factors may be isolated.

And in the first place, what does *having* one's life behind one mean? Sartre has explained this in *L'Etre et le Néant*: one does not possess one's past as one possesses a thing that one can hold and turn in one's hand, inspecting every side of it. My past is the in-itself that I am insofar as I have been outstripped; in order to possess it I must bind it to existence by a project; if this project consists of knowing it then I must make it present to myself by means of bringing it back to my memory. There is a kind of magic in recollection, a magic that one feels at every age. The past was experienced in the *for-itself* mode and yet it has become *in-itself*; in remembering we seem to attain that impossible synthesis of the in-itself and the for-itself that life yearns for but always in vain. (This is why memory shows us the person we were with a fullness of being that endues it with a kind of poetry. Frozen in the past, a pain that we may have had does not cease to have the meaning of a for-itself, and yet it exists in itself with the silent fixity of pain experienced by another, a statue's pain.)

'It is the future that decides whether the past is living or not' says Sartre. A man whose project is to get on, to advance, takes off from his past; he defines his former I as the I that he is no longer and he dissociates himself from it. For some for-itselfs, on the contrary, their project implies the refusal of time and an intimate solidarity with the past. This applies to most old people: they refuse time because they do not wish to decline; they define their former I as that which they still are – they assert their solidarity with their youth. Even if they have overcome the identification-crisis and have accepted a new image of themselves – the dear old grandmother, or the retired person, or the elderly writer – each in his heart preserves the conviction of having remained unalterable:

when they summon their memories they justify this assertion. They set up a fixed, unchanging essence against the deteriorations of age, and tirelessly they tell stories of this being that they were, this being that lives on inside them . . . Once they have recovered the being they were, once they have merged with him, it does not matter whether they are thirty or fifty or even eighty: they have escaped from age.

But what in fact can they recover? How far does memory allow us to retrieve our lives? . . . The images that we can call upon are far from possessing the richness of their original object. An image is the seeing of an absent object by means of an organic and affective analogue. As Sartre says, 'there is a kind of essential poverty' in it . . . An image does not necessarily obey the principle of identity, it produces the object in its general, not its specific aspect; and it appears in an unreal time and space. Our images therefore cannot resuscitate the real world from which they emanate, and that is why we so often find images that we cannot place rising up in our minds. When I was writing my *Mémoires* I would sometimes have brilliant visions of scenes that I could not integrate with the rest of my account because I had no fixes, no coordinates, and so I abandoned them . . . Even when I evoked some particular scene, it was built up from general patterns: in the classroom of our school, the twelve-year-old Zaza thanks me for a bag I have given her – she has the shape and the features of Zaza in her twenties.

These stereotypes persist in the midst of a changing world with the result that in spite of their unalterability they take on a curiously exotic aspect. This would not occur in a repetitive society. If I wore the same traditional clothes as my mother did, a picture of her youth would show me a young woman of today: but fashions have changed, and in her fine jet-black dress she belongs to a past age. A return to my twenties makes me feel as lost as if I were at the other end of the world. I look at a photograph of the old Trocadero, a building whose ugliness I used to love: can I really have seen it with my own eyes? . . . As the years go by, it is always the present moment that appears natural to us; and since the past seems natural too, we have the vague impression that it was the same. But in fact the images that we recover are dated. In this way too our life escapes us – it was freshness, novelty and bloom. And now that freshness is out of date . . .

A friend said to me 'I find old people touching because of the long past they have behind them.' Unfortunately, that is just what they do not have. The past is not a peaceful landscape lying there behind me, a country in which I can stroll wherever I please, and which will gradually show me all its secret hills and dales. As I was moving forward, so it was crumbling. Most of the wreckage that can still be seen is colourless, distorted, frozen: its meaning escapes me . . . The past moves us for the very reason that it is past; but this too is why it so often disappoints us – we lived it in the present, a present rich in the future towards which it was hurrying: and all that is left is a skeleton. That is what makes pilgrimages so pointless. Space takes over time's betrayal: places change. But even those that seem to have remained unaltered are not the same for me. There are streets in Uzerche, Marseilles and Rouen where I can walk about recognizing the houses, the stones. But I shall never find my plans again, my hopes and fears – I shall not find myself . . .

Not only has this past's future ceased to be a future, but in becoming the present, it has often disappointed our hopes. More than once I have known the beginning of what was meant to be an unending friendship; some have fulfilled their promise, others have turned into indifference or even hostility. How are we to interpret an alliance that has been severed by a quarrel? Was it valid at the time but fated to survive no longer than the situation that gave it birth? Was it based upon an illusion? Might it have lasted for ever, instead of being broken by some misunderstanding? No verdict can possibly be final: the meaning of a past event can always be reversed. Not only does the material aspect of the facts escape us, but we cannot decide upon the weight we are to give them; and we are in a continual state of suspended judgment . . .

It is his childhood above all that returns to haunt the aged man . . . The reason why [old men] turn back so readily to their childhood is clear – they are possessed by it. Since it has never ceased to dwell in them they recognize themselves in their childhood, even though for a while they may have chosen to ignore it. And there is another reason: life bases itself upon self-transcendence. But this transcendence comes up against death, particularly when a very great age has been reached. The old person attempts to give his existence a foundation by taking over his birth, or at least his earliest years. The old person, as he is about to step out of this world, recognizes himself in the baby that stepped out of that other unborn world . . .

We also see why old people are not discouraged by the poverty of the images they are capable of summoning up. They are not trying to make a detailed coherent account of their earliest years, but rather to plunge back into them. Again and again they turn over a few themes of great emotional value to them: and far from growing tired of this perpetual repetition, they return to it with an even greater pleasure. They escape from the present; they dream of former happiness; they exorcise past misfortune . . .

The aged man's inward experience of his past takes the form of images, fantasies and emotional attitudes. He is dependent on it in another way; it is the past that defines my present situation and its outlet into the future; it is the admitted fact, the base from which I project myself and which I must go beyond if I am to exist. This is true at all ages. From the past I derive all the mechanisms of my body, the cultural tools I use, my knowledge and my ignorance, my relationship with the outside world, my activities and my duties. Everything I have ever done has been taken back by the past and there, in the past, it has become reified under the form of what Sartre calls the practico-inert. He defines this as the whole formed by those things that are marked by the seal of human activity together with men defined by their relationship with those things: as far as I personally am concerned, the practico-inert is the whole formed by the books I have written, which now outside me constitute my works and define me as their author. 'I am that which I have done and which escapes from me by at once setting me up as Another' (Sartre, *Critique de la raison dialectique*) . . . The older we grow, the more heavily the burden of the practico-inert weighs upon us . . .

Once a certain threshold has been passed – a threshold that varies according to the individual – the elderly man becomes aware of his biological fate: the number of years of life that remain to him is limited. If a year were to seem to a sixty-five-year-old man as long as it was in his childhood, then the lapse of time he could reasonably count upon would still outrun his imagination; but this is not the case. The period seems tragically short to him because time does not flow at the same speed at the different stages of our life: the older one grows the faster it runs.

An hour seems long to a child. The time in which he has his being is a time imposed upon him from without – it is the grownups' time. He can neither measure nor foresee it; he is lost in a continuous happening without beginning or end. I took control of time when I began to give life to my projects, parcelled out according to my curriculum; my weeks took shape round the afternoons when I went to school. Now each day had a past and a future. My coherent, dated memories go back to that time. Then again, minutes drag when we are tense or weary. But because of his weakness, his excitability and the delicacy of his nervous system, a child tires easily. Sixty minutes of reading calls for more sustained effort at five than at ten, and at ten than at twenty. Distances are long, concentration difficult: a child cannot get through his day without fatigue. And above all, the world is then so new, and the impressions it makes upon us so fresh and lively, that, since we gauge its extent by the wealth of contents, we think it far greater than it comes to appear when familiarity has impoverished us . . .

As we leave childhood space draws in, objects grow smaller, the body grows stronger, concentration increases, we get used to clocks and calendars, and memory takes on breadth and precision. But for all that, the seasons go on revolving with a wonderful or a terrible slowness. When I was fifteen and I leafed through my new school-books the journey through the school year seemed to me an immense and passionately interesting voyage. Later, the going back to school plunged me into depression: I felt that I would never get through the ten months that would have to be spent in our dreary flat. But as soon as I recovered from my lowness of spirits the vastness of the future spread out at my feet filled me with enthusiasm. Forty years to live, perhaps even sixty! Since a single one seemed so enormous, this was eternity.

There is more than one reason for the change in the evaluation of time that occurs between youth and age. In the first place it must be pointed out that we always have the whole of our life behind us, reduced to the same form and size at all ages: in perspective, twenty years are equal to sixty, and this gives the units a variable dimension. If a single year amounts to a fifth of our total age, then it seems ten times longer to us than if it represents only the fiftieth part. Clearly, I am not speaking here of precise calculation, but of a spontaneous impression. And then young people's memories give them back the past year with a wealth of detail that spreads over an enormous extent: they therefore suppose that the year to come will have the same dimensions. When we are old, on the other hand, few things make much impression on us; the passing moment brings little new, and upon that little we do not dwell for long. As far as I am concerned, 1968 may be summed up in a few dates, a few patterns, a few facts. And, for me, 1969 has the same label of poverty. I have scarcely returned to Paris in October before it is already July.

There is still another factor that comes into play: I know that in twelve months I shall, at the best, be the same as I am today; whereas when I was twenty, 'being oneself means coming to oneself' as Sartre puts it. One is in a state of waiting for the world and for oneself. Each year brings us a maelstrom of new things and experiences, intoxicatingly delightful, or hideous, and one emerges transformed, with the feeling that the near future will bring about a similar upheaval. It is a period at which one cannot seize and embrace time either by projects or by memory since time tears one from oneself. No person is capable of making its unity real if to begin with the *I* is other than that which it is going to become. An incalculable distance separates the two strangers: or at least that is what they suppose.

The reason why the emotional memories that restore childhood are so treasured is that for a fleeting instant they give us back an endless future. A cock crows in a village whose slate roofs I see in the distance; I am walking in a meadow covered with hoar frost; all at once it is Meyrignac and there is a catch at my heart – this day now just beginning stretches out, a vast expanse, as far as the distant twilight; tomorrow is no more than an empty word; eternity is my portion. And then suddenly it is not; here I am, back in the days when the years go by so fast . . .

The essential difference between the point of view of the old person and that of the child or adolescent is that the first has discovered his finite nature whereas at the beginning of his life he was unaware of it. In those days he saw such manifold and such undefined possibilities lying before him that they seemed limitless; in order to receive them the future in which they had their being had to be broadened to infinity . . . the old person, for his part, knows that his life is accomplished and that he will never refashion it. The future is no longer big with promise: both this future and the being who must live it contract together. Human reality, indeed, possesses a twofold finitude: the one is contingent and it results from facticty [the for-itself as necessarily connection with the in-itself, hence with the world and its own past], the existence of a term imposed from without. The other is an ontological structure of the in-itself. In a man's last years both the one and the other become apparent at the same time; and the one by means of the other . . . Thus the very quality of the future changes between middle-age and the end of one's life. At sixty-five one is not merely twenty years older than one was at forty-five. One has exchanged an indefinite future – and one had a tendency to look on it as infinite – for a finite future. In early days we could see no boundary-mark on the horizon: now we do see one. 'When I used to dream in former times', says Chateaubriand, harking back to his remote past, 'my youth lay before me; I could advance towards the unknown that I was looking for. Now I can no longer take a single step without coming up against the boundary-stone.'

A limited future and a frozen past: such is the situation that the elderly have to face up to. All their plans have been either carried out or abandoned, and their life has closed in about itself. Nothing requires their presence; they no longer have anything whatsoever to do . . .

Modern society, far from providing the aged man with an appeal against his biological fate, tosses him into an outdated past, and it does so while he is still living. The acceleration of history has caused an immense upheaval in the relationship between the aged man and his activities. Formerly it was supposed that with the progress of the years a treasure piled up within him – experience. A certain knowledge of life that was not to be learned from books gradually accumulated in his mind and body, much as crystals are deposited on twigs plunged into petrifying streams. Hegelian philosophy puts forward a . . . justification of this idea according to which every past instant is enfolded in the present instant, which necessarily prepares a still more perfected future, even failures being put right in the end: old age, the final stage of a continual advance, is life's highest pitch of perfection. But in fact this is not how life progresses at all. Its line of advance is perpetually broken by the falling back of our projects into practico-inert reality. At every given moment it provides its own sum, but this summation is never completed . . . That is why our motion is not a firm advance. Old age is not the *summa* of our life. As time gives us the world, so with the same motion it takes it from us. We learn and we forget; we enrich ourselves and we lose our wealth . . .

For the aged person death is no longer a general abstract fate: it is a personal event, an event that is near at hand . . . Every old man knows that he will die soon. But what does knowing mean in this case? . . . The truth of the matter is that the idea of death's coming closer is mistaken. Death is neither near nor far; it is not. Over all living beings, whatever their age, there hangs an inescapable exterior fate: in no case is there a set moment at which this fate will strike. The old man knows that he will die 'soon': the fatality is as present at seventy as it is at eighty, and the word 'soon' remains as vague at eighty as it was at seventy. It is not correct to speak of a relationship with death: the fact is that the old man, like all other men, has a relationship with life and with nothing else. What is in question is his will to survive. The phrase 'putting an end to it all' or 'finishing with life' expresses its meaning very well. The positive significance of accepting or wishing for death is accepting or wishing for 'an end to it all', a 'finishing with life'. It is natural that as the decline of old age grows worse and worse, so life should seem less and less bearable . . .

When the world alters entirely or displays itself in such a way that remaining in it becomes unbearable, a young man can hope for a change: an old man cannot, and all that is left for him is to wish for death, as did Anatole France, Wells and Gandhi . . . Even if the old person is struck by no particular misfortune, he has usually either lost his reasons for living or he has discovered their absence. The reason why death fills us with anxiety is that it is the inescapable reversal of our projects: when a man is no longer active in any way, when he has ceased all undertakings, all plans, then there remains nothing that death can destroy. It is usual to put forward wearing-out and fatigue as an explanation for the way some old people resign themselves to death; but if all a man needed was to vegetate he could put up with his life in slow motion. But for a man, living means self-transcendence. A consequence of biological decay is the impossibility of surpassing oneself and of becoming passionately concerned with anything: it kills all projects, and it is by this expedient that it renders death acceptable . . .

If the moment [of death] were fixed and near at hand, instead of being lost in a misty future, there is no doubt that the old person's attitude would be different. In the *Alcestes*, Euripides observes that old men complain of their state and say that they long for death: when they are brought to the point they change their minds. Admetes' father stubbornly refuses to take his son's place and go down to Hades. The aged Tolstoy said that he did not care one way or the other about dying, but he irritated Sonia by the care he took of his health. This refusal of death is not invariable. But it is quite true that a fair number of old people do hold onto life even when they have lost all reasons for living: in *Une Mort très douce* I described the way my mother, at seventy-eight, clung to it till the very end. So it is the subject's biological state or what is vaguely termed his vitality that determines his refusal or his acceptance. My mother was as religious as my grandmother, for whom leaving the world was restful; yet she had an animal fear of death. Many old people are afraid, and being afraid is the realization in one's own body of the refusal to die. What often makes death easier for old people is the fact that illness wears them out in the end, and that they do not fully understand what is happening to them.

Yet there are clear-minded and peaceful deaths: when all desire to live is physically and spiritually gone, the old person prefers an everlasting sleep to the daily struggle or boredom. The proof that in old age death does not appear as the greatest of evils is the number of old people who decide 'to put an end to it all'. In the conditions that society provides for them today, living on is a pointless trial, and it is understandable that many should choose to shorten it.

IRIS MURDOCH DBE (1919–   )

Iris Murdoch was educated at Somerville College, Oxford of which she has been an Honorary Fellow since 1977. In 1987 she became one of the very few Oxford graduates to receive an honorary degree from her own university. In the same year she became a Dame of the British Empire. After an adventurous war career, she spent two years in Cambridge and then returned to Oxford to teach philosophy at St Anne's College until 1963. Since then she has devoted herself to writing. Besides works on philosophy, she has published poems, plays and a large number of novels, and it is doubtless as a novelist that she is best known. Her novels are full of philosophy, especially of philosophical conversation, and many of them contain a central philosophical figure, sometimes loosely based, it seems, on Wittgenstein, of whose work Iris Murdoch has a great understanding. Her first book, *Sartre* (1953), remains one of the most penetrating studies of the early Sartre; her own philosophical style developed to some extent under his influence. More important, perhaps, has been her deep attraction to, and understanding of, the philosophy of Plato. The project of founding morality not on changing human needs or wishes but on an immutable and absolute idea of goodness has been central to her thought. Both *The Sovereignty of Good* (1970), from which the following extract is taken, and *The Fire and the Sun* (1977) explore this central theme. Her ambitious book *Metaphysics as a Guide to Morals* (1992) showed how this Platonic thought developed through her reading, largely of existentialist, or at any rate European post-Kantian, philosophers. She aimed to found morality on a metaphysical notion of goodness, to replace what she holds to be the unbelievable personal God of Christian theology and religion.

Further Reading

Iris Murdoch, *Under the Net* (London: Chatto & Windus, 1954)
——*The Flight from the Enchanter* (London: Chatto & Windus, 1955)

——*A Word Child* (London: Chatto & Windus, 1975)
——*The Fire and the Sun: Why Plato Banished the Artists* (Oxford: Clarendon Press, 1977)

From Iris Murdoch, The Sovereignty of Good (London: Routledge & Kegan Paul, 1970), chapter 2: 'On "God" and "good" '

To do philosophy is to explore one's own temperament, and yet at the same time to attempt to discover the truth. It seems to me that there is a void in present-day moral philosophy. Areas peripheral to philosophy expand (psychology, political and social theory) or collapse (religion) without philosophy being able in the one case to encounter, and in the other case to rescue, the values involved. A working philosophical psychology is needed which can at least attempt to connect modern psychological terminology with a terminology concerned with virtue. We need a moral philosophy which can speak significantly of Freud and Marx, and out of which aesthetic and political views can be generated. We need a moral philosophy in which the concept of love, so rarely mentioned now by philosophers, can once again be made central.

It will be said, we have got a working philosophy, and one which is the proper heir to the past of European philosophy: existentialism. This philosophy does so far pervade the scene that philosophers, many linguistic analysts for instance, who would not claim the name, do in fact work with existentialist concepts. I shall argue that existentialism is not, and cannot by tinkering be made, the philosophy we need. Although it is indeed the heir of the past, it is (it seems to me) an unrealistic and over-optimistic doctrine and the purveyor of certain false values. This is more obviously true of flimsier creeds, such as 'humanism', with which people might now attempt to fill the philosophical void.

The great merit of existentialism is that it at least professes and tries to be a philosophy one could live by. Kierkegaard described the Hegelian system as a grand palace set up by someone who then lived in a hovel or at best in the porter's ledge. A moral philosophy should be inhabited. Existentialism has shown itself capable of becoming a popular philosophy and of getting into the minds of those (e.g. Oxford philosophers) who have not sought it and may even be unconscious of its presence. However, although it can certainly inspire action, it seems to me to do so by a sort of romantic provocation rather than by its truth; and its pointers are often pointing in the wrong direction. Wittgenstein claimed that he brought the Cartesian era in philosophy to an end. Moral philosophy of an existentialist type is still Cartesian and egocentric. Briefly put, our picture of ourselves has become too grand, we have isolated, and identified ourselves with, an unrealistic conception of will, we have lost the vision of a reality separate from ourselves, and we have no adequate conception of original sin . . .

Kant believed in Reason and Hegel believed in History, and for both this was a form of a belief in an external reality. Modern thinkers who believe in neither, but who remain within the tradition, are left with a denuded self whose only virtues are freedom, or at best sincerity, or, in the case of the British philosophers, an everyday reasonableness. Philosophy, on its other fronts, has been busy dismantling the old substantial picture of the 'self', and ethics has not proved able to rethink this concept for moral purposes. The moral agent then is pictured as an isolated principle of will, or burrowing pinpoint of consciousness, inside, or beside, a lump of being which has been handed over to other disciplines, such as psychology or sociology. On the one hand a Luciferian philosophy of adventures of the will, and on the other natural science. Moral philosophy, and indeed morals, are thus undefended against an irresponsible and undirected self-assertion which goes easily hand in hand with some brand of pseudo-scientific determinism. An unexamined sense of the strength of the machine is combined with an illusion of leaping out of it . . .

The history of British philosophy since Moore represents intensively in miniature the special dilemmas of modern ethics. Empiricism, especially in the form given to it by Russell, and later by Wittgenstein, thrust ethics almost out of philosophy. Moral judgments were not factual, or truthful, and had no place in the world of the *Tractatus*. Moore, although he himself held a curious metaphysic of 'moral facts', set the tone when he told us that we must carefully distinguish the question 'What things are good?' from the question 'What does "good" mean?' The answer to the latter question concerned the will. Good was indefinable (naturalism was a fallacy) because any offered good could be scrutinized by any individual by a 'stepping back' movement. This form of

Kantianism still retains its appeal. Wittgenstein had attacked the idea of the Cartesian ego or substantial self and Ryle and others had developed the attack. A study of 'ordinary language' claimed (often rightly) to solve piecemeal problems in epistemology which had formerly been discussed in terms of the activities or faculties of a 'self'. (See John Austin's book on certain problems of perception, *Sense and Sensibilia*.)

Ethics took its place in this scene. After puerile attempts to classify moral statements as exclamations or expressions of emotion, a more sophisticated neo-Kantianism with a utilitarian atmosphere has been developed. The idea of the agent as a privileged centre of will (for ever capable of 'stepping back') is retained, but, since the old-fashioned 'self' no longer clothes him he appears as an isolated will operating with the concepts of 'ordinary language', so far as the field of morals is concerned. (It is interesting that although Wittgenstein's work has suggested this picture to others, he himself never used it.) Thus the will, and the psyche as an object of science, are isolated from each other and from the rest of philosophy. The cult of ordinary language goes with the claim to be neutral. Previous moral philosophers told us what we ought to do, that is they tried to answer both of Moore's questions. Linguistic analysis claims simply to give a philosophical description of the human phenomenon of morality, without making any moral judgments. In fact the resulting picture of human conduct has a clear moral bias. The merits of linguistic analytical man are freedom (in the sense of detachment, rationality), responsibility, self-awareness, sincerity, and a lot of utilitarian common sense. There is of course no mention of sin, and no mention of love . . .

Linguistic analysis of course poses for ethics the question of its relation with metaphysics. Can ethics be a form of empiricism? Many philosophers in the Oxford and Cambridge tradition would say yes. It is certainly a great merit of this tradition, and one which I would not wish to lose sight of, that it attacks every form of spurious unity. It is the traditional inspiration of the philosopher, but also his traditional vice, to believe that all is one. Wittgenstein says 'Let's see.' Sometimes problems turn out to be quite unconnected with each other, and demand types of solution which are not themselves closely related in any system. Perhaps it is a matter of temperament whether or not one is convinced that all is one. (My own temperament inclines to monism.) But let us postpone the question of whether, if we reject the relaxed empirical ethics of the British tradition (a cheerful amalgam of Hume, Kant and Mill), and if we reject, too, the more formal existentialist systems, we wish to replace these with something which would have to be called a metaphysical theory. Let me now simply suggest ways in which I take the prevalent and popular picture to be unrealistic . . .

Much of contemporary moral philosophy appears both unambitious and optimistic. Unambitious optimism is of course part of the Anglo-Saxon tradition; and it is also not surprising that a philosophy which analyses moral concepts on the basis of ordinary language should present a relaxed picture of a mediocre achievement. I think the charge is also true, though contrary to some appearances, of existentialism. An authentic mode of existence is presented as attainable by intelligence and force of will. The atmosphere is invigorating and tends to produce self-satisfaction in the reader, who feels himself to be a member of the élite, addressed by another one. Contempt for the ordinary human condition, together with a conviction of personal salvation, saves the writer from real pessimism. His gloom is superficial and conceals elation . . . Such attitudes contrast with the vanishing images of Christian theology which represented goodness as almost impossibly difficult, and sin as almost insuperable and certainly as a universal condition.

Yet modern psychology has provided us with what might be called a doctrine of original sin . . . Freud takes a thoroughly pessimistic view of human nature. He sees the psyche as an egocentric system of quasi-mechanical energy, largely determined by its own individual history, whose natural attachments are sexual, ambiguous, and hard for the subject to understand or control. Introspection reveals only the deep tissue of ambivalent motive, and fantasy is a stronger force than reason. Objectivity and unselfishness are not natural to human beings.

Of course Freud is saying these things in the context of a scientific therapy which aims not at making people good but at making them workable. If a moral philosopher says such things he must justify them not with scientific arguments but with arguments appropriate to philosophy; and in fact if he does say such things he will not be saying anything very new, since partially similar views have been expressed before in philosophy, as far back as Plato. It is important to look at Freud and his successors because they can give us more information about a mechanism the general nature of which we may discern without the help of science; and also because the ignoring of psychology may be a source of confusion. Some philosophers (e.g. Sartre) regard traditional psychoanalytical theory as a form of determinism and are prepared to deny it at all levels, and philosophers who ignore it often do so as part of an easy surrender to science of aspects of the mind which ought to interest them. But determinism as a total philosophical theory is not the enemy. Determinism as a philosophical theory is quite unproven, and it can be argued that it is not possible in principle to translate propositions about men making decisions and formulating viewpoints into the neutral languages of natural science ... The problem is to accommodate inside moral philosophy, and suggest methods of dealing with the fact that so much of human conduct is moved by mechanical energy of an egocentric kind. In the moral life the enemy is the fat relentless ego. Moral philosophy is properly, and in the past has sometimes been, the discussion of this ego and of the techniques (if any) for its defeat. In this respect moral philosophy has shared some aims with religion. To say this is of course also to deny that moral philosophy should aim at being neutral.

What is a good man like? How can we make ourselves morally better? *Can* we make ourselves morally better? These are questions the philosopher should try to answer. We realize on reflection that we know little about good men. There are men in history who are traditionally thought of as having been good (Christ, Socrates, certain saints), but if we try to contemplate these men we find that the information about them is scanty and vague, and that, their great moments apart, it is the simplicity and directness of their diction which chiefly colours our conception of them as good. And if we consider contemporary candidates for goodness, if we know of any, we are likely to find them obscure, or else on closer inspection full of frailty. Goodness appears to be both rare and hard to picture. It is perhaps most convincingly met with in simple people – inarticulate, unselfish mothers of large families – but these cases are also the least illuminating.

It is significant that the idea of goodness (and of virtue) has been largely superseded in Western moral philosophy by the idea of rightness, supported perhaps by some conception of sincerity. This is to some extent a natural outcome of the disappearance of a permanent background to human activity: a permanent background, whether provided by God, by Reason, by History, or by the self. The agent, thin as a needle, appears in the quick flash of the choosing will. Yet existentialism itself, certainly in its French and Anglo-Saxon varieties, has, with a certain honesty, made evident the paradoxes of its own assumptions. Sartre tells us that when we deliberate the die is already cast, and Oxford philosophy has developed no serious theory of motivation. The agent's freedom, indeed his moral quality, resides in his choices, and yet we are not told what prepares him for the choices. Sartre can admit, with bravado, that we choose out of some sort of pre-existent condition, which he also confusingly calls a choice, and Richard Hare holds that the identification of mental data, such as 'intentions', is philosophically difficult and we had better say that a man is morally the set of his actual choices. That visible motives do not necessitate acts is taken by Sartre as a cue for asserting an irresponsible freedom as an obscure postulate; that motives do not readily yield to 'introspection' is taken by many British philosophers as an excuse for forgetting them and talking about 'reasons' instead. These views seem both unhelpful to the moral pilgrim and also profoundly unrealistic. Moral choice is often a mysterious matter. Kant thought so, and he pictured the mystery in terms of an indiscernible balance between a pure rational agent and an impersonal mechanism, neither of which represented what we normally think of as personality; much existentialist philosophy is in this respect, though often covertly, Kantian. But should not the mystery of choice be conceived of in some other way?

We have learned from Freud to picture 'the mechanism' as something highly individual and personal, which is at the same time very powerful and not easily understood by its owner. The self of psychoanalysis is certainly substantial enough. The existentialist picture of choice, whether it be surrealist or rational, seems unrealistic, over-optimistic, romantic, because it ignores what appears at least to be a sort of continuous background with a life of its own; and it is surely in the tissue of that life that the secrets of good and evil are to be found. Here neither the inspiring ideas of freedom, sincerity and fiats of will, nor the plain wholesome concept of a rational discernment of duty, seem complex enough to do justice to what we really are. What we really are seems much more like an obscure system of energy out of which choices and visible acts of will emerge at intervals in ways which are often unclear and often dependent on the condition of the system in between the moments of choice.

If this is so, one of the main problems of moral philosophy might be formulated thus: are there any techniques for the purification and reorientation of an energy which is naturally selfish, in such a way that when moments of choice arrive we shall be sure of acting rightly? We shall also have to ask whether, if there are such techniques, they should be simply described, in quasi-psychological terms, perhaps in psychological terms, or whether they can be spoken of in a more systematic philosophical way. I have already suggested that a pessimistic view which claims that goodness is the almost impossible countering of a powerful egocentric mechanism already exists in traditional philosophy and in theology. The technique which Plato thought appropriate to this situation I shall discuss later. Much closer and more familiar to us are the techniques of religion, of which the most widely practised is prayer. What becomes of such a technique in a world without God, and can it be transformed to supply at least part of the answer to our central question?

Prayer is properly not petition, but simply an attention to God which is a form of love. With it goes the idea of grace, of a supernatural assistance to human endeavour which overcomes empirical limitations of personality. What is this attention like, and can those who are not religious believers still conceive of profiting by such an activity? Let us pursue the matter by considering what the traditional object of this attention was like and by what means it affected its worshippers. I shall suggest that God was (or is) a *single perfect transcendent non-representable and necessarily real object of attention*; and I shall go on to suggest that moral philosophy should attempt to retain a central concept which has all these characteristics. I shall consider them one by one, although to a large extent they interpenetrate and overlap.

Let us take first the notion of an object of attention. The religious believer, especially if his God is conceived of as a person, is in the fortunate position of being able to focus his thought upon something which is a source of energy. Such focusing, with such results, is natural to human beings. Consider being in love. Consider too the attempt to check being in love, and the need in such a case of another object to attend to. Where strong emotions of sexual love, or of hatred, resentment, or jealousy are concerned, 'pure will' can usually achieve little. It is small use telling oneself

'Stop being in love, stop feeling resentment, be just.' What is needed is a reorientation which will provide an energy of a different kind, from a different source. Notice the metaphors of orientation and of looking. The neo-Kantian existentialist 'will' is a principle of pure movement. But how ill this describes what it is like for us to alter. Deliberately falling out of love is not a jump of the will, it is the acquiring of new objects of attention and thus of new energies as a result of refocusing. The metaphor of orientation may indeed also cover moments when recognizable 'efforts of will' are made, but explicit efforts of will are only a part of the whole situation. That God, attended to, is a powerful source of (often good) energy is a psychological fact. It is also a psychological fact, and one of importance in moral philosophy, that we can all receive moral help by focusing our attention upon things which are valuable: virtuous people, great art, perhaps (I will discuss this later) the idea of goodness itself. Human beings are naturally 'attached' and when an attachment seems painful or bad it is most readily displaced by another attachment, which an attempt at attention can encourage. There is nothing odd or mystical about this, nor about the fact that our ability to act well 'when the time comes' depends partly, perhaps largely, upon the quality of our habitual objects of attention. 'Whatsoever things are true, whatsoever things are honest, whatsoever things are just, whatsoever things are pure, whatsoever things are lovely, whatsoever things of good report; if there be any virtue, and if there be any praise, think on these things.'

The notion that value should be in some sense *unitary*, or even that there should be a single supreme value concept, may seem, if one surrenders the idea of God, far from obvious. Why should there not be many different kinds of independent moral values? Why should all be one here? The madhouses of the world are filled with people who are convinced that all is one. It might be said that 'all is one' is a dangerous falsehood at any level except the highest; and can that be discerned at all? That a belief in the unity, and also in the hierarchical order, of the moral world has a psychological importance is fairly evident. The notion that 'it all somehow must make sense', or 'there is a best decision here', preserves from despair: the difficulty is how to entertain this consoling notion in a way which is not false. As soon as any idea is a consolation the tendency to falsify it becomes strong: hence the traditional problem of preventing the idea of God from degenerating in the believer's mind. It is true that the intellect naturally seeks unity; and in the sciences, for instance, the assumption of unity consistently rewards the seeker. But how can this dangerous idea be used in morals? It is useless to ask 'ordinary language' for a judgment, since we are dealing with concepts which are not on display in ordinary language or unambiguously tied up to ordinary words. Ordinary language is not a philosopher.

We might, however, set out from an ordinary language situation by reflecting upon the virtues. The concepts of the virtues, and the familiar words which name them, are important since they help to make certain potentially nebulous areas of experience more open to inspection. If we reflect upon the nature of the virtues we are constantly led to consider their relation to each other. The idea of an 'order' of virtues suggests itself, although it might of course be difficult to state this in any systematic form. For instance, if we reflect upon courage and ask why we think it to be a virtue, what kind of courage is the highest, what distinguishes courage from rashness, ferocity, self-assertion, and so on, we are bound, in our explanation, to use the names of other virtues. The best kind of courage (that which would make a man act unselfishly in a concentration camp) is steadfast, calm, temperate, intelligent, loving . . . This may not in fact be exactly the right description, but it is the right sort of description . . .

We have spoken of an 'object of attention' and of an unavoidable sense of 'unity'. Let us now go on to consider, thirdly, the much more difficult idea of 'transcendence'. All that has been said so far could be said without benefit of metaphysics. But now it may be asked: are you speaking of a transcendent authority or of a psychological device? It seems to me that the idea of the transcendent, in some form or other, belongs to morality: but it is not easy to interpret. As with so many of these large elusive ideas, it readily takes on forms which are false ones. There is a false transcendence, as there is a false unity, which is generated by modern empiricism: a transcendence which is in effect simply an exclusion, a relegation of the moral to a shadowy existence in terms of emotive language, imperatives, behaviour patterns, attitudes. 'Value' does not belong inside the world of truth functions, the world of science and factual propositions. So it must live somewhere else. It is then attached somehow to the human will, a shadow clinging to a shadow. The result is the sort of dreary moral solipsism which so many so-called books on ethics purvey.

An instrument for criticizing the false transcendence, in many of its forms, has been given to us by Marx in the concept of alienation. Is there, however, any true transcendence, or is this idea always a consoling dream projected by human need on to an empty sky?

It is difficult to be exact here. One might start from the assertion that morality, goodness, is a form of realism. The idea of a really good man living in a private dream world seems unacceptable. Of course a good man may be infinitely eccentric, but he must know certain things about his surroundings, most obviously the existence of other people and their claims. The chief enemy of excellence in morality (and also in art) is personal fantasy: the tissue of self-aggrandizing and consoling wishes and dreams which prevents one from seeing what is there outside one . . .

It may be agreed that the direction of attention should properly be outward, away from self, but it will be said that it is a long step from the idea of realism to the idea of transcendence. I think, however, that these two ideas are related, and one can see their relation particularly in the case of our apprehension of beauty. The link here is the concept of indestructibility or incorruptibility. What is truly beautiful is 'inaccessible' and cannot be possessed or destroyed. The statue is broken, the flower fades, the experience ceases, but something has not suffered from decay and mortality. Almost anything that consoles us is a fake, and it is not easy to prevent this idea from degenerating into a vague Shelleyan mysticism. In the case of the idea of a transcendent personal God the degeneration of the idea seems scarcely avoidable: theologians are busy at their desks at this very moment trying to undo the results of this degeneration. In the case of beauty, whether in art or in nature, the sense of separateness from the temporal process is connected perhaps with concepts of perfection of form and 'authority' which are not easy to transfer into the field of morals. Here I am not sure if this is an analogy or an instance. It is as if we can see beauty itself in a way in which we cannot see goodness itself. (Plato says this at *Phaedrus* 250 E.) I can *experience* the transcendence of the beautiful, but (I think) not the transcendence of the good. Beautiful things contain beauty in a way in which good acts do not exactly contain good, because beauty is partly a matter of the senses. So if we speak of good as transcendent we are speaking of something rather more complicated and which cannot be experienced, even when we see the unselfish man in the concentration camp. One might be tempted to use the word 'faith' here if it could be purged of its religious associations. 'What is truly good is incorruptible and indestructible.' 'Goodness is not in this world.' These sound like highly metaphysical statements. Can we give them any clear meaning or are they just things one feels inclined to say'?

I think the idea of transcendence here connects with two separate ideas, both of which I will be further concerned with below: *perfection* and *certainty*. Are we not certain that there is a 'true direction' towards better conduct, that goodness 'really matters', and does not that certainty about a standard suggest an idea of permanence which cannot be reduced to psychological or any other set of empirical terms? It is true, and this connects with considerations already put forward under the heading of 'attention', that there is a psychological power which derives from the mere idea of a transcendent object, and one might say further from a transcendent object which is to some extent mysterious. But a reductive analysis in, for instance, Freudian terms, or Marxist terms, seems properly to apply here only to a degenerate form of a conception about which one remains certain that a higher and invulnerable form must exist. The idea admittedly remains very difficult. How is one to connect the realism which must involve a clear-eyed contemplation of the misery and evil of the world with a sense of an uncorrupted good without the latter idea becoming the merest consolatory dream? (I think this puts a central problem in moral philosophy.) Also, what is it for someone, who is not a religious believer and not some sort of mystic, to apprehend some separate 'form' of goodness behind the multifarious cases of good behaviour? Should not this idea be reduced to the much more intelligible notion of the interrelation of the virtues, plus a purely subjective sense of the certainty of judgments?

At this point the hope of answering these questions might lead us on to consider the next, and closely related 'attributes': *perfection* (absolute good) and *necessary existence*. These attributes are indeed so closely connected that from some points of view they are the same. (Ontological proof.) It may seem curious to wonder whether the idea of perfection (as opposed to the idea of merit or improvement) is really an important one, and what sort of role it can play . . .

Let us consider the case of conduct. What of the command 'Be ye therefore perfect?' Would it not be more sensible to say 'Be ye therefore slightly improved?' Some psychologists warn us that if our standards are too high we shall become neurotic. It seems to me that the idea of love arises necessarily in this context. The idea of perfection moves, and possibly changes, us (as artist, worker, agent) because it inspires love in the part of us that is most worthy. One cannot feel unmixed love for a mediocre moral standard any more than one can for the work of a mediocre artist. The idea of perfection is also a natural producer of order. In its *light* we come to see that A, which superficially resembles B, is really better than B. And this can occur, indeed must occur, without our having the sovereign idea in any sense 'taped'. In fact it is in its nature that we cannot get it taped. This is the true sense of the 'indefinability' of the good . . . It lies always beyond, and it is from this beyond that it exercises its *authority*. Here again the word seems naturally in place, and it is in the work of artists that we see the operation most clearly. The true artist is obedient to a conception of perfection to which his work is constantly related and re-related in what seems an external manner . . .

It will be said perhaps: are these not simply empirical generalizations about the psychology of effort or improvement, or what status do you wish them to have? Is it just a matter of 'this works' or 'it is as if this were so'? . . .

A little light may be thrown on the matter if we return now . . . to the idea of '*realism*' which was used earlier in a normative sense: that is, it was assumed that it was better to know what was real than to be in a state of fantasy or illusion. It is true that human beings cannot bear much reality; and a consideration of what the effort to face reality is like, and what are its techniques, may serve both to illuminate the necessity or certainty which seems to attach to 'the Good'; and also to lead on to a reinterpretation of 'will' and 'freedom' in relation to the concept of love. Here again it seems to me that art is the clue. Art presents the most comprehensible examples of the almost irresistible human tendency to seek consolation in fantasy and also of the effort to resist this and the vision of reality which comes with success . . . The appreciation of beauty in art or nature is not only (for all its difficulties) the easiest available spiritual exercise; it is also a completely adequate entry into (and not just analogy of) the good life, since it *is* the checking of selfishness in the interest of seeing the real. Of course great artists are 'personalities' and have special styles . . . But the greatest art is 'impersonal' because it shows us the world, our world and not another one, with a clarity which startles and delights us simply because we are not used to looking at the real world at all. Of course, too, artists are pattern-makers. The claims of form and the question of 'how much form' to elicit constitutes one of the chief problems of art. But it is when form is used to isolate, to explore, to display something which is true that we are most highly moved and enlightened. Plato says (*Republic*, VII, 532) that the *technai* have the power to lead the best part of the soul to the view of what is most excellent in reality. This well describes the role of great art as an educator and revealer. Consider what we learn from contemplating the characters of Shakespeare or Tolstoy or the paintings of Velasquez or Titian. What is learnt here is something about the real quality of human nature, when it is envisaged, in the artist's just and compassionate vision, with a clarity which does not belong to the self-centred rush of ordinary life.

It is important too that great art teaches us how real things can be looked at and loved without being seized and used, without being appropriated into the greedy organism of the self. This exercise of *detachment* is difficult and valuable whether the thing contemplated is a human being or the root of a tree or the vibration of a colour or a sound. Unsentimental contemplation of nature exhibits the same quality of detachment: selfish concerns vanish, nothing exists except the things which are seen. Beauty is that which attracts this particular sort of unselfish attention. It is obvious here what is the role, for the artist or spectator, of exactness and good vision: unsentimental, detached, unselfish, objective attention. It is also clear that in moral situations a similar exactness is called for. I would suggest that the authority of the Good seems to us something necessary because the realism (ability to perceive reality) required for goodness is a kind of intellectual ability to perceive what is true, which is automatically at the same time a suppression of self. *The necessity of the good is then an aspect of the kind of necessity involved in any technique for exhibiting fact*. In thus treating realism, whether of artist or of agent, as a moral achievement, there is of course a further assumption to be made in the fields of morals: that true vision occasions right conduct. This could be uttered simply as an enlightening tautology: but I think it can in fact be supported by appeals to experience. The more the separateness and different-ness of other people is realized, and the fact seen that another man has needs and wishes as demanding as one's own, the harder it becomes to treat a person as a thing. That it is realism which makes great art great remains too as a kind of proof.

If, still led by the clue of art, we ask further questions about the faculty which is supposed to relate us to what is real and thus bring us to what is good, the idea of compassion or love will be naturally suggested. It is not simply that suppression of self is required before accurate vision can be obtained. The great artist sees his objects (and this is true whether they are sad, absurd, repulsive or even evil) in a light of justice and mercy. The direction of attention is, contrary to nature, outward, away from self which reduces all to a false unity, towards the great surprising variety of the world, and the ability so to direct attention is love.

One might at this point pause and consider the picture of human personality, or the soul, which has been emerging. It is in the capacity to love, that is to *see*, that the liberation of the soul from fantasy consists. The freedom which is a proper human goal is the freedom from fantasy, that is the realism of compassion. What I have called fantasy, the proliferation of blinding self-centred aims and images, is itself a powerful system of energy, and most of what is often called 'will' or 'willing' belongs to this system. What counteracts the system is attention to reality inspired by, consisting of, love. In the case of art and nature such attention is immediately rewarded by the enjoyment of beauty. In the case of morality, although there are sometimes rewards, the idea of a reward is out of place. Freedom is not strictly the exercise of the will, but rather the experience of accurate vision which, when this becomes appropriate, occasions action. It is what lies behind and in between actions and prompts them that is important, and it is this area which should be purified. By the time the moment of choice has arrived the quality of attention has probably determined the nature of the act. This fact produces that curious separation between consciously rehearsed motives and action which is sometimes wrongly taken as an experience of freedom. (*Angst.*) Of course this is not to say that good 'efforts of will' are always useless or always fakes. Explicit and immediate 'willing' can play some part, especially as an inhibiting factor. (The daemon of Socrates only told him what not to do.)

In such a picture sincerity and self-knowledge, those popular merits, seem less important. It is an attachment to what lies outside the fantasy mechanism, and not a scrutiny of the mechanism itself, that liberates . . .

I have spoken of the real which is the proper object of love, and of knowledge which is freedom. The word 'good' which has been moving about in the discussion should now be more explicitly considered. Can good itself be in any sense 'an object of attention'? And how does this problem relate to 'love of the real'? Is there, as it were, a substitute for prayer, that most profound and effective of religious techniques? If the energy and violence of will, exerted on occasions of choice, seems less important than the quality of attention which determines our real attachments, how do we alter and purify that attention and make it more realistic? Is the *via negativa* of the will, its occasional ability to stop a bad move, the only or most considerable conscious power that we can exert? I think there is something analogous to prayer, though it is something difficult to describe, and which the higher subtleties of the self can often falsify; I am not here thinking of any quasi-religious meditative technique, but of something which belongs to the moral life of the ordinary person. The idea of contemplation is hard to understand and maintain in a world increasingly without sacraments and ritual and in which philosophy has (in many respects rightly) destroyed the old substantial conception of the self. A sacrament provides an external visible place for an internal invisible act of the spirit. Perhaps one needs too an analogy of the concept of the sacrament, though this must be treated with great caution. Behaviouristic ethics denies the importance, because it questions the identity, of anything prior to or apart from action which decisively occurs, 'in the mind'. The apprehension of beauty, in art or in nature, often in fact seems to us like a temporally located spiritual experience which is a source of good energy. It is not easy, however, to extend the idea of such an influential experience to occasions of thinking about people or action, since clarity of thought and purity of attention become harder and more ambiguous when the object of attention is something moral.

It is here that it seems to me to be important to retain the idea of Good as a central point of reflection, and here too we may see the significance of its indefinable and non-representable character. *Good, not will, is transcendent.* Will is the natural energy of the psyche which is sometimes employable for a worthy purpose. Good is the focus of attention when an intent to be virtuous co-exists (as perhaps it almost always does) with some unclarity of vision. Here, as I have said earlier, beauty appears as the visible and accessible aspect of the Good. The Good itself is not visible. Plato pictured the good man as eventually able to look at the sun. I have never been sure what to make of this part of the myth. While it seems proper to represent the Good as a centre or focus of attention, yet it cannot quite be thought of as a 'visible' one in that it cannot be experienced or represented or defined. We can certainly know more or less where the sun is; it is not so easy to imagine what it would be like to look at it. Perhaps indeed only the good man knows what this is like; or perhaps to look at the sun is to be gloriously dazzled and to see nothing. What does seem to make perfect sense in the Platonic myth is the idea of the Good as the source of light which reveals to us all things as they really are. All just vision, even in the strictest problems of the intellect, and *a fortiori* when suffering or wickedness have to be perceived, is a moral matter. The same virtues, in the end the same virtue (love), are required throughout, and fantasy (self) can prevent us from seeing a blade of grass just as it can prevent us from seeing another person. An increasing awareness of 'goods' and the attempt (usually only partially successful) to attend to them purely, without self, brings with it an increasing awareness of the unity and interdependence of the moral world. One-seeking intelligence is the image of 'faith'. Consider what it is like to increase one's understanding of a great work of art.

I think it is more than a verbal point to say that what should be aimed at is goodness, and not freedom or right action, although right action, and freedom in the sense of humility, are the natural products of attention to the Good. Of course right action is important in itself, with an importance which is not difficult to understand. But it should provide the starting-point of reflection and not its conclusion. Right action, together with the steady extension of the area of strict obligation, is a proper criterion of virtue. Action also tends to confirm, for better or worse, the background of attachment from which it issues. Action is an occasion for grace, or for its opposite. However, the aim of morality cannot be simply action. Without some more positive conception of the soul as a substantial and continually developing mechanism of attachments, the purification and reorientation of which must be the task of morals, 'freedom' is readily corrupted into self-assertion and 'right action' into some sort of *ad hoc* utilitarianism. If a scientifically minded empiricism is not to swallow up the study of ethics completely, philosophers must try to invent a terminology which shows how our natural psychology can be altered by conceptions which lie beyond its range. It seems to me that the Platonic metaphor of the idea of the Good provides a suitable picture here. With this picture must of course be joined a realistic conception of natural psychology (about which almost all philosophers seem to me to have been too optimistic) and also an acceptance of the utter lack of finality in human life. The Good has nothing to do with purpose, indeed it excludes the idea of purpose. 'All is vanity' is the beginning and the end of ethics. The only genuine way to be good is to be good 'for nothing' in the midst of a scene where every 'natural' thing, including one's own mind, is subject to chance, that is, to necessity. That 'for nothing' is indeed the experienced correlate of the invisibility or non-representable blankness of the idea of Good itself.

I have suggested that moral philosophy needs a new and, to my mind, more realistic, less romantic, terminology if it is to rescue thought about human destiny from a scientifically minded empiricism which is not equipped to deal with the real problems. Linguistic philosophy has already begun to join hands with such an empiricism, and most existentialist thinking seems to me either optimistic romancing or else something positively Luciferian. (Possibly Heidegger is Lucifer in person.) However, at this point someone might say, all this is very well, the only difficulty is that none of it is true. Perhaps indeed all is vanity, *all* is vanity, and there is no respectable intellectual way of protecting people from despair. The world just is hopelessly evil and should you, who speak of realism, not go all the way towards being realistic about this? To speak of Good in this portentous manner is simply to speak of the old concept of God in a thin disguise. But at least 'God' could play a real consoling and encouraging role. It makes sense to speak of loving God, a person, but very little sense to speak of loving Good, a concept. 'Good' even as a fiction is not likely to inspire, or even be comprehensible to, more than a small number of mystically minded people who, being reluctant to surrender 'God', fake up 'Good' in his image, so as to preserve some kind of hope. The picture is not only purely imaginary, it is not even likely to be effective. It is very much better to rely on simple popular utilitarian and existentialist ideas, together with a little empirical psychology, and perhaps some doctored Marxism, to keep the human race going. Day-to-day empirical common sense must have the last word. All specialized ethical vocabularies are false. The old serious metaphysical quest had better now be let go, together with the out-dated concept of God the Father.

I am often more than half persuaded to think in these terms myself. It is frequently difficult in philosophy to tell whether one is saying something reasonably public and objective, or whether one is merely erecting a barrier, special to one's own temperament, against one's own personal fears. (It is always a significant question to ask about any philosopher: what is he afraid of?) Of course one is afraid that the attempt to be good may turn out to be meaningless, or at best something vague and not very important, or turn out to be as Nietzsche described it, or that the greatness of great art may be an ephemeral illusion. Of the 'status' of my arguments I will speak briefly below. That a glance at the scene prompts despair is certainly the case. The difficulty indeed is to look at all. If one does not believe in a personal God there is no 'problem' of evil, but there is the almost insuperable difficulty of looking properly at evil and human suffering. It is very difficult to concentrate attention upon suffering and sin, in others or in oneself, without falsifying the picture in some way while making it bearable. [. . .] Only the very greatest art can manage it, and that is the only public evidence that it can be done at all. Kant's notion of the sublime, though extremely interesting, possibly even more interesting than Kant realized, is a kind of romanticism. The spectacle of huge and appalling things can indeed exhilarate, but usually in a way that is less than excellent. Much existentialist thought relies upon such a 'thinking reed' reaction which is nothing more than a form of romantic self-assertion. It is not this which will lead a man on to unselfish behaviour in the concentration camp. There is, however, something in the serious attempt to look compassionately at human things which automatically suggests that 'there is more than this'. The 'there is more than this', if it is not to be corrupted by some sort of quasi-theological finality, must remain a very tiny spark of insight, something with, as it were, a metaphysical position but no metaphysical form. But it seems to me that the spark is real, and that great art is evidence of its reality. Art indeed, so far from being a playful diversion of the human race, is the place of its most fundamental insight, and the centre to which the more uncertain steps of metaphysics must constantly return.

. . . Of course philosophy has its own terminology, but what it attempts to describe need not be, and I think is not in this case, removed from ordinary life. Morality has always been connected with religion and religion with mysticism. The disappearance of the middle term leaves morality in a situation which is certainly more difficult but essentially the same. The background to morals is properly some sort of mysticism, if by this is meant a non-dogmatic essentially unformulated faith in the reality of the Good, occasionally connected with experience . . .

I have throughout this paper assumed that 'there is no God' and that the influence of religion is waning rapidly. Both these assumptions may be challenged. What seems beyond doubt is that moral philosophy is daunted and confused, and in many quarters discredited and regarded as unnecessary. The vanishing of the philosophical self, together with the confident filling in of the scientific self, has led in ethics to an inflated and yet empty conception of the will, and it is this that I have been chiefly attacking. I am not sure how far my positive suggestions make sense. The search for unity is deeply natural, but like so many things which are deeply natural may be capable of producing nothing but a variety of illusions. What I feel sure of is the inadequacy, indeed the inaccuracy, of utilitarianism, linguistic behaviourism, and current existentialism in any of the forms with which I am familiar. I also feel sure that moral philosophy ought to be defended and kept in existence as a pure activity, or fertile area, analogous in importance to unapplied mathematics or pure 'useless' historical research. Ethical theory has affected society, and has reached as far as to the ordinary man, in the past, and there is no good reason to think that it cannot do so in the future. For both the collective and the individual salvation of the human race, art is doubtless more important than philosophy, and literature most important of all. But there can be no substitute for pure, disciplined, professional speculation: and it is from these two areas, art and ethics, that we must hope to generate concepts worthy, and also able, to guide and check the increasing power of science.

MARY MIDGLEY (1919–   )

Mary Midgley, née Scrutton, was educated at Somerville College, Oxford. She has spent all of her professional life as a Senior Lecturer at the University of Newcastle-upon-Tyne, where her husband has also been a professional philosopher. She is a moral philosopher who has developed a particular interest and expertise in matters concerned with evolution and the relation between men and other animals, on which she has written not only books but numerous articles for weeklies such as the *New Statesman*. Everything she has written is grounded on a thorough understanding and a penetrating analysis of the work of moral philosophers who, while having no such specialist interest, seemed relevant to her arguments. Her discussion of Kant and, for example, of G. E. Moore are of particular value. Her book *Beast and Man*, from which the chapter below is taken, was published in 1979. It was written largely while Mary Midgley was in America taking part in seminars at Cornell on Science, Technology and Society. The ethical issues arising out of the relation between man and the rest of the universe, the development of technology and the use of animals, both for food and for research, were beginning to be a matter of great concern and interest both sides of the Atlantic. Mary Midgley brought a fresh eye and a fresh style to the debate. Since the publication of *Beast and Man* there have been innumerable books on the same sort of subject. This book remains not only the most accessible but also the best grounded in philosophy. Chapter 11, which I have extracted, contains its central argument.

Further Reading

Mary Midgley, *Beast and Man: The Roots of Human Nature* (Hassocks: Harvester, 1979)

——*Heart and Mind: The Varieties of Moral Experience* (Brighton: Harvester, 1981)

——*Animals and Why they Matter* (Harmondsworth: Penguin, 1983)

——*Wickedness: A Philosophical Essay* (London: Routledge & Kegan Paul, 1984)

——*Heart and Mind: The Varieties of Moral Experience*, (Fulmer Press, 1981)

Robin Attfield, *The Ethics of Environmental Concern*, 2nd edn (Athens: University of Georgia Press, 1983)

Mary Warnock, *The Uses of Philosophy* (Oxford: Blackwell, 1992), chapters 1,2 and 3

From Mary Midgley, Beast and Man: The Roots of Human Nature *(Hassocks: Harvester, 1979), chapter 11: 'On being animal as well as rational'*

The Unity of Our Nature

This discussion of rationality may strike hasty readers as perverse, because its purpose is so different from that of most treatments of the subject. They are usually concerned essentially to *celebrate* reason, and to stress what is unique about it. This celebration I wholeheartedly accept and take for granted ... My present purpose, however, is the distinct and supplementary one of asking how this unique thing, rationality, is possible in a being that is not just a disembodied intellect, but also and among other things some kind of animal, how it fits into such a life. Thus it will constantly be my business to look at the pattern on the other side of the carpet, at the continuity. I am asking about reason what I have been asking about language, namely, what links it to the rest of nature? what part does it play in our life? To understand this, I shall examine, through animal parallels, what conditions must have been necessary in a prerational creature if reasoning was to develop and what, therefore, must be retained as a setting for reason? I do this, not in the belief that reason can be 'reduced' to nonrational elements, but from the desire to make sense of our nature as a whole – to find how each of us can regard himself as one thing, not two, when part of our nature is prerational ... It is not clear how a creature such as Plato and Descartes described could ever have evolved without celestial interference. Amputating the Cartesian Immortal Soul and leaving the rest of the compound untouched does not, as some people think, help us. The intellect is still left as an alien intruder in the world.

As for celestial interference, it obviously does not make sense in a nonreligious context. But I do not think it does so in a Christian one either. Christianity is not Platonism. If God created through evolution, he surely designed it and used it properly. As I shall suggest, Bishop Butler, who was no atheist, points us toward a far more coherent view of human wholeness than Descartes. How immortality is to be conceived is certainly a difficult problem, but it is so whatever you do. Descartes's shortcut creates as many problems as it solves about *what* survives. Every religion in fact demands that far more should survive than the Intellect.

But the chief difficulty about accepting continuity between man and other species, or between the human intellect and the rest of man, now comes not from traditional religion, but from those who do amputate the soul. It stems from the deep reverence people now feel for human success, and particularly for success in science. In this area, people often do not realize how many of the difficulties raised by religion they are needlessly keeping while officially jettisoning its metaphysics. They revere what they take to be the highest human capacities, particularly the speculative intellect, so deeply that they are inclined to find natural explanations of them quite as blasphemous as religious people used to find natural explanations of the religious faculties. Reverence for humanity, which at first is a most respectable tendency, often slips across into overtly religious form. Thus Auguste Comte instituted a regular 'worship of humanity' with rituals and a temple in Paris. Thus Nietzsche, after killing off God, came near to worshipping the future of the human race in the form of the Superman. And H. G. Wells called one of his utopian future-fantasies *Men Like Gods*. Wells moreover endued man with so much of the divine prerogative that he called upon him to 'bring to trial' every other earthly organism from the rhinoceros to the tubercle bacillus, and alter it to his satisfaction or get rid of it.[1] It is much easier, it seems, to disown a particular God than to get rid of his empty seat and the paranoia that so readily surrounds it. Wells's bold and forceful imagination is very useful to us here, because he made explicit

[1] In *A Modern Utopia* (1906), the work in which the real genius of the early Wells began to give way to 'humanist' paranoia.

what is often covered up – that the only reason for man's having this status was supposed to be what Wells called his intelligence – by which he meant mere cleverness, calculating power, the sort of thing that can be measured by intelligence tests. The future people in *Men Like Gods* are almost purely intellectual – they have, with a few despised exceptions, got rid of 'human weaknesses' such as loving one person better than another. (Significantly, they do not wear clothes.) Wells understood, however, that this meant that any *more* intelligent species, if one appeared, would have the same right to get rid of man. He explained this at the outset of *The War of the Worlds*, where the superintelligent Martians, who are nothing but enormous heads on mechanical trolleys, set out as a matter of course to annihilate the human race without examining it. They are, Wells says, merely exercising the same obvious right we ourselves have always exercised over 'the cow and the cucumber.'

Much science fiction has followed Wells in this competitive way of reasoning, which has obvious attractions for those who like the popping of ray guns and the sound of titles like *Master of a Thousand Universes*. It is, however, very obscure. What is supposed to be *that* good about cleverness? Being clever is not obviously so much more important than being kind, brave, friendly, patient, and generous that it inevitably confers an instant right of general massacre. And those qualities cannot be supposed to follow from cleverness, or be included in it; we know that the two kinds of thing can be found apart. Modern humanists cannot, of course, fall back on Plato's way of talking and say that the intellect is man's divinest faculty, his highest dignity, his link with God, the bridge by which he can approach a reality greater than himself, a mode of action superior to the grossness of physical matter, or anything remotely resembling those notions. If they are good Utilitarians (as Wells was), they should regard it only as one means among others to securing pleasure. And an impartial comparison of hedonic level between intellectuals and other types, or between simple and advanced civilizations, is not likely to suggest that it is an especially efficient one, at least not so much as to settle out of hand and with no reference to any other qualities, the question of who is to exterminate whom. Is there actually anything more to the position that the intellect is primary than the argument which G. E. Moore noted as being relied on against the

North American Indians (we are more advanced than they are because we can kill them faster than they can kill us)? . . .[2]

What this way of talking relies on, of course, is the immense respect that both common sense and the philosophic tradition give to rationality. But rationality is not just cleverness. Even the word *intelligence* is often used to mean a good deal more than what Wells meant. And *rationality* always means more. It includes a definite structure of preferences, a priority system based on feeling. Now that kind of structure is not peculiar to the human race, but is also found in the higher animals.

In the philosophic tradition, Reason, though not always equated with mere intellect, has usually been sharply opposed to Feeling or Desire. This has determined the attitude of most respectable philosophers to the related subjects of animals and human feelings. They have usually just dismissed animal activities from all comparison with human ones, on the general ground that, in man, decision is a formal, rational process, while animals have only feeling, which is a kind of wholly contingent slop or flow, bare matter without form, so that its analysis cannot concern philosophy. Thus, typically, even Hume, who really did want to show that feeling mattered, went to great trouble to show it simply as an undifferentiated physical force, much like gravitation, moving people in much the same sense in which gravitation moved billiard balls. *Understanding* it, for him, simply meant fitting it into a scheme of mechanics, which should be as economical and simple as possible. (Here the modern Emotivists are his successors, boiling down feeling to the straight dynamic function of being for or against something.) Hume wanted to be the Newton of psychology, an ambition that unluckily has survived him. Psychology did not and does not need a Newton. It needed, and still needs, a Darwin – a careful, patient, thorough observer, who would *distinguish* the various forms of motivation, relate and compare them, and eventually work out concepts suitable for classifying and explaining them, rather than imposing slapdash fashion an unsuitable model from an alien science.

Because I need to use the common philosophical language of *form* and *matter*, I must digress here to explain that the traditional use of these terms has been oversimple.

[2] *Principia Ethica*, p. 47.

It will not do to analyze motivation once and for all into Thought as Form, and Feeling as blank, contingent, undifferentiated Matter. It will not do because the distinction of form and matter is never final; it is always a repeatable one. All actual matter has a form; all actual forms fit a matter. For instance, when Aristotle gave the name *hylê, wood*, to matter, he was thinking of a carpenter imposing form on wood by making it into a table. But of course, the wood before that was not just neutral stuff. It already had its own form. It was beech or pine, with a definite grain and structure. If further form was to be imposed on it, the wood would have to be chosen and prepared. (You cannot make a table out of neutral stuff, nor from a transverse slice across a freshly cut pine trunk, nor from chalk or honeycomb either.) And, to look in the other direction, the completed table along with other furniture can be treated as matter, raw material for the art of the moving man, the art historian, or the interior decorator. And so forth. So, though it is quite true that the philosopher's business is with forms, it never follows that he can disregard matter, nor that what is treated as matter for one particular inquiry will not show its formal element in another. It all depends what you are trying to do at the time.

Feeling has its forms, both in man and other species. If it had not, reason could make nothing of it, and rational decision would be impossible. The crude antithesis between feeling and reason, form and matter, is inadequate even to map the human scene – before we start trying to look for some continuity between man and other species, as we must to make evolution intelligible. If you treat morality as entirely a matter of formless feeling (as Hume did) or entirely a formal matter (as Kant did), you oversimplify disastrously. Moreover, bluntly opposing feeling and reason is inclined to lead to personifying them. Hume, who quite rightly said, 'we speak not strictly and philosophically when we talk of the combat of passion and of reason,' nonetheless fell into this trap when he added that 'reason is, and ought only to be, the slave of the passions, and can never pretend to any other office than to serve and obey them.' Making these two abstractions into Employer and Employed is no better than setting them to fight it out like a couple of drunks. 'Reason' is not the name of a character in a drama. It is a name for organizing oneself. When there is a conflict, one desire *must* be restrained to make way for the other. It is the process of *choosing which* that is rightly called reasoning.

But the ill effects of the dramatization constantly appear in Romantic writing, for instance, Blake's *Marriage of Heaven and Hell*:

> Those who restrain desire, do so because theirs is weak enough to be restrained: and the restrainer or reason usurps its place and governs the unwilling.
>
> And being restrained, it by degrees becomes passive, till it is only the shadow of desire.
>
> The history of this is written in *Paradise Lost*, and the Governor or Reason is called Messiah.

Romantics like Blake gave the name Reason to desires they disapproved of – say, caution, or the force of habit, or a mere dreary negativeness – and reserved that of Desire or Passion for the ones they favored. This has become common usage, but it is a mess. Reason and feeling are aspects of all our motives. Feelings themselves have a form, and one that fits the matter. In fact, of course, it can be our duty to *feel* in one way rather than another – something for which the tradition has little room. (Criticism of 'the undeveloped heart' is moral criticism.) Practical reasoning would be impossible were not some preferences 'more rational' than others. Rationality includes having the right priorities. And deep, lasting preferences linked to character traits are formally a quite different proposition from sharp, isolated impulses.

The higher animals have a structure of deep, lasting preferences too.
So in showing the importance of a definite, lasting structure of feeling in human life, we show that we can rightly compare it with the parallel (though distinct) structures found in other species.

We lose nothing by this. It does not infringe on the distinctively human structural properties involved in conceptual thought and language. Acting for the common good deliberately and consciously, with a full understanding that you could do otherwise, and after explicit reflection on the alternatives, is a very different thing from doing it unthinkingly. Backing a principle that you can *state* is a very different thing from just steadily acting on it. All the same – as Kant himself recognized – it is a very narrow notion of value which *confines* it to the rational and deliberate, and does not prize good feeling itself.

Let me try now to explain, however roughly, what I mean by the structure, or constitution of human nature, so as to understand the place of the feelings within it.

I want to get away from the essentially *colonial* picture (used by Blake) in which an imported governor, named Reason, imposes order on a chaotic alien tribe of Passions or Instincts. The colonial picture, which is Plato's, was handed down through the Stoics, Descartes and Spinoza, to Kant. It performed a very good service by honoring Thought. But once doubt arose about how thought could establish values, it ceased to do so. Schopenhauer, Nietzsche and the Existentialists changed the governor's name from Reason to Will. Kant spoke of the will, but he meant by it reason in action – 'the Will is nothing but Practical Reason.' But the will now stands mainly for arrogance, arbitrariness, and contempt for the natural facts.

Instead of being colonial, I want to look at the continuity – to use Bishop Butler's (and to some extent Aristotle's) picture, to talk of what Butler called 'the whole system, as I may speak, of affections, *including rationality*, which constitute the Heart.'[3] I want to consider reason as growing out of and completing a natural balance of parts. I think we all take for granted that there is such a system, and need the idea for our practical thinking. We know that there have to be some things that are naturally more important, more central to human life, than others, and we have a good general idea which sorts of things they are, and how to compare them. We are not really in the helplessly ignorant situation philosophical discussions often suggest, where the only thing that we could safely call important is survival. Of course important things take different forms in different ages and cultures. Of course we must, as it were, keep learning new languages. But where we know the language (as we do in our own culture) we know how to start distinguishing important things from unimportant, and thereby good from evil. Such distinguishing is very often the theme of serious novels and plays. When we are following them we grasp the process very well. It is odd that people are struck with total ignorance when they turn to moral philosophy. Pretending that we do not have this skill is in fact a form of hypocrisy. The hypocrisy of past ages was usually classical and dogmatic, the hypocrisy of this age is romantic and skeptical. We pretend *not* to know. Instead of trying to see, we shut the

---

[3] Sermon 12, 'Upon the Love of our Neighbour,' sec. 11.

curtains and revel in tragic darkness, concentrating carefully on impossible cases and taking the boring possible for granted.

Conflict and Integration

I want to dispense with this hypocrisy in considering briefly how we deal with conflict. It will be helpful to begin by asking a few questions about self-control – about what is controlled, what does the controlling, and what it means to have a controlling center to one's personality. Throughout this section, I am trying to come to grips with the question, what is it, essentially, that we so respect about rationality? What is so good about it? Why, for instance, does Kant sound convincing when he suggests that it is the *only* thing that can command respect?[4] We would not be likely to take this view of mere cleverness. Indeed there is a sense, though a boring one, in which computers can be clever, but only people very deeply misguided and prone to the pathetic fallacy could respect them.

There are, I think, two distinct elements in rationality: cleverness and integration. By integration I mean having a character, acting as a whole, having a firm and effective priority system. The second is a condition of the first, not the other way round. For the full respect that we give to rationality, we need both. But integration alone is something of enormous value, and respect seems a suitable name for the recognition with which we salute it. And integration is not confined to people.

To illuminate these ideas, let us consider what happens when integration fails, first in some animal cases, then in human ones. It will become clear that the problem and the first stage of the solution are common to both.

In Niko Tinbergen's book *The Herring Gull's World* [London: Collins, 1953] there are two especially instructive illustrations. One (p. 145) shows a gull reposing, eyes closed and wings folded, the picture of fatuous parental contentment, on an empty nest, while its eggs addle in the cold, a foot away. Helpful ethologists have removed the eggs to see which the creature would prefer, and it has settled for the nest. The other (p. 209), still more remarkable, shows an oyster catcher trying to perch on top of a monstrous egg, larger than itself, ignoring its own egg and a rather larger gull's egg

[4] *Grundlegung*, chap. 1, sec. 16, note (Paton tr., p. 66).

that is there for further choice. The large egg, a dummy, has been provided by the ethologists to test the bird's powers of discrimination. These are two of many examples where interference has shown how slight, how easily garbled, are the natural cues creatures act on, even in cases essential to survival. Herring gulls, it seems, care more about nests than eggs; oyster catchers like their eggs substantial. And these preferences do no harm in the normal situation where there are no experimenters around, for normally the eggs stay in the nest, and all available eggs are roughly the same size. So there has been no selection pressure to alert gulls about roving eggs, nor to control the romantic dream, which oyster catchers apparently cherish in their hearts, of one day finding an egg really worth sitting on.

Things like outsize eggs are called supernormal stimuli.[5] In these cases, the creature wants what it needs, but wants much *more* of it than it needs – has, in fact, not the slightest idea when to stop. Unlike overeating, which brings on discomfort, or oversleeping, which is broken off naturally, tastes such as outsize-egg-hunger have no built-in corrective. In these situations, tastes depend for their regulation on outside circumstances, which in the course of evolution plainly did not often fail. Their owners simply have no way of knowing when they have had enough of a good thing.

This is sad, we think, and bizarre, but, naturally, nothing to do with *Homo sapiens*.

But isn't it? Might not a species that cannot stop stuffing itself with chocolates, drinking spirits, racing fast cars, gambling, wasting resources, competing, fighting, and watching Miss World on television have something to learn from that unlucky gull and oyster catcher?

Chocolates are in fact an interesting example. A taste for sweetness has some selective values for fruit eaters, because it leads a creature to prefer ripe but not rotten fruit. And of course, in the wild, other sweet things are rare, so no firm safety-stop on sweetness is necessary. This is why, given a supply of sugar, human teeth and human figures are in such danger. The case of Miss World is also instructive. In their strong visual interest, human beings are much nearer to birds than to most animals. In all human cultures, people pay a lot of attention to their own and one

[5] For the term, see *The Herring Gull's World*, pp. 206–8.

another's appearance, and particularly to that of their sexual partners. Cultures differ in what they emphasize, but there is a general tendency to emphasize *something*, to pick out some one set from the repertoire of possible sexual cues and build it up, often beyond what is comfortable, healthy, or (difficult but necessary word) 'balanced.' Tinbergen mentions lipstick, which seems harmless enough. More alarmingly, some peoples pick on a long slender neck, and produce Giraffe Women. The Chinese used to like small feet, and imposed them accordingly. And some African tribes shut up their girls in a fatting house to beautify them before marriage – sometimes so successfully than when the great day comes they are too fat to walk.

Obsessiveness unbalances people's tastes against biological advantage.

In no species do instincts form a perfectly balanced, infallible set, a smooth machine, such as human envy supposes animals to have. Miss World adds an extra twist to this unbalance, in that she is, so to speak, purely visual and speculative, possessing no practical or tactile components. She is doubly abstracted. Voyeurism does not lead anywhere. But this is no different, in principle, from the gull's problem.

Male adornment works differently, partly because women's sexual interest is less visual, but to a greater extent because everywhere men's appearance has an imposing and aggressive, not just a seductive meaning. Male dances are typically war dances. Male ceremonial tends to serve another general interest that can also get out of hand – the competitive taste for impressing, terrifying, and outdoing possible rivals. Where this taste takes charge, people may again be caught in an inconvenient and unbalanced pattern of life. Even if they want to resist it, their obsession traps them. (*Obsession* means a siege; you can't get out.) They are caught by their own inability to resist a particular type of stimulus. So I think it right to link this kind of situation with supernormal stimuli – although of course there is the very important difference that pugnacious exhibitionism is a *much more general* motive. It covers a whole class of stimuli, not just one, like the outsize egg. It appeals not to a single desire, but to a whole character trait. Certainly if we wanted to atomize we could list suitable stimuli for each martial society – the clash of arms, the shouts of the warriors, the gleam of weapons, the enemy's voices – most of all, perhaps, the accepted words and gestures of insulting challenge. (Or, for Academic Man, a bad book, a detested phrase, a pretentious opponent . . .) Such lists sound quite behavioristic. But of course we know that we are speaking of a central uniting factor, the character trait to which all these appeal. We know what it is like to be roused. This is what makes it possible to group the stimuli, and to keep the list open for all sorts of further additions – for instance, on particular occasions, a sudden silence or an especially polite mode of address. All appeal to the pugnacious side of human nature.

That side is real and important. But even for the most pugnacious of us, it is only part of the personality, and often conflicts with more central parts. There is therefore, I think, a characteristic feeling of *exasperation* about these partial stimuli – a feeling of being dragged apart. One side of us has been worked on separately and roused to a feeling that excludes the rest. And our nature fits us to operate as a whole.

We may, of course, deal with this conflict by clamping down sharply on the competing interests, or by trying to make one of them prevail. But one way or another we must try to deal with it, because, unlike the gull and the oyster catcher, *we can see what is going on*, though we often find that we cannot do anything about it. The exasperation is even sharper in a way when the stimuli seem petty and isolated, but still irresistible. Recently I read two furious letters to the newspaper from people wanting particular petty stimuli banned – one a smoker objecting to cigarette advertising, the other a supermarket customer objecting to candy piled at the checkout counter. Both writers said quite honestly that it was not just the simple peasantry they wanted to protect, but themselves. And I think what they wanted protection against was *fragmentation*, not just the ill consequences of smoking or eating candy. ('How dare you set me against myself?') Perhaps this is the basic objection to advertising generally, and indeed to the whole overstimulating surface of our cities – 'stop setting me in conflict.' Perhaps it is a perfectly proper protest against fissiparous forces too strong for the center to cope with. Being torn apart by conflicting motives and unable to hold oneself together can be, as Catullus knew, agonizing:

> Odi at amo; quare id faciam, fortasse requiris.
> Nescio, sed fieri sentio, et excrucior.

(I hate her and I love her. Perhaps you ask me why I do this? I do not know. I only feel it happen, and I am in torment.)

Trivial cases do not, of course, mean agony, but such internal conflict is always confusing, disquieting, and somehow sinister. We are trapped on one side; we cannot pull free. (Supernormal stimuli are, of course, typically the kind of thing used to *bait traps*.) We feel that our nature demands that we should be able to extricate ourselves, to understand what is going on within us and either endorse or control it. We feel that it demands integration.

Self-Control: The Human Solution

Does this feeling make biological sense?

Bishop Butler puts the problem thus:

> Suppose a brute creature by any bait to be allured into a snare, by which he is destroyed. He plainly followed the bent of his nature, leading him to gratify his appetite; there is an entire correspondence between his whole nature and such an action; such action therefore is natural. But suppose a man, foreseeing the same danger of certain ruin, should rush into it for the sake of a present gratification; he in this instance would follow his strongest desire, as did the brute creature; but there would be as manifest a disproportion between the nature of man and such an action, as between the meanest work of art and the skill of the greatest master of that art – Which disproportion arises, not from considering the action singly in itself, or in its consequences, but from comparison of it with the nature of the agent. And since such an action is utterly disproportionate to the nature of man, it is in the strictest and most proper sense unnatural.[6]

About people, Butler is surely right. If a person who had his memory and his intelligence did not *mind* traps, if he had no center, no policy, if he drifted from act to act without any attempt at continuity or interest in relating them, people in any culture would say that he had something wrong with him. We ourselves would probably say there was something medically wrong; we might put it that he was *not all there*. And we would certainly be likely to call him irrational. Sophisticated 'policies of not having a policy' are no exception. If they have some guiding principle, they are only partial; if they really have none, anything can happen. A

[6] Sermon 2, 'Upon Human Nature,' sec. 10.

policy of being flexible on certain selected issues is still a policy; there must be constants elsewhere to call for it. *Integration of the personality is not just an optional extra*. It is a need. Human beings must have a structure, a policy, a continuity. Each has only one life to live. He cannot split up as a coral colony might, into several batches of polyps, each equipped to go their separate ways. Without a lasting character, he cannot even follow out a train of thought – which is why I say that this is a condition of intelligence, not vice versa. Complete disintegration, then, is hard to imagine. But partial cases are very common. Most of us have personalities fairly well integrated on one side, the side we attend to, but fragmented on others, to which we pay less attention.

Butler's idea is that if we reflect on our own nature, if we attend to our neglected outlying motives and relate them to the center, we shall be able to judge them – because the reflective center of our personality has a natural authority, is in a position to judge. 'Had it strength, as it has right, had it force, as it has manifest authority, it would absolutely govern the world.' It 'demands in all cases to govern such a creature as man.'[7]

Butler calls it conscience, not reason, and this has made some people miss his meaning, because they personify Conscience, even more simply and disastrously than Reason, and see it merely as the voice of prejudice, an irresponsible despot. Butler, however, carefully avoids the errors of personifying. He repeatedly explains that he does *not* mean by conscience any unaccountable oracle or intuition, but a reflective faculty at the center of ourselves, by which we can think about our various actions and desires, stamping some with approval and rejecting others. And of course he does not make the mistake of personifying faculties either. For him conscience (or reflection) is simply the man himself in his capacity as decider – each of us, when we think seriously what we are for and against. Just so, Aristotle speaks of the core of the personality as *the man himself*, by contrast to casual impulses, and calls it (or him) *kyrios* – dominant, in charge.[8]

This is the context that justifies Butler's political metaphor of the *authority* of conscience or reflection. What rules us is our own center. It is indeed a 'governor,' but not an alien, colonial one. It is our own sense of how our nature works . . . By reflecting, Butler

---

[7] Sermon 2, sec. 14, and Preface to the *Sermons*, sec. 16.
[8] *Ethics* 9.4, 9.8, 10.7, for example.

says, we stumble on the moral law, because that is the law of our own nature. 'Your obligation to obey this law is, its being the law of your nature.' It is not imposed from without. It is 'the most intimate of all obligations; and which a man cannot transgress without being self-condemned, and unless he has corrupted his nature, without real self-dislike.' He repeatedly points out that it does not depend on any religious sanctions, because it is more fundamental than they. It is as binding on pagans and unbelievers as it is on Christians. 'Man is thus by his very nature a law to himself.'[9]

People are alarmed when Butler speaks of the 'absolute authority' of conscience or reflection over other motives, because they smell political despotism. Now if Butler had meant by conscience what some people mean by it – prejudice, egoism, or fancy – he would, of course, have been cutting short reflection before it could begin. But he means reflection itself. In a full discussion of self-deception, he makes it clear how wrong it is to distort the term conscience by using it to set up any such private oracle. (The position about the infallibility of conscience is rather like that about the infallibility of reason. If people argue confusedly, we do not say that their reason misled them, but that they did not reason properly. Bad argument is by definition *not* the voice of reason, nor, similarly, is bad morality a manifestation of conscience.) What Butler intends is quite different. He is saying that reflection demands action. To put it philosophically, he is pointing out the peculiar 'prescriptive' form in which the conclusions of practical thinking emerge. They are not just theoretical and informative, but imperative and practical as well. If your night's reflection makes clear to you that in your inmost being you loathe and reject the corruption of the city council, then there will follow particular commands – like 'refuse that bribe.' And this command cannot be treated just as one motive among others, a mere impulse to refusal, competing on even terms with other impulses and winning or losing according to its force at the moment.

> Which is to be obeyed, appetite or reflexion? Cannot this question be answered, from the economy and constitution of human nature merely, without saying which is strongest? ... How often soever [impulse] happens to prevail, it is mere *usurpation* ... every instance of

[9] Sermon 3, sec. 5; Preface to the *Sermons*, secs. 28 and 29.

such prevalence is an instance of breaking in upon and violating the constitution of man.

All this is no more than the distinction, which everybody is acquainted with, between *mere power* and *authority*; only instead of being intended to express the difference between what is possible and what is lawful in civil government, here it has been shown applicable to the several principles in the mind of man.[10]

To put the point more psychologically, Butler is pointing out the dangers of a confused personality, remarking that the price of ignoring one's center or refusing to reflect properly is disintegration. In his sermon 'Upon the Character of Balaam,' he looks at the case of a self-deceiving religious obsessive, carefully keeping to the letter of his duty while he violates the spirit of it. This man, he points out, has failed in reflection quite as much as any corrupt contractor. He is deeply disorganized; he is refusing to know what he is about. Butler discusses this phenomenon of self-deception in the next sermon, and finally breaks out: 'If people will be wicked, they had better of the two be so from the common vicious passions without such refinements, than from this deep and calm source of delusion, which undermines the whole principle of good; darkens that light, the *candle of the Lord within*, which is to direct our step, and corrupts conscience, which is the guide of life.'[11]

The formal, philosophical point about the authority of conscience is the same one Kant later put in terms of the claims of practical reason – that our thinking, if it is thorough, will land us with imperatives we cannot dodge, conclusions about what we must do, as well as with unavoidable conclusions about the facts. The distinctive thing about Butler is his managing to combine this formal point with a proper attention to human feeling. He insists that it is our emotional constitution that gives us the material to reflect on. This dependence of thought on feeling is the aspect of the truth which Hume grasped at in saying that 'reason is, and ought only to be, the slave of the passions.' Butler, however, sharply refuses to take sides here, to oppose reason to feeling. He entirely rejects the idea behind Hume's tendentious question, 'concerning the general foundation of Morals, whether they be derived from Reason, or from Sentiment?'[12] Butler saw no reason

[10] Sermon 2, secs. 13–14.
[11] Sermon 10, sec. 16.
[12] *Enquiry Concerning the Principles of Morals*, sec. 134.

to set up a dogfight by regarding these obviously complementary elements as alternatives:

> There are two ways in which the subject of morals may be treated. One begins by enquiring into the abstract relations of things; the other from a matter of fact, namely what the particular nature of man is . . . They both lead us to the same thing . . . The first seems the most direct, formal proof, and in some respects the least liable to cavil or dispute; the latter is in a peculiar manner adapted to satisfy a fair mind . . . and is more easily applicable to the several particular relations and circumstances of life.[13]

This is surely right. Hume's question, indeed, can only appear to make sense by exploiting the extreme looseness of words like *foundation*, *basis*, and *derive*. It is really no better to ask this than to ask 'What are the foundations of physics? Are its truths derived from rational principles, or from the material facts?' The proper answer to such a question is simply 'yes,' which is the treatment Butler gives it. He again sharply refuses to be drawn into this sort of controversy when considering the various names that might be given to Conscience, refusing to classify it as reason or sentiment. It works, he says, 'whether considered as a sentiment of the understanding or a perception of the heart, or, which seems the truth, as including both.'[14] With this deliberate paradox he resists Hume's vicious abstraction. The 'force' Hume enquired about certainly has its emotional side. Good moral arguments do indeed express powerful human tastes and preferences. But it has its rational side too. These arguments *relate* those tastes and preferences in the way our nature as a whole demands. The 'force' this gives them is the force of our demand for wholeness. The sanction of resisting it is not just logical confusion, but disintegration.

This insistence on the emotional element in goodness makes it possible for Butler to make better sense of wickedness than single-minded rationalists like Kant. Kant, in his discussion of the man naturally short of sympathy and 'not exactly framed by nature to be a philanthropist,'[15] seems to suggest that such a man, *whatever* his natural emotional constitution, if he reasons honestly, will see the necessity of virtue, and can act on this insight. But

---

[13] Preface to the *Sermons*, sec. 12.
[14] *Dissertation upon the Nature of Virtue*, sec. 1.
[15] *Grundlegung*, chap. 1, sec. 11 (Paton, tr., p. 64.)

there are intelligent psychopaths. What do we say about them? Rationalists can, I think, fairly point out that we have such difficulty in penetrating their thought that the supposition of its perfect consistency is not a very clear or strong one. Still, the most natural way to describe some psychopathic killers certainly is not in terms of a confusion of thought, but of a *deficiency of feeling*. Other people do not matter to them. They do not care about anybody, they are unable to form personal ties, and so forth. This deficiency deprives them of the premise that Kant rightly thinks essential for rationality – namely, that oneself is not an exception to all rules, that what is sauce for other geese is sauce for this gander. But Butler explicitly recognizes this role of feeling here:

> Reason alone, whatever anyone may wish, is not in reality a sufficent motive of virtue in such a creature as man; but this reason joined with those affections which God has impressed upon his heart . . . Neither is affection itself at all a weakness; nor does it argue defect, any otherwise than our senses and appetites do . . . Both our senses and our passions are a supply to the imperfections of our nature . . . But it is not the supply, but the deficiency, as it is not a remedy, but the disease, which is the imperfection.[16]

Kant takes for granted that his 'naturally unsympathetic' man still comes within the range of emotional normality. So he does not see that normal emotions are as necessary for morality as thought is. Butler simply points this out. By doing so, however, he gives us what we certainly need – language to express the fact that psychopaths are not supermen. The murderer (and indeed the solitary, such as Nietzsche himself) does not have to be seen as a hero, strong enough to dispense with supports on which weaker minds rely. To represent him that way is indeed a piece of sentimental bad faith, unless we actually ourselves accept his option. It is every bit as plausible to see him as we normally see psychopaths, as an emotional cripple, stunted and incomplete because he does not have the normal equipment for a full human life. Intensity in the remaining faculties may to some extent compensate for this handicap in particular cases, as can happen with other handicaps. But all the same a handicap, and not an asset, is what such crippling is . . .

The advantage of Butler's method of making self-control

[16] Sermon 5, sec. 3.

intelligible is that it shows controller and controlled as parts of a single whole. By so doing, it gets rid of any arbitrary, despotic, or miraculous element in our notion of rationality, and shows how our development can be continuous. We begin to see how it is not ridiculous to suppose that we evolved as the kind of creatures that we are. In explaining the work of conscience, Butler's argument indeed is throughout thoroughly biological. It rests on *function*. He asks, what *use* is the conscience? He starts from what he calls a fact, namely the human tendency to reflect on our own and each other's conduct, to judge it, to accuse and excuse ourselves and other people, and to feel *shame* when we ourselves fall short. Shame particularly interests him; he asks quite simply, what is its function? And he notes the great force of such functional arguments in general: 'A man can as little doubt whether his eyes were given him to see with, as he can doubt the truth of the science of optics, deduced from ocular experiments. And allowing the inward feeling, shame, a man can as little doubt whether it was given him to prevent his doing shameful actions, as he can doubt whether his eyes were given him to guide his steps.'[17] The capacity for shame, therefore, is a part of our adaptation as social beings. Putting this question is like asking, why does this creature have legs? If the only intelligible answer is 'to get around with,' it follows that the creature is *designed*, *adapted* or *programmed* to get around; that a stationary life will not suit it, indeed will be bad for it, if only by being a waste of this important resource. Just so with the human capacity for shame and also more generally with the power of reflection – their use is practical. They are fairly central parts of us – not a peripheral one like the appendix or the kiwi's wings. So trying to ignore them will be at best wasteful and probably destructive. So they ought to be used. And in the case of conscience or reflection, Butler suggests, the argument is especially strong, because the position it seems designed for is such a central one. Outlying faculties, if neglected, might atrophy quietly, but, as he says, 'you cannot form a notion of this faculty, conscience, without taking in judgment, direction, superintendency.' Bypassing such a central nexus would be something like deciding to dispense with the central nervous system. Psychosurgery is out of place here.

[17] Sermon 2, sec. 1.

The Shared Solution

As far as people are concerned, Butler's view of how our nature is integrated seems to me thoroughly sensible and a great improvement on the colonial picture. Where it falls short is where all other accounts fall short – in oversimplifying the position about animals for the sake of the contrast.

In the human case, Butler saw plainly that reflection could not work if there were not, so to speak, some unevenness for it to get a grip on, some preexisting balance and structure among the motives, for reflection to discover when it started reflecting. For instance, he thought that both justice and truth-telling were important and valuable elements in human life, quite apart from their tending to make for happiness. It follows that impulses to be fair or truthful have a special value. Reflection recognizes this and does not create it. *Conscience is not a colonial governor imposing alien norms*; it is our nature itself, becoming aware of its own underlying pattern. It does not invent a new set of priorities; it sees those that are called for. It is not free to make up the rules of the value-game. Why, for instance, in Butler's example of entering the snare, is prolonged well-being more important than instant gratification? Because we are 'formed such sort of creatures' as to go in for long schemes, for memory, hope and regret, planning and fruition. (We might not have been.) Why is parricide[18] (another of Butler's examples) *unnatural*? Because we are brood-tending creatures, of a sort that forms bonds of affection, gratitude and cooperation in infancy, bonds that can persist and grow through life, making a great part of the creature's concern and structuring its existence.

Creatures capable of such bonds (they include, I think, all the more intelligent mammals) do not make light of them; their *use* lies in their being central to life. They are part of our animal nature, not a colonial imposition. In *On Aggression* [Konrad Lorenz, *On Aggression*, trans. M. K. Wilson (London: Methuen, 1964)] Lorenz makes this extremely important point well:

> It is a widely held opinion, shared by some contemporary philosophers, that all human behavior patterns which serve the welfare of the community, as opposed to that of the individual, are dictated by

[18] Sermon 2, sec. 17. For the related topics of ingratitude and parental care, see Sermon 1, sec. 8.

specifically human rational thought. Not only is this opinion errone-
ous, but the very opposite is true. If it were not for a rich endowment of
social instincts, man could never have risen above the animal world.
All specifically human faculties, the power of speech, cultural tradition, moral responsibility, could have evolved only in a being which,
before the very dawn of conceptual thinking, lived in well-organized
communities. Our prehuman ancestor was indubitably as true a friend
to his friend as a chimpanzee or even a dog, as tender and solicitous to
the young of his community and as self-sacrificing in its defense, aeons
before he developed conceptual thought and became aware of the
consequence of his actions.   (p. 246)

Hume missed this point by a mile because, as usual, he was trying
to think like a physicist, not like a biologist. He remarked that
parricide was not wrong for trees and would not be so even if they
had 'choice and will.'[19] Therefore, he concluded, its wrongness
for men was just a matter of feeling, and therefore contingent. This
is an excellent example of how *uncontingent* biological truths
really are. They make sense only within their proper context. Items
like 'choice and will' cannot just be tacked on to the notion of a
tree; the phrase 'choosing tree' makes no better sense than 'liquid
tree' or 'invisible elephant.' If someone wrote a story about one of
these, he could of course explain how he conceived it to work – but
he would have to have a point in doing so, and until it is done such
terms are unintelligible. Nothing, or everything equally, follows
from them; they are therefore useless. Until we understand the
nature of a given species, we cannot tell (1) what kind of 'choice' it
might be capable of, (2) what place gratitude and affection, for
instance, have in its life, or (3) whether the notion of a *parent*
makes for it any beyond genetic sense. Codfish do not, in the social
sense, have fathers at all; wolves and beavers do. For bees, the
killing of a genetic father (though never of a mother) could be
considered a duty as well as a pleasure. And many creatures are
quite willing to attack *any* intruding conspecific, and kill it if it
cannot escape. But the more intelligent animals – all those for
whom the notion of deliberate choice might conceivably make
sense – tend strongly to avoid such killing, most particularly in the
case of a close friend or relative. And this tendency is not an
isolated one, but an integral part of their whole pattern of motives.
Social bonds structure their lives. *Communication, and therefore*

---

[19] *Enquiry Concerning the Principles of Morals*, Appendix 1, sec. 243.

intelligence, develops only where there are these long-standing deep relationships. It may be possible for it to occur in another context, but if so, nobody knows what it would be like.

Hume, as so often, is bogged by his mysterious ontology by which 'all beings in the universe, considered in themselves, appear entirely loose and independent of each other.'[20] Not in this universe they don't. Experience does not work like that; it is not atomic. To experience things at all, we have to perceive them within a familiar frame of reference, and relate them to it. No principle, therefore, could be less empiricist than Hume's.

The reason Butler's contrast between man and animal is too simple is, moreover, that animals have frames of reference as well They are not just bundles of disconnected perceptions and motives. They have natures of their own, each according to their species. And actions, which can very well take place, can all the same be contrary to those natures.

Butler's example of the snare is not, in fact, especially typical of animal behavior, at least above the insect level. (It is worth noting that both the snare situation and those of the poor deluded gull and oyster catcher result from human interference, not from conditions normal to the species.) Animals that respond to a supernormal stimulus are indeed somewhat passive. But then, so are people who do so. It is the sort of case where it is only a slight exaggeration to say, with Descartes, that the creature concerned, whether human or not, does not *act*; it is acted upon. The single stimulus drives it to a single, easily predicted piece of behavior. If the whole life of other species were like this and human life never was, the contrast would be fair. But it is not. Actually, as pest-control people know all too well, animals can very often resist traps. Their natures are quite equal to the effort. Exterminating rats, in particular, is extremely hard, because rats learn so quickly from experience; they will not take a bait their leader refuses, and he is remarkably canny at this bit of induction. Loyalty, Prudence, and a little Intelligence among them beat the supernormal stimulus, for that is the nature of the rat. Human beings, on the other hand, quite often do fall into traps, not only into those laid by other human beings, but even those laid by animals, as for instance when a wounded rhinoceros circles round to lie in wait on its own trail and charge the hunter who is following it, or a man-

[20] *Treatise of Human Nature*, Bk. 3, pt. 1, sec. 1.

eating lion ambushes jungle paths. But then here, as usual, theorists are considering animals as they are, and human beings as they should be.

Every species has its own characteristic temperament, of which systematic caution is often a part. Consider, for example, what Richard Carrington says of elephants:

> The caution shown by elephants is a characteristic trait. No animal is more wary of unfamiliar objects, nor more quick to take fright for the most unaccountable reasons . . . Elephants have an instinctive preoccupation with their own safety, which amounts almost to a neurosis. For example, even domesticated elephants who have acquired great confidence in their human masters will often refuse to cross a bridge before they have tested its strength carefully with their fore-feet, or rapped it smartly with the tip of their trunk, rather as a surveyor tests the strength of a plasterboard partition. This is not to say that such behaviour reflects on the elephant's character, and on one view it could be taken as proof of his intelligence. [Richard Carrington, *Elephants* (London: Chatto & Windus, 1958), p. 76]

As elephants can weigh up to twelve tons, the last remark seems reasonable.

Again, on the equally crucial subject of sex, Carrington writes (p. 52): 'Elephants are creatures of affection, and perhaps none of the so-called lower animals enriches the purely mechanical processes of reproduction with a nicer sensibility . . . I learnt myself in India during the war how elephants often showed an affection and solicitude for their mates that could well be held up as an example to members of our own species.'

Elephants, in fact, do *not* simply do the first thing that comes into their heads, even when they are reacting to a strong outside stimulus. They are not mechanical toys. But in any case, much of the time they and other creatures are not reacting to any stimulus at all. A great part of a higher animal's life is spent in positive activity of a kind for which stimulus–response patterns are little help. We could take any stretch of the lively social goings-on watched by Schaller or Jane Goodall. Here each species busies itself according to taste – the quiet, dignified gorillas foraging and exchanging greetings, the lively volatile, outgoing chimps exploring and holding parties. Each member has complex social ties, and develops them according to its character; the conventions are well understood, and *action contrary to the nature* either of the individual or the species can be easily spotted by the experienced observer. It shows up as something *wrong*. The observer then looks for an explanation which is still within the repertory – just as he does in human affairs. (For instance, parricide occurs in humans: it can be explained – but certainly it needs explaining. *The Brothers Karamazov* is quite a long book.) With animals just as with people, the observer can use the individual's character as a guide. He can ask, how natural is it for *this* individual to do *that* surprising thing? and what circumstances might make it natural? But of course, people who do not take a species seriously do not distinguish between individual characters. Just so, Pope wrote:

> Nothing so true as what you once let fall –
> 'Most women have no character at all'.[21]

Again, consider the well-organized wolves Farley Mowat described in *Never Cry Wolf*. Angeline, the she-wolf, gets tired of playing with her cubs. She calls. Out of the den, yawning, comes a young he-wolf, the lodger, evidently sleepy. However, he proceeds to babysit and to play patiently with the cubs while she has a rest. (There are, by the way, no sexual overtones to this story.) Later, Angeline, wanting her lunch, goes down to the lake shore and lures some ducks to the bank by odd behavior which amounts to cleverly feigning madness. She nearly catches one, but it gets away. So, resigning herself to a sandwich, she finds, skillfully catches, and swallows a couple of dozen mice, then returns to the cubs while the others go out to hunt, and return with meat for the family. At another time, when the cubs are older, the adults stage a training hunt for them, carefully driving a few weaker deer toward the cubs while one older wolf remains with them to encourage them, at a time when they would not normally be hunting at all. Nothing is caught, and the adults show no anxiety to catch anything. And this hunt does not take place until George, the father wolf, has repeatedly nudged Angeline and finally stirred her into undertaking it. (Is this 'having an intention'?)

All this behavior is *active*; it is not in the least like getting caught in a snare; it will not break down into passive stimulus–response patterns. It is not mechanical but purposive, and the purpose is linked to lasting character traits expressing priorities. Serious neglect of cubs, or brutal treatment of them, would be thoroughly

---

[21] *Epistle of the Characters of Women*, 1–2.

unnatural among wolves. So would disrespectful or uncooperative behavior to elders. These things sometimes happen. But they are not just unfortunate, they are out of character; they show something *wrong*, something, as Butler said, 'disproportionate to their nature as a whole.'

Stories of this kind often have as their point disputes about intelligence. What I am talking about is, as I have said, something different and much deeper, which is taken for granted; the characteristic basic patterns of motives.

Cub care is *important* to wolves. So is affection for their friends and companions. (Indeed the two things go together; the gestures by which adults show affection are drawn from cub-rearing.) Affection is a prevailing motive. Powerful general motives like this can easily make them delay gratification of immediate desires like hunger or sleepiness. The whole pack is bound together by affection. But this affection too is not 'blind impulse'; it has a *backbone*, a structure that keeps it steady through variations of mood. All wolves have claims, which are generally recognized. And a cross or bored wolf will not just bite another; he quarrels, but he gives warning in a set and intelligible manner. Threats express his irritation; the opponent has time to get out or submit. And submission usually disarms the aggressor. A very interesting thing is that at this point a conflict of motives may be visible; one motive does not necessarily replace another smoothly and unremarked. There is *ambivalence*, conflict behavior. The dominant one refrains from biting, but still growls and snaps over his prostrate enemy, making biting and shaking movements; he won't let the loser get up for a while; when he does get up, he chases him away. Both motives are present together; the wolf is in a way identified with both, yet he must choose one for action. We have all done this. *It is surely the kind of situation out of which a real center to the personality emerges*. The choice we make determines the sort of person we are becoming.

> 'Now see I well,' said Sir Lancelot, 'that such a man I might be, I might have peace, and such a man I might be, that there should be war mortal betwixt us . . .'
>
> (Malory, *Le Morte d'Arthur*)

We tend to think of animals as not having this problem. *They do have the problem. What they do not have is our way of solving it by thinking about it. But they still have a way of solving it –*

namely, by a structure of motives that shapes their lives around a certain preferred kind of solution. If we did not have that too, thinking would get us nowhere.

My point is not just that intelligence, as it develops, is applied to these emotional conflicts. It develops partly as an adaptation to deal with them, for they are quite as serious a threat to life as hunger is, and more serious than the lack of tools. Emotional stability, a solid, continuous character, is necessary to survival. It is quite as necessary as technology, and indeed technology itself depends on it.

So reason does not develop as a neutral, computerlike, technological device, detached from all aims. Form is not a colonial import, to be stamped on brute matter. The only picture that makes evolutionary sense is the Aristotelian one where matter fits its form[22] – not the Platonic one where matter is bare negation, surd, irrational, resistant, indeed the root of all evil. The structure of feeling demands a corresponding structure of thought to complete it. The reason of a social species is not programmable in just any direction. It arises as an aspect of stability and friendliness. So we are not being silly when we expect it to know which way to look for values, what sort of order to demand. We do attach that expectation to terms like intelligence and common sense. We talk of destructive conduct as *stupid* or *irrational*, and undirected conduct as *silly*, *unreasonable*, or *insane*. When human beings reason practically about what would be best to do, they are wondering what would be best 'for such a creature as man.' The range and pattern of possible aims is given with the species. So is a character adapted to them. What counts as help or harm is not a contingent matter. Treating it as contingent, as something logically separate from morality, was Kant's mistake. For once the nature of a species (or any other system) is given, there are limits to the ways in which you can hope to make sense of it.

A computer would see no objection to organizing life on the principle of maximizing noise, getting everything as clean as possible, making everybody always tread on the lines between the paving stones,[23] or minimizing emotion. Computers are not

[22] Aristotle regarded matter as potency – the power to become some particular thing – not as a general neutral stuff (*Metaphysics*, 8.7).
[23] See Philippa Foot, 'When Is a Principle a Moral Principle?' *Proceedings of the Aristotelian Society*, Supplementary Vol. 28 (1954).

rational; they are stupid things. They do not know what *matters*; they are only consistent. The people programming them have to be rational – that is, they must be able to see the priorities among human needs. If the programmer is a simpleminded Utilitarian, he may be hard put to it to see why either justice or art should come into his system. This is because he starts with an artificially simple reduction of human needs to pleasure. *There is absolutely nothing rational about this*. Simple schemes of thought are rational only when they fit the phenomena. Human needs are actually very complex. So any system of thought that is to organize them must admit their complexity.

Yet, having admitted this, it *must* simplify to make choice possible . . . And this, of course, is what makes the colonial image so attractive. Contrasting the roaring confusion of human desires with the simple, neat, infallible system of instincts that we wrongly take animals to have, we feel that the Gordian Knot will have to be cut by some alien force named Reason – a *deus ex machina* to save desire from the consequences of its own folly. But unless you have a suggestion about where the *deus ex machina* can come from, the colonial picture makes no sense. It is quite evident that, as Lorenz says in *On Aggression*, 'like power steering in a modern car, responsible morality derives the energy which it needs to control human behavior from the same primal powers which it was created to keep in rein. Man as a purely rational being, divested of his animal heritage of instincts, would certainly not be an angel – quite the opposite' (p. 247). No carpenter shapes trees; it is the life within them that achieves that, balancing a branch here with another there, sacrificing height to strength, and vice versa. The formula is not imposed; it is essential to the creature. Equally there is nothing but the life within each of us that can resolve our conflicts – though certainly, as compared with trees or even most animals, that life has learned a trick or two. Our intelligence is part of the adaptation by which we do it, but only part. Below that lies our rough natural structure of needs. It *is* very rough. It will not work, at the best, without friction and much sacrifice. But it is there.

We want incompatible things, and want them badly. We are fairly aggressive, yet we want company and depend on long-term enterprises. We love those around us and need their love, yet we want independence and need to wander. We are restlessly curious and meddling, yet long for permanence. Unlike many primates, we do have a tendency to pair-formation, but it is an incomplete one, and gives us a lot of trouble. We cannot live without a culture, but it never quite satisfies us. All this is the commonplace of literature. It is also, to a degree, the problem of the other intelligent species too. In each, a group of counteracting needs and tendencies holds life in a rough but tolerable equilibrium. In each there are endemic conflicts. Yet an individual depends for his satisfaction on the repertory of tastes native to his species; he cannot jump off his feet. What is special about people is their power of understanding what is going on, and using that understanding to regulate it. Imagination and conceptual thought intensify all the conflicts by multiplying the options, by letting us form all manner of incompatible schemes and allowing us to know what we are missing, and also by greatly increasing our powers of self-deception. As against that, they can give us self-knowledge, which is our strongest card in the attempt to sort conflicts out. It is to deepen that self-knowledge that I want to use comparison with other species.

G. E. M. ANSCOMBE (1919–   )

Elizabeth Anscombe was educated at St Hugh's College, Oxford. She held a Research Fellowship at Newnham College, Cambridge, from 1941 until 1944, and it was there that she met Wittgenstein, attended his seminars and became an unusually trusted and faithful disciple. (There is no other way to describe those people who were close to Wittgenstein in Cambridge at this period. But some of them offended him in one way or another, often by borrowing or publicizing his work or allegedly distorting it; and if they offended they were cast off.) In 1946, back in Oxford, Elizabeth Anscombe became a Research Fellow of Somerville, where she remained as a Fellow until 1970, when she was appointed to the Chair of Philosophy in Cambridge. She retired in 1986. She is an Honorary Fellow of New Hall, Cambridge, and of Somerville and St Hugh's in Oxford.

We come here to the undoubted giant among women philosophers, a writer of immense breadth, authority and penetration. Elizabeth Anscombe published *Intention* in 1957, followed by *An Introduction to Wittgenstein's Tractatus* in 1959. In 1961, with her husband, the philosopher Peter Geach, she published *Three Philosophers: Aristotle, Aquinas, Frege*. Her collected philosophical papers are published in three important volumes, *From Parmenides to Wittgenstein*, *Metaphysics and the Philosophy of Mind* and *Ethics, Religion and Politics*. It is from the middle volume that I have taken her Cambridge inaugural lecture. In many ways this lecture is characteristic of her work. It is scholarly (unlike her master, Wittgenstein, she has no inclination to pretend never to have read any earlier philosophers; indeed, all her work is based firmly and explicitly on the insights or the errors of philosophers of the past). It identifies and examines presuppositions, whether those of philosophers or of ordinary language-users, about a central concept, in this case the concept of causality; and it is written with immense care, force and clarity. She is a truly original philosopher, making new connections, constantly opening one's eyes to new questions or to new aspects of the philosophy of the past. She has always been totally dedicated to the dialogue that is central to philosophy.

Further Reading

Wittgenstein, Ludwig, *Notebooks 1914–16*, ed. G. H. von Wright and G. E. M. Anscombe; trans. G. E. M. Anscombe (Oxford: Blackwell, 1961

——[*On Certainty*] *Über Gewissheit*, ed. G. E. M. Anscombe and G. H. von Wright; trans. D. Paul and G. E. M. Anscombe (Oxford: Blackwell, 1969)

——*Philosophical Investigations*, trans. G. E. M. Anscombe, 3rd edn (Oxford: Blackwell, 1968)

——*Remarks on Colour*, ed. G. E. M. Anscombe; trans. Linda L. McAlister and Margarete Schättler (Oxford: Blackwell, 1977)

——[*Remarks on the Foundations of Mathematics*] *Bemerkungen über die Grundlagen der Mathematik*, ed. G. H. von Wright, R. Rhees and G. E. M. Anscombe; trans. G. E. M. Anscombe (Oxford: Blackwell, 1961)

——*Remarks on the Philosophy of Psychology*, ed. G. E. M. Anscombe, G. H. von Wright and Heikki Nyman (Oxford: Blackwell, 1980)

——*Zettel*, ed. G. E. M. Anscombe and G. H. von Wright; trans. G. E. M. Anscombe (Oxford: Blackwell, 1967)

A. Kenny, *Wittgenstein* (London: Allen Lane, 1973)

Intention and Intentionality: Essays in Honour of G. E. M. Anscombe, ed. Cora Diamond and Jenny Teichman (Brighton: Harvester, 1979)

From G. E. M. Anscombe, Metaphysics and the Philosophy of Mind *(Oxford: Blackwell, 1981), chapter 13: 'Causality and determination'*

I

It is often declared or evidently assumed that causality is some kind of necessary connection, or alternatively, that being caused is – non-trivially – instancing some exceptionless generalization saying that such an event always follows such antecedents. Or the two conceptions are combined.

Obviously there can be, and are, a lot of divergent views covered by this account. Any view that it covers nevertheless manifests one particular doctrine or assumption. Namely:

If an effect occurs in one case and a similar effect does not occur in an apparently similar case, there must be a relevant further difference.

Any radically different account of causation, then, by contrast with which all those diverse views will be as one, will deny this assumption. Such a radically opposing view can grant that often – though it is difficult to say generally when – the assumption of relevant difference is a sound principle of investigation. It may grant that there are necessitating causes, but will refuse to identify causation as such with necessitation. It can grant that there are situations in which, given the initial conditions and no interference, only one result will accord with the laws of nature; but it will not see general reason, in advance of discovery, to suppose that any given course of things has been so determined. So it may grant that in many cases difference of issue can rightly convince us of a relevant difference of circumstances; but it will deny that, quite generally, this *must* be so.

The first view is common to many philosophers of the past. It is also, usually but not always in a neo-Humeian form, the prevailing received opinion throughout the currently busy and productive philosophical schools of the English-speaking world, and also in some of the European and Latin American schools where philosophy is pursued in at all the same sort of way; nor is it confined to these schools. So firmly rooted is it that for many even outside pure philosophy, it routinely determines the meaning of 'cause', when consciously used as a theoretical term: witness the terminology of the contrast between 'causal' and 'statistical' laws, which is drawn by writers on physics – writers, note, who would not conceive themselves to be addicts of any philosophic school when they use this language to express that contrast.

The truth of this conception is hardly debated. It is, indeed, a bit of *Weltanschauung*: it helps to form a cast of mind which is characteristic of our whole culture.

The association between causation and necessity is old; it occurs for example in Aristotle's *Metaphysics*: 'When the agent and patient meet suitably to their powers, the one acts and the other is acted on OF NECESSITY.' Only with 'rational powers' an extra feature is needed to determine the result: 'What has a rational power [e.g. medical knowledge, which can kill *or* cure] OF NECESSITY does what it has the power to do and as it has the power, when it has the desire' (Book IX, Chapter v).

Overleaping the centuries, we find it an axiom in Spinoza: 'Given a determinate cause, the effect follows OF NECESSITY, and without its cause, no effect follows' (*Ethics*, Book I, Axiom III). And in the English philosopher Hobbes:

> A cause simply, or an entire cause, is the aggregate of all the accidents both of the agents how many soever they be, and of the patients, put together; which when they are supposed to be present, IT CANNOT BE UNDERSTOOD BUT THAT THE EFFECT IS PRODUCED at the same instant; and if any of them be wanting, IT CANNOT BE UNDERSTOOD BUT THAT THE EFFECT IS NOT PRODUCED.
>
> (*Elements of Philosophy Concerning Body*, Chapter IX)

It was this last view, where the connection between cause and effect is evidently seen as *logical* connection of some sort, that was overthrown by Hume, the most influential of all philosophers on this subject in the English-speaking and allied schools. For he made us see that, given any particular cause . . . and its effect, there is not in general any contradiction in supposing the one to occur and the other not to occur. That is to say, we'd know what was being described – what it would be like for it to be true – if it were reported for example that a kettle of water was put, and kept, directly on a hot fire, but the water did not heat up.

Were it not for the preceding philosophers who had made causality out as some species of logical connection, one would wonder at this being called a discovery on Hume's part: for vulgar humanity has always been over-willing to believe in miracles and marvels and *lusus naturae*. Mankind at large saw no contradiction, where Hume worked so hard to show the philosophic world – the Republic of Letters – that there was none.

The discovery was thought to be great. But as touching the equation of causality with necessitation, Hume's thinking did nothing against this but curiously reinforced it. For he himself assumed that NECESSARY CONNECTION is an essential part of the idea of the relation of cause and effect (*Treatise of Human Nature*, Book I, Part III, Sections ii and vi), and he sought for its nature. He thought this could not be found in the situations, objects or events called 'causes' and 'effects', but was to be found in the human

mind's being determined, by experience of CONSTANT CONJUNC-
TION, to pass from the sensible impression or memory of one term
of the relation to the convinced idea of the other. Thus to say that
an event was caused was to say that its occurrence was an instance
of some exceptionless generalization connecting such an event
with such antecedents as it occurred in. The twist that Hume gave
to the topic thus suggested a connection of the notion of causality
with that of deterministic laws – i.e. laws such that always, given
initial conditions and the laws, a unique result is determined.

The well-known philosophers who have lived after Hume may
have aimed at following him and developing at least some of his
ideas, or they may have put up a resistance; but in no case, so far as
I know, has the resistance called in question the equation of
causality with necessitation.

Kant, roused by learning of Hume's discovery, laboured to
establish causality as an *a priori* conception and argued that the
objective time order consists 'in that order of the manifold of
appearance according to which, IN CONFORMITY WITH A RULE,
the apprehension of that which happens follows upon the
apprehension of that which precedes . . . In conformity with such a
rule there must be in that which precedes an event the condition of
a rule according to which this event INVARIABLY and NECESSA-
RILY follows' (*Critique of Pure Reason*, Book II, Chapter II,
Section iii, Second Analogy). Thus Kant tried to give back to
causality the character of a *justified* concept which Hume's
considerations had taken away from it. Once again the connection
between causation and necessity was reinforced. And this has been
the general characteristic of those who have sought to oppose
Hume's conception of causality. They have always tried to
establish the necessitation that they saw in causality: either *a
priori*, or somehow out of experience.

Since Mill it has been fairly common to explain causation one
way or another in terms of 'necessary' and 'sufficient' conditions.
Now 'sufficient condition' is a term of art whose users may
therefore lay down its meaning as they please. So they are in their
rights to rule out the query: 'May not the sufficient conditions of
an event be present, and the event yet not take place?' For
'sufficient condition' is so used that if the sufficient conditions for
X are there, X occurs. But at the same time, the phrase cozens the
understanding into not noticing an assumption. For 'sufficient
condition' sounds like: 'enough'. And one certainly *can* ask: 'May

there not be *enough* to have made something happen – and yet it not have happened?'

Russell wrote of the notion of cause, or at any rate of the 'law of causation' (and he seemed to feel the same way about 'cause' itself), that, like the British monarchy, it had been allowed to survive because it had been erroneously thought to do no harm. In a destructive essay of great brilliance he cast doubt on the notion of necessity involved, unless it is explained in terms of universality, and he argued that upon examination the concepts of determination and of invariable succession of like objects upon like turn out to be empty: they do not differentiate between any conceivable course of things and any other. Thus Russell too assumes that necessity or universality is what is in question, and it never occurs to him that there may be any other conception of causality ('The Notion of Cause', in *Mysticism and Logic*).

Now it's not difficult to show it prima facie wrong to associate the notion of cause with necessity or universality in this way. For, it being much easier to trace effects back to causes with certainty than to predict effects from causes, we often know a cause without knowing whether there is an exceptionless generalization of the kind envisaged, or whether there is a necessity.

For example, we have found certain diseases to be contagious. If, then, I have had one and only one contact with someone suffering from such a disease, and I get it myself, we suppose I got it from him. But what if, having had the contact, I ask a doctor whether I will get the disease? He will usually only be able to say, 'I don't know – maybe you will, maybe not.'

But, it is said, knowledge of causes here is partial; doctors seldom even know any of the conditions under which one invariably gets a disease, let alone all the sets of conditions. This comment betrays the assumption that there is such a thing to know. Suppose there is: still, the question whether there is does not have to be settled before we can know what we mean by speaking of the contact as cause of my getting the disease.

All the same, might it not be like this: knowledge of causes is possible without any satisfactory grasp of what is involved in causation? Compare the possibility of wanting clarification of 'valency' or 'long-run frequency', which yet have been handled by chemists and statisticians without such clarification; and valencies and long-run frequencies, whatever the right way of explaining them, have been known. Thus one of the familiar philosophic analyses of causality, or a new one in the same line, may be correct, though knowledge of it is not necessary for knowledge of causes.

There is something to observe here, that lies under our noses. It is little attended to, and yet still so obvious as to seem trite. It is this: causality consists in the derivativeness of an effect from its causes. This is the core, the common feature, of causality in its various kinds. Effects derive from, arise out of, come of, their causes. For example, everyone will grant that physical parenthood is a causal relation. Here the derivation is material, by fission. Now analysis in terms of necessity or universality does not tell us of this derivedness of the effect; rather it forgets about that. For the necessity will be that of laws of nature; through it *we* shall be able to derive knowledge of the effect from knowledge of the cause, or vice versa, but that does not show us the cause as source of the effect. Causation, then, is not to be identified with necessitation.

If *A* comes from *B*, this does not imply that every *A*-like thing comes from some *B*-like thing or set-up or that every *B*-like thing or set-up has an *A*-like thing coming from it; or that given *B*, *A* had to come from it, or that given *A*, there had to be *B* for it to come from. Any of these may be true, but if any is, that will be an additional fact, not comprised in *A*'s coming from *B*. If we take 'coming from' in the sense of travel, this is perfectly evident.

'But that's because we can observe travel!' The influential Humeian argument at this point is that we can't similarly observe causality in the individual case (ibid. Book I, Part III, Section ii.) So the reason why we connect what we call the cause and what we call the effect as we do must lie elsewhere. It must lie in the fact that the succession of the latter upon the former is of a kind regularly observed.

There are two things for me to say about this. First, as to the statement that we can never observe causality in the individual case. Someone who says this is just not going to count anything as 'observation of causality'. This often happens in philosophy; it is argued that 'all we find' is such-and-such, and it turns out that the arguer has excluded from his idea of 'finding' the sort of thing he says we don't 'find'. And when we consider what we are allowed to say we do 'find', we have the right to turn the tables on Hume, and say that neither do we perceive bodies, such as billiard balls, approaching one another. When we 'consider the matter with the utmost attention', we find only an impression of travel made by the successive positions of a round white patch in our visual fields . . . etc. Now a 'Humeian' account of causality has to be given in terms of constant conjunction of physical things, events, etc., not of experiences of them. If, then, it must be allowed that we 'find' bodies in motion, for example, then what theory of perception can justly disallow the perception of a lot of causality? The truthful – though unhelpful – answer to the question 'How did we come by our primary knowledge of causality?' is that in learning to speak we learned the linguistic representation and application of a host of causal concepts. Very many of them were represented by transitive and other verbs of action used in reporting what is observed. Others – a good example is 'infect' – form, not observation statements, but rather expressions of causal hypotheses. The word 'cause' itself is highly general. How does someone show that he has the concept *cause*? We may wish to say: only by having such a word in his vocabulary. If so, then the manifest possession of the concept presupposes the mastery of much else in language. I mean: the word 'cause' can be *added* to a language in which are already represented many causal concepts. A small selection: *scrape, push, wet, carry, eat, burn, knock over, keep off, squash, make* (e.g. noises, paper boats), *hurt*. But if we care to imagine languages in which no special causal concepts are represented, then no description of the use of a word in such languages will be able to present it as meaning *cause*. Nor will it even contain words for natural kinds of stuff, nor yet words equivalent to 'body', 'wind', or 'fire'. For learning to use special causal verbs is part and parcel of learning to apply the concepts answering to these and many other substantives. As surely as we learned to call people by name or to report from seeing it that the cat was on the table, we also learned to report from having observed it that someone drank up the milk or that the dog made a funny noise or that things were cut or broken by whatever we saw cut or break them.

(I will mention, only to set on one side, one of the roots of Hume's argument, the implicit appeal to Cartesian scepticism. He confidently challenges us to 'produce some instance, wherein the efficacy is plainly discoverable to the mind, and its operations obvious to our consciousness or sensation' (ibid. Book I, Part III, Section xiv). Nothing easier: is cutting, is drinking, is purring not 'efficacy'? But it is true that the apparent perception of such things may be only apparent: we may be deceived by false appearances. Hume presumably wants us to 'produce an instance' in which *efficacy* is related to sensation as *red* is. It is true that we can't do that; it is not *so* related to sensation. He is also helped, in making his argument that we don't perceive 'efficacy', by his curious belief that 'efficacy' means much the same thing as 'necessary connection'! But as to the Cartesian-sceptical root of the argument, I will not delay upon it, as my present topic is not the philosophy of perception.)

Second, as to that instancing of a universal generalization, which was supposed to supply what could not be observed in the individual case, the causal relation, the needed examples are none too common. 'Motion in one body in all past instances that have fallen under our observation, is follow'd upon impulse by motion in another': so Hume (ibid. Book II, Part III, Section i). But, as is always a danger in making large generalizations, he was thinking only of the cases where we do observe this – billiard balls against free-standing billiard balls in an ordinary situation; not billiard balls against stone walls. Neo-Humeians are more cautious. They realize that if you take a case of cause and effect, and relevantly describe the cause A and the effect B, and then construct a universal proposition, 'Always, given an A, a B follows' you usually won't get anything true. You have got to describe the absence of circumstances in which an A would not cause a B. But the task of excluding all such circumstances can't be carried out. There is, I suppose, a vague association in people's minds between the universal propositions which would be examples of the required type of generalizations, and scientific laws. But there is no similarity.

Suppose we were to call propositions giving the properties of substances 'laws of nature'. Then there will be a law of nature running 'The flash-point of such a substance is . . .', and this will be important in explaining why striking matches usually causes them to light. This law of nature has not the form of a generalization running 'Always, if a sample of such a substance is raised to such a temperature, it ignites'; nor is it equivalent to such a generalization, but rather to: 'If a sample of such a substance is raised to such a temperature and doesn't ignite, there must be a cause of its not doing so.' Leaving aside questions connected with the idea of a pure sample, the point here is that 'normal conditions' is quite properly a vague notion. That fact makes generalizations running 'Always . . .' merely fraudulent in such cases; it will always be necessary for them to be hedged about with clauses referring to normal conditions; and we may not know in advance whether conditions are normal or not, or what to count as an abnormal condition. In exemplar analytical practice, I suspect, it will simply be a relevant condition in which the generalization 'Always if such and such, such and such happens . . .', supplemented with a few obvious conditions that have occurred to the author, turns out to be untrue. Thus the conditional 'If it doesn't ignite then there must be some cause' is the better gloss upon the original proposition, for it does not pretend to say specifically, or even disjunctively specifically, what *always* happens. It is probably these facts which make one hesitate to call propositions about the action of substances 'laws of nature'. The law of inertia, for example, would hardly be glossed: 'If a body accelerates without any force acting on it, there must be some cause of its doing so.' (Though I wonder what the author of *Principia* himself would have thought of that.) On the other hand just such 'laws' as that about a substance's flash-point are connected with the match's igniting because struck.

Returning to the medical example, medicine is of course not interested in the hopeless task of constructing lists of all the sets of conditions under each of which people always get a certain disease. It is interested in finding what that is special, if anything, is always the case when people get a particular disease; and, given such a cause or condition (or in any case), in finding circumstances in which people don't get the disease, or tend not to. This is connected with medicine's concern first, and last, with things as they happen in the messy and mixed-up conditions of life: only between its first and its last concern can it look for what happens unaffected by uncontrolled and inconstant conditions.

II

Yet my argument lies always open to the charge of appealing to ignorance. I must therefore take a different sort of example.

Here is a ball lying on top of some others in a transparent vertical pipe. I know how it got there: it was forcibly ejected with many others out of a certain aperture into the enclosed space above a row of adjacent pipes. The point of the whole construction is to show how a totality of balls so ejected always build up in rough conformity to the same curve. But I am interested in this one ball. Between its ejection and its getting into this pipe, it kept hitting sides, edges, other balls. If I made a film of it I could run it off in slow motion and tell the impact which produced each stage of the journey. Now was the result necessary? We would probably all have said it was in the time when Newton's mechanics was undisputed for truth. It was the impression made on Hume and later philosophers by that mechanics, that gave them so strong a conviction of the iron necessity with which everything happens, the 'absolute fate' by which 'Every object is determin'd to a certain degree and direction of its motion' (*A Treatise of Human Nature*, Book II, Part III, Section i).

Yet no one could have deduced the resting place of the ball – because of the indeterminateness that you get even in the Newtonian mechanics, arising from the finite accuracy of measurements. From exact figures for positions, velocities, directions, spins and masses you might be able to calculate the result as accurately as you chose. But the minutest inexactitudes will multiply up factor by factor, so that in a short time your information is gone. Assuming a given margin of error in your initial figure, you could assign an associated probability to that ball's falling into each of the pipes. If you want the highest probability you assign to be really high, so that you can take it as practical certainty, it will be a problem to reckon how tiny the permitted margins of inaccuracy must be – analogous to the problem: how small a fraction of a grain of millet must I demand is put on the first square of the chess board, if after doubling up at every square I end up having to pay out only a pound of millet? It would be a figure of such smallness as to have no meaning as a figure for a margin of error.

However, so long as you believed the classical mechanics you might also think there could be no such thing as a figure for a difference that had no meaning. Then you would think that though it was not feasible for us to find the necessary path of the ball because our margins of error are too great, yet there *was* a necessary path, which could be assigned a sufficient probability for firm acceptance of it, by anyone (not one of us) capable of reducing his limits of accuracy in measurement to a sufficiently small compass. Admittedly, so small a compass that he'd be down among the submicroscopic particles and no longer concerned with the measurements, say, of the ball. And now we can say: with certain degrees of smallness we get to a region for which Newton's mechanics is no longer believed.

If the classical mechanics can be used to calculate a certain real result, we may give a sense to, and grant, the 'necessity' of the result, given the antecedents. Here, however, you can't use the mechanics to calculate the result, but at most to give yourself a belief in its necessity. For this to be reasonable the system has got to be acknowledged as true. Not, indeed, that that would be enough; but if so much were secured, then it would be worthwhile to discuss the metaphysics of absolute measures of continuous quantities.

The point needs some labouring precisely because 'the system does apply to such bodies' – that is, to moderately massive balls . . . 'The system applies to these bodies' is true only in the sense and to the extent that it yields sufficient results of calculations about these bodies. It does not mean: in respect of these bodies the system is the truth, so that it just doesn't matter that we can't use it to calculate such a result in such a case. I am not saying that a deterministic system involves individual predictability: it evidently does not. But in default of predictability the determinedness declared by the deterministic system has got to be believed because the system itself is believed.

I conclude that we have no ground for calling the path of the ball determined – at least, until it has taken its path – but, it may be objected, is not each stage of its path determined, even though we cannot determine it? My argument had partly relied on loss of information through multiplicity of impacts. But from one impact to the next the path is surely determined, and so the whole path is so after all.

It sounds plausible to say: each stage is determined and so the whole is. But what does 'determined' mean? The word is a curious one (with a curious history); in this sort of context it is often used as if it *meant* 'caused'. Or perhaps 'caused' is used as if it meant 'determined'. But there is at any rate one important difference – a thing hasn't been caused until it has happened; but it may be determined before it happens.

(It is important here to distinguish between being *determined* and being *determinate*. In indeterministic physics there is an apparent failure of both. I am concerned only with the former.)

When we call a result determined we are implicitly relating it to an antecedent range of possibilities and saying that all but one of these is disallowed. What disallows them is not the result itself but something antecedent to the result. The antecedences may be logical or temporal or in the order of knowledge. Of the many –

antecedent – possibilities, *now* only one is – antecedently – possible.

Mathematical formulae and human decisions are limiting cases; the former because of the obscurity of the notion of antecedent possibilities, and the latter because decisions can be retrieved.

In a chess-game, the antecedent possibilities are, say, the powers of the pieces. By the rules, a certain position excludes all but one of the various moves that were in that sense antecedently possible. This is logical antecedence. The next move is determined.

In the zygote, sex and eye-colour are already determined. Here the antecedent possibilities are the possibilities for sex and eye-colour for a child; or more narrowly: for a child of these parents. *Now*, given the combination of this ovum and this spermatozoon, all but one of these antecedent possibilities is excluded.

It might be said that anything was determined once it had happened. There is now no possibility open: it *has* taken place! It was in this sense that Aristotle said that past and present were necessary. But this does not concern us: what interests us is *pre*-determination.

Then 'each stage of the ball's path is determined' must mean 'Upon any impact, there is only one path possible for the ball up to the next impact (and assuming no air currents, etc.).' But what ground could one have for believing this, if one does not believe in some system of which it is a consequence? Consider a steel ball dropping between two pins on a Galton board to hit the pin centred under the gap between them. That it should balance on this pin is not to be expected. It has two possibilities; to go to the right or to the left. If you have a system which forces this on you, you can say: 'There has to be a determining factor; otherwise, like Buridan's ass, the ball must balance.' But if you have not, then you should say that the ball may be undetermined until it does move to the right or the left. Here the ball had only two significant possibilities and was perhaps unpredetermined between them. This was because it cannot be called determined – no reasonable account can be given of insisting that it is so – within a small range of possibility, actualization within which will lead on to its falling either to the right or to the left. With our flying ball there will also be such a small range of possibility. The further consequences of the path it may take are not tied down to just two significant possibilities, as with one step down the Galton board: the range of further possibility gets wider as we consider the paths it may take. Otherwise, the two cases are similar.

We see that to give content to the idea of something's being determined, we have to have a set of possibilities, which something narrows down to one – before the event.

This accords well with our understanding of part of the dissatisfaction of some physicists with the quantum theory. They did not like the undeterminedness of individual quantum phenomena. Such a physicist might express himself by saying 'I believe in causality!' He meant: I believe that the real physical laws and the initial conditions must entail uniqueness of result. Of course, within a range of co-ordinate and mutually exclusive identifiable possible results, only one happens: he means that the result that happens ought to be understood as the only one that was possible before it happened.

Must such a physicist be a 'determinist'? That is, must he believe that the whole universe is a system such that, if its total states at t and t' are thus and so, the laws of nature are such as then to allow only one possibility for its total state at any other time? No. He may not think that the idea of a total state of the universe at a time is one he can do anything with. He may even have no views on the uniqueness of possible results for whatever may be going on in any arbitrary volume of space. For 'Our theory should be such that only the actual result was possible for that experiment' doesn't mean 'Our theory should have excluded the experiment's being muffed or someone's throwing a boot, so that we didn't get the result', but rather: 'Our theory should be such that only this result was possible as *the result of the experiment*.' He hates a theory, even if he has to put up with it for the time being, that essentially assigns only probability to a result, essentially allows of a range of possible results, never narrowed down to one until the event itself.

It must be admitted that such dissatisfied physicists very often have been determinists. Witness Schrödinger's account of the 'principle of causality': 'The exact physical situation at *any* point P at a given moment t is unambiguously determined by the exact physical situation within a certain surrounding of P at any previous time, say $t - \tau$. If τ is large, that is if that previous time lies far back, it may be necessary to know the previous situation for a wide domain around P' (*Science and Humanism*). Or Einstein's more modest version of a notorious earlier claim: if you knew all about the contents of a sphere of radius 186,000 miles, and knew the laws, you would be able to know for sure what would happen at the centre for the next second. Schrödinger says: *any* point *P*; and *a* means *any* sphere of that radius. So their view of causality was not that of my hypothetical physicist, who I said may not have views on the uniqueness of possible results for whatever may be going on in any arbitrary volume of space. My physicist restricts his demand for uniqueness of result to situations in which he has got certain processes going in isolation from inconstant external influences, or where they do not matter, as the weather on a planet does not matter for predicting its course round the sun.

The high success of Newton's astronomy was in one way an intellectual disaster: it produced an illusion from which we tend still to suffer. This illusion was created by the circumstance that Newton's mechanics *had a good model in the solar system*. For this gave the impression that we had here an ideal of scientific explanation; whereas the truth was, it was mere obligingness on the part of the solar system, by having had so peaceful a history in recorded time, to provide such a model. For suppose that some planet had at some time erupted with such violence that its shell was propelled rocket-like out of the solar system. Such an event would not have violated Newton's laws; on the contrary, it would have illustrated them. But also it would not have been calculable as the past and future motions of the planets are presently calculated on the assumption that they can be treated as the simple 'bodies' of his mechanics, with no relevant properties but mass, position and velocity and no forces mattering except gravity.

Let us pretend that Newton's laws were still to be accepted without qualification: no reserve in applying them in electrody-namics; no restriction to bodies travelling a good deal slower than light; and no quantum phenomena. Newton's mechanics is a deterministic system; but this does not mean that believing them commits us to determinism. We could say: of course nothing violates those axioms or the laws of the force of gravity. But animals, for example, run about the world in all sorts of paths and no path is dictated for them by those laws, as it is for planets. Thus in relation to the solar system (apart from questions like whether in the past some planet has blown up), the laws are like the rules of an infantile card game: once the cards are dealt we turn them up in turn, and make two piles each, one red, one black; the winner has the biggest pile of red ones. So once the cards are dealt the game is determined, and from any position in it you can derive all others back to the deal and forward to win or draw. But in relation to what happens on and inside a planet the laws are, rather, like the rules of chess; the play is seldom determined, though nobody breaks the rules.[1]

Why this difference? A natural answer is: the mechanics does not give the special laws of all the forces. Not, for example, for thermal, nuclear, electrical, chemical, muscular forces. And now the Newtonian model suggests the picture: given the laws of all the forces, then there is total coverage of what happens and then the whole game of motion is determined; for, by the first law, any acceleration implies a force of some kind, and must not forces have laws? My hypothetical physicist at least would think so; and would demand that they be deterministic. Nevertheless he still does not have to be a 'determinist'; for many forces, unlike gravity, can be switched on and off, are generated, and also shields can be put up against them. It is one thing to hold that in a clear-cut situation – an astronomical or a well-contrived experimental one designed to discover laws – 'the result' should be determined, and quite another to say that in the hurly-burly of many crossing contingencies whatever happens next must be determined; or to say that the generation of forces (by human experimental procedures, among other things) is always determined in advance of the generating procedure; or to say that there is always a law of composition, of such a kind that the combined effect of a set of forces is determined in every situation.

Someone who is inclined to say those things, or implicitly to assume them, has almost certainly been affected by the impressive relation between Newton's mechanics and the solar system:

> We remember how it was in mechanics. By knowing the position and velocity of a particle at one single instant, by knowing the acting forces, the whole future path of the particle could be foreseen. In Maxwell's theory, if we know the field at one instant only, we can deduce from the equations of the theory how the whole field will change in space and time. Maxwell's equations enable us to follow the history of the field, just as the mechanical equations enabled us to follow the history of material particles . . . With the help of Newton's laws we can deduce

[1] I should have made acknowledgements to Gilbert Ryle (*Concept of Mind*, p. 77) for this comparison. But his use of the openness of chess is somewhat ambiguous and is not the same as mine. For the contrast with a closed card game I was indebted to A. J. P. Kenny.

the motion of the earth from the force acting between the sun and the earth.[2]

'By knowing the acting forces' – that must of course include the *future* acting forces, not merely the present ones. And similarly for the equations which enable us to follow the history of the field; a change may be produced by an external influence. In reading both Newton and later writers one is often led to ponder that word 'external'. Of course, to be given 'the acting forces' is to be given the external forces too and any new forces that may later be introduced into the situation. Thus those first sentences are true, if true, without the special favour of fate, being general truths of mechanics and physics, but the last one is true by favour, by the brute fact that only the force acting between earth and sun matters for the desired deductions.

The concept of necessity, as it is connected with causation, can be explained as follows: a cause C is a necessitating cause of an effect E *when* (I mean: on the occasions when) if C occurs it is certain to cause E unless something prevents it. C and E are to be understood as general expressions, not singular terms. If 'certainty' should seem too epistemological a notion: a necessitating cause C of a given kind of effect E is such that it is not possible (on the occasion) that C should occur and should not cause an E, given that there is nothing that prevents an E from occurring. A non-necessitating cause is then one that can fail of its effect without the intervention of anything to frustrate it. We may discover *types* of necessitating and non-necessitating cause; e.g. rabies is a necessitating cause of death, because it is not possible for one who has rabies to survive without treatment. We don't have to tie it to the occasion. An example of a non-necessitating cause is mentioned by Feynman: a bomb is connected with a Geiger counter, so that it will go off if the Geiger counter registers a certain reading; whether it will or not is not determined, for it is so placed near some radioactive material that it may or may not register that reading.

There would be no doubt of the cause of the reading or of the explosion if the bomb did go off. Max Born is one of the people who has been willing to dissociate causality from determinism: he explicates cause and effect in terms of dependence of the effect on the cause. It is not quite clear what 'dependence' is supposed to be,

[2] Albert Einstein and Leopold Infeld, *The Evolution of Physics* (New York, 1938; paperback edn 1967), p. 146.

but at least it seems to imply that you would not get the effect without the cause. The trouble about this is that you might – from some other cause. That this effect was produced by this cause does not at all show that it could not, or would not, have been produced by something else in the absence of this cause.

Indeterminism is not a possibility unconsidered by philosophers. C. D. Broad, in his inaugural lecture, given in 1934, described it as a possibility; but added that whatever happened without being determined was accidental. He did not explain what he meant by being accidental; he must have meant more than not being necessary. He may have meant being uncaused; but, if I am right, not being determined does not imply not being caused. Indeed, I should explain indeterminism as the thesis that not all physical effects are necessitated by their causes. But if we think of Feynman's bomb, we get some idea of what is meant by 'accidental'. It was random: it 'merely happened' that the radioactive material emitted particles in such a way as to activate the Geiger counter enough to set off the bomb. Certainly the motion of the Geiger counter's needle is caused; and the actual emission is caused too; it occurs because there is this mass of radioactive material here. (I have already indicated that, contrary to the opinion of Hume, there are many different sorts of causality.) But all the same the *causation* itself is, one could say, *mere hap*. It is difficult to explain this idea any further.

Broad used the idea to argue that indeterminism, if applied to human action, meant that human actions are 'accidental'. Now he had a picture of choices as being determining causes, analogous to determining physical causes, and of choices in their turn being either determined or accidental. To regard a choice as such – i.e. any case of choice – as a predetermining causal event, now appears as a naive mistake in the philosophy of mind, though that is a story I cannot tell here.

It was natural that when physics went indeterministic, some thinkers should have seized on this indeterminism as being just what was wanted for defending the freedom of the will. They received severe criticism on two counts: one, that this 'mere hap' is the very last thing to be invoked as the physical correlate of 'man's ethical behaviour'; the other, that quantum laws predict statistics of events when situations are repeated; interference with these, by the *will*'s determining individual events which the laws of nature leave undetermined, would be as much a violation of natural law as would have been interference which falsified a deterministic mechanical law.

Ever since Kant it has been a familiar claim among philosophers that one can believe in both physical determinism and 'ethical' freedom. The reconciliations have always seemed to me to be either so much gobbledegook, or to make the alleged freedom of action quite unreal. My actions are mostly physical movements; if these physical movements are physically predetermined by processes which I do not control, then my freedom is perfectly illusory. The truth of physical indeterminism is thus indispensable if we are to make anything of the claim to freedom. But certainly it is insufficient. The physically undetermined is not thereby 'free'. For freedom at least involves the power of acting according to an idea, and no such thing is ascribed to whatever is the subject (what would be the relevant subject?) of unpredetermination in indeterministic physics. Nevertheless, there is nothing unacceptable about the idea that that 'physical haphazard' should be the only physical correlate of human freedom of action; and perhaps also of the voluntariness and intentionalness in the conduct of other animals which we do not call 'free'. The freedom, intentionalness and voluntariness are not to be analysed as the same thing as, or as produced by, the physical haphazard. Different sorts of pattern altogether are being spoken of when we mention them, from those involved in describing elementary processes of physical causality.

The other objection is, I think, more to the point. Certainly if we have a statistical law, but undetermined individual events, and then enough of these are supposed to be pushed by will in one direction to falsify the statistical law, we have again a supposition that puts will into conflict with natural laws. But it is not at all clear that the same train of minute physical events should have to be the regular correlate of the same action; in fact, that suggestion looks immensely implausible. It is, however, required by the objection.

Let me construct an analogy to illustrate this point. Suppose that we have a large glass box full of millions of extremely minute coloured particles, and the box is constantly shaken. Study of the box and particles leads to statistical laws, including laws for the random generation of small unit patches of uniform colour. Now the box is remarkable for also presenting the following phenomenon: the word 'Coca-Cola' formed like a mosaic, can always be read when one looks at one of the sides. It is not always the same shape in the formation of its letters, not always the same size or in the same position, it varies in its colours; but there it always is. It is not at all clear that those statistical laws concerning the random motion of the particles and their formation of small unit patches of colour would have to be supposed violated by the operation of a cause for this phenomenon which did not derive it from the statistical laws.

It has taken the inventions of indeterministic physics to shake the rather common dogmatic conviction that determinism is a presupposition, or perhaps a conclusion, of scientific knowledge. Not that that conviction has been very much shaken even so. Of course, the belief that the laws of nature are deterministic has been shaken. But I believe it has often been supposed that this makes little difference to the assumption of macroscopic determinism: as if undeterminedness were always encapsulated in systems whose internal workings could be described only by statistical laws, but where the total upshot, and in particular the outward effect, was as near as makes no difference always the same. What difference does it make, after all, that the scintillations whereby my watch dial is luminous follow only a statistical law – so long as the gross manifest effect is sufficiently guaranteed by the statistical law? Feynman's example of the bomb and Geiger counter smashes this conception; but as far as I can judge it takes time for the lesson to be learned. I find deterministic assumptions more common now among people at large, and among philosophers, than when I was an undergraduate.

The lesson is welcome, but indeterministic physics (if it succeeds in giving the lesson) is only culturally, not logically, required to make the deterministic picture doubtful. For it was always a mere extravagant fancy, encouraged in the 'age of science' by the happy relation of Newtonian mechanics to the solar system. It ought not to have mattered whether the laws of nature were or were not deterministic. For them to be deterministic is for them, together with the description of the situation, to entail unique results in situations defined by certain relevant objects and measures, and where no part is played by inconstant factors external to such definition. If that is right, the laws' being deterministic does not tell us whether 'determinism' is true. It is the total coverage of every motion that happens that is a fanciful claim. But I do not mean that any motions lie outside the scope of physical laws, or that one cannot say, in any given context, that certain motions would be violations of physical law. Remember the contrast between chess and the infantile card game.

Meanwhile in non-experimental philosophy it is clear enough what are the dogmatic slumbers of the day. It is over and over again assumed that any singular causal proposition implies a universal statement running 'Always when this, then that'; often assumed that true singular causal statements are derived from such 'inductively believed' universalities. Examples indeed are recalcitrant, but that does not seem to disturb. Even a philosopher acute enough to be conscious of this, such as Davidson, will say, without offering any reason at all for saying it, that a singular causal statement implies *that there is* such a true universal proposition[3] – though perhaps we can never have knowledge of it. Such a thesis needs some reason for believing it! 'Regularities in nature': that is not a reason. The most neglected of the key topics in this subject are: interference and prevention.

[3] 'Causal Relations', *Journal of Philosophy*, 64 (November 1967).

PHILIPPA FOOT (1920–)

Philippa Foot, née Bosanquet, has taught philosophy for all of her professional life, at Somerville College, Oxford, and in the United States. She has written numerous articles and has been a considerable influence on the changing nature of moral philosophy. Her article 'Moral Arguments', reproduced below, can be seen as the first step towards what is now known as moral realism, or cognitivism, the view that there can be true moral propositions, and that values cannot be wholly separated from facts. The belief in the so-called 'Naturalistic Fallacy', the supposed fallacy of 'deriving' judgements of value from judgements of fact, had dominated moral philosophy during the first half of the century. One of its chief exponents was R. M. Hare, whose book *The Language of Morals* was published in 1952 and was followed by further books in which he attempted to show that, even though moral arguments could not be settled in the way arguments about facts could be, they need not on that account be irrational. However, he argued that, in the last analysis, everyone had simply to choose his moral principles. It is against this background that Philippa Foot's article must be read.

Further Reading

Philippa Foot, *Virtues and Vices* (Oxford: Blackwell, 1978). (A collection of her most widely read articles and lectures up to this date.)
——'Moral realism and moral dilemmas', *Journal of Philosophy*, 80 (1983), 379–98
——'Utilitarianism and the virtues', *Mind*, 94 (1985), (196–209)
David Wiggins, *Needs, Values, Truth* (Oxford: Blackwell, 1987), essay
III

From Philippa Foot, 'Moral arguments', Mind, 67 (1958), pp. 502–13

Those who are influenced by the emotivist theory of ethics, and yet wish to defend what Hare has called 'the rationality of moral discourse', generally talk a lot about 'giving reasons' for saying that one thing is right, and another wrong. The fact that moral judgements need defence seems to distinguish the impact of one man's moral views upon others from mere persuasion or coercion, and the judgements themselves from mere expressions of likes and dislikes. Yet the version of argument in morals currently accepted seems to say that, while reasons must be given, no one need accept them unless he happens to hold particular moral views. It follows that disputes about what is right and wrong can be resolved only if certain contingent conditions are fulfilled; if they are not fulfilled, the argument breaks down, and the disputants are left face to face in an opposition which is merely an expression of attitude and will. Much energy is expended in trying to show that no sceptical conclusion can be drawn. It is suggested, for instance, that anyone who has considered all the facts which could bear on his moral position has *ipso facto* produced a 'well-founded' moral judgement; in spite of the fact that anyone else who has considered the same facts may well come to the opposite conclusion. How 'x is good' can be a well-founded moral judgement when 'x is bad' can be equally well founded it is not easy to see.

The statement that moral arguments 'may always break down' is often thought of as something that has to be accepted, and it is thought that those who deny it fail to take account of what was proved once for all by Hume, and elaborated by Stevenson, by Ayer, and by Hare. This article is an attempt to expose the assumptions which give the 'breakdown' theory so tenacious a hold, and to suggest an alternative view.

Looked at in one way, the assertion that moral arguments 'may always break down' appears to make a large claim. What is meant is that they may break down in a way in which other arguments may not. We are therefore working on a model on which such factors as shortage of time or temper are not shown; the suggestion is not that A's argument with B may break down because B refuses for one reason or another to go on with it, but that their positions as such are irreconcilable. Now the question is: how can we assert that any disagreement about what is right and wrong may end like this? How do we know, without consulting the details of each

argument, that there is always an impregnable position both for
the man who says that X is right, or good, or what he ought to do,
and for the man who denies it? How do we know that each is able
to deal with every argument the other may bring?

Thus, when Hare describes someone who listens to all his
adversary has to say and then at the end simply rejects his
conclusion, we want to ask 'How can he?' Hare clearly supposes
that he can, for he says that at this point the objector can only be
asked to make up his mind for himself.[1] No one would ever paint
such a picture of other kinds of argument – suggesting, for
instance, that a man might listen to all that could be said about the
shape of the earth, and then ask why he should believe that it was
round. We should want, in such a case, to know how he met the
case put to him; and it is remarkable that in ethics this question is
thought not to be in place.

If a man making a moral judgement is to be invulnerable to
criticism, he must be free from reproach on two scores: (*a*) he must
have brought forward evidence, where evidence is needed; and (*b*)
he must have disposed of any contrary evidence offered. It is worth
showing why writers who insist that moral arguments may always
break down assume, for both sides in a moral dispute, invulner-
ability on both counts. The critical assumption appears in
different forms because different descriptions of moral arguments
are given; and I shall consider briefly what has been said by
Stevenson and by Hare.

I. Stevenson sees the process of giving reasons for ethical
conclusions as a special process of non-deductive inference, in
which statements expressing beliefs (R) form the premises and
emotive (evaluative) utterances (E) the conclusion. There are no
rules validating particular inferences, but only causal connections
between the beliefs and attitudes concerned. 'Suppose', he writes,
'that a theorist should *tabulate* the "valid" inferences from R's to
E's. It is difficult to see how he could be doing anything more than
specify what R's he thereby resolves to *accept* as supporting the
various E's . . . Under the name of "validity" he will be selecting
those inferences to which he is psychologically disposed to give
assent, and perhaps inducing others to give a similar assent to
them.'[2] It follows that disputes in which each man backs up his

[1] *The Language of Morals*, p. 69.
[2] *Ethics and Language*, pp. 170–1.

moral judgement with 'reasons' may always break down, and this is an implication on which Stevenson insists. So long as he does not contradict himself and gets his facts right, a man may argue as he chooses, or as he finds himself psychologically disposed. He alone says which facts are relevant to ethical conclusions, so that he is invulnerable on counts (a) and (b): he can simply assert that what he brings forward is evidence, and can simply deny the relevance of any other. His argument may be ineffective, but it cannot be said to be wrong. Stevenson speaks of ethical 'inference' and of giving 'reasons', but the process which he describes is rather that of trying to produce a result, an attitude, by means of a special kind of adjustment, an alteration in belief. All that is needed for a breakdown is for different attitudes in different people to be causally connected to the same beliefs. Then even complete agreement in belief will not settle a moral dispute.

II. Hare gives a picture of moral reasoning which escapes the difficulties of a special form of inference without rules of validity. He regards an argument to a moral conclusion as a syllogistic inference, with the ordinary rules. The facts, such as 'this is stealing', which are to back up a moral judgement are to be stated in a 'descriptive' minor premise, and their relevance is to be guaranteed by an 'evaluative' major premise in which that kind of thing is said to be good or bad. There is thus no difficulty about the validity of the argument; but one does arise about the status of the major premise. We are supposed to say that a particular action is bad because it is a case of stealing, and because stealing is wrong; but if we ask why stealing is wrong, we can only be presented with another argument of the same form, with another exposed moral principle as its major premise. In the end everyone is forced back to some moral principle which he simply asserts – and which someone else may simply deny. It can therefore be no reproach to anyone that he gives no reasons for a statement of moral principle, since any moral argument must contain some undefended premise of this kind. Nor can he be accused of failing to meet arguments put forward by opponents arguing from different principles; for by denying their ultimate major premises he can successfully deny the relevance of anything they say.

Both these accounts of moral argument are governed by the thought that there is no logical connection between statements of fact and statements of value, so that each man makes his own decision as to the facts about an action which are relevant to its evaluation. To oppose this view we should need to show that, on the contrary, it is laid down that some things do, and some things do not, count in favour of a moral conclusion, and that a man can no more decide for himself what is evidence for rightness and wrongness than he can decide what is evidence for monetary inflation or a tumour on the brain. If such objective relations between facts and values existed, they could be of two kinds: descriptive, or factual premises might *entail* evaluative conclusions, or they might count as *evidence* for them. It is the second possibility which chiefly concerns me, but I shall nevertheless consider the arguments which are supposed to show that the stronger relationship cannot exist. For I want to show that the arguments usually brought forward do not *even* prove this. I want to say that it has not even been proved that moral conclusions cannot be entailed by factual or descriptive premises.

It is often thought that Hume showed the impossibility of deducing 'ought', from 'is', but the form in which this view is now defended is, of course, that in which it was rediscovered by G. E. Moore at the beginning of the present century, and developed by such other critics of 'naturalistic' ethics as Stevenson, Ayer and Hare. We need therefore to look into the case against naturalism to see exactly what was proved.

Moore tried to show that goodness was a non-natural property, and thus not to be defined in terms of natural properties; the problem was to explain the concept of a 'natural property', and to prove that no ethical definition in terms of natural properties could be correct. As Frankena[3] and Prior[4] pointed out, the argument against naturalism was always in danger of degenerating into a truism. A natural property tended to become one not identical with goodness, and the naturalistic fallacy that of identifying goodness with 'some other thing'.

What was needed to give the attack on naturalism new life was the identification of some deficiency common to the whole range of definitions rejected by Moore, a reason why they all failed. This was provided by the theory that value terms in general, and moral terms in particular, were used for a special function – variously identified as expressing feelings, expressing and inducing attitudes, or commending. Now it was said that words with emotive

---

[3] W. K. Frankena, '*The naturalistic fallacy*', *Mind*, 1939.
[4] A. N. Prior, *Logic and the Basis of Ethics*, chap. 1.

or commendatory force, such as 'good', were not to be defined by the use of words whose meaning was merely 'descriptive'. This discovery tended to appear greater than it was, because it looked as if the two categories of fact and value had been identified separately and found never to coincide, whereas actually the factual or descriptive was defined by exclusion from the realm of value. In the ordinary sense of 'descriptive' the word 'good' is a descriptive word and in the ordinary sense of 'fact' we say that it is a fact about so and so that he is a good man, so that the words must be used in a special sense in moral philosophy. But a special philosopher's sense of these words has never, so far as I know, been explained except by contrasting value and fact. A word or sentence seems to be called 'descriptive' on account of the fact that it is *not* emotive, does *not* commend, does *not* entail an imperative, and so on according to the theory involved. This might seem to reduce the case against naturalism once more to an uninteresting tautology, but it does not do so. For if the non-naturalist has discovered a special feature found in all value judgements, he can no longer be accused of saying merely that nothing is a definition of 'good' unless it is a definition of 'good' and not 'some other thing'. His part is now to insist that any definition which fails to allow for the special feature of value judgements must be rejected, and to label as 'naturalistic' all the definitions which fail to pass this test.

I shall suppose, for the sake of argument, that the non-naturalist really has identified some characteristic (let us call it f) essential to evaluative words; that he is right in saying that evaluations involve emotions, attitudes, the acceptance of imperatives, or something of the kind. He is therefore justified in insisting that no word or statement which does not have the property f can be taken as equivalent to any evaluation, and that no account of the use of an evaluative term can leave out f and yet be complete. What, if anything, follows about the relation between premises and conclusion in an argument designed to support an evaluation?

It is often said that what follows is that evaluative conclusions cannot be deduced from descriptive premises, but how is this to be shown? Of course if a descriptive premise is redefined, as one which does not entail an evaluative conclusion, the non-naturalist will once more have bought security at the price of becoming a bore. He can once more improve his position by pointing to the characteristic f belonging to all evaluations, and asserting that no set of premises which do not entail an f proposition can entail an evaluation. If he takes this course he will be more like the man who says that a proposition which entails a proposition about a dog must be one which entails a proposition about an animal; he is telling us what to look out for in checking the entailment. What he is not so far telling us is that we can test for the entailment by looking to see whether the premise itself has the characteristic f. For all that has yet been shown it might be possible for a premise which is not f to entail a conclusion which is f, and it is obviously this proposition which the non-naturalist wants to deny.

Now it may seem obvious that a non-evaluative premise could not entail an evaluative conclusion, but it remains unclear how it is supposed to be proved.

In one form, the theory that an evaluative conclusion of a deductive argument needs evaluative premises is clearly unwarrantable; I mention it only to get it out of the way. We cannot possibly say that at least one of the premises must be evaluative if the conclusion is to be so; for there is nothing to tell us that whatever can truly be said of the conclusion of a deductive argument can truly be said of any one of the premises. It is not necessary that the evaluative element should 'come in whole', so to speak. If f has to belong to the premises it can only be necessary that it should belong to the premises *together*, and it may be no easy matter to see whether a set of propositions has the property f.

How in any case is it to be proved that if the conclusion is to have the characteristic f the premises taken together must also have it? Can it be said that unless this is so it will always be possible to assert the premises and yet deny the conclusion? I shall try to show that this at least is false, and in order to do so I shall consider the case of arguments designed to show that a certain piece of behaviour is or is not rude.

I think it will be agreed that in the wide sense in which philosophers speak of evaluation, 'rude' is an evaluative word. At any rate it has the kind of characteristics upon which non-naturalists fasten: it expresses disapproval, is meant to be used when action is to be discouraged, implies that other things being equal the behaviour to which it is applied will be avoided by the speaker, and so on. For the purpose of this argument I shall ignore the cases in which it is admitted that there are reasons why something should be done in spite of, or even because of, the fact that it is rude. Clearly there are occasions when a little rudeness is in place, but this does not alter the fact that 'rude' is a condemnatory word.

It is obvious that there is something else to be said about the word 'rude' besides the fact that it expresses, fairly mild, condemnation: it can only be used where certain descriptions apply. The right account of the situation in which it is correct to say that a piece of behaviour is rude, is, I think, that this kind of behaviour causes offence by indicating lack of respect. Sometimes it is merely conventional that such behaviour does indicate lack of respect (*e.g.* when a man keeps his hat on in someone else's house); sometimes the behaviour is naturally disrespectful, as when one man pushes another out of the way. (It should be mentioned that rudeness and the absence of rudeness do not exhaust the subject of etiquette; some things are not rude, and yet are 'not done'. It is rude to wear flannels at a formal dinner party, but merely not done to wear a dinner jacket for tennis.)

Given that this reference to offence is to be included in any account of the concept of rudeness, we may ask what the relation is between the assertion that these conditions of offence are fulfilled – let us call it O – and the statement that a piece of behaviour is rude – let us call it R. Can someone who accepts the proposition O (that this kind of offence is caused) deny the proposition R (that the behaviour is rude)? I should have thought that this was just what he could not do, for if he says that it is not rude, we shall stare, and ask him what sort of behaviour would be rude; and what is he to say? Suppose that he were to answer 'a man is rude when he behaves conventionally', or 'a man is rude when he walks slowly up to a front door', and this not because he believes that such behaviour causes offence, but with the intention of leaving behind entirely the usual criteria of rudeness. It is evident that with the usual criteria of rudeness he leaves behind the concept itself; he may say the words 'I think this rude', but it will not on that account be right to describe him as 'thinking it rude'. If I *say* 'I am sitting on a pile of hay' and bring as evidence the fact that the object I am sitting on has four wooden legs and a hard wooden back, I shall hardly be described as thinking, even mistakenly, that I am sitting on a pile of hay; all I am doing is to use the *words* 'pile of hay'.

It might be thought that the two cases were not parallel, for while the meaning of 'pile of hay' is given by the characteristics which piles of hay must possess, the meaning of 'rude' is given by the attitude it expresses. The answer is that if 'thinking a thing rude' is to be described as having a particular attitude to it, then having an attitude presupposes, in this case, believing that certain conditions are fulfilled. If 'attitudes' were solely a matter of reactions such as wrinkling the nose, and tendencies to such things as making resolutions and scolding, then thinking something rude would not be describable solely in terms of attitudes. Either thinking something rude is not to be described in terms of attitudes, or attitudes are not to be described in terms of such things. Even if we could suppose that a particular individual could react towards conventional behaviour, or to walking slowly up to an English front door, *exactly* as most people react to behaviour which gives offence, this would not mean that he was to be described as thinking these things rude. And in any case the supposition is nonsense. Although he could behave in some ways as if he thought them rude, *e.g.* by scolding conventional or slow-walking children, but not turning daughters with these proclivities out of doors, his behaviour could not be just as if he thought them rude. For as the social reaction to conventional behaviour is not the same as the social reaction to offensive behaviour, he could not act in just the same way. He could not for instance apologise for what he would call his 'rudeness', for he would have to admit that it had caused no offence.

I conclude that whether a man is speaking of behaviour as rude or not rude, he must use the same criteria as anyone else, and that since the criteria are satisfied if O is true, it is impossible for him to assert O while denying R. It follows that if it is a sufficient condition of P's entailing Q that the assertion of P is inconsistent with the denial of Q, we have here an example of a non-evaluative premise from which an evaluative conclusion can be deduced.

It is of course possible to admit O while refusing to assert R, and this will not be like the refusal to say about prunes what one has already admitted about dried plums. Calling an action 'rude' is using a concept which a man might want to reject, rejecting the whole practice of praising and blaming embodied in terms such as 'polite' and 'rude'. Such a man would refuse to discuss points of etiquette, and arguments with him about what is rude would not so much break down as never begin. But once he did accept the question 'Is this rude?', he would have to abide by the rules of this kind of argument; he could not bring forward any evidence he liked, and he could not deny the relevance of any piece of evidence brought forward by his opponent. Nor could he say that he was unable to move from O to R on this occasion because the belief in O had not induced in him feelings or attitudes warranting the assertion of R. If he had agreed to discuss rudeness he had committed himself to accepting O as evidence for R, and evidence is not a sort of medicine which is taken in the hope that it will work. To suggest that he could refuse to admit that certain behaviour was rude because the right psychological state had not been induced, is as odd as to suppose that one might refuse to speak of the world as round because in spite of the good evidence of roundness a feeling of confidence in the proposition had not been produced. When given good evidence it is one's business to act on it, not to hang around waiting for the right state of mind. It follows that if a man is prepared to discuss questions of rudeness, and hence to accept as evidence the fact that behaviour causes a certain kind of offence, he cannot refuse to admit R when O has been proved.

The point of considering this example was to show that there may be the strictest rules of evidence even where an evaluative conclusion is concerned. Applying this principle to the case of moral judgements, we see that – for all that the non-naturalist has proved to the contrary – Bentham, for instance, may be right in saying that when used in conjunction with the principle of utility 'the words *ought* and *right* and *wrong*, and others of that stamp, have a meaning: when otherwise they have none'.[5] Anyone who uses moral terms at all, whether to assert or deny a moral proposition, must abide by the rules for their use, including the rules about what shall count as evidence for or against the moral judgement concerned. For anything that has yet been shown to the contrary these rules could be entailment rules, forbidding the assertion of factual propositions in conjunction with the denial of moral propositions. The only recourse of the man who refused to accept the things which counted in favour of a moral proposition as giving him a reason to do certain things or to take up a particular attitude, would be to leave the moral discussion and abjure altogether the use of moral terms.

To say what Bentham said is not, then, to commit any sort of 'naturalistic fallacy'. It is open to us to enquire whether moral terms do lose their meaning when divorced from the pleasure

[5] *Principles of Morals in Legislation*, chap. I, x.

principle, or from some other set of criteria, as the word 'rude' loses its meaning when the criterion of offensiveness is dropped. To me it seems that this is clearly the case; I do not know what could be meant by saying that it was someone's duty to do something unless there was an attempt to show why it mattered if this sort of thing was not done. How can questions such as 'what does it matter?' 'what harm does it do?' 'what advantage is there in . . . ?' 'why is it important?', be set aside here? Is it even to be suggested that the harm done by a certain trait of character could be taken, by some extreme moral eccentric, to be just what made it a virtue? I suggest that such a man would not even be a moral eccentric, any more than the man who used the word 'rude' of conventional behaviour was putting forward strange views about what was rude. Both descriptions have their proper application, but it is not here. How exactly the concepts of harm, advantage, benefit, importance, etc., are related to the different moral concepts, such as rightness, obligation, goodness, duty and virtue, is something that needs the most patient investigation, but that they are so related seems undeniable, and it follows that a man cannot make his own personal decision about the considerations which are to count as evidence in morals.

Perhaps it will be argued that this kind of freedom of choice is not ruled out after all, because a man has to decide for himself what is to count as advantage, benefit, or harm. But is this really plausible? Consider the man described by Hare as thinking that torturing is morally permissible.[6] Apparently he is not supposed to be arguing that in spite of everything torture is justifiable as a means of extracting confessions from enemies of the state, for the argument is supposed to be at an end when he has said that torturing people is permissible, and his opponent has said that it is not. How is he supposed to have answered the objection that to inflict torture is to do harm? If he is supposed to have said that pain is good for a man in the long run, rather than bad, he will have to show the benefits involved, and he can no more choose what shall count as a benefit than he could have chosen what counted as harm. Is he supposed perhaps to count as harm only harm to himself? In this case he is guilty of *ignoratio elenchi*. By refusing to count as harm anything except harm to himself, he puts himself

---

[6] 'Universalisbility', *Proceedings of the Aristotelian Society*, 1954–5, p. 304.

outside the pale of moral discussion, and should have explained that this was his position. One might compare his case to that of a man who in some discussion of common policy says 'this will be the best thing to do', and announces afterwards that *he* meant best for himself. This is not what the word 'best' does mean in the context of such a discussion.

It may be objected that these considerations about the evidence which must be brought for saying that one thing is good and another bad, could not in any case be of the least importance; such rules of evidence, even if they exist, only reflecting the connection between our existing moral code and our existing moral terms; if there are no 'free' moral terms in our language, it can always be supposed that some have been invented – as indeed they will have to be invented if we are to be able to argue with people who subscribe to a moral code entirely different from our own. This objection rests on a doubtful assumption about the concept of *morality*. It assumes that even if there are rules about the grounds on which actions can be called good, right, or obligatory, there are no rules about the grounds on which a principle which is to be called a moral principle may be asserted. Those who believe this must think it possible to identify an element of feeling or attitude which carries the meaning of the word 'moral'. It must be supposed, for instance, that if we describe a man as being for or against certain actions, bringing them under universal rules, adopting these rules for himself, and thinking himself bound to urge them on others, we shall be able to identify him as holding moral principles, whatever the content of the principle at which he stops. But why should it be supposed that the concept of morality is to be caught in this particular kind of net? The consequences of such an assumption are very hard to stomach; for it follows that a rule which was admitted by those who obeyed it to be completely pointless could yet be recognised as a moral rule. If people happened to insist that no one should run round trees left handed, or look at hedgehogs in the light of the moon, this might count as a basic moral principle about which nothing more need be said.

I think that the main reason why this view is so often held in spite of these difficulties, is that we fear the charge of making a verbal decision in favour of our own moral code. But those who bring that charge are merely begging the question against arguments such as those given above. Of course if the rules we are refusing to call moral rules can really be given this name, then we are merely legislating against alien *moral codes*. But the suggestion which has been put forward is that this could not be the right description for rules of behaviour for which an entirely different defence is offered from that which we offer for our moral beliefs. If this suggestion is right, the difference between ourselves and the people who have these rules is not to be described as a difference of moral outlook, but rather as a difference between a moral and a non-moral point of view. The example of etiquette is again useful here. No one is tempted to say that the ruling out, *a priori*, of rules of etiquette which each man decides on for himself when he feels so inclined, represents a mere verbal decision in favour of our kind of socially determined standards of etiquette. On what grounds could one call a rule which someone was allowed to invent for himself a rule of *etiquette*? It is not just a fact about the use of our words 'rude', 'not done', etc., that they could not be applied in such a case; it is also a fact about etiquette that if terms in another language did appear in such situations they would not be terms of etiquette. We can make a similar point about the terms 'legal' and 'illegal' and the concept of law. If any individual was allowed to apply a certain pair of terms expressing approval and disapproval off his own bat, without taking notice of any recognised authority, such terms could not be legal terms. Similarly it is a fact about etiquette and law that they are both conventional as morality is not.

It may be that in attempting to state the rules which govern the assertion of moral propositions we shall legislate against a moral system radically opposed to our own. But this is only to say that we may make a mistake. The remedy is to look more carefully at the rules of evidence, not to assume that there cannot be any at all. If a moral system such as Nietzsche's has been refused recognition as a moral system, then we have got the criteria wrong. The fact that Nietzsche was a moralist cannot, however, be quoted in favour of the private enterprise theory of moral criteria. Admittedly Nietzsche said 'You want to decrease suffering; I want precisely to increase it' but he did not *just* say this. Nor did he offer as a justification the fact that suffering causes a tendency to absent-mindedness, or lines on the human face. We recognise Nietzsche as a moralist because he tries to justify an increase in suffering by connecting it with strength as opposed to weakness, and individuality as opposed to conformity. That strength is a good thing can only be denied by someone who can show that the strong man overreaches himself, or in some other way brings harm to himself or other people. That individuality is a good thing is something that has to be shown, but in a vague way we connect it with originality, and with courage, and hence there is no difficulty in conceiving Nietzsche as a moralist when he appeals to such a thing.

In conclusion it is worth remarking that moral arguments break down more often than philosophers tend to think, but that the breakdown is of a different kind. When people argue about what is right, good, or obligatory, or whether a certain character trait is or is not a virtue, they do not confine their remarks to the adducing of facts which can be established by simple observation, or by some clear-cut technique. What is said may well be subtle or profound, and in this sort of discussion as in others, in the field of literary criticism for instance, or the discussion of character, much depends on experience and imagination. It is quite common for one man to be unable to see what the other is getting at, and this sort of misunderstanding will not always be resolvable by anything which could be called argument in the ordinary sense.

JUDITH JARVIS THOMSON (1929–   )

Judith Thomson is Professor of Philosophy in the Department of Linguistics and Philosophy at the Massachusetts Institute of Technology. She has spent her professional life in the United States, though she has travelled widely and has spent some time in Oxford. The article I have chosen to include below was first published in 1971 in the journal *Philosophy and Public Affairs*. It was written at the beginning of the widespread and often violent debate on abortion in America, and soon after the passage of the Abortion Act (1967) in Britain. Since then there has been an enormous amount written on the rights and wrongs of abortion, and Judith Thomson's article has become a frequently quoted classic. It was, indeed, one of the first writings in the newly 'applied' moral philosophy. Since that time she has written on many currently controversial issues, such as the right of self-defence, and on preferential hiring, or a quota-system for the employment of blacks and women. Her collected papers were published in 1986. She herself, in the Afterword to that volume, expressed awareness, if not dismay, at the extreme complexity required of a moral theory if it is to be used to cover the vast variety of moral dilemmas that exist. She is also dubious, indeed sceptical, about the language of rights, arguing that it is not clear what is being claimed when someone claims a right. In the light of both these anxieties, she argues that in moral philosophy the use of stories, narrative examples, whether derived from real life or fictional, is necessarily of supreme importance.

Further Reading

Judith Jarvis Thomson, *Rights, Restitution, and Risk: Essays in Moral Theory*, ed. William Parent (Princeton, NJ: Princeton University Press, 1986)

*Judith Jarvis Thomson, 'A defense of abortion';
reprinted from her* Rights, Restitution, and Risk:
Essays in Moral Theory, *ed. William Parent
(Princeton, NJ: Princeton University Press, 1986),
chapter 1*

Most opposition to abortion relies on the premise that the fetus is a
human being, a person, from the moment of conception. The
premise is argued for, but, as I think, not well. Take, for example,
the most common argument. We are asked to notice that the
development of a human being from conception through birth into
childhood is continuous; then it is said that to draw a line, to
choose a point in this development and say 'before this point the
thing is not a person, after this point it is a person' is to make an
arbitrary choice, a choice for which in the nature of things no good
reason can be given. It is concluded that the fetus is, or anyway
that we had better say it is, a person from the moment of
conception. But this conclusion does not follow. Similar things
might be said about the development of an acorn into an oak tree,
and it does not follow that acorns are oak trees, or that we had
better say they are. Arguments of this form are sometimes called
'slippery slope arguments' – the phrase is perhaps self-explanatory
– and it is dismaying that opponents of abortion rely on them so
heavily and uncritically.

I am inclined to agree, however, that the prospects for 'drawing
a line' in the development of the fetus look dim. I am inclined to
think also that we shall probably have to agree that the fetus has
already become a human person well before birth. Indeed, it
comes as a surprise when one first learns how early in its life it
begins to acquire human characteristics . . . On the other hand, I
think that the premise is false, that the fetus is not a person from
the moment of conception. A newly fertilized ovum, a newly
implanted clump of cells, is no more a person than an acorn is an
oak tree. But I shall not discuss any of this. For it seems to me to be
of great interest to ask what happens if, for the sake of argument,
we allow the premise. How, precisely, are we supposed to get from
there to the conclusion that abortion is morally impermissible?
Opponents of abortion commonly spend most of their time
establishing that the fetus is a person, and hardly any time

explaining the step from there to the impermissibility of abortion. Perhaps they think the step too simple and obvious to require much comment. Or perhaps instead they are simply being economical in argument. Many of those who defend abortion rely on the premise that the fetus is not a person, but only a bit of tissue that will become a person at birth; and why pay out more arguments than you have to? Whatever the explanation, I suggest that the step they take is neither easy nor obvious, that it calls for closer examination than it is commonly given, and that when we do give it this closer examination we shall feel inclined to reject it.

I propose, then, that we grant that the fetus is a person from the moment of conception. How does the argument go from here? Something like this, I take it. Every person has a right to life. So the fetus has a right to life. No doubt the mother has a right to decide what shall happen in and to her body; everyone would grant that. But surely a person's right to life is stronger and more stringent than the mother's right to decide what happens in and to her body, and so outweighs it. So the fetus may not be killed; an abortion may not be performed.

It sounds plausible. But now let me ask you to imagine this. You wake up in the morning and find yourself back to back in bed with an unconscious violinist. A famous unconscious violinist. He has been found to have a fatal kidney ailment, and the Society of Music Lovers has canvassed all the available medical records and found that you alone have the right blood type to help. They have therefore kidnapped you, and last night the violinist's circulatory system was plugged into yours, so that your kidneys can be used to extract poisons from his blood as well as your own. The director of the hospital now tells you, 'Look, we're sorry the Society of Music Lovers did this to you – we would never have permitted it if we had known. But still, they did it, and the violinist now is plugged into you. To unplug you would be to kill him. But never mind, it's only for nine months. By then he will have recovered from his ailment, and can safely be unplugged from you.' Is it morally incumbent on you to accede to this situation? No doubt it would be very nice of you if you did, a great kindness. But do you *have* to accede to it? What if it were not nine months, but nine years? Or longer still? What if the director of the hospital says, 'Tough luck, I agree, but you've now got to stay in bed, with the violinist plugged into you, for the rest of your life. Because remember this. All persons have a right to life, and violinists are persons. Granted you have a right to decide what happens in and to your body, but a person's right to life outweighs your right to decide what happens in and to your body. So you cannot ever be unplugged from him.' I imagine you would regard this as outrageous, which suggests that something really is wrong with that plausible-sounding argument I mentioned a moment ago.

In this case, of course, you were kidnapped; you didn't volunteer for the operation that plugged the violinist into your kidneys. Can those who oppose abortion on the ground I mentioned make an exception for a pregnancy due to rape? Certainly. They can say that persons have a right to life only if they didn't come into existence because of rape; or they can say that all persons have a right to life, but that some have less of a right to life than others, in particular, that those who come into existence because of rape have less. But these statements have a rather unpleasant sound. Surely the question of whether you have a right to life at all, or how much of it you have, shouldn't turn on the question of whether or not you are the product of a rape. And in fact the people who oppose abortion on the ground I mentioned do not make this distinction, and hence do not make an exception in case of rape.

Nor do they make an exception for a case in which the mother has to spend the nine months of her pregnancy in bed. They would agree that would be a great pity, and hard on the mother; but all the same, all persons have a right to life, the fetus is a person, and so on. I suspect, in fact, that they would not make an exception for a case in which, miraculously enough, the pregnancy went on for nine years, or even the rest of the mother's life.

Some won't even make an exception for a case in which continuation of the pregnancy is likely to shorten the mother's life; they regard abortion as impermissible even to save the mother's life. Such cases are nowadays very rare, and many opponents of abortion do not accept this extreme view. All the same, it is a good place to begin: a number of points of interest come out in respect to it.

1. Let us call the view that abortion is impermissible even to save the mother's life 'the extreme view.' I want to suggest first that it does not issue from the argument I mentioned earlier without the addition of some fairly powerful premises. Suppose a woman has become pregnant, and now learns that she has a cardiac condition

such that she will die if she carries the baby to term. What may be done for her? The fetus, being a person, has a right to life, but as the mother is a person too, so has she a right to life. Presumably they have an equal right to life. How is it supposed to come out that an abortion may not be performed? If mother and child have an equal right to life, shouldn't we perhaps flip a coin? Or should we add to the mother's right to life her right to decide what happens in and to her body, which everybody seems to be ready to grant – the sum of her rights now outweighing the fetus's right to life?

The most familiar argument here is the following. We are told that performing the abortion would be directly killing the child, whereas doing nothing would not be killing the mother, but only letting her die. Moreover, in killing the child, one would be killing an innocent person, for the child has committed no crime, and is not aiming at his mother's death. And then there are a variety of ways in which this might be continued. (1) But as directly killing an innocent person is always and absolutely impermissible, an abortion may not be performed. Or, (2) as directly killing an innocent person is murder, and murder is always and absolutely impermissible, an abortion may not be performed. Or, (3) as one's duty to refrain from directly killing an innocent person is more stringent than one's duty to keep a person from dying, an abortion may not be performed. Or, (4) if one's only options are directly killing an innocent person or letting a person die, one must prefer letting the person die, and thus an abortion may not be performed.

Some people seem to have thought that these are not further premises which must be added if the conclusion is to be reached, but that they follow from the very fact that an innocent person has a right to life. But this seems to me to be a mistake, and perhaps the simplest way to show this is to bring out that while we must certainly grant that innocent persons have a right to life, the theses in (1) through (4) are all false. Take (2), for example. If directly killing an innocent person is murder, and thus is impermissible, then the mother's directly killing the innocent person inside her is murder, and thus is impermissible. But it cannot seriously be thought to be murder if the mother performs an abortion on herself to save her life. It cannot seriously be said that she *must* refrain, that she *must* sit passively by and wait for her death. Let us look again at the case of you and the violinist. There you are, in bed with the violinist, and the director of the hospital says to you, 'It's all most distressing, and I deeply sympathize, but you see this is putting an additional strain on your kidneys, and you'll be dead within the month. But you *have* to stay where you are all the same. Because unplugging you would be directly killing an innocent violinist, and that's murder, and that's impermissible.' If anything in the world is true, it is that you do not commit murder, you do not do what is impermissible, if you reach around to your back and unplug yourself from that violinist to save your life.

The main focus of attention in writings on abortion has been on what a third party may or may not do in answer to a request from a woman for an abortion. This is in a way understandable. Things being as they are, there isn't much a woman can safely do to abort herself. So the question asked is what a third party may do, and what the mother may do, if it is mentioned at all, is deduced, almost as an afterthought, from what it is concluded that third parties may do. But it seems to me that to treat the matter in this way is to refuse to grant to the mother that very status of person which is so firmly insisted on for the fetus. For we cannot simply read off what a person may do from what a third party may do. Suppose you find yourself trapped in a tiny house with a growing child. I mean a very tiny house, and a rapidly growing child – you are already up against the wall of the house and in a few minutes you'll be crushed to death. The child on the other hand won't be crushed to death; if nothing is done to stop him from growing he'll be hurt, but in the end he'll simply burst open the house and walk out a free man. Now I could well understand it if a bystander were to say, 'There's nothing we can do for you. We cannot choose between your life and his, we cannot be the ones to decide who is to live, we cannot intervene.' But it cannot be concluded that you too can do nothing, that you cannot attack it to save your life. However innocent the child may be, you do not have to wait passively while it crushes you to death. Perhaps a pregnant woman is vaguely felt to have the status of house, to which we don't allow the right of self-defense. But if the woman houses the child, it should be remembered that she is a person who houses it.

I should perhaps stop to say explicitly that I am not claiming that people have a right to do anything whatever to save their lives. I think, rather, that there are drastic limits to the right of self-defense. If someone threatens you with death unless you torture someone else to death, I think you have not the right, even to save your life, to do so. But the case under consideration here is very different. In our case there are only two people involved, one whose life is threatened, and one who threatens it. Both are innocent: the one who is threatened is not threatened because of any fault, the one who threatens does not threaten because of any fault. For this reason we may feel that we bystanders cannot intervene. But the person threatened can.

In sum, a woman surely can defend her life against the threat to it posed by the unborn child, even if doing so involves its death. And this shows not merely that the theses in (1) through (4) are false; it shows also that the extreme view of abortion is false, and so we need not canvass any other possible ways of arriving at it from the argument I mentioned at the outset.

2. The extreme view could of course be weakened to say that while abortion is permissible to save the mother's life, it may not be performed by a third party, but only by the mother herself. But this cannot be right either. For what we have to keep in mind is that the mother and the unborn child are not like two tenants in a small house which has, by an unfortunate mistake, been rented to both: the mother *owns* the house. The fact that she does adds to the offensiveness of deducing that the mother can do nothing from the supposition that third parties can do nothing. But it does more than this: it casts a bright light on the supposition that third parties can do nothing. Certainly it lets us see that a third party who says 'I cannot choose between you' is fooling himself if he thinks this is impartiality. If Jones has found and fastened on a certain coat, which he needs to keep him from freezing, but which Smith also needs to keep him from freezing, then it is not impartiality that says 'I cannot choose between you' when Smith owns the coat. Women have said again and again 'This body is *my* body!' and they have reason to feel angry, reason to feel that it has been like shouting into the wind. Smith, after all, is hardly likely to bless us if we say to him, 'Of course it's your coat, anybody would grant that it is. But no one may choose between you and Jones who is to have it.'

We should really ask what it is that says 'no one may choose' in the face of the fact that the body that houses the child is the mother's body. It may be simply a failure to appreciate this fact. But it may be something more interesting, namely the sense that one has a right to refuse to lay hands on people, even where it would be just and fair to do so, even where justice seems to require that somebody do so. Thus justice might call for somebody to get Smith's coat back from Jones, and yet you have a right to refuse to be the one to lay hands on Jones, a right to refuse to do physical violence to him. This, I think, must be granted. But then what should be said is not 'no one may choose,' but only '*I* cannot choose,' and indeed not even this, but '*I* will not *act*,' leaving it open that somebody else can or should, and in particular that anyone in a position of authority, with the job of securing people's rights, both can and should. So this is no difficulty. I have not been arguing that any given third party must accede to the mother's request that he perform an abortion to save her life, but only that he may.

I suppose that in some views of human life the mother's body is only on loan to her, the loan not being one which gives her any prior claim to it. One who held this view might well think it impartiality to say 'I cannot choose.' But I shall simply ignore this possibility. My own view is that if a human being has any just, prior claim to anything at all, he has a just, prior claim to his own body. And perhaps this needn't be argued for here anyway, since, as I mentioned, the arguments against abortion we are looking at do grant that the woman has a right to decide what happens in and to her body.

But although they do grant it, I have tried to show that they do not take seriously what is done in granting it. I suggest the same thing will reappear even more clearly when we turn away from cases in which the mother's life is at stake, and attend, as I propose we now do, to the vastly more common cases in which a woman wants an abortion for some less weighty reason than preserving her own life.

3. Where the mother's life is not at stake, the argument I mentioned at the outset seems to have a much stronger pull. 'Everyone has a right to life, so the unborn person has a right to life.' And isn't the child's right to life weightier than anything other than the mother's own right to life, which she might put forward as ground for an abortion?

This argument treats the right to life as if it were unproblematic. It is not, and this seems to me to be precisely the source of the mistake.

For we should now, at long last, ask what it comes to, to have a right to life. In some views having a right to life includes having a right to be given at least the bare minimum one needs for continued life. But suppose that what in fact *is* the bare minimum a man needs for continued life is something he has no right at all to be given? If I am sick unto death, and the only thing that will save my life is the touch of Henry Fonda's cool hand on my fevered brow, then all the same, I have no right to be given the touch of Henry Fonda's cool hand on my fevered brow. It would be frightfully nice of him to fly in from the West Coast to provide it. It would be less nice, though no doubt well meant, if my friends flew out to the West Coast and carried Henry Fonda back with them. But I have no right at all against anybody that he should do this for me. Or again, to return to the story I told earlier, the fact that for continued life that violinist needs the continued use of your kidneys does not establish that he has a right to be given the continued use of your kidneys. He certainly has no right against you that *you* should give him continued use of your kidneys. For nobody has any right to use your kidneys unless you give him such a right; and nobody has the right against you that you shall give him this right – if you do allow him to go on using your kidneys, this is a kindness on your part, and not something he can claim from you as his due. Nor has he any right against anybody else that *they* should give him continued use of your kidneys. Certainly he had no right against the Society of Music Lovers that they should plug him into you in the first place. And if you now start to unplug yourself, having learned that you will otherwise have to spend nine years in bed with him, there is nobody in the world who must try to prevent you, in order to see to it that he is given something he has a right to be given.

Some people are rather stricter about the right to life. In their view, it does not include the right to be given anything, but amounts to, and only to, the right not to be killed by anybody. But here a related difficulty arises. If everybody is to refrain from killing that violinist, then everybody must refrain from doing a great many different sorts of things. Everybody must refrain from slitting his throat, everybody must refrain from shooting him – and everybody must refrain from unplugging you from him. But does he have a right against everybody that they shall refrain from unplugging you from him? To refrain from doing this is to allow him to continue to use your kidneys. It could be argued that he has a right against us that *we* should allow him to continue to use your kidneys. That is, while he had no right against us that we should give him the use of your kidneys, it might be argued that he anyway has a right against us that we shall not now intervene and deprive him of the use of your kidneys. I shall come back to third-party interventions later. But certainly the violinist has no right against you that *you* shall allow him to continue to use your kidneys. As I said, if you do allow him to use them, it is a kindness on your part, and not something you owe him.

The difficulty I point to here is not peculiar to the right of life. It reappears in connection with all the other natural rights; and it is something which an adequate account of rights must deal with. For present purposes it is enough just to draw attention to it. But I would stress that I am not arguing that people do not have a right to life – quite to the contrary, it seems to me that the primary control we must place on the acceptability of an account of rights is that it should turn out in that account to be a truth that all persons have a right to life. I am arguing only that having a right to life does not guarantee having either a right to be given the use of or a right to be allowed continued use of another person's body – even if one needs it for life itself. So the right to life will not serve the opponents of abortion in the very simple and clear way in which they seem to have thought it would.

4. There is another way to bring out the difficulty. In the most ordinary sort of case, to deprive someone of what he has a right to is to treat him unjustly. Suppose a boy and his small brother are jointly given a box of chocolates for Christmas. If the older boy takes the box and refuses to give his brother any of the chocolates, he is unjust to him, for the brother has been given a right to half of them. But suppose that, having learned that otherwise it means nine years in bed with that violinist, you unplug yourself from him. You surely are not being unjust to him, for you gave him no right to use your kidneys, and no one else can have given him any such right. But we have to notice that in unplugging yourself, you are killing him; and violinists, like everybody else, have a right to life, and thus in the view we were considering just now, the right not to be killed. So here you do what he supposedly has a right you shall not do, but you do not act unjustly to him in doing it.

The emendation which may be made at this point is this: the right to life consists not in the right not to be killed, but rather in the right not to be killed unjustly. This runs a risk of circularity, but never mind: it would enable us to square the fact that the violinist has a right to life with the fact that you do not act unjustly toward him in unplugging yourself, thereby killing him. For if you do not kill him unjustly, you do not violate his right to life, and so it is no wonder you do him no injustice.

But if this emendation is accepted, the gap in the argument against abortion stares us plainly in the face: it is by no means enough to show that the fetus is a person, and to remind us that all persons have a right to life – we need to be shown also that killing the fetus violates its right to life, that is, that abortion is unjust killing. And is it?

I suppose we may take it as a datum that in a case of pregnancy due to rape the mother has not given the unborn person a right to the use of her body for food and shelter. Indeed, in what pregnancy could it be supposed that the mother has given the unborn person such a right? It is not as if there were unborn persons drifting about the world, to whom a woman who wants a child says 'I invite you in.'

But it might be argued that there are other ways one can have acquired a right to the use of another person's body than by having been invited to use it by that person. Suppose a woman voluntarily indulges in intercourse, knowing of the chance it will issue in pregnancy, and then she does become pregnant; is she not in part responsible for the presence, in fact the very existence, of the unborn person inside her? No doubt she did not invite it in. But doesn't her partial responsibility for its being there itself give it a right to the use of her body? If so, then her aborting it would be more like the boy's taking away the chocolates, and less like your unplugging yourself from the violinist – doing so would be depriving it of what it does have a right to, and thus would be doing it an injustice.

And then, too, it might be asked whether or not she can kill it even to save her own life: If she voluntarily called it into existence, how can she now kill it, even in self-defense?

The first thing to be said about this is that it is something new. Opponents of abortion have been so concerned to make out the independence of the fetus, in order to establish that it has a right to life, just as its mother does, that they have tended to overlook the possible support they might gain from making out that the fetus is *dependent* on the mother, in order to establish that she has a special kind of responsibility for it, a responsibility that gives it rights against her which are not possessed by any independent person – such as an ailing violinist who is a stranger to her.

On the other hand, this argument would give the unborn person a right to its mother's body only if her pregnancy resulted from a voluntary act, undertaken in full knowledge of the chance a pregnancy might result from it. It would leave out entirely the unborn person whose existence is due to rape. Pending the availability of some further argument, then, we would be left with the conclusion that unborn persons whose existence is due to rape have no right to the use of their mothers' bodies, and thus that aborting them is not depriving them of anything they have a right to and hence is not unjust killing.

And we should also notice that it is not at all plain that this argument really does go even as far as it purports to. For there are cases and cases, and the details make a difference. If the room is stuffy, and I therefore open a window to air it, and a burglar climbs in, it would be absurd to say, 'Ah, now he can stay, she's given him a right to the use of her house – for she is partially responsible for his presence there, having voluntarily done what enabled him to get in, in full knowledge that there are such things as burglars, and that burglars burgle.' It would be still more absurd to say this if I had had bars installed outside my windows, precisely to prevent burglars from getting in, and a burglar got in only because of a defect in the bars. It remains equally absurd if we imagine it is not a burglar who climbs in, but an innocent person who blunders or falls in. Again, suppose it were like this: people-seeds drift about in the air like pollen, and if you open your windows, one may drift in and take root in your carpets or upholstery. You don't want children, so you fix up your windows with fine mesh screens, the very best you can buy. As can happen, however, and on very, very rare occasions does happen, one of the screens is defective; and a seed drifts in and takes root. Does the person-plant who now develops have a right to the use of your house? Surely not – despite the fact that you voluntarily opened your windows, you knowingly kept carpets and upholstered furniture, and you knew that screens were sometimes defective. Someone may argue that you are responsible for its rooting, that it does have a right to your house, because after all you *could* have lived out your life with bare floors and furniture, or with sealed windows and doors. But this won't do – for by the same token

anyone can avoid a pregnancy due to rape by having a hysterec-
tomy, or anyway by never leaving home without a (reliable!)
army.

It seems to me that the argument we are looking at can establish
at most that there are *some* cases in which the unborn person has a
right to the use of its mother's body, and therefore *some* cases in
which abortion is unjust killing. There is room for much
discussion and argument as to precisely which, if any. But I think
we should side-step this issue and leave it open, for at any rate the
argument certainly does not establish that all abortion is unjust
killing.

5. There is room for yet another argument here, however. We
surely must all grant that there may be cases in which it would be
morally indecent to detach a person from your body at the cost of
his life. Suppose you learn that what the violinist needs is not nine
years of your life, but only one hour: all you need do to save his life
is to spend one hour in that bed with him. Suppose also that letting
him use your kidneys for that one hour would not affect your
health in the slightest. Admittedly you were kidnapped. Admittedly you did not give anyone permission to plug him into you.
Nevertheless it seems to me plain you *ought* to allow him to use
your kidneys for that hour – it would be indecent to refuse.

Again, suppose pregnancy lasted only an hour, and constituted
no threat to life or health. And suppose that a woman becomes
pregnant as a result of rape. Admittedly she did not voluntarily do
anything to bring about the existence of a child. Admittedly she
did nothing at all which would give the unborn person a right to
the use of her body. All the same it might well be said, as in the
newly emended violinist story, that she *ought* to allow it to remain
for that hour – that it would be indecent in her to refuse.

Now some people are inclined to use the term 'right' in such a
way that it follows from the fact that you ought to allow a person
to use your body for the hour he needs, that he has a right to use
your body for the hour he needs, even though he has not been given
that right by any person or act. They may say that it follows also
that if you refuse, you act unjustly toward him. This use of the
term is perhaps so common that it cannot be called wrong;
nevertheless it seems to me to be an unfortunate loosening of what
we would do better to keep a tight rein on. Suppose that box of
chocolates I mentioned earlier had not been given to both boys

jointly, but was given only to the older boy. There he sits, stolidly eating his way through the box, his small brother watching enviously. Here we are likely to say 'You ought not to be so mean. You ought to give your brother some of those chocolates.' My own view is that it just does not follow from the truth of this that the brother has any right to any of the chocolates. If the boy refuses to give his brother any, he is greedy, stingy, callous – but not unjust. I suppose that the people I have in mind will say it does follow that the brother has a right to some of the chocolates, and thus that the boy does act unjustly if he refuses to give his brother any. But the effect of saying this is to obscure what we should keep distinct, namely the difference between the boy's refusal in this case and the boy's refusal in the earlier case, in which the box was given to both boys jointly, and in which the small brother thus had what was from any point of view clear title to half.

A further objection to so using the term 'right' that from the fact that A ought to do a thing for B, it follows that B has a right against A that A do it for him, is that it is going to make the question of whether or not a man has a right to a thing turn on how easy it is to provide him with it; and this seems not merely unfortunate, but morally unacceptable. Take the case of Henry Fonda again. I said earlier that I had no right to the touch of his cool hand on my fevered brow, even though I needed it to save my life. I said it would be frightfully nice of him to fly in from the West Coast to provide me with it, but that I had no right against him that he should do so. But suppose he isn't on the West Coast. Suppose he has only to walk across the room, place a hand briefly on my brow – and lo, my life is saved. Then surely he ought to do it, it would be indecent to refuse. Is it to be said 'Ah, well, it follows that in this case she has a right to the touch of his hand on her brow, and so it would be an injustice in him to refuse'? So that I have a right to it when it is easy for him to provide it, though no right when it's hard? It's rather a shocking idea that anyone's rights should fade away and disappear as it gets harder and harder to accord them to him.

So my own view is that even though you ought to let the violinist use your kidneys for the one hour he needs, we should not conclude that he has a right to do so – we should say that if you refuse, you are, like the boy who owns all the chocolates and will give none away, self-centered and callous, indecent in fact, but not unjust. And similarly, that even supposing a case in which a woman pregnant due to rape ought to allow the unborn person to use her body for the hour he needs, we should not conclude that he has a right to do so; we should conclude that she is self-centered, callous, indecent, but not unjust, if she refuses. The complaints are no less grave; they are just different. However, there is no need to insist on this point. If anyone does wish to deduce 'he has a right' from 'you ought,' then all the same he must surely grant that there are cases in which it is not morally required of you that you allow that violinist to use your kidneys, and in which he does not have a right to use them, and in which you do not do him an injustice if you refuse. And so also for mother and unborn child. Except in such cases as the unborn person has a right to demand it – and we were leaving open the possibility that there may be such cases – nobody is morally *required* to make large sacrifices, of health, of all other interests and concerns, of all other duties and commitments, for nine years, or even for nine months, in order to keep another person alive.

6. We have in fact to distinguish between two kinds of Samaritan: the Good Samaritan and what we might call the Minimally Decent Samaritan. The story of the Good Samaritan, you will remember, goes like this:

> A certain man went down from Jerusalem to Jericho, and fell among thieves, which stripped him of his raiment, and wounded him, and departed, leaving him half dead.
>
> And by chance there came down a certain priest that way; and when he saw him, he passed by on the other side.
>
> And likewise a Levite, when he was at the place, came and looked on him, and passed by on the other side.
>
> But a certain Samaritan, as he journeyed, came where he was; and when he saw him he had compassion on him.
>
> And went to him, and bound up his wounds, pouring in oil and wine, and set him on his own beast, and brought him to an inn, and took care of him.
>
> And on the morrow, when he departed, he took out two pence, and gave them to the host, and said unto him, 'Take care of him; and whatsoever thou spendest more, when I come again, I will repay thee.'
>
> (Luke 10:30-35)

The Good Samaritan went out of his way, at some cost to himself, to help one in need of it. We are not told what the options were, that is, whether or not the priest and the Levite could have helped by doing less than the Good Samaritan did, but assuming they could have, then the fact they did nothing at all shows they were not even Minimally Decent Samaritans, not because they were not Samaritans, but because they were not even minimally decent.

These things are a matter of degree, of course, but there is a difference, and it comes out perhaps most clearly in the story of Kitty Genovese, who, as you will remember, was murdered while thiry-eight people watched or listened, and did nothing at all to help her. A Good Samaritan would have rushed out to give direct assistance against the murderer. Or perhaps we had better allow that it would have been a Splendid Samaritan who did this, on the ground that it would have involved a risk of death for himself. But the thirty-eight not only did not do this, they did not even trouble to pick up a phone to call the police. Minimally Decent Samaritanism would call for doing at least that, and their not having done it was monstrous.

After telling the story of the Good Samaritan, Jesus said 'Go, and do thou likewise.' Perhaps he meant that we are morally required to act as the Good Samaritan did. Perhaps he was urging people to do more than is morally required of them. At all events it seems plain that it was not morally required of any of the thirty-eight that he rush out to give direct assistance at the risk of his own life, and that it is not morally required of anyone that he give long stretches of his life – nine years or nine months – to sustaining the life of a person who has no special right (we were leaving open the possibility of this) to demand it.

Indeed, with one rather striking class of exceptions, no one in any country in the world is *legally* required to do anywhere near as much as this for anyone else. The class of exceptions is obvious. My main concern here is not the state of the law in respect to abortion, but it is worth drawing attention to the fact that in no state in this country is any man compelled by law to be even a Minimally Decent Samaritan to any person; there is no law under which charges could be brought against the thirty-eight who stood by while Kitty Genovese died . . .

I should think, myself, that Minimally Decent Samaritan laws would be one thing, Good Samaritan laws quite another, and in fact highly improper. But we are not here concerned with the law. What we should ask is not whether anybody should be compelled by law to be a Good Samaritan, but whether we must accede to a situation in which somebody is being compelled – by nature, perhaps – to be a Good Samaritan. We have, in other words, to look now at third-party interventions. I have been arguing that no person is morally required to make large sacrifices to sustain the life of another who has no right to demand them, and this even where the sacrifices do not include life itself; we are not morally required to be Good Samaritans or anyway Very Good Samaritans to one another. But what if a man cannot extricate himself from such a situation? What if he appeals to us to extricate him? It seems to me plain that there are cases in which we can, cases in which a Good Samaritan would extricate him. There you are, you were kidnapped, and nine years in bed with that violinist lie ahead of you. You have your own life to lead. You are sorry, but you simply cannot see giving up so much of your life to the sustaining of his. You cannot extricate yourself, and ask us to do so. I should have thought that – in light of his having no right to the use of your body – it was obvious that we do not have to accede to your being forced to give up so much. We can do what you ask. There is no injustice to the violinist in our doing so.

7. Following the lead of the opponents of abortion, I have throughout been speaking of the fetus merely as a person, and what I have been asking is whether or not the argument we began with, which proceeds only from the fetus's being a person, really does establish its conclusion. I have argued that it does not.

But of course there are arguments and arguments, and it may be said that I have simply fastened on the wrong one. It may be said that what is important is not merely the fact that the fetus is a person, but that it is a person for whom the woman has a special kind of responsibility issuing from the fact that she is its mother. And it might be argued that all my analogies are therefore irrelevant – for you do not have that special kind of responsibility for that violinist, Henry Fonda does not have that special kind of responsibility for me. And our attention might be drawn to the fact that men and women both *are* compelled by law to provide support for their children.

I have in effect dealt (briefly) with this argument in section 4 above; but a (still briefer) recapitulation now may be in order. Surely we do not have any such 'special responsibility' for a person unless we have assumed it, explicitly or implicitly. If a set of parents do not try to prevent pregnancy, do not obtain an abortion, and then at the time of birth of the child do not put it out for adoption, but rather take it home with them, then they have assumed responsibility for it, they have given it rights, and they cannot *now* withdraw support from it at the cost of its life because they now find it difficult to go on providing for it. But if they have taken all reasonable precautions against having a child, they do not simply by virtue of their biological relationship to the child who comes into existence have a special responsibility for it. They may wish to assume responsibility for it, or they may not wish to. And I am suggesting that if assuming responsibility for it would require large sacrifices, then they may refuse. A Good Samaritan would not refuse – or anyway, a Splendid Samaritan, if the sacrifices that had to be made were enormous. But then so would a Good Samaritan assume responsibility for that violinist; so would Henry Fonda, if he is a Good Samaritan, fly in from the West Coast and assume responsibility for me.

8. My argument will be found unsatisfactory on two counts by many of those who want to regard abortion as morally permissible. First, while I do argue that aborton is not impermissible, I do not argue that it is always permissible. There may well be cases in which carrying the child to term requires only Minimally Decent Samaritanism of the mother, and this is a standard we must not fall below. I am inclined to think it a merit of my account precisely that it does *not* give a general yes or a general no. It allows for and supports our sense that, for example, a sick and desperately frightened fourteen-year-old schoolgirl, pregnant due to rape, may *of course* choose abortion, and that any law which rules this out is an insane law. And it also allows for and supports our sense that in other cases resort to abortion is even positively indecent. It would be indecent in the woman to request an abortion, and indecent in a doctor to perform it, if she is in her seventh month, and wants the abortion just to avoid the nuisance of postponing a trip abroad. The very fact that the arguments I have been drawing attention to treat all cases of abortion, or even all cases of abortion in which the mother's life is not at stake, as morally on a par ought to have made them suspect at the outset.

Secondly, while I am arguing for the permissibility of abortion in some cases, I am not arguing for the right to secure the death of the unborn child. It is easy to confuse these two things in that up to a certain point in the life of the fetus it is not able to survive outside the mother's body; hence removing it from her body guarantees its death. But they are importantly different. I have argued that you are not morally required to spend nine months in bed, sustaining the life of that violinist; but to say this is by no means to say that if, when you unplug yourself, there is a miracle and he survives, you then have a right to turn round and slit his throat. You may detach yourself even if this costs him his life; you have no right to be guaranteed his death, by some other means, if unplugging yourself does not kill him. There are some people who will feel dissatisfied by this feature of my argument. A woman may be utterly devastated by the thought of a child, a bit of herself, put out for adoption and never seen or heard of again. She may therefore want not merely that the child be detached from her, but more, that it die. Some opponents of abortion are inclined to regard this as beneath contempt – thereby showing insensitivity to what is surely a powerful source of despair. All the same, I agree that the desire for the child's death is not one which anybody may gratify, should it turn out to be possible to detach the child alive.

At this place, however, it should be remembered that we have only been pretending throughout that the fetus is a human being from the moment of conception. A very early abortion is surely not the killing of a person, and so is not dealt with by anything I have said here.

ONORA O'NEILL (1941–   )

Onora O'Neill was educated at Somerville College, Oxford, and went to Harvard to do postgraduate work, receiving a Ph.D. from that university. She was supervised there by John Rawls, one of the first twentieth-century philosophers to be part of the revival of moral and political philosophy. His book *A Theory of Justice* and the shorter (and perhaps more lucid) articles which preceded it were immensely influential. Onora O'Neill taught for many years at the University of Essex, where she became Professor of Philosophy, and greatly influenced the development of what was a relatively new department. In 1992 she was elected Principal of Newnham College, Cambridge. In 1986 she published *Faces of Hunger: An Essay on Poverty, Development and Justice* and in 1989 *Constructions of Reason: Explorations of Kant's Practical Philosophy*. Onora O'Neill has been involved in numerous ethics committees, and is especially concerned with medical ethics at the present time. She has a theoretical interest in the processes of resolving disputes, and the role of reason in such resolutions. The article I have selected, however, is concerned with the fundamental nature of morality and the moral vocabulary. It formed a lecture delivered to the Royal Institute of Philosophy and was published as part of a supplement to the periodical *Philosophy*, entitled *Ethics* (edited by A. Phillips Griffiths) in 1993.

Further Reading

John Rawls, *A Theory of Justice* (Oxford: Basil Blackwell, 1971)
Alasdair MacIntyre, *After Virtue* (Notre Dame, Ind.: University of Notre Dame Press, 1981)
Bernard Williams, *Ethics and the Limits of Philosophy* (London: Fontana, 1985)

Onora O'Neill, 'Duties and virtues'; reprinted from
Ethics, *ed, A. Phillips Griffiths, Royal Institute of*
Philosophy Supplements 35 (Cambridge: Cam-
bridge University Press, 1993), pp. 107–20

Duty versus Virtue

Duty and virtue are no longer the common coin of daily
conversation. Both terms strike many of us as old-fashioned and
heavy handed. Yet we incessantly talk about what ought and
ought not to be done, and about the sorts of persons we admire or
despise. As soon as we talk in these ways we discuss topics
traditionally dealt with under the headings of duty and of virtue. If
we no longer use these terms, it may be because we associate them
with heavily moralistic approaches to life, with obsolete codes and
ideals, with 'Victorian' values and attitudes, rather than because
the concerns our predecessors discussed in these terms have
vanished from our lives.

Moralizers in each age latch on to established moral vocabularies to confine them for their own purposes; in doing so they may
make those vocabularies less useful and less appealing to others
who do not share their views. Those who want to think more
critically or openly about the same topics then often find it useful
to adopt a new or extended vocabulary which is less freighted with
attitudes they reject. So it is not surprising that today when people
talk about the topics that traditionally fell under the heading of
duty, they seldom use the term. Instead they discuss moral
requirements using the vocabulary of right action, indeed often
specifically of rights, of norms, rules and principles of action, of
conceptions of justice and of legal, professional and moral
obligations, and of promises and commitments, of autonomy and
of respect for persons. Nor is it surprising that we have come to
talk about topics traditionally associated with virtue using a
variety of other terms. Although explicit use of the term *virtue* has
become more common in philosophical writing in the last decade,
contemporary discussion of good lives, characters and communities often concentrates on particular traits or dispositions, or on
the tact, care, sensitivity, perception and responsiveness to
difference which such traits demand. Questions about duty, about

what we are required to do, have been recast in discussions about right action; questions about virtue, about what it is good to be, have given way to discussions of character, relationships and communities.

It is surely not surprising that concern with these topics has outlasted various traditional ways of approaching them. Presumably we will always have reason to be interested both in the right and in the good, both in what is required and in what is excellent. The two concerns have been linked throughout Western traditions of philosophical, theological and popular writing since classical antiquity. Virtually everybody who wrote about what ought to be done also wrote about the sorts of lives it would be good to lead. Yet recently this has changed. Many philosophers writing in English in the last two decades apparently assume that we must approach the moral life *either* through the categories of duty, obligation and right action, among which they think justice of prime importance, *or* through those of good character, hence of the virtues, and that these two approaches are not complementary but incompatible.

To some extent these two groups of writers lay claim to different territories. The advocates of justice and right action – of duty – dominate political philosophy and jurisprudence, as well as applied ethics, which has dealt mainly with areas of life that are most regulated by law and state. The friends of the virtues are most concerned with the ethics of personal life and of relationships; conception of the more public side of life centres on the notion of community and does not engage much with questions of state or legal order. Contemporary partisans of duty and of virtue at least agree on one matter: they do not see these differences as mere division of labour. Many from both camps see writing of the other sort as both philosophically and morally defective, *a fortiori* as dispensable. At the limit some hold that a serious concern for duty precludes us from saying anything about the virtues, and vice versa.

For example, some recent theorists of justice contend that we can establish no objective account of the good life; we can hope to establish only an account of the principles of justice (of course, even these are hotly disputed). Although people will have conceptions of the good, these must remain subjective and contentious. Philosophical writing can only be 'agnostic about the good for man', so must see the domain of life not constrained by obligations of justice as available for the pursuit not of virtue, but of preference. In so far as they discuss recent philosophical work on virtue ethics, the theorists of justice criticize it as lacking sound principles and rigorous argument, as failing to establish which life or lives are good or best, as alarmingly casual about justice, and as giving unwarranted weight to community standards, traditions, or to ordinary processes of deliberation or moral perception, whose moral authority (rather than corruption) they blandly assume rather than demonstrate. At the limit, they see much recent work in virtue ethics as condemned by its communitarian commitments to relativism, and at its worst as a repository of conservative, ethnocentric and often elitist prejudice.

Virtue ethicists have correspondingly sharp objections to make against those who think that the moral life is centrally a matter of justice, right action and of principle, rather than of good character. They charge (with some truth) that contemporary advocates of duty and right action are in fact narrowly obsessed with rights – that is specifically with those duties that can be claimed of others. They allege that the arguments which supposedly establish universal principles of duty, and specifically of justice, are not merely inadequate but deeply misguided. The conception of life as guided by rules or principles is ethically crippled, and perhaps ultimately incoherent. The ethical deficiency of rule-based ethics is supposedly its rigorism: it cannot take account of differences and always prescribes with rigid uniformity, so denying the sensitivity and perception which virtue ethics treats as central to the moral life. The deeper incoherence, which I shall not address directly here, is supposedly that the very idea of following a rule overlooks the unavoidable indeterminacy of rules, whose interpretation is always open, which therefore can offer no guidance. (The charges of rigidity and of incoherence are, of course, incompatible: if rules prescribe nothing determinate, they won't prescribe with rigid uniformity.)

Principles of Duty and of Virtue

The writers whose positions I have been sketching make varied further claims. Here I shall pursue neither textual accuracy nor case by case criticism. My aim is rather to suggest that without some rather extraordinary assumptions the claim that we must choose between duty and virtue because they are incompatible is wholly implausible. The clusters of ethical concerns which we associate with the two terms are close allies rather than irreconcil-able rivals. Both clusters depend on viewing action as informed by principles which constrain but do not and cannot wholly deter-mine what ought to be done and what it would be good to be.

I shall first argue for this central claim in a rather spare and elementary way and then sketch an alternative picture of some of the differences between concern for duty and for virtue. Of course, even if the arguments are convincing, they will not show that or how we can vindicate an integrated account of the right and the good. But they may at least show that it would not be foolish to aim to produce such an account.

Consider first the central objections aimed at theories of justice by some of those recent critics who take virtue to be the heart of ethical concern. These criticisms start from the fact that any account of what is ethically required (of the right, of justice, of duties) must focus on rules or principles. For example, such positions may claim that justice permits each to speak freely, or that we have a duty to rescue those whom we can easily help, or that we have a right that others be prevented from injuring us. In each case, *modal* claims are made about action informed by certain principles: action of a specified type is said to be required or permitted some agent, with the corollary that others are required not to prevent enactment of that requirement or permission; treatment of a certain type is said to be a matter of entitlement, with the corollary that some or all must be obliged to meet those entitlements. Principles of right – above all of justice – constitute a modal web of requirements, permissions and entitlements which must be internally consistent. The articulation of these modal consistency requirements for sets of principles that are to hold universally for some domain of agents – e.g. citizens of one state, or human beings – has been the focus of much of the most acute writing on justice, rights and obligations in recent decades. Universal permissions would be incoherent without universal obligations to respect those permissions; universal entitlements are nonsense unless there are counterpart obligations to meet those entitlements.

Many critics of theories of justice object to the very idea of universal rights, obligations or entitlements; more generally they object to the idea that there are universal ethical principles, often on the grounds that universal principles will demand action that is uniform, so necessarily enjoin lives of numbing rigidity, in which the particularities of persons and predicaments are systematically brushed aside. At the least, the result is insensitivity; at worst a callous inhumanity.

Yet is it true that any ethical conception which takes universal rules or principles as central must prescribe with rigid uniformity? There is, to be sure, a common use of the notion of a rule, which associates it with rigidity, and with uniformity. However, there is no reason at all to suppose that ethical rules – principles of duty or of justice, for example – have to be rules of that sort. Plenty of quite important and widely accepted moral rules do very little to impose rigid uniformity on life or action. All of us who refrain from perjury and injury keep within the requirements of two rather important moral rules: but unsurprisingly we can nevertheless lead rather varied lives. Evidently rules that state permissions will leave much open; but even those which prescribe or proscribe do not rule out varied response since they prescribe or proscribe only some aspects of what is to be done or shunned. Since rules are basically practical principles, incorporating certain act descriptions, and act descriptions are intrinsically indeterminate, it should not be surprising that rules too underdetermine action, and that any application of a rule requires judgment, and that judgment may well differ when cases differ – or even when they do not. Rules are universal provided that all cases within a certain domain fall within their scope; they prescribe uniformly when they demand that the treatment of those cases be the same in all respects. Any universal rule which is indeterminate will demand no more than that some, perhaps very minor, aspects of action be uniform, and will leave other matters open, hence in particular open for non-uniformity.

Of course, some rules incorporate a lot more detail than others, and perhaps those who worry about the rigidity of moral rules – of principles of duty or of obligation – fear that the only moral rules that can be vindicated are of this type, and so must mandate regimented action. Perhaps they fear above all that those who advocate any sort of ethics of rules or principles will in some way be recommending a particular sort of algorithmic rule. There are two points to be made here. First, strictly speaking, algorithms belong in formal systems, and there can be no algorithms for action precisely because there cannot be exhaustive descriptions of action. Second, less strictly speaking, there can of course be heavy-handed and intrusive rules, rules that demand too much or regiment life excessively, which we might think of as quasi-algorithms; and I have offered no argument to show that ethical rules are not of that sort. Nor on the other hand do those who insist that duties and rights must prescribe uniformity prove that ethical rules must be of this type.

The fear that the principles of ethics are heavy-handed quasi-algorithms which threaten a stultifying uniformity of life has various sources. One may be a consequentialist line of thought which, if taken to a theoretical extreme, suggests that ethics can be reduced to calculation, hence to quasi-algorithms. For example, the rule 'maximize utility' would (if it could be operationalized) point to one, or at most very few, permissible actions in any situation. However, such reasoning is (in principle, at least) sensitive to minute variation of circumstances – consequentialists often prize sensitivity to empirical circumstances – so there is little reason to suppose that its quasi-algorithms must regiment life by mandating uniformity of action where situations differ. The quasi-algorithms of felicific calculation for varied circumstances can hardly fail to map onto highly differentiated action. Quasi-algorithms need not regiment. The way in which utilitarian or other consequentialist reasoning may more plausibly be thought to regiment is rather that, since it takes sub-optimal action as wrong, any optimal act will be not merely permitted but required, so that once it has been performed another optimal act may loom up, which once again is required. The so-called 'overload of obligations' problem, which erodes the merely permissible, is instantly generated. A burdensome sense that all of life is divided into the forbidden and the required may then fuel a fear that such reasoning leads towards a moral gulag. But these reasons for thinking that utilitarian or other consequentialist reasoning demands too much have nothing to do with the fear that principles or rules regiment: indeed, this sort of excess demand is a more troubling feature of act than of rule utilitarianism. Rule utilitarians have long pointed out that within a consequentialist framework a focus on rules and rights rather than on acts provides a superior framework for withstanding the domination of life by utilitarian demands.

Despite these theoretical points, there is little reason to fear that consequentialist reasoning *as it actually gets done* will tend to commend uniform solutions. Actual consequentialist reasoning is much less ambitious. Since it is impossible to generate a complete list of 'options', from which an optimal act is to be chosen, it has to work within the assumption that there are certain available or attractive options (real options), and it is only among these that consequences are to be reckoned and optima computed. Since options will differ with situations, the starting points for real-life consequentialist reasoning will always be adapted to actual situations, so that fears of uniform prescription are, at the least, exaggerated. This may detract from the purity and ambition of consequentialist reasoning – but it at least puts worries about its supposed demand for uniformity into context.

However, worries about the structure of consequentialist thought are not the decisive context for understanding whether duty and its allies regiment life. Consequentialists see good results rather than duty and right action as morally fundamental. It is a standard complaint of those who take the right, and with it the web of moral requirement, as the central ethical category that consequentialist reasoning subverts what they take to be most central to the moral life by subjecting it to a calculus of tradeoffs between expected results.

If it were true that an ethic of rules must regiment, that it demands uniformity, then this would have to be because, as it happens, the ethical principles advocated by those who think duty and rights fundamental prescribe rigid uniformities. But why should we think this likely? It is true that the advocates of duty and right action commend universal principles: but universality does not entail uniformity. For principles to be universal is simply for them to apply to all cases that fall under the agent description they embody. In the case of negative prescriptions even a rather demanding principle will not get far towards imposing uniformity: in not committing perjury, or not coercing others, we conform to demanding moral proscriptions, and yet our lives become uniform only in very minor ways. However, it is theoretically possible that a positive prescription of a very specific character might impose far more in the way of uniformity (although strict uniformity would not, of course, be mandated even by quasi-algorithms, since even these are unavoidably less than fully determinate). If the most fundamental moral principles were, for example, to *require* marriage between cousins, or to *require* tithing of income, or *require* adherence to sumptuary laws, a considerable degree of uniformity at least for certain aspects of life would be prescribed. However, contemporary work on fundamental moral requirements, and indeed modern moral philosophy in general, does not advocate specific fundamental requirements. On the contrary, it has advocated rather indeterminate prescriptions and proscriptions for the construction of institutions, rather abstract human rights and the equally abstract obligations that are their counterparts. (This abstraction is not denied by those who worry lest rules and principles mandate uniformity: the very same writers often object that duty and rights provide too abstract an approach to ethics.)

These indeterminate principles are put forward as the framework within which more specific and more constraining requirements (laws, institutions, roles, practices) may be identified as required in particular situations. However, these derivative, more specific requirements are not to be taken as holding without variation for all situations or for all moral agents: we cannot simply infer uniformity of requirement from the fact that a certain universal principle forms the backdrop for judging the diversity of cases occurring within some domain. Background principles may do no more than define a context for debate about the construction of institutions, the framing of laws and the forming of practices, within which particular cases will be handled. The elaboration and interpretation of such principles may lead to quite determinate requirements in some cases, or even to uniform treatment of certain ranges of cases; but it can also lead to diversification of treatment of other cases. The inference from universal moral requirement to required uniformity of practice can fail at *many* stages.

At this point it is clear that the gap between the sort of practical reasoning that supposedly underlies moral requirements and that which underlies judgments about good lives and characters is greatly narrowed. Given that principles of action, and with them moral requirements, are not algorithms, practical reasoning that refers to principles can never dispense with judgment and sensitivity to the varieties of cases. Some of the central concerns of contemporary virtue ethics, including its emphasis on judgment and discrimination of cases, are not therefore alien but indispensable to a consideration of duty. This should surprise nobody; Kant, the greatest exponent of an ethics of duty, was also the first to insist that rules cannot determine their own application and that judgment is indispensable in all following of rules.

Looked at from the other direction, I believe it is equally clear that judgments about good characters and good lives cannot be solely a matter of responsiveness to the particularities of cases. None of the virtues is a matter of *mere* responsiveness to the particularities of situations. Virtuous lives show *principled* responsiveness to situations, not mere registration of differences. To be courageous or caring or honest is not just to respond with discrimination and sensitivity to the variety of life and situation, but to do so in distinctive, characteristic, in short, principled ways. Of course, this is not to suggest that virtuous action is uniform: here too there can be principle without uniformity. The point is only that virtue is never unprincipled – just as duty is subverted rather than completed without elements of perception and judgment, so virtue is subverted by lack of principle. This is not, of course, to say that the virtuous can formulate or are conscious of their virtuous principles: they are more likely to have them well internalized. Nor is it to say that each good act is proof of virtue: on the way to embedding principles in character many good acts may, as Aristotle insists, precede the achievement of virtue.

In order to sustain the view that concern with the right and with the good are incompatible we would, it now appears, have to take a surprisingly divergent view of practical reasoning in the two domains. We would have to view reasoning about moral require-ments not merely as informed by principles, but as wholly determined by those principles and as by-passing judgement and sensitivity. In short, we would have to suppose that the practices of interpretation and debate that we take to be part and parcel even of those domains of life which are most explicitly rule-governed, such as legal and bureaucratic life, are dispensable in favour of mere, sheer uniformity of response. On the other hand, we would have to suppose that the sort of responsiveness to cases and particularities which is most admired by those who are concerned with the virtues wholly dispenses with principles or standards, and is guided by unmediated apprehension of cases, so that there is no principle behind the various categories of virtue which we distinguish and discuss.

Conflicts and Consistencies between Duties and Virtues

It may seem that this rapprochement has gone too far. I said at the beginning that I would argue that concern for what is morally required and for what is excellent might be compatible, by showing that certain recent depictions of their incompatibility were illusory. It appears that I have now argued that both the right and the good must be understood as expressed in action informed by principles which underdetermine judgment of cases, hence underdetermine action. Yet there is surely a difference between these two domains of moral concern. In the rest of this paper I want to suggest some useful distinctions between duty and virtue.

Part of the difference is I think, simply one of modality. As soon as we raise questions about duty, or any of its contemporary derivatives, we raise questions about what is morally required. Our basic question has to be put modally. It may be the Kantian 'What ought I do?', or a less individualistic 'What ought we do?', or a more impersonal 'What is to be done?' Alternatively the question may be posed from the point of view of the recipient rather than the agent: 'What are my rights?' or 'What are we entitled to?' However, in every case the question has a modal structure. The answers to such questions must therefore be answers that speak to systems of requirements for pluralities of agents. If we either ought or are permitted to do X, others cannot be permitted to prevent us from doing X. If we have a right that Y be done to or for us, then there must be others who have the counterpart obligations so to do. The modal character of deontic claims – of claims about obligations and rights – means that they require us to think about systematic structures that mesh together the moral lives of many agents. If we are to call duty into question, we must call into question not principles and universality, but the claim that part of what is morally significant has this systematic, deontic structure.

This structure has indeed been called into question. So-called 'conflicts of obligation' will, it is argued, undermine any would-be account of moral requirements. By contrast, the less exigent structure of claims about what is good or excellent, which do not or need not interlock with claims about what is good or excellent for others, may seem less problematic. Classical discussions of the different 'lives' illustrate the less demanding structure of claims about virtue. We can grasp and appreciate both the life of honour and the life of contemplation as excellent lives, although they are incompatible in the sense that nobody can live both fully at the same time. In more contemporary terms, we can grasp and appreciate that both modesty and assertiveness, both care and fairness, can be virtues without thinking that both can be manifest in one life at all times. If we thought that both members of such pairs of virtues were matters of requirement in the same situations, our grasp of what an ethical requirement could be would collapse. Here at least is a clear difference between claims about the right and the good: the latter do not consist of deontic claims, and so there can be a plurality of good lives, no one of which is required.

It has sometimes been suggested that the modal structure of claims about right action and duty not merely differentiate these concerns from concern with virtue and excellence, but lead to conceptual shipwreck. Since any set of ethical requirements will generate conflicts of obligation, the underlying constellation of ideas to which notions such as duty, right and justice belong, will, it is said, prove irredeemably incoherent. It is certainly the case that, for any two principles stating ethical requirements, cases will arise in which it is impossible to honour both. For example, I may in a particular situation be able to save a life only by telling a lie, or to keep a promise only at the expense of causing great grief. Worse still, in some situations we will find that we cannot live up even to one principle without also violating that very principle. Conflicts of loyalty may reveal that we can honour one promise only by breaking another, sustain one relationship only by harming another. Does this show that although the idea of principled action is coherent, the idea of principles of moral requirement is not? I believe that it does not. The only case in which a conflict of moral requirements would be intrinsically incoherent is the case where the act descriptions embodied in the two requirements *cannot* be simultaneously satisfied. Anybody who aims to be both popular and a recluse, or to eat both abstemiously and gluttonously, or to be both celibate and sexually active, makes claims that, taken literally, are incoherent. No possible course of action can sustain both sides of these claims. However, in such cases the incoherence has nothing to do with the modal structure that is distinctive of duty and its cognates: it arises quite simply out of the attempt to combine commitments that are intrinsically incompatible.

It is quite a different matter to try to combine requirements that are not intrinsically incompatible. We constantly find ourselves committed to principles that may contingently rather than intrinsically come into conflict, and although this is a source of pain and difficulty in many lives, it is in no way incoherent. Principles generate conflicts in certain situations; even commitment to a single principle can do so. Conflicts of moral requirement may lead us to revise our plans and even plunge us into anguish: but they do not show that the principles (or principle) involved are senseless, dispensable or worthless. To take a well-known example, Sartre's student had to choose between filial and patriotic duty. In his actual situation, unlike many others, these two were in sharp conflict. But it does not follow that both principles, or either principle, is worthless or to be discarded. Since principles are indeterminate, they can be lived up to in many ways, and unsurprisingly some ways of living up to them will conflict with some ways of living up to other principles. Often we are fortunate and find adequate ways of meeting the requirements of a plurality of principles. In a fortunate life all fundamental moral requirements can be met without great difficulty or sacrifice, in a well-lived life action that lives up to all fundamental moral requirements is discerned and taken even when not easy or obvious. In an unfortunate life there may be deep, perhaps irresolvable, difficulty in finding any way of living up to all fundamental moral requirements, although these are intrinsically coherent. In short, the possibility of some cases of irremovable conflict does not make the idea of moral requirement incoherent or redundant. Only those sets of requirements which could never be lived up to are incoherent. These considerations show, I think, that there is no basic incoherence in the idea of a set of principles which state moral requirements. Of course, they do not show that moral requirements can be justified or what they are or whether they are all that is morally important: they just show that it is hard to live up to principles, even when these principles are matters of requirement.

Moreover, the very same considerations about conflict and consistency will arise in any account of virtue. In many situations it will prove hard to manifest both of two virtues: it is often hard to show justice and mercy, to combine fairness and solidarity. But it is not always impossible, and when it is done we admire the doing. What would, by contrast, be impossible is adopting two dispositions which always and by their very nature pulled in contrary directions. It is not an option to be secretive and open, to be taciturn and loquacious, to be firm and pliable in all situations: at best we can manifest one of these conflicting tendencies in one situation and the other in another. An account of the virtues, like an account of duty and right, has to argue for a coherent set of virtues. However, coherence is not a matter of contriving a world in which the demands of all virtues are readily enacted in all situations. There is no such world. Coherence is only a matter of commitment to virtues which could be enacted, given good fortune and good judgment. One way in which that commitment is expressed is in shaping our lives so that intrinsically coherent moral requirements do not contingently come into conflict, for example, by making no promises or commitments that will clash.

Perfect and Imperfect Duties

The fact that the demands of consistency and coherence weigh on duty and on virtue in parallel ways shows that it is not specifically the modal structure of the requirements of duty that makes the two different. However, an important difference between duty and virtue lies in a feature closely connected to that modal structure. A significant feature of deontic principles is that they *link pluralities of agents in structures of requirement*. Our duties are mirrored in others' permissions and rights; our permissions and rights in their duties. There may indeed be duties to self; but, these apart, every right, duty and permission implies a constellation of rights, duties and permissions in others. It is this feature of moral requirement that leads us to distinguish duty from virtue, and to link discussions of some important duties closely with the ethics of a legal order and social structure in which reciprocal requirements are tightly specified, in particular with the ethics of public life and of social roles; it is the absence of this feature which makes it possible to think of virtue as embodied at least in large measure in character, and even of some virtues as lying outside social relations and reflected in matters such as personal style, intellectual or spiritual commitment and aesthetic orientation.

However, this contrast between duty and virtue should not be exaggerated or oversimplified. While some duties define tight and symmetrical links of moral requirement between agent and recipient, others define less exigent structures. If A has a right, then either all others or specified others (depending on the sort of right) must have an obligation to respect that right. Where duties have counterpart rights we may think of them as completely specified, or, using an older vocabulary, as *perfect duties*. Unless rights have counterpart obligations, which are allocated either to all or to specified others, they amount to nothing more than rhetoric, and at worst to a callous and dangerous rhetoric which ascribes entitlements but is vague or cavalier about what it would take to meet those entitlements. At best such a proleptic proclamation of rights might be used to urge people to seek to secure rights by determining some allocation of the corresponding obligations.

However, not all duties exhibit this strong modal structure: some are reflected in a less complete structure of ethical requirements and are often thought of as being virtues as well as duties. Unlike rights, certain sorts of duty require no fixed allocation among recipients. Duties of charity or beneficence are often construed like this: the duty is universal in that it is ascribed to all, but its allocation remains at each agent's discretion. One use of the traditional term *imperfect duty* has been to distinguish duties that are unallocated in this way. Some contemporary advocates of justice hold that there are no imperfect duties: they think that duties are always the mirror image of rights, so that those who are obliged have no discretion in the allocation of their duty. In the stark and simplified accounts of duty offered by some libertarians, we are obliged only to respect the rights of others, and everything else is a matter of preference.

However, in more traditional accounts of duty, two types of ethical requirements are often distinguished. *Perfect duties* will be matched by rights to have those duties performed. They will form a tight network of moral requirement which links agents and recipients in a web of reciprocal ties. Imperfect duties will not be matched by rights to have those duties performed. Although they are duties, hence required of agents, they lack counterpart rights: nobody can lay claim to performance. Many of the duties traditionally classified as imperfect have often also been classified as virtues. Kant, for example, was merely following tradition when he wrote on *duties of virtue*. Like many others he sees the social virtues as a matter of duty, but of duties without counterpart rights or entitlements.

The fact that duty and virtue can be seen as closely linked in these ways does not show that the good can be reduced to the right, or that virtue is simply duty without rights. The argument shows only that we can coherently speak of duties that are also virtues, in that both are matters of differentiated enactment of principle, that neither mandates uniform or rigid action. However, there may well be many other virtues which are not moral requirements at all. It may be that there are many ways of leading good lives, which are compatible with but go far beyond the limits of ethical requirement.

The fact that some recent writers on justice have been sceptical about establishing any account of duties without rights, and others sceptical about establishing an account of virtues which are not duties, shows that it will not be a simple matter to establish an integrated account of duty and of virtue. However, recent claims that this traditional ambition is not merely difficult but intrinsically incoherent cannot be sustained: in large measure it is based on no more than a wholly unlikely conception of the sorts of rules that are most important in human lives.

SUSAN HAACK (1945–   )

Susan Haack was educated at St Hilda's College, Oxford. She did postgraduate work in Oxford and went to the University of Warwick as a Lecturer and later Professor of Philosophy. She is now a Professor at the University of Miami. Her work has been mainly in the theory of knowledge, and the book *Evidence and Inquiry: Towards Reconstruction in Epistemology*, from which I have extracted the first chapter, is a critical examination of recent epistemology, together with a development of her own theory. It must be read against the background of a generally accepted dichotomy between what is known as foundationalism and on coherentism. The first is the view that knowledge, if it is to be justified, must be founded on certain evident truths and built up from them (a view adopted and defined by Descartes, for example); the second is the view that no such foundation exists or is possible, knowledge consisting in whatever beliefs are consistent one with another, and accepted by a particular group of like-minded people. Susan Haack rejects this dichotomy, defending instead an amalgam of both which she calls 'foundherentism' (neologisms are a feature of all her writings). In articulating this theory she describes herself as 'trying to make explicit what is implicit in our commonsense appraisals of evidence as . . . strong or weak'. If challenged, as the coherentists would, on what she means by 'our' in this context, she rejects the notion that all criteria of what counts as evidence are culture-related or relative. In particular, she refuses to accept the proposition of feminist epistemologists that there exist truths evident to women but not to men. To throw light on the structure of knowledge, she uses the analogy of solving a crossword puzzle. Even if two people differ about the answer to a particular clue, they are using the same framework, and their aim is identical, to solve the whole puzzle. Susan Haack's is a comparatively new but highly influential 'voice'.

Further Reading

J. Pollock, *Contemporary Theories of Knowledge* (London: Hutchinson, 1987)

W. V. Quine, *Theories and Things* (Cambridge, Mass., and London: Harvard University Press, 1981)

R. Rorty, *Philosophy and the Mirror of Nature* (Princeton, NJ: Princeton University Press, 1979)

——*Objectivity, Relativism and Truth: Philosophical Papers 1* (Cambridge: Cambridge University Press, 1991)

S. Haack, *Evidence and Inquiry: Towards Reconstruction in Epistemology* (Oxford: Blackwell, 1993)

From Susan Haack, Evidence and Inquiry: Towards Reconstruction in Epistemology *(Oxford: Blackwell, 1993) chapter 1: 'Foundationalism versus coherentism: a dichotomy disclaimed'*

> One seems forced to choose between the picture of an elephant which rests on a tortoise (What supports the tortoise?) and the picture of a great Hegelian serpent of knowledge with its tail in its mouth (Where does it begin?). Neither will do.
>
> Sellars, 'Empiricism and the Philosophy of Mind'

Once upon a time – not so long ago, in fact – the legitimacy of epistemology was undisputed, the importance to epistemology of such concepts as evidence, reasons, warrant, justification was taken for granted, and the question of the relative merits of foundationalist and coherentist theories of justification was acknowledged as an important issue. Now, however, it seems that disenchantment reigns. The most disenchanted insist that the problems of epistemology are misconceived and should be abandoned altogether, or else that they should be replaced by natural-scientific questions about human cognition. The somewhat disenchanted, though still willing to engage in epistemology, want to shift the focus away from the concepts of evidence or justification and onto some fresher concept: epistemic virtue, perhaps, or information. Even those who still acknowledge that the concepts of evidence and justification are too central to be ignored are mostly disenchanted enough to want to shift the focus away from the issues of foundationalism versus coherentism and onto some fresher dimension: deontologism versus consequentialism, perhaps, or explanationism versus reliabilism. A great clamour of disenchantment fills the air, to the effect that the old epistemological pastures are exhausted and that we must move on to fresher fields.

I disagree.

A full explanation of the now-fashionable disenchantment would no doubt be quite complex, and would require appeal to factors external to the philosophical arguments, as well as to those arguments themselves. I don't think it is unduly cynical to speculate that part of the explanation of the urge to move away from familiar epistemological issues towards questions more amenable to resolution by cognitive psychology or neurophysiology or AI, for example, lies in the prestige those disciplines now enjoy. But part of the explanation, and the part which concerns me here, lies in a widely-held conviction that the familiar epistemological issues have proved to be hopelessly recalcitrant, and, most particularly, that neither foundationalism nor coherentism will do.

I agree that neither foundationalism nor coherentism will do. Obviously, however, no radical conclusion follows about the bona fides of the concept of justification, let alone about the legitimacy of epistemology, unless foundationalism and coherentism exhaust the options. But, as I shall argue, they do not; and, as I shall also argue, there is an intermediate theory which can overcome the difficulties faced by the familiar rivals.

So my first moves 'towards reconstruction in epistemology' will take the old, familiar debates between foundationalism and coherentism as their starting point.

Lest I raise false expectations, I had better say right away that I can offer neither a fell swoop nor a full sweep. The former would require perfectly precise characterizations of foundationalism and coherentism and knock-down, drag-out arguments against both rivals, neither of which I am in a position to supply. The latter would require a comprehensive examination of all the variants of foundationalism and coherentism, which, again, is beyond my powers (and your tolerance). What I offer is a compromise, a hodgepodge of the two desirable but impossible strategies. In the

present chapter I shall characterize foundationalism and coherentism as sharply as I can, and state the sturdiest arguments in the
field as strongly as I can, hoping to show at least that there seem to
be powerful arguments against each of the traditional rivals,
which, however, the intermediate theory looks to be able to
withstand; that, in other words, there is a pull towards the middle
ground of foundherentism . . .

One last preliminary: something should be said about how one
should judge the correctness or incorrectness of a theory of
justification. This task is surprisingly, but instructively, far from
straightforward. In offering an explication of our criteria of
justification the epistemologist is aiming to spell out with some
precision and theoretical depth what is implicit in judgements that
this person has excellent reasons for this belief, that that person
has unjustifiably jumped to a conclusion, that another person has
been the victim of wishful thinking . . . and so forth and so on. I
call this project 'explication', rather than 'analysis', to indicate
that the epistemologist will have to do more than faithfully
describe the contours of usage of phrases like 'justified in
believing' and its close relatives; since such usage is vague, shifting,
and fuzzy at the edges, the task will involve a lot of filling in,
extrapolation, and plain tidying up. But one way in which a theory
of justification may be inadequate is by failing to conform, even in
clear cases, to our pre-analytic judgements of justification.

But this is only part of the story. The concept of justification is
an *evaluative* concept, one of a whole mesh of concepts for the
appraisal of a person's epistemic state. To say that a person is
justified in some belief of his, is, in so far forth, to make a
favourable appraisal of his epistemic state. So the task of
explication here calls for a *descriptive* account of an *evaluative*
concept.

The evaluative character of the concept imposes a different kind
of constraint on theories of justification. To believe that p is to
accept p as true; and strong, or flimsy, evidence for a belief is
strong, or flimsy, evidence for its truth. Our criteria of justification, in other words, are the standards by which we judge the
likelihood that a belief is true; they are what we take to be
indications of truth. Another way in which a theory of justification
may be inadequate, then, is that the criteria it offers are such that
no connection can be made between a belief's being justified, by
those criteria, and the likelihood that things are as it says.

Satisfaction of both constraints would be the ideal. Not, of course, that there is any guarantee in advance that what we take to be indications of the truth of a belief really are such. But, if there is one, an account which satisfies both the descriptive and the evaluative constraints is what we are after.

The tricky part is to get the two kinds of constraint in the right perspective, neither excessively pollyannish nor excessively cynical. For now, let me just say that the epistemologist can be neither an uncritical participant in, nor a completely detached observer of, our pre-analytic standards of epistemic justification, but a reflective, and potentially a revisionary, participant. The epistemologist can't be a completely detached observer, because to do epistemology at all (or to undertake *any* kind of inquiry) one must employ some standards of evidence, of what counts as a reason for or against a belief – standards which one takes to be an indication of truth. But the epistemologist can't be a completely uncritical participant, because one has to allow for the possibility that what pre-analytic intuition judges strong, or flimsy, evidence, and what really is an indication of truth, may fail to correspond. In fact, however, I don't think this possibility is realized; I think pre-analytic intuition conforms, at least approximately, to criteria which are, at least in a weak sense, ratifiable as genuinely truth-indicative. Foundherentism, I shall argue, satisfies both constraints.

I

Before offering a characterization of the distinctive features of foundationalism and coherentism, I should explain my strategy for dealing with two initial difficulties which this enterprise faces. The main problem is that there is much variety and considerable vagueness in the way the terms 'foundationalism' and 'coherentism' are used in the literature. To protect myself, so far as this is possible, from the accusation that my characterization supports my thesis that foundationalism and coherentism do not exhaust the options simply as a matter of verbal stipulation, I can only do my best to ensure that my characterizations are in line with other attempts to go beyond the rather casual definitions sometimes assumed, and that they categorize as foundationalist those theories which are ordinarily and uncontroversially classified as foundationalist, and as coherentist those theories which are ordinarily and uncontroversially classified as coherentist.

A minor complication is that both 'foundationalism' and

'coherentism' have other uses besides their use in the context of theories of justification. Sometimes they are used to refer to theories of knowledge rather than of justification specifically, but this is not a significant problem for the present enterprise. Nor is the fact that 'coherentism' has a distinct use as a term for a certain style of theory of truth. Potentially the most confusing ambiguity is that, besides referring to a certain style of theory of justification, and a corresponding style of theory of knowledge, 'foundationalism' also has two meta-epistemological uses: to refer to the idea that epistemic standards are objectively grounded or founded; and to refer to the idea that epistemology is an a priori discipline the goal of which is to legitimate or found our presumed empirical knowledge . . .

But here and throughout the book, 'foundationalism' will refer to theories of justification which require a distinction, among justified beliefs, between those which are basic and those which are derived, and a conception of justification as one-directional, i.e., as requiring basic to support derived beliefs, never vice versa. This, rough as it is, is sufficient to capture something of the metaphorical force of the term 'foundationalism'; the basic beliefs constitute the foundation on which the whole superstructure of justified belief rests. I shall say that a theory qualifies as foundationalist which subscribes to the theses:

(FD1) Some justified beliefs are basic; a basic belief is justified independently of the support of any other belief;

and:

(FD2) All other justified beliefs are derived; a derived belief is justified via the support, direct or indirect, of a basic belief or beliefs.

(FD1) is intended to represent the minimal claim about the requirements for a belief to qualify as basic. It is a claim about *how basic beliefs are (and how they are not) justified*. Many foundationalists have also held that basic beliefs are privileged in other ways: that they are certain, incorrigible, infallible . . . i.e., that it is impossible that they be falsely held. 'Infallibilist foundationalism' will refer to theories which make this additional claim. (But theories which postulate certain or infallible beliefs, but do not take such beliefs to be required for the justification of all other beliefs, or do not require such beliefs to be justified independently of the support of any other beliefs, will not qualify as foundationalist.)

(FD1) admits of many and various variations. One dimension of variation concerns the material character of the beliefs claimed to be basic. Fundamental is the distinction between those foundationalist theories which take the basic beliefs to be empirical, and those which take them to be non-empirical. I distinguish:

> (FD1^{NE}) Some beliefs are basic; a basic belief is justified independently of the support of any other belief; basic beliefs are non-empirical in character.

Proponents of (FD1^{NE}) usually have in mind simple logical or mathematical truths, often thought of as 'self-evident', as basic.

> (FD1^{E}) Some beliefs are basic; a basic belief is justified independently of the support of any other beliefs; basic beliefs are empirical in character.

'Empirical', here, should be understood as roughly equivalent to 'factual', not as necessarily restricted to beliefs about the external world. In fact, one style of empirical foundationalism takes beliefs about the subject's own, current, conscious states as basic, another takes simple beliefs about the external world as basic, and a third allows both.

I shall restrict my discussion, in what follows, to empirical foundationalism, leaving non-empirical foundationalism (and the possible variant which allows both empirical and non-empirical basic beliefs) out of account.

A different dimension of variation runs obliquely to this. It concerns the explanation given to the claim that a basic belief is 'justified, but not by the support of any other belief'. There seem to be three significantly different kinds of account: according to the experientialist version of empirical foundationalism, basic beliefs are justified, not by the support of other beliefs, but by the support of the subject's (sensory and/or introspective) experience; according to the extrinsic version of empirical foundationalism, basic beliefs are justified because of the existence of a causal or law-like connection between the subject's having the belief and the state of affairs that makes it true; and according to the intrinsic or self-justificatory version of empirical foundationalism, basic beliefs are justified because of their intrinsic character, their content is the guarantee of their justification. Thus:

(FD$\text{1}^\text{E}_\text{EXP}$) Some justified beliefs are basic; a basic belief is justified, not by the support of any other belief, but by the subject's experience

represents the first of these, while:

(FD$\text{1}^\text{E}_\text{EXT}$) Some justified beliefs are basic; a basic belief is justified, not by the support of any other belief, but because of a causal or law-like connection between the subject's belief and the state of affairs which makes it true

represents the second, and:

(FD$\text{1}^\text{E}_\text{SJ}$) Some justified beliefs are basic; a basic belief is justified, not by the support of any other belief, but in virtue of its content, its intrinsically self-justifying character

represents the third.

The intrinsic or self-justifying style of explanation of the justification of basic beliefs is, naturally, also attractive to those non-empirical foundationalists who would explain the justification of basic logical beliefs as resulting from their intrinsic character or content (or, more likely, their lack of content). But this need not be pursued here.

Experientialist empirical foundationalism may be restricted to relying on the subject's introspective experience, or may be restricted to relying on his sensory experience, or may allow both kinds; depending on which it does, it is likely to class as basic beliefs about the subject's own, current, conscious states, or simple perceptual beliefs, or both. Extrinsic foundationalism and self-justificatory foundationalism, likewise, cut across the sub-categories of empirical foundationalism with respect to the kinds of belief they take as basic.

The main reason I use the expression 'empirical foundationalism' rather than 'a posteriori foundationalism' should now be apparent. One reason, of course, is that 'a posteriori' versus 'a priori ' does not lend itself to convenient abbreviation. The more substantial reason, however, is that, unlike the experientialist version, neither extrinsic nor self-justificatory foundationalism gives a justificatory role to the subject's experience. This leads to another significant point: that while experientialist foundationalism connects justification to the subject's experience, and extrinsic foundationalism connects justification to states of affairs in the world, self-justificatory foundationalism makes justification a matter solely of beliefs: their intrinsic character where the basis is concerned, and their support relations where the superstructure is concerned.

(FD1^E) also admits of variation with respect to the strength of the claim it makes about the justification of basic beliefs. The stronger version claims that basic beliefs are, simply, justified, independently of the support of any other beliefs; weaker versions, that they are justified prima facie but defeasibly, or to some degree but less than fully, independently of any other beliefs. As should be apparent, the weaker versions may, though they need not, require acknowledgement of degrees of justification. I distinguish:

> (FD1_s) Some justified beliefs are basic; a basic belief is (decisively, conclusively, completely) justified independently of the support of any other belief

and:

> (FD1_w) Some justified beliefs are basic; a basic belief is justified prima facie but defeasibly/to some degree but not completely, independently of the support of any other belief.

'Strong foundationalism' will refer to the first style, 'weak foundationalism' to the second.

(FD2) also admits of variations. According to the pure version, derived beliefs are always justified *wholly* by means of the support of basic beliefs; according to the impure version, derived beliefs are always justified *at least in part* by means of the support of basic beliefs, but the possibility is allowed that they may get part of their justification by means of mutual support among themselves. I distinguish:

> (FD2^P) All other justified beliefs are derived; a derived belief is justified wholly via the support, direct or indirect, of a basic belief or beliefs

and:

> (FD2^I) All other justified beliefs are derived; a derived belief is justified at least in part via the support, direct or indirect, of a basic belief or beliefs.

'Pure foundationalism' will refer to the first of these, 'impure foundationalism' to the second.

Like one variant of weak foundationalism, impure foundationalism is committed, at least implicitly, to recognizing degrees of
justification.

The distinctions so far made permit a whole range of permuta-
tions. For example, the pair of distinctions strong/weak, pure/
impure gives the fourfold classification: strong, pure, foundationalism; weak, pure, foundationalism; strong, impure, foundationalism; weak, impure, foundationalism.

The characteristic theses of coherentist theories of justification
are that justification is exclusively a matter of relations among
beliefs, and that it is the coherence of beliefs within a set which
justifies the member beliefs. I shall say that a theory qualifies as
coherentist if it subscribes to the following thesis:

(CH) A belief is justified iff it belongs to a coherent set of beliefs.

Of course, there is room for variation as to just what set of beliefs
is held to be relevant, and as to the exact content of the
requirement that the set be coherent. It is usually agreed that
consistency is necessary; most also require comprehensiveness; a
more recently fashionable gloss is 'explanatory coherence'. But the
most important distinction for present purposes is between those
uncompromisingly egalitarian forms of coherentism which insist
that all the beliefs in a coherent set are exactly on a par with respect
to their justification, and those moderated, inegalitarian forms
which do not. The uncompromising version disallows the possibilities both that any belief could have a distinguished initial status,
independently of its relations to other beliefs, and that any belief
could be more intimately interlocked in a set of beliefs than other
members of the set. The moderated version comes in two styles.
One results from allowing the first possibility, that some beliefs
may have an initially distinguished status, independently of their
relations to other beliefs, so that relations of mutual support must
be weighted, with interconnections with initially distinguished
beliefs counting for more than other interconnections. The other
style of moderated coherentism results from allowing the second
possibility, that, though no beliefs have any initial distinction,
some may be more deeply embedded in a coherent set of beliefs
than others. So I characterize 'uncompromising coherentism' thus:

(CH^U) A belief is justified iff it belongs to a coherent set of beliefs, no belief having a distinguished epistemic status and no belief having a distinguished place within a coherent set.

'Moderated coherentism' will refer to any theory which accepts the first part of (CH^U) but denies the second. 'Moderated, weighted coherentism' will be:

(CH^M_W) A belief is justified iff it belongs to a coherent set of beliefs, some beliefs having a distinguished initial status, and justification depending on weighted mutual support

and 'moderated, degree-of-embedding coherentism' will refer to:

(CH^M_D) A belief is justified iff it belongs to a coherent set of beliefs, some beliefs being distinguished by being more deeply embedded in a coherent set than others.

Moderated coherentism, unlike the uncompromising kind, suggests an implicit acknowledgement of the possibility of degrees of justification.

With the various refinements, qualifications and modifications mentioned, the rival theories have come, in a way, closer together. Weighted coherentism and weak, self-justificatory foundationalism – especially impure, weak, self-justificatory foundationalism – bear more than a passing resemblance to each other. Self-justificatory foundationalism makes justification derive from relations among beliefs, as does coherentism in all its forms; weighted coherentism allows that some beliefs have an epistemic distinction not dependent on their relations to other beliefs, as does foundationalism in all its forms. But the theories remain distinct. Weighted coherentism allows for pervasive mutual support; even impure, weak, self-justificatory foundationalism insists on one-directionality, denying that a basic belief could receive any justification from the support of a non-basic belief.

From here, it will not take very elaborate argument to establish the main thesis of this section, that foundationalism and coherentism do not exhaust the options. It is necessary, though, by way of preliminary, to make it clear that my thesis concerns foundationalism and coherentism *qua* rival theories of empirical justification. The idea that, for example, some form of coherentism might be correct as an account of a priori justification, and some form of foundationalism of an empirical stripe be correct as an account of empirical justification, is not presently at issue. Considered as theories of empirical justification, the point is, foundationalism and coherentism do not exhaust the options; there is logical space in between. At its simplest, the argument is this: foundationalism requires one-directionality, coherentism does not; coherentism requires justification to be exclusively a matter of relations among beliefs, foundationalism does not. (Matters are not perfectly symmetrical, since foundationalism only *allows*, but does not *require*, non-belief input; but this asymmetry does not affect the issue.) So: a theory which allows non-belief input cannot be coherentist; a theory which does not require one-directionality cannot be foundationalist. A theory such as the one I favour, which allows the relevance of experience to justification, but requires no class of privileged beliefs justified exclusively by experience with no support from other beliefs, is neither foundationalist nor coherentist, but is intermediate between the traditional rivals.

Foundherentism may be approximately characterized thus:

(FH1) A subject's experience is relevant to the justification of his empirical beliefs, but there need be no privileged class of empirical beliefs justified exclusively by the support of experience, independently of the support of other beliefs

and:

(FH2) Justification is not exclusively one-directional, but involves pervasive relations of mutual support.

This is only a *very* rough first approximation; the task of working out the details and making this more precise is yet to be undertaken. But from even this very sketchy characterization it will be apparent that, since the subject's experience is to play a role, the account will be personal rather than impersonal, and that, since beliefs will be seen to be justified partially by experience and partially by other beliefs, the account will be gradational rather than categorical; the preferred *explicandum*, in short, will be: 'A is more/less justified in believing that p depending on . . .'

Foundherentism is not, of course, the only 'third alternative' theory of justification to be suggested: contextualism is a more familiar third possibility. The characteristic feature of contextualist accounts is that they define justification in terms of conformity to the standards of some epistemic community. It is not unusual for contextualist accounts, once they go beyond this very general thesis, to have a two-level, one-directional structure reminiscent of foundationalism, but there is a very important difference: a contextualist may posit 'basic' beliefs by which all justified beliefs must be supported, but these will be construed, not as beliefs justified otherwise than by the support of other beliefs, but as beliefs which, in the epistemic community in question, *do not stand in need of justification*.

It is sometimes felt that contextualism does not really address the same question as the traditionally rival theories, a feeling sometimes expressed in the suggestion that contextualists are focused, not on the explication of 'A is justified in believing that p', but on the explication of 'A can justify his belief that p (to the members of C)', or, less charitably, that they have confused the two. The diagnosis of confusion of *explicanda* is not without merit, in my view, and there is indeed something about contextualism which sets it apart not only from foundationalism and coherentism but also from foundherentism: it leads in short order to the thesis that epistemic standards are not objective but conventional. And this means that contextualism is covertly anti-epistemological; it would undermine the legitimacy of the project of ratification. This is the first clue to why it has been thought – in my view, of course, wrongly – that, if neither foundationalism nor coherentism will do, the whole epistemological enterprise comes under threat.

That contextualism has radical consequences is no argument that it is mistaken. I think it *is* mistaken, but I shall not discuss it in any detail until much later. For the moment, since the purpose of the present chapter is to make a prima facie case for foundherentism, the point that needs emphasis is that the difficulties I shall identify in foundationalism and coherentism are clearly such as to point in the direction of foundherentism, not contextualism, as the most promising route to a successful resolution.

II

The goal, then, is to make a prima facie case for foundherentism. The strategy will be to examine the most significant arguments in the debate between foundationalism and coherentism with the aim of showing how they push one towards the middle ground of foundherentism.

Most, though not all, of the arguments to be considered are

quite familiar; but I shall have to engage in a certain amount of rational reconstruction to get these familiar arguments into their strongest forms. Despite this, I can claim only to make a prima facie case, because the arguments under consideration are, even in their rationally reconstructed versions, seldom watertight; and it would be less than candid to disguise the fact that sometimes it is a matter of judgement whether a difficulty faced by the one style of theory, regarded by proponents of the other style as insuperable, is more reasonably regarded as a decisive objection or as a challenging, but superable, obstacle.

My meta-argument begins with a consideration of the **infinite regress argument**, which has often been supposed to show that some form of foundationalism must be accepted. The argument goes somewhat as follows: it is impossible that a belief should be justified by being supported by a further belief, that further belief being supported by a further belief . . . and so on, for unless this regress of reasons for a belief comes to an end, the first belief would not be justified; so there must be, as foundationalism holds, basic beliefs which are justified otherwise than by the support of other beliefs, and which serve as the ultimate justification of all other justified beliefs. There must be basic beliefs, in the foundationalist's sense, in other words, because there cannot be an infinite regress of reasons. Suppose it is granted that a person could not be justified in a belief if the chain of reasons for that belief never came to an end. The argument is still inconclusive as it stands, for it requires the assumption that the reasons for a belief form a chain which either ends with a basic belief, or doesn't end at all; and these are obviously not the only options. Perhaps the chain of reasons comes to an end with a belief which is not justified; perhaps the chain ends with the belief with which it begins, with the initial belief supported by further beliefs which it, in turn, supports . . .

Of course, the foundationalist would regard these options as no more palatable than an infinite regress. So a stronger version of the argument may be constructed – which, however, it no longer seems appropriate to call the 'infinite regress argument', since an infinite regress is only one of several possibilities it holds to be unacceptable. I will call this reconstructed argument the **no tolerable alternatives argument**. It would run like this:

Suppose A believes that p. Is he justified in believing that p?

Well, suppose he believes that p on the basis of his belief that q.

Then he is not justified in believing that p unless he is justified in believing that q.

Suppose he believes that q on the basis of his belief that r.

Then he is not justified in believing that q, and hence not justified in believing that p, unless he is justified in believing that r.

Suppose he believes that r on the basis of his belief that s.

Then he is not justified in believing that r, and hence not justified in believing that q, and hence not justified in believing that p, unless . . .

Now either (1) this series goes on without end; or (2) it ends with a belief which is not justified; or (3) it goes round in a circle; or (4) it comes to an end with a belief which is justified, but not by the support of any further beliefs.

If (1), if the chain of reasons never ends, A is not justified in believing that p.

If (2), if the chain of reasons ends with a belief which is not justified, A is not justified in believing that p.

If (3), if the chain goes round in a circle, with the belief that p depending on the belief that q, the belief that q depending on the belief that r . . . and the belief that z depending on the belief that p, A is not justified in believing that p.

If (4), however, if the chain ends with a belief which is justified, but not by the support of any further beliefs, A is justified in believing that p.

So, since (4) is precisely what foundationalism claims, only if foundationalism is true is anyone ever justified in any belief. (Foundationalism is the only tolerable – the only non-sceptical – alternative.)

This argument is still – though no longer, perhaps, obviously – inconclusive. I grant, once again, that a person would not be justified in a belief if the chain of reasons for that belief did not come to an end; I grant, also, that he would not be justified in a belief if the chain of reasons for that belief came to an end with a belief which was not justified. I even grant that if the chain of beliefs went round in a circle, with the further beliefs supporting the initial belief themselves ultimately supported by that very belief, he would not be justified in the initial belief. What I deny is that there need be a chain of reasons at all.

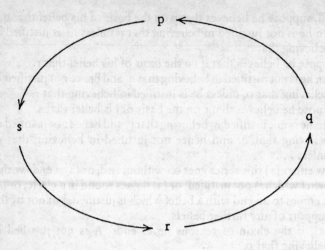

Figure 1.1

A significant clue to what has gone wrong is this: foundationalists suggest that 'going round in a circle' is the picture of
justification that a coherentist must be offering, and that it is
obviously unsatisfactory; coherentists are apt to respond by
protesting that – though indeed they insist on the pervasiveness of
relations of mutual support among beliefs – there is all the
difference in the world between legitimate mutual support and a
vicious circle of reasons. And here, I think, though rarely if ever do
they manage to say just what this 'all the difference in the world'
amounts to, the coherentists are in the right.

To repeat, there is a false assumption built into the no tolerable
alternatives argument, but built in so integrally as to be almost
invisible: that the reasons for a belief must constitute a chain – a
series, that is, with the belief that p supported by the belief that q
supported by the belief that r . . . and so on. *If* the reasons for a
belief had to be a chain, a series, then mutual support would
indeed have to be a circle, as in figure 1.1; and it is indeed
impossible to accept that this kind of circle of reasons could be
justifying.

But the chain analogy is wrong even by the foundationalist's own
lights. The appropriate picture for the structure the foundationalist envisages would be, not a chain, but a pyramid or inverted tree

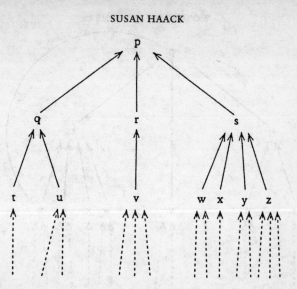

Figure 1.2

– as: belief that p based on beliefs q, r and s, belief that q based on beliefs t and u, belief that r based on belief that v . . . etc., as in figure 1.2; and it is *not* intuitively clear why it could not be the case that A is justified in believing that p even if part of A's justification for the belief that p is the belief that z, and part of A's justification for the belief that z is the belief that p – as in figure 1.3. It seems entirely plausible to suppose that the degree to which A is justified in a belief depends (at least) on how well his reasons support that belief, and on how justified he is, independently of that belief, in believing those reasons. If so, he can be justified, not completely but to however high a degree you like short of that, in the presence of such loops of justification.

In fact, the impure form of foundationalism allows the possibility of just such loops of reasons; though, according to impure foundationalism, all justification rests at least in part on the support of basic beliefs, mutual support among derived beliefs can contribute to their justification. So even some foundationalists admit – as coherentists and foundherentists maintain – that there can be legitimate mutual support, that the interpenetration of beliefs need not necessarily involve a vicious circularity.

Other foundationalist arguments against coherentism are, I think, more damaging. I consider first the argument that consistency (which is assumed by coherentists to be a necessary

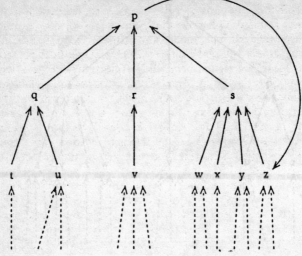

Figure 1.3

condition of coherence) is too strong a requirement for justification. The point of this objection – I shall call it the **too much to ask
objection** – is quite simple. Coherentism seems to entail that a
subject who has inconsistent beliefs, and hence an incoherent
belief-set, is not justified in any of his beliefs. But this is excessively
demanding; probably no one has a completely consistent set of
beliefs, and in any case the mere fact that there is, say, a hidden
contradiction within the corpus of my beliefs about the geography
of Russia is, surely, no reason for saying that I am not justified in
believing that snow is white, that there is a piece of paper before
me, that my name is SH . . . Since it is hardly a serious option to
discard consistency as a necessary condition of coherence, the only
escape route open to the coherentist might be to rule that the set of
beliefs coherence of which is to constitute justification, is to be, not
the subject's whole belief-set, but some sub-set of that set. Indeed,
the thought is plausible that even if (as I believe) a justified belief
will always be one enmeshed in a whole complex of other beliefs,
nevertheless not *all* of a person's beliefs are relevant to the
justification of *every* belief of his.

A coherentist who subscribed to the idea that the best defence is
a strong offence might point out that there is a certain awkward-
ness about the foundationalist picture which also relates, though
in a slightly different way, to the matter of inconsistency among a

subject's beliefs. Foundationalism, to be sure, does not imply (as the usual forms of coherentism do) that if a subject's beliefs are inconsistent, he is not justified in any of them. It focuses, not on the whole belief-set, but on the sub-set which plays a role in the tree of reasons for the particular belief the justificational status of which is at issue. So far, so good; foundationalism is not too high-minded about inconsistencies in a subject's belief-set. But it is a bit too low-minded about the possibility of inconsistencies in a person's reasons for a belief. All foundationalists, so far as I am aware, take it that if the reasons for a belief deductively imply it, they are conclusive; hence, since inconsistent propositions deductively imply any proposition whatsoever, inconsistent reasons for a belief must be deemed conclusive. Of course, the foundationalist doesn't have to say that if a person's reasons for a belief are inconsistent, and hence conclusive, he is thereby justified in the belief; on the contrary, one can confidently expect him to say that the subject is *not* justified in the belief, since he is not justified in believing the reasons for the belief. Still, the idea that reasons which are inconsistent are *eo ipso* conclusive is surely counter-intuitive, and should if possible be avoided.

To return, though, to the main thread of the discussion, which is presently focused on objections to coherentism: even if a restricted form of coherentism were possible which operated in terms of clumps of mutually relevant beliefs, it would still face other foundationalist objections. The too much to ask objection urges that consistency is too strong a requirement for justification; the next objection to be considered, which I shall call the **consistent fairy story objection**, urges that it is too weak. Coherentism cannot be correct, the argument goes, because the consistency of a set of beliefs is manifestly insufficient to guarantee, or to be an indication of, their truth. It might be thought that this is unfair, since coherentists usually require more than simple consistency of a coherent belief-set. But it is clear on very little reflection that adding a requirement of comprehensiveness doesn't make matters any better – at any rate, that a set of beliefs is consistent and large is no more a guarantee, or indication, of its truth than that it is, simply, consistent. Once again, however, as with the accusation that his conception of mutual support is a matter of 'going round in a circle', the coherentist is likely to protest that what he really proposes is not so simple-minded; perhaps he will insist that 'comprehensive' means not just 'large' but 'covering a significant range of topics', or perhaps he will claim that explanatory coherence, at any rate, is a more sophisticated conception which does not fall to any simple, easy objection along these lines. The foundationalist objector, on the other hand, is likely to be sceptical that elaboration of the concept of coherence will fix the problem. Are we, then, at a stalemate?

I think not; for what may lie behind the foundationalist's conviction that nothing like coherence, however sophisticated an elaboration of that concept is offered, can guarantee the required connection between justification and likely truth, is a further argument, and this time, to my mind, a pretty persuasive one. The fundamental problem with coherentism, according to this argument, lies precisely in the fact that it tries to make justification depend solely on relations among beliefs. The point is expressed vaguely but vividly by C. I. Lewis when he protests that the coherentist's claim that empirical beliefs can be justified by *nothing but* relations of mutual support is as absurd as suggesting that two drunken sailors could support each other by leaning back to back – when neither was standing on anything!

To get this objection to coherentism in as strong a form as possible, it is desirable (though I shall continue to call it the **drunken sailors argument**) to spell it out literally. The fundamental objection is this: that because coherentism allows no non-belief input – no role to experience or the world – it cannot be satisfactory; that unless it is acknowledged that the justification of an empirical belief requires such input, it could not be supposed that a belief's being justified could be an indication of its truth, of its correctly representing how the world is.

In the end, I believe, this argument really is fatal to coherentism. A theory couched in terms exclusively of relations among a subject's beliefs faces an insuperable difficulty about the connection between the concepts of justification and truth. How could the fact that a set of beliefs is coherent, to whatever degree and in however sophisticated a sense of 'coherent', be a guarantee, or even an indication, of truth?

Well, coherentists, of course, think it *could*. On the face of it, at least, their most promising strategy is, while acknowledging that the objection may be fatal to uncompromising coherentism, to argue that a moderated, weighted form can avoid it. For the initial distinction accorded by this style of coherentism to a sub-class of beliefs, and the weighting of relations of mutual support, is intended precisely to make it plausible that justification is truth-indicative. But the appearance that this response solves the problem seems to be *mere* appearance. The objector will not fail to notice that weighted coherentism proposes to distinguish the very kinds of beliefs which foundationalism takes as basic, and will not fail to press the question: where, or how, do initially distinguished beliefs get their epistemic distinction? If the coherentist offers no answer, he is vulnerable to the objection that his initial distinctions among beliefs, and his weighting of support relations, is arbitrary; but if he answers, plausibly enough, that he distinguishes simple perceptual beliefs, say, because of their closeness to the subject's experience, then, while the objection that no place has been allowed for input from the world is met, the objection that he has covertly sacrificed the coherentist character of his theory is inevitable. In fact, moderated, weighted 'coherentism', when combined with this kind of rationale for its initial epistemic weightings, starts to look nearly indistinguishable from foundherentism.

Of course, even if this is sufficient to discredit the weighted coherentist response to the drunken sailors argument, it is not sufficient to establish that *no* plausible response is available to the coherentist . . . However, I want to point out that *if* the drunken sailors argument is a good argument against coherentism, which I think it is, it is also a good argument against self-justificatory foundationalism; for in that form foundationalism, just like coherentism, makes justification exclusively a matter of relations among beliefs. One way of putting it might be to say that self-justificatory foundationalism, like weighted coherentism, is obliged to motivate the idea that some beliefs are epistemically distinguished in virtue of their intrinsic character, their content. *Perhaps*, in the case of some non-empirical beliefs, this is not hopelessly implausible (what makes the belief that eggs are eggs self-justifying, it might be said, is precisely its obvious lack of content); one gloss on 'self-evident', after all, is 'such that failure to accept its truth is an indication of failure to understand it'. But in the case of empirical beliefs this recourse is not available. The basic beliefs of self-justificatory empirical foundationalism will have to have *some* content. And it is not clear how self-justificatory foundationalism is better equipped than weighted coherentism to avoid the dilemma that, if the choice of initially distinguished beliefs is not arbitrary, it must be covertly motivated by an assumed connection with experience or the world.

Extrinsic and experientialist versions of foundationalism, however, are not, like self-justificatory versions, susceptible to the side-
effects (hangover?) of the drunken sailors argument. But they face
other objections. The exact statement of the most important
argument against extrinsic foundationalism – I shall call it the
evidentialist objection – will depend on the exact formulation of
the connection between the subject's belief and the state of affairs
that makes it true which the extrinsic foundationalist is offering;
but the main thrust is to the effect that extrinsic foundationalism
violates the intuition that what justifies a belief should be
something of which – as the etymology of 'evidence' suggests – the
subject is aware. In its strongest version, the evidentialist objection
is that extrinsic foundationalism violates intuition two ways,
being both too weak and too strong, allowing that a basic belief is
justified if there is an appropriate connection between the belief-
state and the state of affairs that makes it true, even when the
subject has no evidence for the belief or has evidence against it, and
denying this if there is no such connection, even when the subject
has good evidence for the belief. I note that the experientialist
foundationalist is precluded from using this objection – for it
implicitly repudiates the one-directionality on which, *qua* foundationalist, he insists. Though it would require further development
to establish that no revised extrinsic formula would avoid it, my
feeling is that the evidentialist objection is very damaging to
extrinsic foundationalism.

This leads me to a familiar coherentist argument which, if it
worked, would rule out experientialist as well as extrinsic
foundationalism. For simplicity, and because I regard the evidentialist objection as already precluding extrinsic foundationalism, I
state this argument in the form in which it applies to experientialist
foundationalism. Experientialist foundationalism claims that
basic beliefs are justified by the subject's experience. But while
there can be *causal* relations, there cannot be *logical* relations
between a person's experiences and his beliefs. Hence, since
justification is a logical matter, it must be a matter exclusively of
relations among beliefs.

The first premiss of the argument is true. A's seeing a dog may
cause him to believe that there is a dog present, but it cannot *entail
or confirm the proposition* that there is a dog present. But the
argument that this shows that the subject's experiences are
irrelevant to the justification of his beliefs – the irrelevance of

causation argument – is inconclusive, because it requires the further premiss that justification is exclusively a logical matter, which is false. What justifies A in believing there is a dog present? – his seeing the dog, the fact that he sees the dog, is a natural answer. What this argument really shows is not that experience is irrelevant to justification, but that we stand in need of an account of how it is relevant, of the relations between the causal and the logical aspects of the concept of justification. And there is already a clue as to how one might go about constructing such an account in the coherentist's premiss that there can be only causal, not logical, relations between a subject's experiences and his beliefs. For in this premiss the term 'belief' is ambiguous (as my elaboration of the argument made apparent): there can be causal relations between a belief-*state*, *someone's believing something*, and that person's experiences; there can be logical relations between a belief-*content, a proposition, what someone believes*, and other belief-contents, other propositions. This suggests that an adequate account of how the fact that a person's having certain experiences contributed causally to his believing something could make it more or less likely that what he believes is true, will need to exploit the distinction between belief-states and belief-contents.

The most that has to be conceded by the experientialist in response to the irrelevance of causation argument is that only an account which combines logical and causal elements can allow the relevance of experience to justification. I say 'the most' because we have already, in the brief discussion of the mismatch between deductive consequence and conclusiveness in the presence of inconsistency, encountered one reason to doubt whether 'logical' is quite the right word for the non-causal, evaluative component of the concept of justification; and subsequently, when I come to argue the mismatch between 'inductive logic', so called, and supportiveness of evidence, we shall encounter another. The appropriate response to the irrelevance of causation argument, therefore, is to insist on the 'double-aspect', or 'state-content', character of the concept of justification; acknowledging, of course, that an adequate account of how experience is relevant to justification will require an articulation of how the two aspects interrelate. Experientialist foundationalism usually leaves all this implicit; but it is not fatally damaged by the irrelevance of causation argument.

Foundherentism, as characterized in section I, is experientialist;

so it too will require a double-aspect, state-content approach; when it comes to articulating the theory in detail, I shall make this as explicit as possible.

A second influential argument against foundationalism points out that it requires that basic beliefs be both secure (plausibly claimed to be justified independently of the support of any other beliefs) and rich (plausibly claimed to be capable of supporting a substantial body of other beliefs); and urges that no belief can fulfil both these requirements. For, the argument goes, these two requirements are in competition with each other; the first can be satisfied only by stripping down, the second only by beefing up, the content of the basic beliefs.

This argument seems to me extremely persuasive with respect to a restricted class of foundationalist theories, those, namely, which claim that the basic beliefs have to be certain or infallible, incapable of being false. But infallibilism is inessential to foundationalism, so the interesting question is what sort of force this argument has against other forms. A reasonable initial response is that while there is plausibility in the suggestion that the requirement of security is apt to compete with the requirement of richness (a plausibility vividly illustrated by the history of foundationalist programmes, which have indeed shown a marked tendency to swing back and forth between insisting on security at the expense of content, and insisting on content at the expense of security), it is unproven that the tension is irresoluble. Further reflection suggests that this argument – the **swings and roundabouts argument** – is the more plausible the more strongly privileged basic beliefs are required to be, and the more of the responsibility for the support of all other justified beliefs they are required to bear. This means that the argument is likely to be less effective against weak foundationalism than against strong foundationalism (since the former does not require basic beliefs to be absolutely justified independently of the support of other beliefs), and less effective against impure foundationalism than against pure foundationalism (since the former does not require basic beliefs to do all the work of supporting the superstructure of derived beliefs); least effective, therefore, against weak, impure foundationalism. In fact, I am reasonably confident that this argument is quite *in*effective against weak, impure foundationalism – and of course entirely confident that it has *no* force against foundherentism, which requires no privileged class of basic beliefs at all.

It remains to explain what persuades me that foundherentism is more plausible even than the modest forms of foundationalism which seem capable of withstanding the swings and roundabouts argument. Here I rely on an interlocking pair of arguments, not, so far as I am aware, previously deployed in the debate between foundationalism and coherentism. The first points to a lacuna in weak foundationalism which cannot be filled except by abandoning the one-directional character of justification; the second points to the lack of a cogent rationale for weakening one-directionality, as impure foundationalism does, without abandoning it altogether. I shall call these the **up and back all the way down arguments**.

According to weak foundationalism, a basic belief is justified prima facie but defeasibly, or to some degree but not completely, by something other than a belief. This sounds, at first blush, a sensible account of the following, common enough, kind of situation: suppose A believes that there is a dog present, and that he believes this because of his current sensory experience (his seeing what appears to be a dog); then A is justified prima facie, or justified to a considerable degree, in believing that there is a dog before him – but not indefeasibly justified, not fully justified, because appearances could be misleading. At second blush, however, an awkward question arises: would not A be *more* justified, or more securely justified, in believing that there is a dog before him if he also justifiedly believed that his eyes are working normally, that he is not under the influence of post-hypnotic suggestion, that there are no very lifelike toy dogs around, etc., etc.? Surely, he would. But the weak foundationalist cannot allow this, for his story is that basic beliefs get their justification exclusively from something other than the support of further beliefs; to allow that they get some justification from experience and some from the support of other beliefs would violate the one-directional character of justification, on which, *qua* foundationalist, he insists. And if this possibility were allowed, weak, experientialist foundationalism would be transmuted into a form of foundherentism.

The problem with impure foundationalism is, rather, that it lacks a cogent rationale. Unlike the pure foundationalist, who insists that justification always goes from basic to derived beliefs, the impure foundationalist maintains one-directionality only in the form of the negative thesis that justification never goes from derived to basic beliefs. But why, then, does he still insist that there must be a distinct, privileged class of basic beliefs which get their justification entirely without the support of any other beliefs, and which must contribute to the justification of all other beliefs? Perhaps the response will be: because there must be a role for input from outside the subject's beliefs. But this, though true, is obviously insufficient to establish that there must be a privileged class of basic beliefs which get *all* their justification from such input. And without this assumption, for which no reason has been given, impure experientialist foundationalism would be transmuted into a form of foundherentism.

The infinite regress argument for foundationalism is inconclusive, and so, too, is its stronger variant, the no tolerable alternatives argument. The too much to ask argument seriously damages the usual, holistic forms of coherentism, though it might possibly be avoided by retreat to a restricted, quasi-holistic version; it also suggests awkward questions about the foundationalist's own attitude to inconsistency. The drunken sailors argument, however, is decisive against coherentism; and the attempt to avoid it by a shift from the uncompromising, egalitarian form to a moderated, weighted variant turns out to amount, in the only form in which it has any prospect of success, to the adoption of a disguised form of foundherentism. So coherentism won't do.

The drunken sailors argument turns out to do as much damage to self-justificatory foundationalism as it does to coherentism. And the evidentialist objection is fatal to extrinsic foundationalism. But the irrelevance of causation argument is not fatal to experientialist foundationalism, but only points to the need for a double-aspect, state-content approach. The swings and roundabouts argument succeeds against infallibilist foundationalism and, probably, against strong and pure foundationalism. Weak and impure forms probably survive it. They succumb, however, to the up and back all the way down arguments. So foundationalism won't do.

So neither foundationalism nor coherentism will do.

Since it allows the relevance of non-belief input to justification, foundherentism survives the decisive argument against coherentism, the drunken sailors argument. It is untouched by the evidentialist objection to extrinsic foundationalism, and, like experientialist foundationalism, can survive the irrelevance of causation argument by adopting a double-aspect approach. Since it requires no privileged class of basic beliefs, it is under no threat from the swings and roundabouts argument. And its superiority to even weak and impure forms of experientialist foundationalism is exhibited by its ability, and their inability, to accommodate the up and back all the way down arguments. So foundherentism looks to be able to survive both the strongest arguments against foundationalism and the strongest arguments against coherentism.

This constitutes my prima facie case for foundherentism.

ACKNOWLEDGEMENTS

The editor and publishers are grateful to all of the living authors here represented who have given permission for their work to be included.

The editor and publishers would also like to thank the following for permission to use copyright material: Blackwell Publishers for Elizabeth Anscombe, Chapter 13: 'Causality and determination' of *Metaphysics and Philosophy of Mind*, Blackwell, 1981; Cambridge University Press for Onora O'Neill, 'Duties and virtues' reprinted from *Ethics*, ed. A. Phillips Griffiths, Royal Institute of Philosophy Supplements 35, Cambridge University Press, 1993; Harcourt Brace & Company for Hannah Arendt, excerpt from *On Violence*, copyright © 1969, 1970 Hannah Arendt; Harvard University for material from Susanne K Langer, *Philosophy in a New Key: A Study in the Symbolism of Reason, Rite and Art*, Cambridge, Mass.: Harvard University Press, Copyright © 1942, 1951, 1957 by the President and Fellows of Harvard College, renewed 1970, 1979 by Susanne Knauth Langer, 1985 by Leonard C R Langer; Kluwer Academic Publishers for Anne Conway, *The Principles of the Most Ancient and Modern Philosophy*, ed Peter Loptson, Martinus Nijhoff, 1982, pp. 175–208; Oxford University Press for Philippa Foot, 'Moral Arguments', *Mind*, 67, 1958; Penguin Books Ltd for material from Simone de Beauvoir, *Old Age*, translated by Patrick O'Brian (Penguin Books 1977, this translation first published by André Deutsch and Weidenfeld & Nicolson 1972, first published as *La Viellesse* by Éditions Gallimard 1970), copyright © Éditions Gallimard, 1970, English translation copyright © André Deutsch, Weidenfeld & Nicolson and G P Putnam's Sons, 1972; Princeton University for J. J. Thomson, 'A Defense of Abortion' from *Rights, Restitution and Risk: Essays and Moral Theory*, ed. William Parent, © 1971 by Princeton University Press; Routledge for Mary Midgley, Chapter 11: 'On being animal as well as rational' from